Economic Liberalization and Turkey

The liberalization of the Turkish economy is a key factor affecting Turkey's application to join the European Union. This book examines the impact of economic liberalization in Turkey and Turkey's approach to the elimination of barriers to trade. It focuses on the liberalization of trade in Turkey's agricultural and industrial commodities sector and key services such as telecommunications, electricity, natural gas, banking and transport. The chapters include thorough discussions on World Trade Organization and European Union approaches for the elimination of barriers to trade, international and EU rules and regulations in the various service sectors, and the methods for estimating the tariff equivalents of barriers to trade in the different service sectors as well as methods for estimating the benefits of liberalization of services for Turkey. The experience of Turkey, its approach to liberalization and its measures to eliminate barriers to trade serve as a useful model for other neighbouring countries of the European Union.

Sübidey Togan is Professor of Economics and the Director of the Centre for International Economics at Bilkent University, Turkey. His recent publications include (as co-editor) *Macroeconomic Policies for EU Accession*; *Turkey: Economic Reform and Accession to the European Union* and *Turkey and Central and Eastern European Countries in Transition: Towards Membership of the EU*.

The Routledge Political Economy of the Middle East and North Africa series

Edited by Hassan Hakimian

London Middle East Institute, School of Oriental and African Studies, University of London

Trade Policy and Economic Integration in the Middle East and North Africa
Economic boundaries in flux
Edited by Hassan Hakimian and Jeffrey B. Nugent

State Formation in Palestine
Viability and governance during a social transformation
Edited by Mushtaq Husain Khan

Palestinian Labour Migration to Israel
Land, labour and migration
Leila H Farsakh

Islam and the Everyday World
Public policy dilemmas
Edited by Sohrab Behdad and Farhad Nomani

Monetary Policy and Central Banking in the Middle East and North Africa
Edited by David Cobham and Ghassan Dibeh

Economic Performance in the Middle East and North Africa
Institutions, corruption and reform
Edited by Serdar Sayan

Economic Liberalization and Turkey
Sübidey Togan

Economic Liberalization and Turkey

Sübidey Togan

LONDON AND NEW YORK

First published 2010
by Routledge
2 Park Square, Milton Park, Abingdon, Oxon, OX14 4RN

Simultaneously published in the USA and Canada
by Routledge
270 Madison Avenue, New York, NY 10016

*Routledge is an imprint of the Taylor & Francis Group, an informa
business*

© 2010 Sübidey Togan

Typeset in Times New Roman by Prepress Projects Ltd, Perth, UK
Printed and bound in Great Britain by CPI Antony Rowe, Chippenham,
Wiltshire

British Library Cataloguing in Publication Data
A catalogue record for this book is available from the British Library

Library of Congress Cataloging in Publication Data
Togan, Sübidey
Economic liberalization and Turkey/Sübidey Togan.
p. cm. – (The Routledge political economy of the Middle East and North
Africa series; 7)
Includes bibliographical references and index.
1. Turkey – Commercial policy. 2. Turkey – Economic policy. 3. Free
trade – Turkey. 4. Trade regulation – Turkey. I. Title.
HF1583.4.T624 2010
330.9561 – dc22
2009039071

ISBN10: 0-415-49595-4 (hbk)
ISBN10: 0-203-85509-4 (ebk)

ISBN13: 978-0-415-49595-0 (hbk)
ISBN13: 978-0-203-85509-6 (ebk)

Contents

Figures

Tables

Preface and acknowledgements

This book is about economic liberalization. It covers issues related to the liberalization of trade in agricultural and industrial goods, the liberalization of services, and the role of regulatory institutions in trade liberalization.

The author's previous work on economic liberalization concentrated mainly on the liberalization of trade in agricultural and industrial goods with emphasis on tariffs and tariff-like measures. Work on services started only recently with the Forum Euro-Mediterranée des Instituts Economiques (FEMISE) project 'Impact of Liberalization of Trade in Services: Banking, Telecommunications and Maritime Transport in Egypt, Morocco, Tunisia and Turkey' (FEM22–02). The financial support from FEMISE, supported by the European Commission, is greatly appreciated. The views expressed in this book in no way reflect the official opinion of the Commission. The study was extended later with the Economic Research Forum (ERF) project 'Quantifying the Impact of Liberalization of Services and Network Industries within the Context of EU Integration in Turkey' (ERF Project No. ERF 03-TK-2002). The author is grateful to the ERF for the financial support. He also would like to express his gratitude to Bernard Hoekman and Ismail Arslan of the World Bank for getting him involved in issues related to the liberalization of services.

This book may carry the author's name alone but its contents were shaped by the contributions and insights of various collaborators he has been lucky to work with in recent years. It is a pleasant duty to acknowledge them here (in alphabetical order): Erkan Akdemir, Sare Arıcanlı, Erdem Başçı, Hakan Berument, Saadettin Doğan, Hasan Ersel, Bartlomiej Kaminski, Jan Michalek, Cenk Pala and Osman Sevaioğlu. It should be noted that Chapter 2 is an updated and extended version of a paper published originally in 2005 in *World Economy* as 'Turkey: Trade Policy Review' and Chapter 3 is based partially on the paper 'Turkey: Trade Policy Review, 2007', which will appear in *World Economy* during 2010. Similarly, Chapter 4 is an updated and extended version of a paper published originally in 2007 in *World Economy* as 'Telecommunications Policy Reform in Turkey', co-authored with E. Akdemir and E. Başçı. Finally, Chapter 8 is based largely on 'EU Maritime Rules and Transport Sector Policy Reform in Turkey', published in *Economic Development through World Trade: A Developing World Perspective*, edited by Yong-Shik Lee. I thank Professor Yong-Shik Lee for giving me permission to include a revised version of the paper in this book.

1 Introduction

The aim of economic activity is to generate wealth for a country's citizens through the achievement of relatively high but sustainable economic growth measured by growth in real per capita income. Views on market-oriented policies to achieve this aim have converged recently into a set of policy principles that are termed the 'Washington Consensus' and later revised as the 'Post-Washington Consensus'. According to Rodrik (2007a), the 'universal' principles of sound economic policy consist of allocative efficiency, macroeconomic and financial stability and social inclusion. Allocative efficiency requires protection of property rights, contract enforcement, rule of law, market-based competition, appropriate incentives, liberalization of foreign trade and liberalization of foreign direct investment (FDI). Macroeconomic and financial stability require sound money, prudent supervision, fiscal sustainability and current account sustainability. Finally, social inclusion requires social safety nets and targeted poverty-reduction programmes.

Market economy is embedded in five sets of non-market institutions: institutions for securing property rights, regulatory institutions, institutions for macroeconomic stabilization, institutions for social insurance, and institutions of conflict management.[1] In a market economy entrepreneurs need to have adequate control over the returns to the assets, and private appropriability of the returns to accumulation is an essential requirement for achieving allocative efficiency. Because markets fail when participants engage in fraudulent or anticompetitive behaviour, every market economy needs also to be overseen by regulatory institutions. Establishment of appropriate institutions that will attain sound money, prudent supervision, fiscal sustainability and current account sustainability are requirements for achieving macroeconomic stabilization. In addition, social insurance in a market economy is needed to achieve social stability and social cohesion. Finally, for conflict management, market economies need the rule of law, a high-quality judiciary and an effective police force.

This study on economic liberalization is concerned with the liberalization of foreign trade, the liberalization of foreign direct investment, and the role of regulatory institutions in trade liberalization. In the case of agricultural and industrial commodities, most of the discussion on liberalization of trade focuses on the elimination of tariffs and non-tariff barriers of trade. On the other hand, in the case of services, barriers to trade are regulatory in nature, and outcomes of services liberalization depend heavily on the regulatory environments.

To emphasize the role of regulatory environments in the liberalization of services we note that 'services' cover a broad range of industries, encompassing 'network industries' such as electricity, natural gas and telecommunications, other 'intermediate services' such as transport, financial intermediation, distribution, construction and business services, and 'final demand services' such as education, health, recreation, environmental services, tourism and travel. Services for a long time were believed to be non-tradable, but technological changes over the past decades have made trade in many services feasible, increasing the importance of services in international trade.

In a world where countries have different regulatory regimes in the service sectors, often have little interest in each other's regulatory regimes, have little confidence in the quality of other countries' regulatory regimes and are in general reluctant to change their own regulatory regimes, achieving liberalization of services is a challenging task. As long as the qualifications of different countries differ substantially and the associated complying costs are country-specific, they become market-entry costs and they may turn out to be prohibitive, hampering exports and investment.

In principle, countries can choose to liberalize the markets for services unilaterally by adopting and implementing international norms such as the Basic Agreement on Telecommunications, Energy Charter Treaty and Basel Core Principles.[2] Alternatively and also simultaneously, countries can use multilateral engagement through negotiations under the World Trade Organization's (WTO) General Agreement on Trade in Services (GATS). Finally, the third alternative to liberalization of services is through regional cooperation. But each of these approaches has its problems.

Unilateral liberalization of the markets for services may lead to efficiency gains, but liberalization in this case can be constrained if the country cannot on its own gain improved access to larger foreign markets. On the other hand the multilateral approach to services liberalization under GATS may lead not only to efficiency gains but also to improved access to larger foreign markets and to reduced compliance costs.

GATS's objective is to open the borders of the WTO member nations to trade in all types of services, and GATS applies to all possible modes of delivering services, including:

- *Cross-border supply.* This is analogous to trade in goods and arises when a service crosses a national frontier, for example air or maritime transport across borders, purchase of software or insurance by a consumer from a supplier located abroad, and legal advice from abroad given by letter or telephone.
- *Consumption abroad.* This occurs when the consumer travels to the territory of the service supplier, for example when purchasing tourism, education or health services or a visit to a law office abroad.
- *Commercial presence.* This involves foreign direct investment, for example when a foreign bank or telecommunications or electricity firm establishes a branch, subsidiary or plant in the territory of another country.

- *Movement of individuals.* This occurs when independent service providers or employees of a multinational firm temporarily move to another country for business consulting or construction.

GATS contains four sets of obligations for WTO members with respect to trade in services. The first set of rules, called horizontal obligations, involves the general obligations that apply to all measures affecting trade in services. The second set of rules governs the making of specific market access and national treatment commitments by WTO members, which arise from voluntary undertakings by members and apply only to service sectors specified in the commitments. The third set of rules lays out the obligation of WTO members to engage in successive rounds of negotiations with a view to achieving progressively higher levels of liberalization in trade in services. Finally, the fourth set of rules establishes the institutional framework for GATS and links the treaty to the WTO's dispute settlement mechanism.

The 'general obligations' include Article II on the most-favoured nation (MFN) treatment, Article VI on domestic regulation, Article VIII on monopolies and service suppliers and Article XIV on general exceptions. The MFN principle requires that with respect to any measure covered by GATS, each WTO member shall accord immediately and unconditionally to services and service suppliers of any other WTO member treatment no less favourable than that it accords to like services and service suppliers of any other country. According to the domestic regulation obligation each member shall ensure that all measures of general application affecting trade in services in sectors, where specific commitments are undertaken, are administered in a reasonable, objective and impartial manner. The Council for Trade in Services shall develop any necessary disciplines on measures relating to qualification requirements, technical standards and licensing requirements to ensure that such measures do not constitute unnecessary barriers to trade in services. Such disciplines shall aim to ensure that such requirements are, *inter alia*, not more burdensome than necessary to ensure the quality of the service. The monopolies and exclusive service suppliers condition requires that if a WTO member grants monopoly or exclusive service rights regarding the supply of a service covered by specific commitments then that WTO member must make compensatory arrangements with any WTO member adversely affected by such granting of monopoly or exclusive service rights. Finally, according to the general exceptions, WTO members may restrict trade in specific services in violation of general obligations or specific commitments when such restrictive measures are necessary to protect human, animal or plant life or health, and the application of which does not constitute a means of arbitrary or unjustifiable discrimination or a disguised restriction on trade in services.

Regarding 'specific commitments' we note that GATS creates a structure for countries to make specific market access (Article XVI) and national treatment (Article XVII) commitments in service sectors in which they wish to liberalize trade. GATS Article XVI prohibits specific limitations (e.g. quotas) on the number of suppliers; on the total value of service transactions or assets, including needs tests; on the total number of service operations or total quantity of service output; on the total number of people that may be employed; on the types of legal entities or joint ventures through which a service can be supplied; and on the participation of foreign capital. Thus, in sectors in which liberal market access commitments are undertaken, WTO members may not maintain or adopt laws that: (1) limit the number of service suppliers via quotas, monopolies or exclusive service suppliers, (2) limit the total value of service transactions, (3) limit the total number of service operations or the total quantity of service output, (4) limit the total number of natural persons who may be employed in a particular service sector, (5) restrict or require specific types of legal entities or joint ventures through which a service supplier may supply a service and (6) limit the participation of foreign capital in terms of maximum percentage limits on foreign shareholding or the total value of individual or aggregate foreign investment. On the other hand, according to the national treatment principle, each WTO member in the sectors inscribed in its Schedule of Specific Commitments, and subject to any conditions and qualifications set out therein, shall accord to the services and service suppliers of any other WTO member, in respect of all measures affecting the supply of services, treatment no less favourable than that it accords to its own like services and service suppliers.

Under GATS, each WTO member decides for itself whether to make binding market access and national treatment commitments. When making these commitments, countries have to list all measures that they wish to retain which would otherwise violate the specific commitments being made. As the commitments each apply to the four modes of supply, trading conditions are ultimately defined in the form of eight entries per sector. These may vary within a spectrum whose opposing ends are guaranteed market access and/or national treatment without limitations (full commitments) and the denial of any such guarantees (no commitments). While the relevant entry would be 'none' in the former case, the absence of commitments would be indicated as 'unbound'. The non-scheduling of a sector or a non-commitment on a particular mode does not imply that the relevant policies are beyond all GATS disciplines. Some basic obligations such as the MFN principle apply regardless of such circumstances. Any form of discrimination between trading partners on grounds of nationality is prohibited. The only exemptions relate to mutual preferences between participants in economic integration agreements and to recognition measures in the areas of licensing, certification and technical standards. Exemptions from MFN treatment could have been sought for a period not exceeding ten years in principle at the date of entry into force of the agreement or, for new WTO members, at the date of accession. The market access and national treatment commitments are inscribed in national Schedules of Specific Commitments, which are annexed to GATS; the Schedules also specify any limitations on market access or national treatment commitments that a country chooses to maintain in one or more of the four modes of supply.

The 'progressive liberalization commitments' include Article XIX on negotiation of specific commitments and Article XXI on modification of schedules. While Article XIX requires that WTO members shall enter into successive rounds of negotiations with a view to achieving a progressively higher level of liberalization in trade in services, Article XXI states that to withdraw or modify a Schedule of Specific Commitments a WTO member must make compensatory arrangements for WTO members adversely affected by such withdrawal or modification (and such compensatory arrangements are then available to all WTO members on a MFN basis).

The 'institutional provisions' in GATS include Article XXIII on dispute settlement and enforcement, and Article XXIV on the Council for Trade in Services. According to Article XXIII, disputes that arise under GATS are subject to the WTO Dispute Settlement Understanding. Violations or non-compliance with GATS provisions found by dispute settlement panels of the WTO will require action to curtail trade-distorting behaviour. If not resolved, members will have the right to impose retaliatory tariffs against nations found in violation of the GATS. Finally, note that according to Article XXIV, the Council for Trade in Services shall facilitate the operation of GATS and advance its objectives.

For the multilateral negotiations to be fruitful, the different countries have to recognize mutual interests in reciprocal liberalization. Recognizing these potential mutual gains will allow reciprocal 'concessions' that would benefit all. But the achievement of multilateral liberalization of services seems to be possible only in the long term. On the other hand, liberalization of services through regional cooperation may be feasible in the short term. As an example of regional cooperation consider the European Union's (EU) European Neighbourhood Policy (ENP). The ENP presents an opportunity to deepen the market integration of the EU's southern and eastern neighbouring countries with the EU, to increase their participation in global production networks. The perspective of progressively participating in the Internal Market is the most far-reaching aspect of the ENP. The objective is to gradually create an economically integrated space, with free movement of goods, services and factors of production between those countries and the EU. To have free trade in services the neighbouring countries of the EU are expected to adopt and implement the European Community's rules and regulations in the specific service sectors.[3]

The above considerations reveal that the liberalization of services, whether pursued through unilateral or multilateral engagement, or through regional cooperation, is a challenging task. Consider the case of two trucking companies, one a Turkish trucking company established in Turkey and the other a German trucking company established in Germany. The Turkish company is subject to Turkish rules that regulate market access, competition, prices, fiscal conditions, social conditions, technical conditions and safety in the road freight transportation sector in Turkey. Similarly, the German company is subject to German rules that regulate market access, competition, prices, fiscal conditions, social conditions, technical conditions and safety in the road freight transportation sector in Germany. Before the achievement of liberalization of trade in road freight transportation services between the two countries, suppose that Germany is satisfied with its own regulatory regime, that rules are implemented strictly in each country, and that German rules and regulations are in general much stricter than those prevailing in Turkey.

In such a case how can the two countries achieve liberalization of trade in road freight services?

If Turkey wants to liberalize its road freight transportation services, it could unilaterally adopt and implement international norms developed for the road freight transportation sector such as those of the United Nations Economic Commission for Europe (UNECE) Inland Transport Committee.[4] If Turkey adopts and implements these norms, will trade in road freight transportation services be liberalized between the two countries? The answer is probably no as Germany would regard the UNECE Inland Transport Committee norms as not as comprehensive enough as those prevailing in Germany. Let us first be clear about what liberalization of road freight transportation services between Turkey and Germany entails.

We say that road freight transportation services between Turkey and Germany are liberalized if there are no restrictions on the operations of the Turkish and German trucking companies between the two countries (cross-border supply). The Turkish trucking company should be able to freely carry freight between, for example, Istanbul and Frankfurt, and also between Frankfurt and Istanbul. Similar conditions should apply for the German trucking company carrying freight between Frankfurt and Istanbul, and also between Istanbul and Frankfurt. Liberalization further requires that no restrictions are placed on freight transportation by the Turkish company between, for example, Frankfurt and Hamburg, and no restrictions are placed on freight transportation by the German company between, for example, Istanbul and Antalya, Turkey. In addition, liberalization requires that there should be no restrictions on the establishment of Turkish trucking companies in Germany, and no restrictions on the establishment of German trucking companies in Turkey (commercial presence). Finally, liberalization requires that Turkish road freight transportation service providers or Turkish employees of the Turkish trucking company should be able to move freely for relatively short periods (temporarily) from Turkey to Germany and also within the EU. Similarly, German road freight transportation service providers or German employees of the German trucking company should be able to move freely for relatively short periods (temporarily) from Germany to Turkey and within Turkey.

Under these assumptions, liberalization of trade in road freight transportation services between Turkey and Germany would be achieved if Turkey adopted and strictly implemented all of the rules and regulations in the road freight transportation sector prevailing in Germany, the country with stricter policies, and Germany determined that this was indeed the case. Thus, generalizing from this simple case we note that liberalization of services involves the reduction of regulatory barriers to market access and the reduction of discriminatory national treatment across all four modes of supply. The focus is to ensure that existing regulations do not discriminate against foreign participation in the markets of domestic and foreign countries. Moving to a non-discriminatory regulatory regime can thus require significant changes in how some service sectors are currently regulated in the particular country under consideration.

In this study on economic liberalization we consider the case of Turkey, a developing country interested in closing the economic gap between itself and the rich countries of the world. It tries to achieve this goal though implementation of market-oriented policies and trade liberalization. The policy of opening up the economy has been pursued through membership in the WTO and close association with the EU. Turkey realizes that the main factors that will ensure convergence with the living standards of advanced countries is acquiring high-quality institutions and following the 'universal' principles of sound economic policy.

The book consists of three parts. Part I considers the liberalization of trade in agricultural and industrial commodities, Part II the liberalization of services, and Part III the impact of economic liberalization.

Part I consists of two chapters. While the first chapter discusses the liberalization of trade in agricultural and industrial commodities, the second chapter is on the elimination of technical barriers to trade.

According to Chapter 2 the main pillar defining Turkey's trade policy is the Customs Union Agreement with the EU covering trade in industrial goods. The Agreement has contributed as emphasized by Kaminski and Ng (2007) to a significant increase in the contestability of the domestic Turkish industrial goods markets through infusing predictability, transparency and stability to trade policy as well as by liberalizing market access. Turkish producers of industrial goods are protected, in terms of tariffs, from external competition to exactly the same extent as the EU producers are. However, they are not protected by tariffs from competition from duty-free imports of industrial goods from world-class EU firms. In return, industrial producers have duty-free market access, unrestrained by the rules of origins and tariffs, to the European Economic Area, Croatia and Macedonia. In addition, tariff rates on imports from third countries are not only low but also predictable and stable. Because these tariffs are tied to EU tariffs, as well as to comprehensive EU commitments under the WTO agreements, they are resistant to domestic pressures for tariff protection. Furthermore, Turkey has taken up the EU rules of origin and EU customs procedures including customs valuations, customs declaration, release for free circulation and duty suspension arrangements. The Agreement has also triggered reforms of competition policy infrastructure.

Chapter 2 is structured as follows. After discussing the main developments in Turkey's trade regime, the chapter considers Turkish trade performance. Thereafter, the chapter examines trade policy under the headings of measures affecting imports of agricultural and industrial goods, exports of agricultural and industrial goods, and foreign direct investment.

Chapter 3 deals with the elimination of technical barriers to trade (TBT). It describes how TBTs in Turkey have significantly declined with the country's gradual transition to the EU's technical standards regime. Analyzing how Turkey made large strides in establishing a modern, market-based regime of technical regulations and standards, the chapter notes how the adoption of international and European standards, as well as improved procedures for admitting goods into Turkey, not only increased contestability in domestic markets but also created conditions for increased competitiveness of domestic firms in foreign markets. The chapter is structured as follows. After considering product standards, technical regulations and conformity assessment systems in general terms, the chapter studies the multilateral regulations for the elimination of TBTs within the context of the WTO. Thereafter the chapter analyzes the EU and Turkish approaches adopted to eliminate TBTs.

Part II of the study is on liberalization of services. It consists of six chapters analyzing liberalization in key backbone services, namely telecommunications, electricity, natural gas, banking, maritime freight transport and road freight transport.

For almost a century, telecommunications industries were organized as state monopolies. In the late 1970s the basic tenets of the monopoly model started to be challenged because of major technological developments. Industry organizations in sectors subject to fierce international competition argued that they were being penalized by the high cost of telecommunications. Consumers also started to complain about the poor performance of monopolies as prices tended to be high and the quality of service poor. Over time, the view that liberalization of the industry is the best way to induce better prices, improve quality of service and stimulate innovation started to gain prominence. Chapter 4 discusses the liberalization of telecommunications services starting with an analysis of distinctive features of the telecommunications industry. Thereafter it considers first the international regulatory regime in the telecommunications sector, and next the regulatory regimes in the EU and Turkish telecommunications sectors respectively.

Until recently, the electricity sector was typically vertically integrated with a captive franchise market, either state-owned or under regulated private ownership. Investment in generation and transmission were chosen to deliver the least-cost expansion plan (in theory), financed by low-cost borrowing underwritten by the franchise revenue base. The last few decades have seen a dramatic change in views of how the electricity sector should be owned, organized and regulated. Today, many of these monopolies have been broken up, and the electricity industry in a large number of countries has been reorganized around markets. Chapter 5 considers the policy reforms introduced in the electricity sector. After discussing the basic characteristics of the sector, the chapter studies the problems and obstacles of liberalizing the electricity sector, emphasizing the experience of the United Kingdom. Thereafter the chapter studies the main principles of the electricity market reform introduced in the EU and Turkey respectively.

For a long time it was considered that natural gas lacked the prerequisites for competition to function on an open market. A key reason was the need for a grid to deliver the energy. As a result, the theory of natural monopoly in the grid-based energy industry was considered sacrosanct up until the middle of the 1980s. Competition was regarded as impractical and market thinking as superfluous. Since the mid-80s, however, there has been a trend towards the liberalization of natural gas markets. A number of countries have launched extensive structural reforms aimed at introducing competition, which is expected to bring economic benefits to consumers. Chapter 6 considers policy reform in the natural gas sector. After analyzing the conditions for competitive gas markets, the chapter studies first the regulatory framework prevailing at the global level and then considers the EU regulations and Turkish regulations in the natural gas sector respectively.

In a large number of low- and middle-income countries, entry into the banking sector was for a long time tightly controlled by regulatory boards that limited the ability of providers to offer a full range of banking services and also limited market access. In those countries, banks were the main sources of domestic financing for governments. Many countries had high reserve, liquidity and portfolio requirements that necessitated significant holdings of cash and government bonds. Banks were used to finance government expenditures directly, and also for directing credit to preferred ends, which often included political supporters of government circles. Lately, objectives such as boosting economic development, preventing and mitigating costly crises and protecting consumers have become important policy goals, and liberalizing banking services is considered essential to achieving these objectives. Chapter 7 considers the liberalization of banking services, including the lessons learned from the recent global financial crisis. After considering banking regulations in general terms, the chapter studies first the global regulation of the banking sector within the framework of the Basel Committee and negotiations under the WTO. Thereafter, the chapter discusses bank regulations introduced in the EU and Turkey respectively.

Chapter 8 considers liberalization in the maritime freight transport sector. Because maritime transport is inherently international in character and vessels on most voyages must operate under the regulatory requirements of many jurisdictions, there is an inherent need for harmonization between countries. Thus, to liberalize the sector, countries must adopt not only the international norms, but also, in the case of a regional alternative, the regulations of those countries with stricter rules. After studying the international regulatory regime the chapter studies the regulatory regimes in the EU and Turkey respectively.

Goods need to be moved, domestically and internationally, freely, reliably and efficiently while minimizing the impact on other transport users and the environment, as well as as safely as possible. As lack of accessibility or poor road conditions are barriers to the trade of agricultural and industrial goods and hinder a country's development efforts, efficient freight transport is essential to achieving prosperity in those countries. Such systems give the countries a competitive edge in moving goods economically. Studies reveal that countries that have liberalized their road freight transport services have done well economically. Chapter 9 studies the liberalization of road freight transportation services. After discussing the international norms in the road freight transportation sector, the chapter analyzes the EU's rules and regulations and finally the Turkish rules and regulations.

Part III is on the quantification of the impact of economic liberalization and consists of Chapter 10 only.

To design successful reform strategies it is crucial that the effects of economic liberalization be analyzed thoroughly. To do that we first need to quantify the trade barriers in different tradable sectors. Thus, the first part of Chapter 10 is on the quantification of barriers to trade in Turkish telecommunications, electricity, natural gas, banking, maritime freight transportation and road freight transportation services. The following section then assesses quantitatively the effects of economic liberalization on the Turkish economy.

The ten chapters of this book cover issues related to liberalization of foreign trade, liberalization of foreign direct investment and the role of regulatory institutions in trade liberalization. Although Turkey is a candidate country for EU accession, the experience of Turkey and the approach to liberalization of goods and services adopted by the country could serve as a useful model for other neighbouring countries of the EU, where liberalization of goods and services is high on the agenda, and could also point out the various difficulties faced during economic liberalization. This study should be of value to both policy makers and academics in the neighbouring countries of the EU and Turkey.

Part I

Liberalization of trade in goods

2 The foreign trade regime and trade liberalization in Turkey

(co-authored with Bartlomiej Kaminski)

After pursuing inward-oriented development strategies for 50 years, Turkey has begun switching to outward-oriented policies since the 1980s. The policy of opening up the economy was pursued with the aim of integrating into the world economy through meeting the requirements of membership in the World Trade Organization (WTO) and close association with the European Union (EU). The latter has also driven multilateral liberalization simply because—in contrast to preferential arrangements with now-EU members from Central Europe—it has entailed the establishment of a customs union between Turkey and the EU beginning in 1996 rather than bilateral reductions in tariff rates. The implementation of a customs union agreement with the EU has resulted in the adoption by Turkey of the EU's much more liberal most-favoured nation (MFN) tariffs on industrial products. This in turn has dramatically increased the openness of the Turkish economy over the last decade. Turkey's applied MFN tariff rates for industrial products, the same as those in the EU's Common External Tariffs, represent now one of the lowest, if not the lowest, levels of MFN tariff protection among economies at a similar stage of economic development.

The purpose of this chapter is to analyze the implications of membership in the WTO and close association with the EU for Turkey's performance in trade in goods. The chapter is structured as follows. The first section describes the main developments in Turkey's trade regime and the second section considers Turkish trade performance. The third section examines the trade policy under the headings of measures affecting imports, exports and foreign direct investment. Finally, the fourth section offers conclusions.

Main developments

Until the early 1980s, Turkey was a fairly closed economy. During the 1960s and 1970s, all imports into Turkey were regulated by annual import programmes. Each programme was published in the *Official Gazette*. The import programme itemized commodities under the liberalization list, the quota list and a list enumerating the commodities to be imported under bilateral trade arrangements. Importation of goods not enumerated in any of the lists was prohibited. The liberalization list was further divided into a free import list (Liberalization List

I) and a restricted list (Liberalization List II). Commodities on the free import list consisted of raw materials and spare parts. Commodities on the restricted list were mainly processed and semi-processed goods and raw materials. The quota list covered commodities for which there was some domestic production or which were considered not essential by plan objectives, such as consumer goods. As soon as domestic production of an import-competing product began, the import was transferred from the liberalized list to the quota list. When domestic production of a commodity was sufficient to meet the domestic demand, the item was removed from the quota list. As commodities not specified on the import lists could not be imported, complete protection was granted to local producers.

By the late 1970s, it was apparent that the strategy of economic growth based on import substitution characterized by fixed exchange rates, regulation of imports through quotas and high nominal and effective protection rates was no longer sustainable. During the 1970s, the increase in prices of oil and other imported commodities and the consequent world recession had adversely affected the Turkish economy. Instead of adjusting to these external shocks Turkey attempted to preserve its growth momentum through rapid reserve decumulation and massive external borrowing. As a result of the oil price shock, the inefficiencies of the long-standing inward-looking development strategy and inflationary financing of growing public sector deficits, the country faced a crisis towards the end of the 1970s. Social and political tensions increased.

In January 1980 the government introduced a comprehensive policy package to address the worsening economic situation. The immediate goals of the reforms were twofold: combatting inflation and reducing the balance-of-payments deficit. The policy makers further aimed at making the economy responsive to market forces in the long run, and in turn more dynamic and efficient. To this end Turkey attempted to foster competition. It was recognized that international trade would be the most effective means to introduce competition in the economy.

Hence, the 1980 reform package called for the gradual liberalization of the Turkish foreign trade regime. In 1981 the quota list was partly phased out, with a large number of commodities transferred from Liberalization List II to Liberalization List I. A major reform was introduced in January 1984 when all imports were classified into three lists: the 'prohibited' list, the 'imports subject to permission' list and the 'liberalized' list. Commodities that could not be imported under any circumstances, such as arms and ammunitions, were specified on the prohibited list. The imports subject to permission list specified the items that could be imported with prior official permission, and the liberalized list enumerated commodities that could be freely imported. According to Togan (1994), the economy-wide nominal protection rate (NPR) amounted to 70.19 per cent and the economy-wide effective protection rate (EPR) 74.71 per cent in 1984.

Liberalization of the foreign trade regime combined with macroeconomic stability positively impacted external performance. By 1985, Turkey's current account deficit was a manageable US$1 billion. The balance-of-payments turnaround during the 1980s was achieved largely by dramatic improvements in exports. Exports increased from US$2.9 billion in 1980 to US$13.6 billion in

1991. This increase in exports was achieved through consistent export promotion and credit policies in addition to fiscal incentives. According to Togan (1994), the economy-wide nominal export subsidy rate (NSR) amounted to 31.98 per cent and the economy-wide effective subsidy rate 37.52 per cent in 1983.

Liberalization of foreign trade intensified during 1988–9 as revealed by the substantial decrease in NPRs and NSRs. While the economy-wide NPR decreased from 70.19 per cent in 1984 to 55.42 in 1988 and to 28.68 per cent in 1990, the economy-wide EPR declined from 74.71 per cent in 1984 to 68.56 per cent in 1988 and to 39.12 per cent in 1990. On the other hand, while the economy-wide NSR declined from 31.98 per cent in 1983 to 13.04 per cent in 1990, the economy-wide effective subsidy rate declined from 37.52 per cent in 1983 to 12.25 in 1990.

Turkey, which had acceded to the General Agreement on Tariffs and Trade (GATT) in 1951 under the Torquay Protocol, participated in all subsequent rounds of multilateral trade negotiations and became an original member of the WTO on 26 March 1995. In order to meet the provisions of the Uruguay Round Agreements, which established the WTO and extended multilateral disciplines, Turkey amended legislation in the areas of intellectual property, safeguards, anti-dumping and countervailing measures. Turkey is not a signatory to any of the plurilateral agreements that resulted from the Uruguay Round but has an observer status in the Committees on Government Procurement and is party to the Information Technology Agreement.

Turkey applied for associate membership in the EU – then the European Economic Commission (EEC) – as early as 1959 (Box 2.1). The application resulted in an Association Agreement in 1963 whereby Turkey and the EU would conditionally and gradually create a customs union by 1995 at the latest. The

---

Box 2.1 The 'EU' factor in Turkey's regional and multilateral liberalization

1959   Turkey requests the signing of an Association Agreement with the European Economic Community (EEC)

1964   Association Agreement (also known as the Ankara Agreement), signed in 1963, enters into force. It established a preferential regime for Turkey's exports of selected products (hazelnuts, tobacco, raisins, dried figs). It also opened the possibility of accession, linking it to the progress that would 'justify envisaging full acceptance by Turkey of the obligations arising of the [Rome] Treaty ...'. (Article 28). According to the Agreement, the association process was to be accomplished in three stages: a preparatory stage, a transitional stage and a final stage

1965   Association Council's meeting agrees on the establishment of a customs union between the EEC and Turkey starting on 1 January 1996

1971	The European Communities (EC) eliminates customs duties and charges having an equivalent effect on industrial imports (except some oil products over a fixed quota, clothing and textiles and steel products) from Turkey
1973	The Additional Protocol, signed in 1970, comes into force. It set out the steps towards the establishment of a customs union within 22 years for industrial products, the elimination of import quotas, the gradual establishment of a preferential trading regime for agricultural products with a free movement once Turkey accepted the Common Agricultural Policy (by 1995) and the establishment of the free movement of labour by 1 December 1986. The protocol also called for the liberalization of trade in services
1973	EC countries introduce restrictions on the recruitment of labour from non-EC member states
1978	Turkey invokes Article 60 of the Additional Protocol, suspending the implementation of the customs union and other bilateral trade liberalization measures for five years
1987	Turkey applies for full membership in the EC and resumes the implementation of tariff reductions on imports from the EC 'frozen' since 1978
1988	Turkey announces that it will fulfil customs union provisions of the Additional Protocol, that is, full alignment of the Turkish MFN tariff schedule with the EC's Common External Tariff (CET), to be completed by the end of 1995
1989	European Council decides not to open accession negotiations with Turkey pointing to the state of flux in European internal architecture caused by the 1986 Single Act
1996	Customs Union Agreement enters into force with transitions: until 1 January 2001 to apply higher tariffs for products agreed by the Association Council (Article 15) and to align progressively with the preferential customs regime of the Community, including its provisions concerning rules of origin
1999	Turkey becomes part of the pan-European cumulation system created in 1997 on the basis of the European Economic Area (EEA) Agreement (1994) between the EC, the European Free Trade Association (EFTA) countries, the Central European countries and the Baltic states, subsequently widened to Slovenia
1999	The European Council, held in Helsinki on 10–11 December 1999, officially recognizes Turkey as a candidate state. In consequence,

	parts of the acquis communautaire covered by the Customs Union Decision are extended to the whole acquis
2001	The Accession Partnership, approved by the European Council (8 March 2001), sets the road map for Turkey's accession and the framework for the EU's financial assistance
2001	National Program for the Adoption of the Acquis (19 March 2001) announced
2001	Turkish tariff rates on industrial products fully aligned with the EU's Common External Tariff
2003	Incorporation of most New Approach EU Directives on technical regulations into Turkey's internal legal order
2003	Revised National Program for the Adoption of the Acquis adopted
2004	Turkey fully adopts the EU's General System of Preferences (GSP) (25 August 2004)
2004	Turkey signs Customs Union Additional Protocol extending Customs Union Decision to ten new EU member countries, including the Greek Cypriot side of Cyprus
2004	The December 2004 Council decides to start membership talks with Turkey on 3 October 2005
2006	The completion by the European Commission of the screening process covering all 35 accession chapters, and suspension on 14–15 December 2006 of negotiations on eight chapters relevant to Turkey's restrictions with regard to the Republic of Cyprus

Sources: Arısan (1999); Bourguignon (1990); Togan (2000); Turkish News Agency Anatolia (http://www.aa.com.tr), European Commission website (http://ec.europa.eu/enlargement/candidate-countries/turkey/relation/index_en.htm).

customs union was seen as a step towards full membership at an unspecified future date. The EU unilaterally granted Turkey preferential tariffs and financial assistance, but the process of staged, mutual reductions in tariffs and in non-tariff barriers was delayed in the 1970s because of economic and political conditions in Turkey. Turkey applied for full membership in 1987. The response in 1990 was that accession negotiations could not be undertaken at that time as the EU was engaged in major internal changes as well as in the transition of Eastern Europe. However, the EU was prepared to extend economic relations without explicitly rejecting the possibility of full membership at a future date.

In 1995 it was agreed at the Association Council meeting that Turkey would create a customs union between Turkey and the EU starting on 1 January 1996. According to the Customs Union Decision (CUD) of 1995, all industrial goods [except for products of the European Coal and Steel Community (ECSC)] complying with the European Community (EC) norms could circulate freely between Turkey and the EU as of 1 January 1996. For ECSC products, Turkey signed a free trade agreement (FTA) with the EU in July 1996, and, as a result, ECSC products have received duty-free treatment between the parties since 1999. The CUD required that Turkey implement the EC's Common Customs Tariffs (CCT) on imports of industrial goods from third countries as of 1 January 1996; adopt by 2001 all of the preferential trade agreements that the EU concluded until then; and implement commercial policy measures similar to those of the EC. Adhering to the stipulations of the CUD, Turkey maintained rates of protection above those specified in the CCT for certain 'sensitive' products until 2001.

As a result of adopting all of the preferential trade agreements that the EU concluded and bringing its commercial policy in line with that of the EU, Turkey over time signed FTAs with the European Free Trade Association (EFTA) countries, Israel, Macedonia, Croatia, Bosnia-Herzegovina, the Palestinian Authority, Tunisia, Morocco, Syria, Egypt, Albania and Georgia. Under these agreements, bilateral trade in industrial goods was to be liberalized at the end of a transition period, and mutual concessions were granted on selected agricultural and processed agricultural goods.[1] As part of the CUD, Turkey has based its Generalized System of Preferences (GSP) on the EC's. Under Turkey's GSP regime, preferences are granted to selected non-agricultural goods, including raw materials and semi-finished goods. On the commercial policy side, Turkey has adopted the EC competition law, established the Competition Board, adopted EC rules on protection of intellectual and industrial property rights, and established the Patent Office. Turkey has also taken up EU customs procedures (customs valuations, customs declaration, release for free circulation and duty suspension arrangements).

An important aspect of Turkey's integration into European markets was its accession to the Pan-European Agreement on Cumulation of the Rules of Origin (PACO) in 1999. Countries benefiting from preferential access are subject to rules of origin. These may be so strict (constraining) that countries are forced to pay an MFN tariff because they cannot satisfy the requirements.[2] The significance of the PACO is that it addresses the barrier stemming from requirements associated with meeting the rules of origin in preferential agreements, thanks to diagonal cumulation rules of origin among PACO participants significantly simplifying the procedures involved. The objective of the PACO, which came into effect on 1 January 1997, was to encourage Europe-wide industrial cooperation by diagonal cumulation that would allow treating imports from parties of the agreement as local inputs. The PACO system has encouraged intra-industry trade, exports and foreign direct investment (FDI) inflows. The Agreement paved the way for the establishment in 2002 of a single European trading block for industrial products, encompassing the EU-15, EFTA and ten Central European countries (Bulgaria, Czech Republic, Estonia, Hungary, Latvia, Lithuania, Poland, Romania, Slovakia and Slovenia). This new arrangement, allowing unfettered distribution of production capacities in the territory of each signatory of the Pan-European Agreement without worrying about meeting the rules of origin requirements, has created a very attractive environment for trade.

On 10–11 December 1999, the European Council meeting held in Helsinki produced a breakthrough in Turkey–EU relations. Turkey was officially recognized as a candidate state for accession, on equal footing with other candidate states. It now has a so-called Accession Partnership with the EU, which means that the EU is working together with Turkey to enable it to adopt the *acquis communautaire*, the legal framework of the EU. In contrast to other candidate countries, Turkey did not receive a timetable for accession. After the approval of the Accession Partnership by the Council and the adoption of the Framework Regulation on 26 February 2001, the Turkish government announced its own National Program for the adoption of the *acquis communautaire* on 19 March 2001. Progress towards accession continues along the path set by the National Program.

In late 2004 another milestone was reached: the Copenhagen European Council in December 2002 had concluded that 'if the European Council in December 2004, on the basis of a report and a recommendation from the Commission, decides that Turkey fulfils the Copenhagen political criteria, the European Union will open accession negotiations with Turkey without delay' (Council of the European Union 2003: 5). The December 2004 Council decided to start membership talks with Turkey on 3 October 2005, acting upon the recommendation of the Commission of the EC that the European Council endorse the launching of formal accession negotiations with Turkey and establish a timetable for accession. With this decision, the last hurdle to begin accession negotiations disappeared.

The screening process started right after the official launching of the EU accession negotiations and lasted until October 2006. Thereafter, the Commission prepared the screening reports for each of the 35 policy chapters. The first chapter to be negotiated, Chapter 25, on science and research, was opened and provisionally closed on 12 June 2006. In November 2006, the EU expressed concern over restrictions to the free movement of goods, including restrictions on means of transport, to which Turkey had committed by signing the Additional Protocol to the Ankara Agreement. With no solution found, the European Council decided on 14–15 December 2006 to suspend negotiations on eight chapters relevant to Turkey's restrictions with regard to the Republic of Cyprus.[3] It was also decided that no chapter would be provisionally closed until Turkey fulfilled its commitments under the Additional Protocol to the EU–Turkey Association Agreement. However, this did not mean that the process of negotiations was blocked. As of January 2007, the negotiations were back on track on the chapters that were not suspended.[4]

The EU–Turkey CUD and more recently the Accession Partnership have been major instruments of integration into the EU and global markets, offering powerful tools to reform the Turkish economy. The former has credibly locked Turkey into a liberal foreign trade regime for industrial goods and holds a promise of Turkey's participation in the EU internal market for industrial products (Kaminski 2005).[5] The latter extends liberal commitments of reforms to other spheres, determining openness of domestic markets to competition from imports as well as the scope of distortions generated by domestic institutions and policies (e.g. monopolistic arrangements or subsidies). In contrast to the CUD imposing legally binding commitments on Turkey, the Accession Partnership provides merely a venue for cooperation and assisting Turkey to adopt the *acquis communautaire*. The extent of its use hinges upon the political will of both sides. As a result of these agreements, Turkish producers of industrial goods have become exposed to competition from imports and operate in one of the largest, if not the largest, free trade areas for industrial products in the world. Turkish producers of industrial goods are now protected by tariffs from external competition to exactly the same extent as EU producers are. Moreover, they are not protected by tariffs and have to face competition from duty-free imports of industrial goods from world-class pan-European firms. In return, industrial producers have duty-free market access, unrestrained by the rules of origins and tariffs, to the European Economic Area (EU-27 and EFTA). The area was recently extended to Mediterranean countries that signed the Barcelona Declaration, namely Algeria, Egypt, Israel, Jordan, Lebanon, Morocco, Syria, Tunisia and the Palestinian Authority of the West Bank and Gaza Strip.

In addition to its trade relations with the EC, Turkey also participates in the Economic Cooperation Organization (ECO), the Black Sea Economic Cooperation (BSEC), and the Euro-Mediterranean Partnership. The ECO is an inter-governmental regional organization established in 1985 by Iran, Pakistan and Turkey for the purpose of sustainable socio-economic development of member states. In 1992, the Organization was expanded to include Afghanistan, Azerbaijan, Kazakhstan, Kyrgyz Republic, Tajikistan, Turkmenistan and Uzbekistan. On 17 July 2003, the ECO Trade Agreement (ECOTA) was signed between Afghanistan, Iran, Pakistan, Tajikistan and Turkey. The Agreement foresees the reduction of tariffs to a maximum of 15 per cent within a maximum period of eight years. ECOTA has binding provisions on state monopolies, state aid, protection of intellectual property rights and dumping and anti-dumping measures. On the other hand, the BSEC aims to improve and diversify economic and trade relations between its 11 members. The member countries are Albania, Armenia, Azerbaijan, Bulgaria, Georgia, Greece, Moldavia, Romania, the Russian Federation, Turkey and Ukraine. The BSEC Declaration was signed on 25 June 1992, and on 7 February 1997 a declaration of intent for the establishment of a BSEC free trade area was adopted. Recently, the BSEC launched projects to eliminate non-tariff barriers on regional trade and to harmonize trade documents in the region. Finally, the Euro-Mediterranean Partnership is a political, economic and social programme aimed at creating an area of shared prosperity, including a Euro-Mediterranean FTA by 2010.

Trade performance and investment

Until the early 1980s Turkey, as emphasized above, was a fairly closed economy. At that time – as part of more wide-ranging economic reforms – the trade policy of protection and import substitution was replaced by a much more open trade regime. As a result, exports and imports increased considerably over time. Whereas Turkey's merchandise exports (imports) amounted to US\$2.9 (US\$7.9) billion in 1980, they increased to US$131.97 (US$201.96) billion in 2008. On the other hand, exports (imports) of goods and services increased from US$3.4 (US$8.3) billion in 1980 to US187.2 (US$227.7) billion in 2008. This amounts to an average annual rate of growth of merchandise exports (imports) of 14.6 (12.3) per cent, and of exports (imports) of goods and services of 15.4 (12.5) per cent. As a per cent of gross domestic product (GDP), merchandise exports (imports) increased from 4.5 (12.1) per cent in 1980 to 16.6 (25.4) per cent in 2008, and exports (imports) of goods and services increased from 5.2 (12.8) per cent in 1980 to 23.6 (28.7) per cent in 2008. These are remarkable increases by any standards achieved within the context of a liberal trade regime.

Table 2.1 shows that in 2008 exports to the EU-15 formed 48.4 per cent of total exports. The table further reveals that the three export commodities with the highest shares in total exports were automotive products, with a share of 13.4 per cent, iron and steel, with a share of 12.6 per cent, and clothing, with a share of 10.2 per cent. The three export commodities with the highest shares in exports to the EU were automotive products, with a share of 20.8 per cent, clothing, with a share of 17.1 per cent, and other semi-manufactures, with a share of 7.9 per cent. During the period 1995–2008, total exports grew at an annual rate of 13.9 per cent. The export commodities with the highest annual growth rates were other products, with a growth rate of 41.9 per cent, automotive products, with a growth rate of 27.6 per cent, and other transport equipment, with a growth rate of 21.4 per cent. Similarly the export commodities to the EU with the highest growth rates were automotive products, with a growth rate of 32.8 per cent, other products, with a growth rate of 29.4 per cent, and office machines and equipment, with a growth rate of 20.8 per cent. Finally, we note that the share of the EU in total sectoral exports has been highest in the cases of office machines and telecommunications equipment, with a share of 85.5 per cent, clothing, with a share of 81.1 per cent, and automotive products, with a share of 75.2 per cent. Among the sectors considered, the share of the EU in total sectoral exports has been the lowest in the cases of other products, iron and steel and other chemicals.

Table 2.2 shows that imports from the EU-15 formed 37.2 per cent of total imports. The table further reveals that the three import commodities with the highest shares in total imports were fuels, with a share of 23.8 per cent, automotive products, with a share of 7.5 per cent, and iron and steel, with a share of 7.4 per cent. The three import commodities with the highest shares in imports from the EU were automotive products, with a share of 15.7 per cent, other non-electrical machinery, with a share of 12.7 per cent, and other semi-manufactures, with a share of 7 per cent. During the period 1995–2008, total imports grew at an annual rate of 12.4 per cent. The imported commodities with the highest annual growth rates were other products, with a growth rate of 36.2 per cent, clothing, with a growth rate of 22.9 per cent, and non-ferrous metals, with a growth rate of 17.5 per cent. Similarly the imported commodities from the EU with the highest growth rates were fuels, with a growth rate of 18.9 per cent, pharmaceuticals, with a growth rate of 17.4 per cent, and automotive products, with a growth rate of 15.7 per cent. Finally, we note that the share of the EU in total sectoral imports

Table 2.1 Exports from Turkey

SITC	Commodity	Total exports 2008 (US$ million)	Percentage distribution, total exports	Annual growth rate of exports 1995–2008 (%)	Exports to the EU 2008 (US$ million)	Percentage distribution, exports to EU	Share of sectoral exports to EU (%)	Annual growth rate of exports to EU 1995–2008 (%)
	Agricultural products							
0+1+4+22	Food	10,694	8.02	6.33	4,238	6.57	39.63	6.84
2–22–27–28	Agricultural raw materials	768	0.58	6.31	332	0.52	43.28	4.88
	Mining products							
27+28	Ores and other minerals	2,463	1.85	13.28	838	1.30	34.02	10.75
3	Fuels	7,531	5.65	21.21	2,073	3.21	27.52	9.36
68	Non-ferrous metals	2,094	1.57	15.31	1,169	1.81	55.83	17.66
	Manufactures							
67	Iron and steel	16,844	12.63	15.84	3,550	5.50	21.08	18.98
	Chemicals							
51	Organic chemicals	462	0.35	8.15	287	0.44	62.17	9.41
57+58	Plastics	2,365	1.77	19.67	876	1.36	37.06	20.42
52	Inorganic chemicals	673	0.50	4.32	256	0.40	38.08	2.20
54	Pharmaceuticals	470	0.35	13.98	193	0.30	41.04	16.88
53+55+56+59	Other chemicals	2,152	1.61	12.15	540	0.84	25.08	20.52
6–65–67–68	Other semi-manufactures	12,254	9.19	16.78	5,090	7.89	41.54	16.27

Machinery and transport equipment

71–713	Power-generating machinery	2,369	1.78	20.92	1,494	2.32	63.04	17.13
72+73+74	Other non-electrical machinery	6,097	4.57	20.57	2,451	3.80	40.20	20.27
75+76+776	Office machines and tel. equipment	2,433	1.82	19.13	2,081	3.23	85.53	20.84
77–776–7783	Electrical machinery and apparatus	7,062	5.30	17.71	3,520	5.46	49.85	17.82
78–785–786+7132+7783	Automotive products	17,845	13.38	27.61	13,415	20.79	75.17	32.83
79+785+786+7131+7133+7138+7139	Other transport equipment	4,674	3.51	21.44	3,036	4.70	64.94	20.28
65	Textiles	9,403	7.05	10.22	4,795	7.43	50.99	10.04
84	Clothing	13,595	10.20	7.22	11,027	17.09	81.11	9.23
8–84–86–891	Other consumer goods	6,896	5.17	17.83	2,970	4.60	43.08	20.31
9+891	*Other products*	4,208	3.16	41.93	291	0.45	6.91	29.43
Total		133,352	100	13.87	64,520	100	48.38	14.74

Source: Own calculations based on data provided by the State Institute of Statistics.

Note
SITC, Standard International Trade Classification.

Table 2.2 Imports to Turkey

SITC	Commodity	Total imports 2008 (US$ million)	Percentage distribution, total imports	Annual growth rate of imports 1995–2008 (%)	Imports from EU 2008 (US$ million)	Percentage distribution, imports from EU	Share of sectoral imports from EU (%)	Annual growth rate, imports from EU 1995–2008 (%)
	Agricultural products							
0+1+4+22	Food	8,502	4.20	6.69	1,887	2.51	22.20	6.76
2–22–27–28	Agricultural raw materials	4,535	2.24	7.09	1,418	1.88	31.26	6.83
	Mining products							
27+28	Ores and other minerals	10,345	5.11	15.57	3,965	5.27	38.33	12.30
3	Fuels	48,207	23.81	12.97	3,531	4.69	7.32	18.94
68	Non-ferrous metals	6,382	3.15	17.50	1,452	1.93	22.76	13.11
	Manufactures							
67	Iron and steel	15,031	7.42	15.61	5,070	6.74	33.73	12.83
	Chemicals							
51	Organic chemicals	4,169	2.06	9.21	2,026	2.69	48.60	8.65
57+58	Plastics	8,486	4.19	15.63	4,749	6.31	55.97	13.15
52	Inorganic chemicals	1,667	0.82	8.67	537	0.71	32.22	6.28
54	Pharmaceuticals	4,738	2.34	16.51	3,250	4.32	68.59	17.36
53+55+56+59	Other chemicals	6,481	3.20	10.04	3,884	5.16	59.93	9.67
6–65–67–68	Other semimanufactures	9,071	4.48	11.74	5,267	7.00	58.06	10.90

	Machinery and transport equipment							
71–713	Power-generating machinery	2,991	1.48	10.59	1,740	2.31	58.19	11.51
72+73+74	Other non-electrical machinery	14,767	7.29	9.16	9,524	12.66	64.49	8.80
75+76+776	Office machines and tel. equipment	8,079	3.99	11.62	2,535	3.37	31.38	4.76
77–776–7783	Electrical machinery and apparatus	6,869	3.39	13.67	3,562	4.73	51.86	10.07
78–785–786+ 7132+7783	Automotive products	15,155	7.49	15.47	11,794	15.67	77.82	15.72
79+785+786+ 7131+7133+ 7138+7139	Other transport equipment	4,327	2.14	5.10	2,478	3.29	57.26	9.47
65	Textiles	5,797	2.86	9.64	1,713	2.28	29.55	7.00
84	Clothing	2,216	1.09	22.89	465	0.62	20.97	13.04
8–84–86–891	Other consumer goods	8,961	4.43	12.41	4,133	5.49	46.12	10.20
9+891	*Other products*	5,685	2.81	36.16	269	0.36	4.74	15.44
Total		202,461	100.00	12.42	75,249	100.00	37.17	11.19

Source: Own calculations based on data provided by the State Institute of Statistics.

Note
SITC, Standard International Trade Classification.

has been highest in the cases of automotive products, with a share of 77.8 per cent, pharmaceuticals, with a share of 68.6 per cent, and other non-electrical machinery, with a share of 64.5 per cent. Among the sectors considered, the share of the EU in total sectoral imports has been lowest in the cases of other products, fuels and clothing.

Kaminski and Ng (2007), highlighting the recent trade performance of Turkey, note that the country has become highly integrated into the world economy. Adopting a taxonomy developed by Landesmann and Stehrer (2003), the authors assess the technological content of Turkish exports in three categories: low technology and unskilled labour-intensive activities, medium-to-high technology activities and resource-intensive activities. The last covers either extraction of mineral resources or unprocessed agricultural products whereas the low technology and unskilled labour-intensive activities group includes textiles and clothing, wood products, chemicals, tyres, etc. The medium-to-high technology group includes machinery and equipment, transport equipment, electrical and optical equipment, pharmaceuticals, etc. The authors found that EU-oriented exports show a dramatic shift towards medium and high technology products, although low technology and unskilled labour-intensive products remain as major areas of specialization. According to the authors, the shift has led to higher wages in higher technology sectors, which in turn has led to higher wages in services and unskilled labour-intensive sectors with obvious implications for their international competitiveness.

Kaminski and Ng (2007) emphasize that network trade has been the driving force for the Turkish economy's integration into global markets. Integration into EU-27 production and distribution value chains and networks structures has been the driver of Turkey's increasing participation in the division of labour based on outsourcing and production fragmentation. The authors define 'buyer-driven' commodity chains as networks that tend to exist in industries in which large retailers, branded marketers and branded manufacturers play the pivotal roles in setting up decentralized production networks in a variety of exporting countries. They point out that this pattern has become common in Labour-intensive, consumer goods sectors such as textiles and clothing, footwear and furniture. On the other hand, the authors note that production fragmentation in vertically integrated sectors has led to the emergence of 'producer-driven' network trade, which, differing from 'buyer-driven' global value chains, includes two-way flows of parts and components across firms located in various countries for further processing, and development occurring at several tiers with large multinational corporations playing a central role in coordinating the production process. 'Producer-driven' networks are mainly present in capital- and skilled labour-intensive industries such as automobiles, computers, semi-conductors and heavy machinery. The authors note that the share of 'buyer-driven' network exports in total Turkish exports has dramatically declined in recent years, but they still account for a large portion of all network exports. In Turkey there was a clear shift towards specialization in higher value-added 'producer-driven' networks. The major driver of change, overall, has been the automotive network, but strongly supported by the expansion in exports of information and communication technology network final products.

Turning to consideration of FDI flows, we note that Turkey until recently was not successful in attracting FDI inflows. Annual FDI inflows amounted to only US$791 million during 1990–2000. The country's failure to attract large foreign investment inflows was mainly due to economic and political uncertainties surrounding the country in the 1990s and early 2000s, and the investment climate, which was particularly unfavourable to foreign investors. With the introduction of the 2001 programme of economic stabilization, implementation of its privatization programme, the EU's 2004 decision to begin membership negotiations with Turkey, and liberalization measures introduced during the last seven years, FDI inflows increased considerably. They reached US$20.2 billion in 2006, US$22.1 billion in 2007 and US$18.2 billion in 2008.

Table 2.3, showing the sectoral distribution of FDI inflows into Turkey over the period 2004–8, reveals that during the last five years the sectors attracting the

Table 2.3 Sectoral distribution of foreign direct investment inflows (US$ million)

Sectors	2004	2005	2006	2007	2008
Agriculture, hunting and forestry	4	5	5	5	26
Fishing	2	2	1	3	19
Mining and quarrying	73	40	122	336	173
Manufacturing	190	785	1,866	4,210	3,828
Manufacture of food products and beverages	78	68	608	766	1,279
Manufacture of textiles	9	180	26	232	190
Manufacture of chemicals and chemical products	38	174	601	1,109	202
Manufacture of machinery and equipment	6	13	54	48	223
Manufacture of electrical optical equipment	2	13	53	117	243
Manufacture of motor vehicles, trailers and semi-trailers	27	106	63	70	67
Other manufacturing	30	231	461	1,868	1,624
Electricity, gas and water supply	66	4	112	567	1,053
Construction	3	80	222	285	720
Wholesale and retail trade	72	68	1,166	169	2,073
Hotels and restaurants	1	42	23	33	27
Transport, storage and communications	639	3,285	6,696	1,116	169
Financial services	69	4,018	6,957	11,662	5,925
Real estate, renting and business activities	3	29	99	560	673
Health and social services	35	74	265	177	150
Other community, social and personal service activities	33	103	105	13	59
Total	1,190	8,535	17,639	19,136	14,895

Source: Undersecretariat for the Treasury.

highest amount of FDI have been services and manufacturing. While the average share of services in total FDI inflows over the period 2006–8 amounted to 79.2 per cent, the average share of manufacturing in total FDI inflow over the same period was 19.4 per cent. In services, 'financial services' and 'transport, storage and communications' received the highest amount of investment, with 59.7 per cent and 17.3 per cent respectively. In manufacturing, the highest amount of investment was received by 'manufacture of food products and beverages' and 'manufacture of chemicals and chemical products', with 28.1 per cent and 21.3 per cent respectively. Table 2.4, showing the FDI inflows by country of origin over the period 2004–8, reveals that the EU was the largest investor in Turkey. While the share of the EU in total FDI inflows over the period 2006–8 amounted to 74.6 per cent, the share of the United States was 10.9 per cent and the share of Gulf countries 8.2 per cent. The largest investors from the EU have been those from the Netherlands, with a share of 31.2 per cent in total FDI inflows from the EU over the period 2006–8, and the United Kingdom, with a share of 10.1 per cent.

Finally, we note that Turkey's annual FDI outflows amounted to US$0.92 billion in 2006, US$2.11 billion in 2007 and US$2.59 billion in 2008, averaging US$1.87 billion over the period 2006–8.

Table 2.4 Foreign direct investment inflows by country of origin (US$ million)

Country	2004	2005	2006	2007	2008
EU countries	1,027	5,006	14,489	12,600	11,281
Germany	73	391	357	954	1,217
France	34	2,107	439	368	685
Netherlands	568	383	5,069	5,443	1,738
United Kingdom	126	166	628	702	2,294
Italy	14	692	189	74	222
Other EU countries	212	1,267	7,807	5,059	5,125
Other European countries	6	1,646	85	373	291
African countries	–	3	21	5	82
United States	36	88	848	4,212	863
Canada	61	26	121	11	24
Americas	–	8	33	494	60
Asia	60	1,756	1,927	1,405	2,292
Near and Middle Eastern countries	54	1,678	1,910	608	2,132
Gulf countries	43	1,675	1,783	311	1,911
Other Near and Middle Eastern countries	11	2	3	196	96
Other Asian countries	6	78	17	797	160
Other countries	–	2	115	36	2
Total	1,190	8,535	17,639	19,136	14,895

Source: Undersecretariat for the Treasury.

Trade policy

Over the last 13 years Turkey has been quite successful in amending its domestic legislation to reflect both its EU and WTO commitments. Both border measures and behind-the-border regulations have been brought in conformance not only with the WTO agreements but also with those with the EU. The latter have called for a much deeper and wider liberalization of foreign trade than envisaged under the WTO agreements. The EU–Turkey CUD has not only called for the adoption of the EU's MFN applied tariff rates on industrial products but also for bringing Turkey's commercial policy in line with that of the EU as well as harmonization with the *acquis communautaire* in many other areas relevant to the EU single market including technical standards and customs procedures. Turkey's participation in the Pan-European/Med Agreement on Cumulation of the Rules of Origin also removes some tools of foreign trade policy from the available menu, for example, the agreement explicitly prohibits the use of duty drawbacks.

The largest discretion in policy making is in agricultural products. While they are subject to bilateral liberalization measures negotiated between Turkey and its foreign trade partners, they are not part of customs union arrangements and respective regulations vary between Turkey and the EU. In addition, as the EU–Turkey CU went into effect after the completion of the Uruguay Round of multilateral trade negotiations, Turkey's tariff commitments differ from those of the EU.

The above has the following two implications: first, the use of a wide range of measures with both a direct and an indirect impact on foreign trade is either banned by existing international agreements or significantly curtailed; and, second, the bulk of Turkey's foreign trade is subject to preferential arrangements and is mostly free of both duties and other trade-restraining measures.

Measures affecting imports

Goods imported into Turkey are subject to various charges: customs duties, levies such as the Mass Housing Fund levy, and internal taxes such as excise duties [special consumption tax (SCT), value added tax (VAT) and stamp duty].[6] As of 2009, Turkey's tariff comprises 16,800 lines at the Harmonized Commodity Description and Coding System (HS) 12-digit level. As a result of the Uruguay Round, 46.3 per cent of tariff lines in Turkey are now bound (all tariff lines for agricultural products and some 36 per cent of the lines for non-agricultural products). Final bindings range from zero to 225 per cent on agricultural products, and from zero to 102 per cent on non-agricultural goods. The simple average bound tariff rate amounts to 33.9 per cent.

In Turkey, besides bound tariff rates, there are two other sets of tariff rates. These are the applied tariff rates and the statutory tariff rates. Law No. 474 of the Customs Tariff Schedule has set the so-called statutory tariff rates. The law enables the government to increase the applied MFN tariff rates for a given year when they are deemed not high enough to provide 'adequate' protection to domestic industries. Under the law, the government can replace applied MFN tariff rates by 150 per cent of the corresponding rates of the statutory tariff, with a view to ensuring higher protection to local industries. In the case of products subject to tariff bindings, when the new rate is higher than the corresponding bound tariff rate, the latter applies. But in cases in which the tariff rate is specified as 'exempt', the equivalent applied tariff rate is zero per cent and the government cannot increase the applied tariff rate above zero per cent. Hence, the 'exempt' status in the tariff schedule provides added protection to Turkey's trade liberalization commitments.

The Turkish applied tariff schedule is rather complex.[7] It consists of a large number of lists specifying the tariff lines classified at the HS 12-digit level for different country groups and countries. List I displays customs duties applied to imports of agricultural products, excluding fish and fishery products. List II shows customs duties to be applied to imports of industrial products and products covered by the ECSC. Lists III lays down customs duties applied to imports of processed agricultural products, and List IV the customs duties applied to imports of fish and fishery products. List V displays reduced customs duties applied to imports of certain products used as raw materials in the fertilizer, chemicals, plastics, textile and electrical machinery industries. Finally, List VI lists the commodities that can be imported by the civil air transportation sector with zero tariff rates. The six lists are accompanied by six annexes. Annexes 1 and 2 show the specific tariff rates applied to imports of processed agricultural products distinguished by their content of milk fat and cornstarch/glucose. Annex 3 lists the three groups of countries benefitting from the GSP regime, and Annexes 4 and 5 list the sensitive and non-sensitive sectors benefitting again from the GSP regime.

Turkey's tariff comprises ad valorem and non-ad valorem rates consisting of specific, mixed, compound and formula duties. Most of the tariffs are ad valorem. Specific taxes (Mass Housing Fund levy) are applied on the imports of certain fish and fishery products specified in List IV as well as on the imports of certain products specified in List II. The mixed, compound and formula duties are applied on processed agricultural commodities specified in List III. In List III the duties range between 0 and 368.25 euro/100 kg depending on the content of milk fat and cornstarch/glucose.[8] Finally, we note that products listed in List V are in general more specific than those listed in List II. For products listed in both List V and List II we take the minimum of the two tariff rates.

For the calculation of nominal protection rates we introduce the following notation. Let t_c^i denote the rate of ad valorem customs duty on commodity i, M_i c.i.f. the value of the import of commodity i measured in Turkish liras, m_i the quantity of the import of commodity i measured in units the Mass Housing Fund levy is reported in, $FUND_1^i$ the Mass Housing Fund levy on commodity i, $FUND_2^i$ the ad valorem Mass Housing Fund tax rate on commodity i, and E the exchange rate (Turkish liras per euro).[9] The base of the customs duty on commodity i is the c.i.f. value of the import of commodity i. Therefore, this duty is calculated as $t_c^i M_i$. The Mass Housing Fund levy is usually specific. For these specific tariff rates the ad valorem equivalents of these rates need to be calculated. Given the foreign price of the commodity

$$p_j^{Euro} = \frac{M_j}{m_j E}$$

the Turkish lira equivalent of the euro-denominated levy is calculated from the relation

$$FUND_1^i m_i E = \left(M_i \left(FUND_1^i / p_i^{Euro} \right) \right)$$

Hence, the ad valorem equivalent is given by ($FUND_1^i/p_i^{Euro}$). On the other hand, when the Mass Housing Fund tax is specified in ad valorem terms the equivalent tariff revenue is given by $FUND_2^i M_i$. The sum total of all of the above taxes and surcharges is then denoted by:

$$t_i = \left(t_c^i + \left(FUND_1^i / p_i^{Euro} \right) + FUND_2^i \right).$$

On imported commodities Turkey imposes VAT as well as SCT. The base of SCT is the value of imported commodities inclusive of import taxes and surcharges, that is, $(1+t_i)M_i$. On the other hand the base of VAT is the value of imported commodities inclusive of import taxes, surcharges and the SCT. Letting vat_i be the value added tax rate on commodity i, and sct_i the special consumption tax rate on commodity i, the special consumption tax rate on imported commodity i is calculated as:

$$SCT_i = sct_i \left(1 + t_c^i + \left(FUND_1^i / p_i^{Euro} \right) + FUND_2^i \right)$$

Similarly, the VAT rate on imported commodity i is determined as:

$$VAT_i = vat_i \left[\left(1 + t_c^i + \left(FUND_1^i / p_i^{Euro} \right) + FUND_2^i \right) + SCT_i \right]$$

Noting that domestically produced commodities are subject to VAT and SCT at the rates vat_i and sct_i, respectively, the nominal protection rate on imported commodity i (NPR_i), measuring the protection provided to commodity i relative to domestic production of commodity i, equals:

$$NPR_i = t_i + SCT_i + VAT_i - vat_i(1 + sct_i) - sct_i$$

When we consider the average protection rate in a particular sector j with k commodities in the sector the simple average protection rate is calculated as

$$\sum_{i=1}^{k} NPR_i^j / k$$

where NPR_i^j denotes the average protection rate on commodity i of sector j.

It was stated above that Annexes 1 and 2 show among others the specific tariff rates applied to imports of processed agricultural products distinguished by the content of milk fat and cornstarch/glucose, and that the specific tariff rate for a specific 12-digit HS commodity indicated as T1 and T2 in List III may vary between 0 and 368.25 euro/100 kg depending on the content of milk fat and cornstarch/glucose. Thus, one cannot obtain the ad valorem equivalent of the specific tariff rate for these 12-digit HS commodities unless one has information on the milk fat and cornstarch/glucose contents of the commodities imported. To obtain the ad valorem equivalent of the specific tariff rates for each 12-digit HS commodity in List III, for which the specific tariffs are stated as T1 and T2, we first determine the total Housing Fund taxes collected on each 12-digit HS commodity under consideration by country groups (EU + EFTA, and other countries). Next we divide the Housing Fund tax collected on each 12-digit HS commodity under consideration by country groups by the value of import of the corresponding 12-digit HS commodity again by country group, and obtain the ad valorem tariff equivalent for each 12-digit HS commodity in List III, for which the specific tariffs are stated as T1 and T2.[10]

Table 2.5 shows the NPRs prevailing in 2009, in which all non-ad valorem tariffs have been converted to ad valorem equivalents and incorporated into NPRs. In the table average tariffs for two groups of countries are listed. These are the EU, and countries for which the MFN tariffs apply. In the table the average NPRs are shown for 19 aggregated HS commodity groups such as chemical products, textile and textile articles and transport equipment. The table reveals that in trade with the EU the overall simple average NPR is 9.12 per cent and the overall simple average MFN protection rate is 13.86 per cent.

In trade with the EU, 17 out of the total of 19 sectors have zero NPRs. The highest protection rates apply in the cases of agricultural commodities and chemical products. In those cases the NPRs are 52.22 per cent and 0.08 per cent respectively. In the case of trade with countries for which the MFN tariffs apply, the NPR on agricultural products is 56.5 per cent, textiles and textile articles 8.93 per cent, and footwear and miscellaneous manufactures 8.03 per cent. The figures show that in Turkey the agricultural sector is heavily protected.

Table 2.6 shows the NPRs for the agricultural commodities in more detail. The table reveals that in trade with the EU the simple average NPR is 50.7 per cent, and in trade with countries for which MFN tariffs apply it is 54.85 per cent. In the case of trade with the EU the highest average protection rates apply in the cases of meat and edible offal, milk and dairy products; eggs; honey and products made from meat, fish and crustacea. In these cases the NPRs are 147.65 per cent, 104.01 per cent and 102.63 per cent respectively. In the case of trade with countries for which the MFN tariffs apply the highest average NPRs are imposed on meat and edible offal, products made from meat, fish and crustacea, and milk and dairy products; eggs; honey. These protection rates are not much different from the protection rates that apply on imports from the EU.

Comparison of the protection rates reported in Tables 2.5 and 2.6 with those given in the *Trade Policy Review: Turkey 2007* (WTO 2008) reveals that our protection rates are higher for some of the commodity groups for MFN tariff countries. Although the figures in WTO (2008) refer to the year 2007 and our data to the year 2009, the difference in the result is due mainly to the way that the protection rates in the two studies have been estimated. It is interesting to note that, whereas the overall MFN simple average tariff rate in WTO (2008) is 11.6 per cent, it is 13.86 per cent in our case. Furthermore, when the WTO definition of agricultural products is used, the overall MFN simple average protection rate in agriculture is calculated as 47.6 per cent in WTO (2008), whereas it is 54.85 per cent in our case.[11] Divergence of the NPRs calculated in the two different studies is more pronounced in sectors in which the tariff rates inclusive of all other taxes and surcharges, VAT rates and SCT rates are relatively high as in the case of 'vehicles other than railway or tramway rolling stock, and parts and accessories thereof' (HS 87).

In Turkey, import prohibitions apply to ten broad product categories such as narcotics, arms and ammunitions, and ozone-depleting substances, for reasons such as protection of the environment, public security, health and public morals. Regarding licensing, we note that import licences are required for several categories of products, including some motor vehicles, transmission apparatus, chemicals, fertilizers, endangered species of wild fauna and flora, solvent and petroleum products, and certain sugar substitutes. Importers of these items must obtain permission from the relevant authorities. In addition, the importation of pharmaceuticals, drugs, some medical products, cosmetics, detergents, foodstuffs and packaging materials, fishery products, and agricultural, animal and veterinary products is subject to health and sanitary controls. Imports of agricultural products and foodstuffs require a 'control certificate' issued by the Ministry of Agriculture and Rural Affairs (MARA) and imports of pharmaceutical products, drugs, certain consumable medical products, cosmetics and detergents require a control certificate issued by the Ministry of Health.[12] Finally, we note that measuring and weighing instruments to be released for free circulation in Turkey are subject to control by the Directorate General of Measures and Standards of the Ministry of Industry and Trade; and carrying materials comprising cinematographic and musical works are inspected and examined by the Directorate of Copyright and Cinema with the aim of combating piracy. Tariff preferences on agricultural products, granted under Turkey's trade agreements, are generally subject to quotas. Tariff quotas are applied on imports of various agricultural and processed agricultural products from the EU, Israel, Macedonia, Croatia, Bosnia-Herzegovina, Morocco, Syria, Tunisia, Egypt and Albania. In addition, Turkey is applying import quotas on certain textile and clothing products as a requirement for harmonizing its import policy with that of the EC. Licensing is used again whenever quotas are imposed.

Article 36 of the CUD of 1995 specifies that as long as a particular practice is incompatible with the competition rules of the customs union as specified in Articles 30–32 of the CUD and 'in the absence of such rules if such practice causes or threatens to cause serious prejudice to the interest of the other Party or material injury to its domestic industry' the Community or Turkey may take

Table 2.5 Nominal protection rates, 2009 (%)

HS code	Commodity description	Number of tariff lines	Applied mean tariffs (simple), EU	Range of tariff, EU	Standard deviation, EU	Mean MFN tariffs (simple), others	Range of tariff, non-EU	Standard deviation, non-EU	Imports 2008 (US$ million)
01–24	Agricultural products	2,931	52.22	0–243	54.54	56.50	0–243	55.08	8,758.8
25–27	Mineral products	414	0.00	0–0	0.00	1.26	0–14.8	2.02	49,555.2
28–38	Chemical products	3,072	0.08	0–18.4	1.10	5.41	0–40.8	3.23	17,384.7
39–40	Plastics and rubber	543	0.00	0–0	0.00	4.54	0–7.0	2.88	11,604.7
41–43	Leather and travel goods	218	0.00	0–0	0.00	3.46	0–10.6	2.92	1,158.0
44–46	Wood products	320	0.00	0–0	0.00	2.23	0–11.8	2.91	1,178.5
47–49	Cellulose products, paper and paper products	446	0.00	0–0	0.00	0.00	0–0	0.00	3,246.6
50–63	Textile and textile articles	2,341	0.00	0–0	0.00	8.93	0–14.2	3.98	9,630.0
64–67	Footwear and miscellaneous manufactures	156	0.00	0–0	0.00	8.03	0–18.4	5.69	769.2
68–70	Articles of stone, ceramics, glass and glass products	437	0.00	0–0	0.00	4.36	0–15.6	3.39	1,403.1
71	Precious and semi-precious articles	104	0.00	0–0	0.00	1.20	0–4.7	1.91	5,653.8

72–83	Base metals and articles of base metal	1,915	0.00	0–0	0.00	5.36	0–27.6	6.41	33,417.3
84	Non-electric machinery	1,479	0.00	0–0	0.00	1.95	0–10.5	1.69	22,515.4
85	Electric machinery	977	0.00	0–0	0.00	3.30	0–19.8	3.82	13,868.0
86–89	Transport equipment	466	0.00	0–0	0.00	6.36	0–38.2	6.56	15,593.2
90–92	Precision	591	0.00	0–0	0.00	2.55	0–11.8	2.25	3,711.9
93	Arms and ammunitions	33	0.00	0–0	0.00	2.85	0–4.5	1.39	60.2
94–96	Miscellaneous manufactured articles	343	0.00	0–0	0.00	3.05	0–9.1	1.90	1,900.1
97	Art and antiques	14	0.00	0–0	0.00	0.00	0–0	0.00	414.2
	Total	16,800	9.12	0–243	30.2	13.86	0–243	30.5	201,822.9

Source: Own calculations.

Table 2.6 Protection in agriculture, 2009 (%)

HS code	Description	Number of tariff lines	Applied mean tariffs (simple), EU	Range of tariff, EU	Standard deviation, EU	Mean MFN tariffs (simple), others	Range of tariff, non-EU	Standard deviation, non-EU	2008 imports (US$ million)
I.	Live animals and animal products								
1	Live animals	83	44.84	0–136.4	51.40	44.84	0–136.4	51.40	41.45
2	Meat and edible offal	235	147.65	25.3–243	80.66	147.72	25.3–243	80.57	0.91
3	Fish and sea products	336	36.88	0–64.9	14.52	47.05	0–76.7	17.99	119.77
4	Milk and dairy products; eggs; honey	209	104.01	0–183.6	65.05	105.93	0–183.6	63.33	126.94
5	Other animal products	38	1.92	0–23.6	5.75	2.08	0–23.6	5.78	28.54
II.	Vegetable products								
6	Plants and floriculture products	52	20.05	2.6–55.2	22.96	20.64	4.2–55.2	22.52	57.75
7	Vegetable, plants, roots and tubers	166	20.74	0–50	10.33	20.80	0–50	10.23	400.25
8	Edible fruits; citrus fruits	148	42.08	15.6–147.3	22.98	42.08	15.6–147.3	22.98	318.63
9	Coffee, tea, spices	57	40.93	0–156.6	35.72	41.20	0–156.6	35.51	72.74
10	Cereals	65	58.05	0–140.4	48.81	58.09	0–140.4	48.77	2,137.32
11	Products of the milling industry	102	42.18	4.3–82.8	15.39	42.46	4.3–82.8	15.14	25.19
12	Oilseeds, various seeds/fruits; industrial plants	125	19.01	0–41.3	11.63	19.94	0–41.3	11.63	1,465.17
13	Vegetable lacquers, resins, balsams	35	2.70	0–23.6	7.62	4.97	0–29.5	9.96	25.68
14	Vegetable plaiting materials	21	0.00	0–0	0.00	0.00	0–0	0.00	4.92

III.		Animal or vegetable oils and fats								
	15	Animal or vegetable oils and fats	198	25.43	0–59	19.55	26.13	0–59	18.90	1,657.56
IV.		Foodstuffs, beverages, tobacco								
	16	Products made from meat, fish, crustacea	134	102.63	43.2–131.2	34.14	109.12	58.3–131.2	26.90	2.47
	17	Sugar and sweets	64	73.07	0–145.8	69.21	78.28	0–145.8	64.93	86.84
	18	Cocoa and cocoa products	29	8.58	0–28.1	7.61	10.53	0–32.1	6.32	284.17
	19	Cereal products, wheat floor, pastries	88	6.20	0–40.0	9.19	16.24	4.1–68.2	12.65	151.28
	20	Foods made of vegetable, fruits and other plants	371	58.60	0–146.8	19.31	59.16	0–146.8	17.95	87.64
	21	Various foods	63	5.88	0–63.2	15.98	14.77	0–63.18	15.73	387.18
	22	Alcoholic and non-alcoholic beverages	201	46.41	0–96.2	45.51	66.05	0–134.6	62.82	111.79
	23	Residues of food industry; fodders	83	9.44	0–15.9	5.02	10.17	0–15.9	4.86	772.97
	24	Processed tobacco and substitutes	28	12.64	0–29.5	14.87	61.51	18.6–139.6	48.04	391.69
V.		Hides, wool and cotton								
	4101–4103	Hides and skin	31	0.00	0–0	0.00	0.00	0–0	0.00	235.46
	5101–5103	Wool and animal hair	44	0.00	0–0	0.00	0.00	0–0	0.00	46.67
	5201–5203	Cotton	13	0.00	0–0	0.00	0.00	0–0	0.00	1,005.81
Total			3019	50.7	0–243	54.46	54.85	0–243	55.1	10,046.78

Source: Own calculations.

appropriate measures. Article 42 allows anti-dumping actions as long as Turkey fails to implement effectively the competition rules of the customs union and other relevant parts of the *acquis communautaire*. In those cases, Article 47 of the Additional Protocol signed in 1970 between Turkey and the EC remains in force. According to this article, if the Association Council finds dumping it shall address recommendations to the persons with whom such practices originate. The injured party may take suitable measures if: (1) the Council has taken no decision within three months and (2) the dumping practices continue. In the case of the need for immediate action, the party may introduce an interim protection measure such as anti-dumping duties for a limited duration. But the Council may recommend the abolition of these interim measures. Finally, Article 61 is about safeguards, and states that safeguard measures specified in Article 60 of the Additional Protocol will remain valid. According to Article 60, the Community (Turkey) may take necessary protective measures if serious disturbances occur in a sector of the economy of the Community (Turkey) or prejudice the external financial stability of one or more member states (Turkey), or if difficulties arise that adversely affect the economic situation in a region of the Community (Turkey).

Regarding the contingency measures, we note that as of the end of 2008 Turkey had 107 anti-dumping duties in force. Most of the anti-dumping duties were imposed on imports from China (42 duties), Indonesia (ten duties), Chinese Taipei (nine duties), Thailand (eight duties) and India (seven duties), and measures have affected mostly textiles and clothing. The majority are specific duties, and some ad valorem duties are as high as 100 per cent. Turkey is an important user of anti-dumping measures. As of December 31, 2008 it had 32 anti-dumping investigations in progress, and most of these investigations concerned imports from China. On the other hand Turkey did not make extensive use of countervailing measures and safeguard actions. It has reported only one countervailing measure against imports from India, and it has not taken any safeguard actions under GATT Article XIX.

Measures affecting exports

In Turkey, exporting certain commodities is subject to registration, and exporting other commodities is prohibited because of environmental, health or religious reasons. All other commodities can be exported freely. Exporters are required to register with the Exporters Union and their local chamber of commerce. According to the regulations of the export regime, export prohibitions have been imposed on antiques and archaeological works, Indian hemp, tobacco seedlings and tobacco plants, Angora goats, game and wild animals, walnut, mulberry, cherry, pear, plum, badger, ash, elm and lime in logs, in timber, in plank and in sketch, natural flower bulbs, wood and wood charcoal, plants of olive, fig, hazelnut, pistachio and grapevine, sahlep, *Liquidambar orientalis* and *Pterocarya carpinifolia*.

Export licences are required for 26 categories of products. Exporters of these items must obtain permission from the relevant authorities. The 26 categories include as of 2009 commodity groups such as military weapons and ammunition, opium and poppy seeds, addictive and psychotropic substances, seeds, feeds covered by Feed Law, pharmaceuticals for veterinary purposes, technology and equipment used for nuclear purposes, goods covered by the Missile Technology Controlling Regime and sugar. Finally, we note that Turkey applies export taxes at the rate of US$0.04 per kg on shelled hazelnuts, US$0.08 per kg on unshelled hazelnuts, and US$0.5 per kg on raw skins (HS 41.01, 41.02 and 41.03, excluding processed raw skins).

Regarding export incentives we note that, as a result of the customs union between the EU and Turkey as well as Turkey's commitments vis-à-vis the WTO, Turkey has progressively revamped the incentives provided to exporters. Currently, export subsidies are provided through the following programmes: cash subsidies, the Investment Encouragement Program (IEP), the Inward-Processing (IP) scheme, state aid programmes under the Ministerial Council Resolution on State Aids Related to Exports of 1994, the export credit scheme of the Turk Eximbank (Export Credit Bank of Turkey), and free zones.

Cash subsidies are extended to a number of agricultural products and processed agricultural goods including cut flowers, frozen vegetables, frozen fruit and olive oil. Table 2.7 shows the subsidies extended to these commodities. From the table it follows that subsidies are quite substantial for various commodities, but that the applied subsidy rates cannot exceed specified maximum rates. These rates are set between 5 per cent and 20 per cent of the value of exports, and between 14 and 100 per cent of the quantities exported.

Duty concessions are granted under the IEP, which merged the previous General Investment Encouragement Program and the Aids Granted to Small and Medium Enterprises (SMEs) Investments. The purpose of IEP is to encourage and orient investments in order to reduce regional imbalances within the country, and to create new employment opportunities while using technologies with greater value added. To qualify for the IEP, potential investors must apply for an investment encouragement certificate to be issued by the Undersecretariat for the Treasury. In principle, all investment projects are eligible. If granted a certificate, the project can benefit from incentives that cover: (1) exemption from customs duties and fund levies on imported machinery and equipment that are part of the investment project and appear on the machinery and equipment list approved by the Undersecretariat for the Treasury, (2) VAT exemption for imported and locally purchased machinery and equipment, (3) 'interest support' (by certain percentage points of the interest rate) on credit obtained on commercial terms by investors to finance their investment projects and (4) electricity cost support for tourism investments and establishments. Furthermore, foreign exchange earning activities are exempt from stamp duties and related charges. SMEs Investments can also benefit from the encouragement measures offered under the IEP.

In addition to the IEP scheme, the IP scheme also benefits exporters. Goods imported under the IP scheme are intended for re-export from the customs territory of Turkey in the form of 'compensating products'.[13] The system works through suspension of duties and VAT until the exportation of the products, or reimbursement based on a drawback method. The suspension system is used whenever there

Table 2.7 Cash export subsidies

HS code	Commodity	Cash subsidies	Share of exported quantity eligible for the subsidy (%)	Maximum subsidy rate (%)
0207	Meat and edible offal of poultry (excluding 02071391, 02071399, 02071491, 02072691, 02072699, 020734, 02073591, 02072791, 02072799, 02073599, 02073681, 02073685, 02073689)	US$186/tonne	14	20
040700	Eggs	US$15/1000 units	78	10
040900	Honey	US$65/tonne	32	10
060311, 12, 13, 14, 19	Fresh cut flowers and flower buds of a kind suitable for bouquets	US$205/tonne	37	10
0710	Vegetables (uncooked or cooked by steaming or boiling in water) (excluding 071010)	US$79/tonne	27	12
0712	Dried vegetables, whole, cut, sliced, broken or in powder	US$370/tonne	20	10
080810	Apples	US$50/tonne	March–May 2009	15
0811	Fruits and nuts, uncooked or cooked by steaming or boiling	US$78/tonne	41	8
1509	Olive oil (including 151620910014 and 151620980011)	US$180/tonne	100	5
16010099, 160231, 160232	Sausages made of poultry	US$250/tonne	40	10
1604	Prepared or preserved fish	US$200/tonne	100	5

1806	Chocolate and other food preparations containing cocoa	US$119/tonne	48	6
1902	Pasta	US$66/tonne	32	10
190531, 32	Sweet biscuits; waffles (including 19059045, 1905906000, 1905906014)	US$119/tonne	18	8
2001, 2002, 2003, 2004, 2005, 2006, 2008	Vegetables, fruits, nuts and other edible parts of plants, tomatoes prepared or preserved, mushrooms, truffles, other vegetables prepared or preserved. Fruits, nuts, and other edible parts of plants (frozen) (excluding 200811, 20081911, 200819130011, 200819190014, 200819190039, 200819190049, 20081991, 200819930011, 200819950014, 200819950039, 200819950049, 20081999)	US$75/tonne	51	15
2007	Jams, fruit jellies, marmalades, fruit or nut puree (excluding 20079920, 200799970018)	US$63/tonne	35	5
2009	Fruit juices	US$150/tonne	15	12

Source: http://www.igeme.gov.tr.

is 'substantiated' intention to re-export the goods in the form of compensating products. Under the drawback system, used mainly for inward processing, repayment of the import duty and VAT can be claimed when the compensating products are exported.

Under the Ministerial Council Resolution on State Aids Related to Exports of 1994 Turkey provides nine different state aid programmes, carried out by various public bodies/institutions and organizations. The programmes are 'state aid for organizing domestic fairs with international participation'; 'state aid for environmental protection activities'; 'state aid for research and development projects'; 'state aid for encouraging employment in sectoral foreign trade companies'; 'state aid for participation in international fairs and exhibitions'; 'state aid for operating stores abroad'; 'state aid for promoting Turkish trademarks and improving the image of Turkish goods'; 'state aid for market research projects'; and 'state aid for vocational training'.[14]

Preferential export credits are extended by the Turk Eximbank, which operates a large number of export credit, guarantee and insurance schemes. Short-term financial assistance through Turk Eximbank is made available to exporters at the pre-shipment and post-shipment stages with a term of up to 360 days for credits in Turkish lira and 540 days for credits in foreign currency. Credits are allocated through the Turkish commercial banks or directly by the Turk Eximbank. Turk Eximbank's medium- and long-term financial support programmes have been developed mainly for the export of capital goods and turnkey investment projects to be undertaken by Turkish and Turkey-based contractors. The majority of these programmes involve extending financing facilities to buyers outside of Turkey for the purchase of Turkish goods and/or services. For many medium- and long-term operations, a sovereign guarantee in favour of Turk Eximbank has been a prerequisite for extension of the facility. Moreover, export receivables are discounted in order to promote sales on deferred payment conditions and to increase export trade volumes. The Turk Eximbank also offers Turkish exporters, investors and overseas contractors a variety of insurance policies against commercial and political risks. Commercial risk-based losses are indemnified by Turk Eximbank from its own resources, whereas political risks are, in principle, backed by the government. Since 2000, short-term political risks have also been ceded to the reinsurance panel within certain country limits.

Since the passage of the law on free zones in 1985, 20 zones have been established in Turkey. The zones are open to a wide range of activities. Offshore banking, insurance businesses and customs brokers are not allowed, but all industrial and other commercial and service operations deemed appropriate by the Supreme Planning Board may be conducted. There is no limitation on foreign capital participation in investment within the free zones, and 100 per cent repatriation of capital is allowed without prior permission, tax, duty or fee. In addition, financial incentives are available to free zone companies, and these include exemption from payment of customs duties and fees and value added taxes, and no restrictions on profit transfer or foreign exchange transactions. Under Law No. 5084 of 2004 on the Encouragement of Investments and Employment only free zone users who operate under a production licence are exempted from income or corporate taxes until the end of the taxation period of the year in which Turkey becomes a full member of the EC.[15] For other free zone users who obtained an operating licence before February 2004, the income or corporate tax exemption will apply for the validity period of the operating licence. Free zone users who obtained an operating licence other than for production after February 2004 do not enjoy income or corporate tax exemption. In contrast to most other free zones, sales to the Turkish domestic market are allowed, but goods and revenues transported from the zones into Turkey are subject to all relevant import regulations.

Foreign direct investment framework

As shown earlier, until very recently, annual FDI inflows into Turkey amounted to less than US$1 billion. This was mainly because of economic and political uncertainties surrounding the country and the enormous institutional, legal and judicial obstacles faced by foreign investors in Turkey. Furthermore, the inadequate functioning of regulatory bodies that oversaw competition in service and infrastructure industries such as telecommunications, energy and finance made entry and exit into these markets extremely difficult.[16]

The Decree on Improving the Investment Environment in Turkey was enacted at the end of 2001 as a part of the national strategy to increase domestic and foreign investments by improving the business environment, increasing the overall level of income and productivity and raising the level of competitiveness. The Decree also established the Coordination Council for the Improvement of the Investment Environment and technical subcommittees to identify and remove the remaining regulatory and administrative barriers to private investment. Since then, the authorities have implemented several legislative measures to further improve the business and investment climate.

Foreign-owned firms in Turkey had long been subject to special authorizations and sectoral limitations. In 2001 the Turkish government requested the Foreign Investment Advisory Service of the World Bank to conduct a study on the business environment affecting FDI firms in Turkey. The study was conducted in cooperation with the Undersecretariat for the Treasury. According to the Foreign Investment Advisory Service (2001a,b) seven major problems impeded the operations of FDI enterprises up until the early 2000s: (1) political instability, (2) government hassle, (3) a weak judicial system, (4) heavy taxation, (5) corruption, (6) deficient infrastructure and (7) competition from the informal economy. On the basis of this work, a new law on FDI and important amendments in various laws (commercial law and in the laws concerning the employment of foreigners, the registry of title deeds and public procurement) were adopted by Parliament in 2003.

The aim of the 2003 Foreign Direct Investment Law is to: (1) encourage FDIs in the country, (2) protect foreign investors' rights, (3) bring investors and investments in line with international standards, (4) establish a notification-based rather than approval-based system for FDIs and (5) increase the volume of FDI through established policies. The law provides a definition of foreign investors and FDIs, and explains the important principles of FDIs, such as freedom to invest, national treatment, expropriation and nationalization, transfers, access to real estate, dispute settlement, valuation of non-cash capital, employment of expatriates and liaison offices. The new law has removed the screening and pre-approval procedures for FDI projects, redesigned the company registration process to provide equality between domestic and foreign firms, facilitated the hiring of foreign employees, included FDI firms in the definition of 'domestic tenderer' in public procurement, and authorized foreign persons and companies to acquire real estate in Turkey. All companies established under the rules of the Turkish Commercial Code are regarded as Turkish companies. Therefore, equal treatment is applicable to all such companies, both in rights and responsibilities, as stated in the Constitution and other laws. According to the law, a company can be 100 per cent foreign owned in almost all sectors of the economy. However, a number of sectors are still subject to FDI restrictions. Establishments in broadcasting, aviation, maritime transportation, port services, fishing, accounting, auditing and book-keeping services, the financial sector, petroleum, mining, electricity, education and private employment offices require special permission according to the applicable laws. Finally, regarding acquisition of land, we note that, until 2003, foreigners were not allowed to acquire property in Turkey. With the new FDI Law, foreigners can acquire land in accordance with the mutuality principle, but acquisition of land of between 2.5 and 30 hectares is subject to permission from the Council of Ministers.[17]

In June 2006 the Turkish Investment Support and Promotion Agency was established, which provides information to interested investors as well as incentives such as the provision and development of investment sites for specific investment projects. The agency aims to function in the future as a one-stop shop where all bureaucratic procedures can be handled within a very short period of time. Finally, note that Turkey has been a member of the International Centre for Settlement of Investment Disputes and the Multilateral Investment Guarantee Agency since 1987. Furthermore, since 1991 Turkey has been a member of the Convention on the Recognition and Enforcement of Foreign Arbitral Awards, and of the European Convention on International Commercial Arbitration. In addition, Turkey has developed since 1962 an impressive network of bilateral agreements with 80 countries, the main purpose of which has been to promote investment flows between parties, ensure a more stable investment environment, provide economic and legal assurance to foreign investors and establish a favourable environment for economic cooperation. Turkey has also signed double taxation prevention treaties with 68 countries that enable tax paid in one of two countries to be offset against tax payable in the other, thus preventing double taxation. It has also signed social security agreements with 22 countries, which make it easier for expatriates to move between countries.

Although the investment climate in Turkey has improved considerably over the last seven years, the change is still not reflected in various international competitiveness studies such as the IMD (International Institute for Management

Development) World Competitiveness Report. Turkey was ranked forty-eighth in the IMD World Competitiveness Report in 2001, 2007 and 2008, and it is lagging far behind many of its competitors. In 2008, the Czech Republic ranked twenty-eighth, the Slovak Republic thirtieth, Spain thirty-third, Portugal thirty-seventh, Hungary thirty-eighth, Greece forty-second, and Poland forty-fourth. Turkey's poor impression is repeated by the Doing Business Survey of the World Bank, which ranked Turkey fifty-seventh among 178 countries. According to a 2006 study conducted by the Organization for Economic Co-operation and Development's (OECD) overall FDI Regulatory Restrictiveness Index, Turkey's most restrictive sectors are air and maritime transport, followed by electricity, and its most liberal sectors are in manufacturing, together with some services subsectors such as telecommunications, insurance services and certain business services.[18]

With the introduction of the 2001 programme of economic stabilization, implementation of its privatization programme, the EU's 2004 decision to begin membership negotiations with Turkey and liberalization measures introduced during the last few years, the FDI inflows into Turkey increased, as emphasized above, to US$20.2 billion in 2006, US$22.1 billion in 2007 and US$18.2 billion in 2008. But an important shortcoming of these inflows has been their composition. Almost all of the FDI inflows over the last four years have been composed of mergers and acquisitions and directed towards service sectors and real estate. From a longer-term growth perspective Turkey needs to attract greenfield investments.[19] To put Turkey in international producers' networks the current investment environment should be further improved by implementing long-delayed judicial and legal reforms.

Conclusion

Kaminski and Ng (2007) note that countries successfully take advantage of opportunities offered by global markets as long as three conditions are satisfied: macroeconomic stability, the presence of contestable and competitive domestic markets that are open to external competition, and well-functioning backbone services. Although Turkey had historically failed the macroeconomic test, that condition now seems to be satisfied after the stabilization measures taken during and after 2001 – at least until the global financial crisis of 2008. The liberalization measures taken during the 1980s and the CUD and the EU accession process have contributed immensely to the emergence of contestable domestic markets and to improved efficiency in services sectors.

The CUD has contributed to a significant increase in the contestability of domestic Turkish markets through infusing predictability, transparency and stability to trade policy as well as by liberalizing market access. As of 2009, Turkish protection rates are very low except in agricultural commodities, hence one could state that tariffs for Turkey are largely a non-issue in the non-agricultural sector. Currently there is free movement of industrial products between the EU and Turkey, with the exception of contingent protectionism measures and technical legislation. Regarding contingent protectionism, we note that both the EU and Turkey have been active users of such measures, but more so the EU. The formation of the customs union has not provided protection from EC anti-dumping, and the EU has continued to protect its sensitive sectors through contingent protectionism. On the other hand, technical barriers to trade have significantly declined with Turkey's gradual transition to the EU's technical standards regime.[20]

3 Standards, conformity assessment and technical barriers to trade

(co-authored with Saadettin Doğan[1])

As markets continue to integrate and tariff barriers are progressively eliminated, standards and conformity assessment procedures have begun to surface as barriers to trade. This chapter focuses on technical barriers to trade (TBTs). The first section considers product standards, technical regulations and conformity assessment systems, whereas the second section studies the multilateral regulations for the elimination of TBTs within the context of the World Trade Organization (WTO). This is followed by a section analyzing the European Union's (EU) approach to eliminating TBTs and a section on the policies and approaches adopted by Turkey for the elimination of TBTs. The chapter ends with some concluding remarks.

Standards, conformity assessment and trade

Product standards, technical regulations and conformity assessment systems are essential ingredients of functioning modern economies.[2] A 'standard' is defined as a set of characteristics or quantities that describes features of a product, process, service or material, whereas 'technical regulation' is a mandatory requirement imposed by public authorities. Technical regulations and standards, despite many similarities, have different impacts. If a product does not fulfil the requirements of a technical regulation, it will not be allowed to be put on sale. In the case of standards, non-complying products will be allowed on the market but the volume of sales may be affected if consumers prefer products that meet the standards. Although the distinction between product standards and technical regulations is useful for policy purposes, in the following we use the term 'standards' to refer to both mandatory requirements and voluntary specifications. Finally, 'conformity assessment' is the comprehensive term for measures taken by manufacturers, their customers, regulatory authorities and independent third parties to assess conformity to standards.

Product and process standards serve the functions of fostering commercial communication, diffusing technology, raising productive efficiency, enhancing market competition, ensuring physical and functional compatibility, and enhancing public welfare.[3] Standards reduce the transaction costs for buyer and seller by conveying information regarding the inherent characteristics and quality of products. They facilitate market transactions. Under standardization, products become closer substitutes, increasing the elasticity of substitution in demand between versions of similar products. As a result, standards enhance competition by allowing products that conform to a given standard to compete directly with each other. Moreover, standardization in manufacturing enables efficiency-increasing measures such as repetitive production, reduced inventories and flexibility in substituting components on the assembly line, bringing about significant economies of scale. The economies of scale, in turn, benefit the producer through cost reductions, which can then be passed on to the consumer as lower prices. In addition, compatibility standards are important in industries that are organized into networks, such as telecommunications. The more widespread a given network standard becomes, the greater the incentive becomes for additional users to adopt that standard. Moreover, standards diffuse technical information embodied in products and processes, when a technological advance by a designer, researcher or developer at one firm is incorporated into a standard used by others. Thereby, standards help to raise productivity and industrial competitiveness. They also contribute to the provision of public goods. While emission standards can contribute to cleaner air, health standards can raise the average heath status in the economy. Because a standard can be used any number of times without depleting its utility, it is also a public good, raising questions about the provision of standards by the private sector only.

Standards are developed in three main ways. First, a standard may arise from a formal coordinated process, in which key participants in a market, such as producers, designers, consumers, corporate and government purchasing officials, and regulatory authorities, seek consensus on the best technical specifications to meet customer, industry and public needs. The resulting standards are then published for voluntary use throughout industry. Second, a standard may arise from uncoordinated processes in the competitive marketplace. When a particular set of products or process specifications gains market share, such that it acquires influence, the set of specifications is considered a de facto standard. Third, a standard may be set by the government for which compliance is required, either by regulation or in order to sell products or services to government agencies. In this context, a procurement standard may specify requirements that must be met by suppliers to the government, and a regulatory standard may set safety, environmental or related criteria.

On the international level, the three predominant standards-setting bodies are the International Standardization Organization (ISO), the International Electrotechnical Commission (IEC) and the International Telecommunications Union (ITU). The ISO was formed in 1947. The impetus for the establishment of the ISO came from the United Nations, following the breakdown of certain earlier standards organizations during World War II. The jurisdiction of the ISO is unlimited, and, in principle, the ISO may undertake standardization initiatives relating to any product or service market. It is dedicated to voluntary standardization. The development process is lengthy and requires a majority consensus of technical committee members. Only after consensus has been reached is the standard published by the ISO Council as an International Standard. The IEC, established in 1908, resulted from the rapid technical progress in electrical technology at the time and the perception that standards were necessary to maintain a reasonable level of compatibility among electrical products. The IEC is now affiliated with the ISO. The development process in the IEC is again a lengthy one. The technical work is carried out by technical committees, subcommittees and working groups. The IEC, relying on some form of consensus as the decision-making mechanism, issues publications and recommendations for international standards and promotes safety and compatibility. Finally, the ITU, based in Geneva, is the leading United Nations agency for information and communication technologies. As the global focal point for governments and the private sector, the ITU's role in helping the world communicate spans three core sectors: radio communication, standardization and development. The ITU typically develops recommendations that are implemented as national standards by national telecommunications authorities. The administrative structure at the ITU that directs the standards-setting process also consists of committees, subcommittees and working groups and relies on some form of consensus as the decision-making mechanism.

Conformity assessment enhances the value of standards by increasing the confidence of buyers, users and regulators that products actually conform to claimed standards. Over time, the definition of conformity assessment has gained different meanings, as developments occurred in conformity assessment procedures. Currently, it requires the close inter-relation between 'parties assessing conformity to standards', accreditation, calibration and metrology.

Testing is the determination of the characteristics of a product, process or service, according to certain procedures, methodologies or requirements; the aim of testing may be to check whether a product fulfils specifications such as safety requirements or characteristics relevant for commerce and trade. The extent of the controls that a product must undergo varies according to the risk attached to the use of the product. Requirements may range from a declaration by the manufacturer stating that certain standards have been applied to extensive testing and certification. In a large number of cases, tests are carried out by the manufacturer, based on internal testing and quality assurance mechanisms. In such cases, the purchaser takes the manufacturer's word that the product conforms. However, in more risky situations, the manufacturer's declaration of conformity may not be sufficient. The use of independent laboratories may be required by the customer as a condition of sale or mandated by a regulatory agency. Alternatively, through testing and other means, the purchaser may insist on formal verification by an unbiased third party that a product conforms to specific standards. In this case, certification is the procedure by which a third party gives written assurance that a product, process or service conforms to specified requirements. In sectors with high demands for safety and reliability, certifiers may require a relatively intensive certification process involving multiple tests, one or more factor inspections, and testing large numbers of product samples.

Conformity assessment systems consist not only of testers and of certifiers evaluating products, processes and services, they also incorporate accreditation and recognition. Whereas accreditation refers to the procedure by which an authoritative body gives formal recognition that a body responsible for conformity assessment is competent to carry out specific tasks, recognition is the evaluation of the competence of the accreditors. Many large manufacturers require their suppliers' testing laboratories to be accredited as a condition for accepting suppliers' products. As emphasized by the National Academy of Sciences (1995), accreditation of a laboratory's or certifier's competence in a particular field typically involves a review of technical procedures, staff qualifications, product sample handling, test equipment calibration and maintenance, quality control, independence, and financial stability. To maintain accredited status, periodic reassessment, with follow-up testing and site visits, may also be required.

One of the most significant factors in any conformity assessment system is the reliability of measurements. This reliability can only be achieved by calibrating the measuring devices. Almost all countries have national metrology centres, the main objectives of which are to build and maintain national standards for all measurements carried out within the country and to calibrate the measurement standards and devices of lower-level laboratories. National centres with accredited laboratories form the national measurement system and coordinate their activities. Thus, metrology delivers the basis for the comparability of test results, for example by defining the units of measurement and by providing traceability and associated uncertainty of the measurement results. In many countries, a national metrology institute exists, which maintains primary standards of measurement used to provide traceability to customer's instruments through calibration.[4]

The benefits of standards and conformity assessment systems apply also across borders. However, standards and conformity assessment systems can also impose additional costs to exporters and act as barriers to trade. TBTs are said to exist as long as countries impose different product standards as conditions for the entry, sale and use of commodities; as long as the different countries have different legal regulations on health, safety and environmental protection; and as long as different parties have dissimilar procedures for testing and certification to ensure conformity to existing regulations or standards.[5]

Stephenson (1997) points out that many disputes over technical barriers arise from mandatory government requirements for standards, due to differing national interpretations of the reasonableness of the regulations in question, such as the scientific interpretation of tolerable health and safety risks for consumers of various products. Non-tariff barriers also arise through increased product costs created by the often redundant testing and certification for different national markets; increased transportation costs, if the product is deemed not to comply with the importer's regulatory requirements; and time and administrative delays caused by costly and lengthy inspection visits by the importing country's authorities.

Technical barriers have two aspects: (1) the content of the norms (regulations and standards) and (2) the testing procedures needed to demonstrate that a product complies with a norm. The TBTs thus come in two basic forms, content-of-norm TBTs and testing TBTs. In either case, the costs of the product design adaptations, the reorganization of production systems, and the multiple testing and certification needed by exporters can be high. These costs are on the one hand upfront and one-time and on the other hand ongoing. While the upfront costs are associated with learning about the regulations and bringing the product into conformity with the regulations, the ongoing costs are related to periodic testing. TBTs are said to distort trade when they raise the costs of foreign firms relative to those of domestic firms. As emphasized by Baldwin (2001), liberalization requires closing the gap between the costs of the foreign and domestic firms. The two main dimensions to such a step are liberalization of the content of norms and liberalization of conformity assessment. Liberalization of the content of norms involves making product norms more cosmopolitan and, thus, narrowing the cost advantage of domestic firms. Liberalization of conformity assessment involves lowering the excess costs that foreign firms face in demonstrating the compliance of their goods to accepted norms.

World Trade Organization framework

Since World War II, considerable progress has been made in lowering international trade barriers, particularly those associated with tariffs. As tariff barriers have decreased, the relative significance of non-tariff barriers to trade, including those related to standards, has increased. These developments led the General Agreement on Tariffs and Trade (GATT) contracting parties to address the topic of standards in the Tokyo Round of trade negotiations, as the provisions of GATT 1947 contained only a general reference to technical regulations and standards and did not treat these in detail.[6] After prolonged negotiations in the Tokyo Round of trade negotiations, a plurilateral agreement was concluded in 1979, dubbed the Standards Code, which established rules for the preparation, adoption and application of technical regulations, standards and conformity assessment procedures for industrial and agricultural goods.[7] The idea of the Standards Code was to ensure that international trade would not be hampered by standards drawn up to preserve health, safety and the environment. With only a few signatories and lacking a strong enforcement mechanism, the code nevertheless provided a good testing ground for how best to discipline the use of technical regulations and standards.[8]

In 1994, a major multilateral trade agreement was concluded in the Uruguay Round, which made significant progress in addressing the rise of non-tariff trade barriers (WTO 2002). The WTO Agreement on Technical Barriers to Trade strengthened the GATT provisions on standards and conformity assessment-related barriers to trade, combined with the establishment of new enforcement mechanisms through the WTO.

The TBT Agreement is applicable to 'technical regulations', 'standards', and 'conformity assessment procedures', defined in Annex I of the Agreement.[9] These definitions establish the general scope of the Agreement. Technical regulations are dealt with in Articles 2 and 3, and standards are governed by Article 4, which makes an explicit reference to Annex 3, which contains the *Code of Good Practice for the Preparation, Adoption and Application of Standards* (*Code*). It is in the Code where almost all of the substantive provisions governing the treatment of standards are found. Articles 5–9 of the *TBT Agreement* set forth provisions relevant to determining the scope and applicability of the *Agreement* to conformity assessment procedures, and the principles and rules discussed in Articles 10–15 of the *Agreement* are applicable to each of these areas.[10]

The general aim of the TBT Agreement is to ensure that technical regulations and standards, as well as testing and certification procedures, do not create unnecessary obstacles to international trade. The *Agreement* has certain common principles and rules that are applicable throughout. These principles, as emphasized by UNCTAD (2003), are non-discrimination, the prevention of unnecessary obstacles to international trade, harmonization, equivalence and mutual recognition, and transparency.

The non-discrimination obligation has two elements: 'most-favoured-nation (MFN) treatment' and 'national treatment'. Whereas the MFN treatment is an obligation not to discriminate between 'like products' imported from different WTO members, national treatment is an obligation not to discriminate between domestic and imported 'like products'. To determine whether different products are like products, their physical properties and tariff classifications, the consumer tastes and habits vis-à-vis these products, and the end uses of these products are examined.

The preamble to the TBT Agreement states that:

> no country should be prevented from taking measures necessary to ensure the quality of its exports, or for the protection of human, animal, and plant life or health, of the environment, or for the prevention of deceptive practices, at the levels it considers appropriate.
>
> (WTO 2002: 121)

Nevertheless, standards and conformity assessment procedures must not be prepared, adopted or applied to create unnecessary obstacles to international trade. The prevention of such obstacles is a principle applicable to standards and conformity assessment procedures. With respect to 'technical regulations', the prevention of unnecessary obstacles to trade is defined in Article 2.2 to mean that technical regulations must not be more trade restrictive than necessary to achieve a policy goal and must fulfil a legitimate objective, accounting for the risks that non-fulfillment would create. Elements that members can use for risk assessment are available scientific and technical information related to processing technology or the intended end uses of products. On the other hand, the prevention of unnecessary obstacles to international trade in the case of 'standards' is not defined in the TBT Agreement or in the Code of Good Practice. Thus, it seems that the same definition would be applicable as in the case of technical regulations. Finally, with respect to 'conformity assessment procedures', the phrase 'unnecessary obstacles to international trade' is defined in Article 5.1.2, which states that conformity assessment procedures should not be more strict or be applied more strictly than is necessary to give the importing member adequate confidence that the products conform with the applicable technical regulations or standards, accounting for the risks that non-conformity would create.

Harmonization is a central pillar of the TBT Agreement. Members are encouraged to use agreed international standards as a basis for domestic technical regulations and standards. The emphasis on harmonization is based on the view that trade is disrupted less if members use internationally agreed standards as a basis for domestic regulations and standards and that a degree of harmonization benefits producers and consumers as a result of economies of scale and technical compatibility respectively. Failing to use international standards might constitute an unnecessary obstacle to trade. It is stressed that widespread participation in international standardizing bodies such as the ISO, IEC and ITU can ensure that international standards reflect country-specific production and trade interests. Hence, the TBT Agreement encourages members to participate, within the limits of their resources, in the work of international bodies for the preparation of standards and guides or of recommendations for conformity assessment procedures.

The TBT Agreement encourages members to accept foreign technical regulations as 'equivalent' to their own, provided they fulfil the same objectives. Likewise, members are encouraged to accept foreign conformity assessment procedures as 'equivalent' to their own procedures provided those procedures ensure conformity with standards and technical regulations equivalent to their own procedures. Although the notion of equivalence is not mentioned in the Code of Good Practice, the principle of equivalence is made applicable to standards through Article 6.1. Members are encouraged to enter into negotiations for the mutual recognition of the results of conformity assessment procedures. It is emphasized that members, by accepting the results of another member's conformity assessment procedures, can reduce the testing costs. Thus, confidence in a trading partner's testing procedures is a prerequisite for the acceptance of a mutual recognition agreement.

Finally, the Agreement requires an appropriate level of transparency. Transparency is the process whereby the creation, terms and application of technical regulations, standards and conformity assessment procedures are made public; opportunities are provided for the public, including other members, to comment on proposed technical regulations, standards and conformity assessment procedures.[11]

According to Article 1.5 of the TBT Agreement, the provisions of the Agreement do not apply to sanitary and phyto-sanitary measures as defined in Annex A of the WTO Agreement on the Application of Sanitary and Phyto-Sanitary Measures (SPS Agreement), with special implications for global agricultural trade.[12] The TBT Agreement is also not applicable to purchasing specifications prepared by governmental bodies for the production or consumption requirements of governmental bodies, as such measures fall under the WTO Agreement on Government Procurement.

Last, it should be emphasized that during the Uruguay Round negotiations the signatories were able to conclude a new Understanding on Rules and Procedures Governing the Settlement of Disputes. The disputes settlement understanding allows complainants to obtain a dispute resolution panel essentially as a matter of right, as well as for appellate review. It provides that panel reports will be adopted as definitive by the signatories, unless they decide not to do so by consensus or the report is appealed. In addition, it provides that appellate reports will be adopted as definitive by the signatories unless they decide not to do so by consensus. Finally, it provides for sanctions if a signatory does not abide by dispute resolution findings.

The above considerations reveal that protectionist technical measures exist if: (1) the measure or its enforcement is purely cost-raising, and it is inefficient, (2) a measure is set at a level that is stronger than required to achieve a policy objective, and it increases domestic profits at the expense of foreign profits, (3) a measure is discriminatory in application or effect between domestic and foreign firms, (4) a measure is not the one least disruptive to trade among available policies and (5) a measure mandates excessive caution in relation to reliable scientific measures of risk.[13] Alternatively, following RAND Science and Technology (2004), one may pose a series of questions to find out whether the requirements of the TBT Agreement have been violated:

- Is there a legitimate and defensible rationale for preparing, adopting and applying standards, conformity assessment procedures or technical regulations that are not based on international standards, recommendations and guides?
- Does the technical regulation, standard or conformity assessment procedure apply equally to all suppliers regardless of national origin?
- Was the measure introduced after imports began to take an appreciable share of the local market?
- Were there domestic pressures or sources of influence leading to the adoption of the regulation?
- Are the standards, conformity assessment procedures or technical regulations unduly onerous with no opportunity for graduated application?
- Is the net effect of the technical regulation, conformity assessment procedure or standard to prevent foreign entrants into a national market?

In cases of affirmative answers, one might apply more narrow tests to see if a TBT exists according to the terms of the Agreement and take appropriate action in response, invoking WTO's dispute settlement procedures.

The EU approach to eliminating technical barriers to trade

The European Commission (1998a) divides traded products into regulated and non-regulated commodities. Regulated products are those whose commercialization is governed by the regulations of member states, and non-regulated products are those for which no regulations have an impact on commercialization. Regulated products are further divided into commodities under the harmonized sphere and those under the non-harmonized sphere. Products under the harmonized sphere are covered by European rules for the harmonization of regulations and mandatory specifications, and commodities under the non-harmonized sphere are governed by national rules.[14]

Mutual recognition principle

Mutual recognition refers to the principles enshrined in the Treaty of Rome, interpreted by the European Court of Justice, as set out in the 1979 Cassis de Dijon judgment. In this ruling, the court stated that Germany could prohibit imports of a French beverage (Cassis de Dijon) only if it could invoke mandatory requirements such as public health, protection of the environment, and fairness of commercial transactions. In other words, the court introduced a broad definition of Article 28 (ex 30) of the Treaty of Rome, which prohibits quantitative restrictions on imports between member states and 'all measures having equivalent results'. Because of this ruling, the European Commission stated that a product lawfully produced and marketed in one member state should be admitted to other member states for sale, except in cases of mandatory requirements. Thus, the basic EU approach under the mutual recognition principle (MRP), considered as the first line of defence against technical barriers in the regulated non-harmonized sphere, has been to promote the idea that products manufactured and tested in accordance with a partner country's regulations could offer levels of protection equivalent to those provided by corresponding domestic rules and procedures. Mutual recognition, in other words, reflects the existence of *ex ante* trust between the trading partners.

The Directive 98/34/EC, covering all industrial and agricultural commodities that fall outside the 'harmonized' area, aims to eliminate or reduce the barriers to the free movement of goods which can arise from the adoption of different national technical regulations, by encouraging transparency of national initiatives vis-à-vis the European Commission, European standardization bodies and other member states. According to the directive, member states are obliged to notify to the Commission, in draft, proposed technical regulations, and to observe a three-month standstill period before a regulation is made or brought into force.[15] The Commission circulates the notified drafts to all member states. To allow the Commission and other member states to react, the member states must refrain from adopting any draft technical regulations for three months from the date of receipt by the Commission. The standstill period is extended to four months for drafts in the form of a voluntary agreement and for six months for all others in which the Commission delivers a detailed opinion indicating that the draft may impede the free movement of goods. This notification procedure is to provide an opportunity for the Commission and other member states to comment if they consider that the proposed regulation has the potential to create a technical barrier to trade.

According to the European Commission (2007a) national technical rules adopted by various member states lead to substantial obstacles to the free movement of goods within the EU, resulting in extra administrative controls and tests, and the system of market surveillance needed considerable improvement, as there was no consistency of approach. As a result, the European Parliament and the Council adopted Resolution (EC) No. 764/2008, which defines the rights and obligations of national authorities and enterprises wishing to sell in a member state products lawfully marketed in another member state, when the competent authorities intend to take restrictive measures about the product in accordance with national technical rules. The regulation concentrates on the burden of proof by setting out the procedural requirements for denying mutual recognition.

Harmonization of national regulations and standards

EU legislation on harmonizing technical specifications has followed two distinct approaches: the old approach and the new approach.

The old approach was based on the idea that the EU would become a unified economic area functioning like a single national economy. It dealt with the content-of-standards issue via negotiated harmonization. The regulations were implemented by the directives of the European Council, and the designated bodies in EU nations performed the conformity assessments. Technical regulations were harmonized using the old approach for food stuffs, motor vehicles, chemicals, pharmaceuticals, cosmetics, textiles, footwear labelling, crystal glass, legal metrology and pre-packaging. Under this approach, separate directives for different products detailed EU specifications that applied to the related products and their testing requirements. Under the old approach, European standards institutions such as CEN (Comité Européen de Normalisation), CENELEC (Comité Européen de Normalisation Electrotechnique) and ETSI (European Telecommunications Standards Institute) were not mandated to draw up supplementary technical specifications.[16] The old approach involved extensive product-by-product or even component-by-component legislation, and was carried out by detailed directives. Achieving this type of harmonization was slow, as emphasized by the World Bank (2005a), for two reasons. First, the process of harmonization became highly technical, with attention given to very detailed product categories. Consultations were often drawn out. Second, the adoption of directives required unanimity in the Council, which meant that they were slow to be adopted.[17] Over time, the need was recognized by economic units to reduce the intervention of public authorities prior to a product being placed on the market and to change the decision-making procedure to allow for the adoption of harmonization directives by a qualified majority. Therefore, the new approach was adopted, and it applied to products with 'similar characteristics' that were subject to a widespread divergence of technical regulations in EU countries.

Under the new approach, only 'essential requirements' are indicated. This approach gives manufacturers greater freedom on how they satisfy those requirements by dispensing with the 'old' type of exhaustively detailed directives. Directives under the new approach provide for more flexibility, by using the support of the established standardization bodies – CEN, CENELEC, ETSI and the national standard bodies. This standardization work is easier to update and involves greater participation from industry.

Under the new approach, the European Council issues a directive that outlines 'essential requirements'. So far, 26 directives have been adopted based on this approach, and 21 of these directives require the affixing of the CE (Conformité Européene) marking, explained in more in the following section. This new approach to product legislation covers the areas of non-automatic weighing instruments and measuring instruments, low voltage equipment, electromagnetic compatibility, toys, machinery, lifts, noise emissions by outdoor equipment, emissions of pollutants from non-road mobile machinery engines, personal protective equipment, equipment and protective systems intended for use in explosive atmospheres, medical devices, gas appliances, pressure vessels, cableway installations, construction products, recreational craft, eco-design requirements for energy-using products, and radio and telecommunications terminal equipment. Once a new approach directive has been issued, member states must make their national laws and regulations conform to it. The European Commission is empowered to determine whether the national measures are equivalent to the 'essential requirements'. The Council refers the task of formulating detailed standards that meet the essential requirements to CEN, CENELEC and ETSI.

Conformity assessment

To ensure that products meet the requirements laid down in the new approach directives, special conformity assessment procedures have been established. They describe the controls to which products must be subjected before they are considered compatible with the essential requirements and thus placed on the internal market. The extent of the controls that a product must undergo varies, according to the risk attached to the use of the product. Requirements may range from a declaration by the manufacturer stating that certain standards have been applied, to extensive testing and certification by third parties, called notified bodies in the EU.[18]

In 1993, Council Decision 93/465/EEC was adopted in connection with the new approach directives. It provides an overview of all conformity assessment procedures available under the directives, divided up into modules and grouped by category of risk. By standardizing the conformity assessment procedures the Decision ensures coherence and transparency in the application of the directives. It divides conformity assessment into eight different modules, which cover the design and production phases. The modules specify how conformity assessment procedures used in new approach directives are organized. In setting the range of possible choices open to the manufacturer, the directives: (1) take into consideration, in particular, such issues as the appropriateness of the modules to the types of products, the nature of the risks involved, the economic infrastructures of the given sector, the types and importance of production, etc., and (2) attempt to leave as wide a choice to the manufacturer as is consistent with ensuring compliance with the requirements. The specifications of the eight modules are as follows:

- Under Module A on 'internal control of production', covering internal design and production control, the manufacturer prepares technical documentation and declares conformity with the directive.[19] The module does not require intervention by a notified body.
- Under Module B on 'EC type-examination', covering the design phase, the manufacturer prepares technical documentation and the notified body

ascertains conformity. The module is followed by one of the Modules C, D, E or F providing for assessment in the production phase.

- Module C on 'conformity to type' provides for conformity with type as described in the EC type-examination certificate issued according to Module B. The module does not require the intervention of a notified body.[20]
- Module D on 'production quality assurance' derives from the quality assurance standard EN ISO 9002, with the intervention of a notified body responsible for approving and controlling the quality system for production, final product inspection and testing set up by the manufacturer.
- Module E on 'product quality assurance' derives from quality assurance standard EN ISO 9003, with the intervention of a notified body responsible for approving and controlling the quality system for final product inspection and testing set up by the manufacturer.
- Under Module F on 'product verification', a notified body controls conformity to type as described in the EC type-examination certificate issued according to Module B, and issues a certificate of conformity.
- Module G on 'unit verification' covers the design and production phases. Each individual product is examined by a notified body, which issues a certificate of conformity.
- Finally, Module H on 'full quality assurance' covers the design and production phases. It derives from quality assurance standard EN ISO 9001, with the intervention of a notified body responsible for approving and controlling the quality system for design, manufacture, final product inspection and testing set up by the manufacturer.

The new approach directives oblige the manufacturer to draw up a technical file (technical documentation), which provides information on the design and manufacturing phases of the product. The contents of the technical documentation are laid down with the requirements of the directive to be assessed.[21] The details included in the documentation depend on the nature of the product and on what is considered necessary, from a technical point of view, for demonstrating the conformity of the product to the essential requirements of the relevant directive. The manufacturer must also draw up an EC declaration of conformity as part of the conformity assessment procedure provided for in the new approach directives. The EC declaration of conformity should contain all relevant information to identify the directives according to which it is issued, as well as the manufacturer, the notified body if applicable, the product and, when appropriate, a reference to harmonized standards or other normative documents.[22] The technical file and the EC declaration of conformity must be kept for at least ten years from the last date of manufacture of the product, unless the directive expressly provides for any other duration, and this is the responsibility of the manufacturer.

For products regulated by the new approach directives, the mandatory CE marking confirms conformity with the essential requirements of the directives and is required for a product to be placed on the internal market. The CE marking indicates not only that the product has been manufactured in conformity with the requirements of the directive, but also that the manufacturer has followed all of the prescribed procedures for conformity assessment. It ensures free access to all of the EU.

The above considerations reveal that conformity assessment varies in levels of difficulty and complexity depending on the level of risk associated with the product. For example, Module A permits the manufacturer to assume total responsibility for conformity assessment. If the product is manufactured to harmonized standards, and if the risk is not unusually high, the manufacturer may rely on internal manufacturing checks. The manufacturer compiles the technical file, issues a declaration of conformity to the appropriate directives and, if appropriate, standards, applies the CE marking, and places the product on the market. As the risk of injury associated with a product increases, the level of complexity of the conformity assessment process and the associated costs increase with it. Certain high-risk products may not be self-certified, but must be subjected to an EC type-examination. This examination involves the inspection of a representative sample by a notified body.[23]

Notified bodies are independent testing houses, laboratories or product certifiers authorized by the EU member states to perform the conformity assessment tasks specified in directives. A notified body is designated by a member state and must have the necessary qualifications to meet the testing and/or certification requirements set forth in a directive. A notified body not only needs to be technically competent and capable of carrying out the specified conformity assessment procedures, but also must demonstrate independence, impartiality and integrity. Accreditation, according to the EN ISO 45000 series of standards, is a support to the technical part of notification and, although it is not a requirement, it remains an important and privileged instrument for evaluating the competence, impartiality and integrity of the bodies to be notified.

In order to build and maintain confidence between the member states concerning the assessment of notified bodies, it is essential to apply the same assessment criteria. It is also important that the bodies performing the assessment of notified bodies have the capability to do so and can demonstrate an equivalent competence and operate according to the same criteria, and that such requirements are laid down in EN ISO 45003 and EN ISO 45010. The European Commission (1997) emphasizes that accreditation systems at a national level should be set up under the aegis of the public authorities. It maintains that accreditation systems must be commercially independent and that accreditation services be offered in a competent, transparent, neutral, independent and non-discriminatory manner. Furthermore, the national accreditation bodies should become members of a European organization covering all countries of the EU and EFTA, to ensure proper coordination as well as the development of appropriate mutual recognition mechanisms. Such an organization was formed in 2000 as the European Co-operation for Accreditation (EA), which resulted from the merger of the European Accreditation of Certification (EAC) and the European Co-operation for Accreditation of Laboratories (EAL).

Finally, note that conformity assessment procedures differ for classical approach and new approach directives. The above text describes the procedures for new approach directives. The general procedures also apply to a large extent for bodies working with conformity assessments under old approach directives; however, there are some differences. As the old approach directives contain specified technical requirements, 'product standards' as defined formally above are used to a very limited extent. Conformity assessment bodies that deal with new approach directives are officially named 'notified bodies', whereas bodies working with old approach directives are officially named 'technical services'. The new approach directives are based on essentially private pre-market certification. However, notified bodies may also be public. Thus, in the new approach, pre-market certification is competitive as opposed to exclusively public authority-based certification in the old approach.

Market surveillance

The final stage of implementation of the new approach system consists of market surveillance procedures that develop a common approach to enforcement. The main objective of market surveillance is to place only safe products on the market. Market surveillance consists of the control that the relevant authorities in the member states are required to carry out to ensure that the criteria for CE marking have been satisfied – after the products have been placed on the market.

For areas under the new approach directives, the system in use is in-market control. Under this system, the responsibility for placing a product on the market is left to the producer, as long as the product is certified to satisfy the minimum requirements set under the directives. Market surveillance is the responsibility of public authorities. As emphasized by the European Commission (2000), each member state can decide upon the market surveillance infrastructure. There is no limitation on the allocation of responsibilities between authorities on a functional or geographical basis, as long as surveillance is efficient and covers the whole territory. Market surveillance authorities must perform their operations in an impartial and non-discriminatory way. They must have the power, competence and resources to visit commercial, industrial and storage facilities regularly; to visit regularly, if appropriate, workplaces and other premises where products are put into service to organize random checks and spot checks; to take samples of products and subject them to examination and testing; and to require all necessary information. Thus, market surveillance is carried out in the form of random inspections to ensure that the technical documentation, as required by the directive, is available, but it also may include examination of the documentation or the product itself. The control is intended to prevent misuse of the CE marking, to protect consumers and to secure a level playing field for producers. New approach directives provide for two different tools that enable surveillance authorities to receive information on the product: the EC declaration of conformity and the technical documentation. These must be made available by the manufacturer, the authorized representative established within the community or, under certain circumstances, the importer or person responsible for placing the product on the market. Monitoring of products placed on the market may be divided between several authorities on the national level, for example, functionally or geographically. When the same products are subject to control by more than one authority, coordination between services within a member state is necessary.

The coordination task between different market surveillance bodies in a member state can be accomplished by a market surveillance authority. Regarding personnel resources, this authority needs to have, or have access to, a sufficient number of suitably qualified and experienced staff, with the necessary professional integrity. The testing facilities should comply with the relevant criteria of the EN ISO 45001 standard. The authority should be independent and carry out its operations in an impartial and non-discriminatory way.[24] For market surveillance to be efficient, resources should be concentrated where risks are likely to be higher or non-compliance more frequent, or where a particular interest can be identified.

Through the market surveillance system described above, measures are taken in the EU to ensure that products meet the requirements of the applicable directives, that action is taken to bring non-compliant products into compliance, and that sanctions are applied when necessary. Member states are free to choose the type of sanction to use. The only requirement is that the penalties be effective, proportionate and dissuasive. But the above text describes the surveillance procedures for the new approach directives. For other commodities, surveillance could be discussed in terms of the general safety directive (2001/95/EC), rapid exchange of information (RAPEX), and the principle of product liability as developed by the directive 85/374/EEC.

The General Product Safety Directive 2001/95/EC is aimed at ensuring that consumer products placed on the market are safe. The directive obliges the member states to take the measures necessary to enforce the safety requirements for which it provides and to notify any such measures taken. To that effect, the directive sets up a system for rapid exchange of information (RAPEX) concerning products posing a serious risk to consumers.[25] The directive also imposes obligations on producers and distributors. Producers and distributors are to inform the national authorities if they know or ought to know, on the basis of information in their possession and as professionals, that a product they have placed on the market is dangerous. On the other hand, the Directive 85/374/EEC establishes the principle of objective liability or liability without fault of the producer in cases of damage caused by a defective product. According to the directive people injured by defective products may have the right to sue for damages, the injured person can take action against producers as well as importers, and liability applies to all goods used at a place of work and food.

Relations with third countries

In EU's relations with third countries, one can distinguish between the EFTA countries and the remaining countries. In 1992 the European Economic Area (EEA) Agreement was signed between the EFTA countries and the EU. In extending the EU single market to the EFTA countries, the EU felt that ongoing and effective surveillance and enforcement were essential. Accordingly, the EFTA Court of Justice and the EFTA Surveillance Authority were established in 1992. Through the EEA Agreement, the EFTA countries of Iceland, Lichtenstein and Norway participate fully in the EU internal market and thus in the establishment of common product requirements and methods of conformity assessment. Outside the areas covered by EEA legislation related to product requirements, EEA states are permitted to introduce national product requirements, if it can be proved that such requirements are needed to meet public health, environmental, safety and other social considerations. To ensure transparency, the EEA states are required to notify the EFTA Surveillance Authority and the European Commission of all draft national technical rules for products. Finally, the EEA Agreement forces EFTA countries to accept future European Council directives on the single market without formal participation in the formation of these new laws.

In its relations with third countries other than the EFTA countries, the European Community has advocated the use of Mutual Recognition Agreements (MRAs) in many regional or bilateral forums. These agreements are based on the mutual acceptance of test reports, certificates and marks of conformity issued by the conformity assessment bodies of one of the parties to the agreement, in compliance with the legislation of the other party. Such agreements were signed with Australia, Canada, Israel, Japan, New Zealand, Switzerland and the United States. In addition, the European Community negotiated protocols to the European Agreements on Conformity Assessment and Acceptance of Industrial Products (PECAs) with some of the candidate countries at that time. The PECAs represent the recognition of progress made in adopting and implementing the relevant Community legislation on industrial products and in creating the necessary administrative infrastructure. The agreements cover a wide range of sectors, from medical devices to pressure vessels and electrical equipment.[26]

As can be seen from the above considerations, the MRAs have been implemented mostly between developed countries, and they are applicable only in certain sectors. For example, bilateral negotiations between the United States and the EU aiming to recognize each other's conformity assessment procedures, test results, controls and product certification started in 1992. The negotiations were completed in 1997, and the agreement covered telecommunication equipment, medical devices and pharmaceuticals. During the negotiations, the differences between the test and certification systems of the United States and those of the EU were emphasized, and the EU side noted the complexity of the US standards system, the changeability of the certification programmes and the differences between the legal environments at the federal, state and even local levels, because of the non-harmonization of the standardization systems. In response to the EU arguments, the US side claimed that the EU system was designed for the benefit of companies located in the EU, that it constituted an unfair trade barrier for non-EU companies and that it made mandatory product certification by notified bodies located in the EU or its representatives. As all of these measures are cost increasing, non-EU companies that intend to enter the EU market would face barriers to trade because of the cost disadvantage. With the conclusion of negotiations, it was decided that the agreement would be implemented on the above-mentioned sectors after a transition period.

The negotiations between the United States and the EU form a model for countries that will pursue MRAs. However, companies from both sides, which benefit from the advantages of two different conformity assessment systems, resist the change. As MRAs bring two different regulatory systems to recognize the other's standardization system simultaneously, it is difficult to reconcile the differences between the regulatory systems, and a lengthy negotiation process is necessary. Thus, it is a difficult process to form MRAs between countries at different development levels, as is the case in the WTO negotiations. For example, the WTO International Telecommunications Agreement aims to remove the TBTs and create free trade among the countries who are party to it, by applying the international standards. Even though telecommunications is a sector in which the rate of standards harmonization is the highest in the world, it is difficult to say that success has been achieved in meeting the objectives of the agreement.

In summary, MRAs seek to facilitate trade while safeguarding the health, safety and environmental objectives of each party. Each party is free to set its health, consumer protection, environmental or other regulations at whatever level it deems necessary, as long as they comply with international obligations. These obligations require that each side have full confidence that the certification process on the other side can wholly satisfy its requirements.

Epilogue

According to the European Commission (2007a), almost all of the promises on the internal market for goods that were made in the 1985 White Paper on the completion of the internal market were kept. Almost all technical barriers to intra-EU trade in goods were eliminated through the application of Articles 28–30 of the EC Treaty and through secondary EC legislation. After determining that the internal market for goods was still not complete as of 2007, a new legislative framework was adopted in 2008. The new package of measures has the objective of removing the remaining obstacles to free circulation of products. The legal texts include Regulation (EC) No. 765/2008 setting out the requirements for accreditation and market surveillance relating to the marketing of products, and Regulation (EC) No. 768/2008 on a common framework for the marketing of products. The objective of the package is to facilitate the functioning of the internal market for goods and to strengthen and modernise the conditions for placing a wide range of industrial products on the EU market. The package builds upon existing systems to introduce clear Community policies that will strengthen the application and enforcement of internal market legislation.

Turkish approach to elimination of technical barriers to trade

Different approaches are available for countries to raise standards and to address TBTs. Countries can unilaterally upgrade standards by adopting international standards. However, some of the returns from adopting international standards – in terms of greater market access – only materialize if the country's trading partners also accept products produced to that standard in the country under consideration. A second approach requires cooperation between countries to upgrade standards by agreeing that products satisfying particular standards will be accepted in each other's markets.[27] Turkey adopted the second approach for the elimination of TBTs when it formed the customs union with the EU in 1995.

Legislative alignment

According to Decision 1/95 of the EC–Turkey Association Council of 1995 establishing the customs union, Turkey must harmonize its technical legislation with that of the EU.[28] Decision 2/97 of the Association Council of 1997 listed the areas in which Turkey must align its legislation. This work should have been finalized before the end of 2000, but, unfortunately, because of the lack of suitable legal infrastructure, it was not completed during the specified period. According to Annex II of Decision 2/97, Turkey was supposed to incorporate into its internal legal order 300 instruments that correspond to various EEC or EC regulations and directives. Currently, Turkey has incorporated into its legal order only 259 of these instruments.

Turkey has adopted all 21 new approach directives that require affixing the CE conformity marking, and 20 of the directives have entered into force up to the present time. They cover commodities and product groups such as low-voltage equipment, toys, simple pressure vessels, electromagnetic compatibility, gas appliances, personal protective equipment, machinery, medical devices, non-automatic weighing instruments, telecommunications terminal equipment, hot water boilers, civil explosives, lifts and recreational crafts.

To align with the *acquis*, Law No. 4703 on the Preparation and Implementation of Technical Legislation on Products, published in 2001, entered into force in January 2002, and it has been supplemented by secondary legislation. This greatly enhanced harmonization works, as it provides the legal basis for harmonization with the EC legislation. It defines the principles for product safety and for implementation of the old and new approach directives, including the conditions for placing products on the market; the obligations of the producers and distributors, conformity assessment bodies, and notified bodies; market surveillance and inspection; withdrawal of products from the market; and notification procedures.[29] The legislation on market surveillance, the use and affixing of the CE conformity mark, working principles and procedures for the conformity assessment bodies and notified bodies and notification procedures between Turkey and the EU for technical regulations and standards, which apply to the non-harmonized regulated area, entered into force during 2002.[30]

Quality infrastructure

In the EU, national quality infrastructures are critical to the free circulation of goods in the single market. Turkey, as a member of a customs union with the EU and as a candidate country, must align its national quality infrastructure with the European one. It has to complete the establishment of the so-called quality infrastructure, a generic term encompassing the operators and operation of standardization, testing, certification, inspection, accreditation and metrology. Products manufactured in Turkey must satisfy the same requirements prevailing in the EU, and conformity to these requirements must be demonstrated in the same way and according to the same principles. Furthermore, it is important to create confidence on an international level in the testing, inspection and certification bodies in Turkey and to create reliability in the tests they perform and in the certificates they issue.

After the formation of the customs union in 1995, private conformity assessment bodies started to invest in Turkey in order to provide international certificates and markings such as the ISO 9000 series and CE marking for Turkish producers. The Turkish Accreditation Agency (TURKAK), founded in 1999, started accepting accreditation applications for conformity assessment bodies in 2001.[31-33] Accreditation is not compulsory for notified bodies, but public authorities request – as emphasized by the European Commission (2007a) – that candidate notified bodies comply with EN ISO 45000 standards. The relevant ministries are responsible for appointing notified bodies in their field of competence. These authorities work in cooperation with TURKAK to assess the capacity of the notified bodies, or accept those that are to be notified to the European Commission. In particular, the Ministry of Industry and Trade, the Ministry of Labour and Social Security, the Ministry of Health, the Ministry of Public Works and Settlements, the Undersecretariat for Maritime Affairs and the Telecommunications Authority have established cooperation protocols with TURKAK in this context. In 2002, TURKAK became a full member of the European Co-operation for Accreditation (EA). However, becoming a member of an international organization is not sufficient to achieve international recognition of accreditation certificates, as an accreditation body must also be a signatory to specific multilateral agreements (MLAs) with other accreditation bodies.

In the past, the relatively large Turkish firms wishing to obtain CE marking for products exported to the EU market contacted the local subsidiaries of the European notified bodies who used their European laboratories for testing. However, for other Turkish companies, this process was expensive and slow. The small and medium-sized enterprises (SMEs) that export products to the EU found it particularly difficult to pay the high costs.[34] In Turkey, marking and certification parallel to the EU system were implemented only in the automotive sector, which is subject to the old approach directives.[35] In addition, Turkey suffered for a long time from a lack of certification bodies.[36] Although Turkey opened up the certification, testing and calibration market to other actors, Turkish firms were reluctant to enter the market for conformity assessment bodies as long as uncertainties prevailed regarding the acceptance of notified bodies by the European Commission.

In April 2006, TURKAK signed four out of seven MLAs with EA members. These four MLAs cover the areas of test laboratories, calibration laboratories, quality systems management certification bodies, and inspection bodies. Hence, since April 2006, certificates issued by all test, calibration, quality systems management and inspection bodies accredited by TURKAK are recognized within the EU. With the signing of the remaining three MLAs in 2008 TURKAK's full international recognition has been completed. These three MLAs are those for product certification, personnel certification and environmental management systems certification. Finally, we note that the right of Turkey to assign notified bodies was officially recognized by the EU by virtue of the Association Council Decision No. 1/2006.[37] Thereafter Turkish authorities have assigned a number of Turkish notified bodies for several new approach directives.[38]

Over time, competition among potential Turkish notified bodies will ensure lower costs for conformity assessment. The expense, time and unpredictability incurred in obtaining approvals will then be reduced by having products evaluated in Turkey. These savings can be particularly important when rejection of products in the EU can create delays and necessitate additional shipping or other costs. In addition, the SMEs can benefit from procedures in which all testing and certification steps are carried out locally at lower costs. Turkish firms, and in particular the SMEs, can then be expected to increase their competitiveness in the EU market, and more and more Turkish firms can be expected to participate in the free circulation of goods between Turkey and the EU.

Finally, note that the Turkish National Metrology Institute (UME) was founded in 1992 as part of the Scientific and Technological Research Council of Turkey (TUBITAK). The objectives of the UME are to: (1) establish and maintain national measurement standards in accordance with the International System of Units, (2) ensure the traceability of national measurement standards to international standards, (3) establish a national measurement system and provide services to the laboratories within this system in terms of calibration, training, consultancy and other mechanisms, (4) ensure the suitability of the laboratories that apply to join the Turkish Calibration Service and organize their accreditation, (5) contribute to research and development in the areas of measurement techniques, calibration and basic metrology at the international level, (6) develop high technology products and disseminate them via its developed infrastructure, (7) increase the quality of products produced in Turkey by providing the measurement infrastructure through the national measurement system and (8) represent Turkey at an international level in the field of metrology.

The above considerations reveal that, as of 2009, there is a relatively well-functioning quality certification system in place in Turkey, comprising the accreditation agency TURKAK, the National Metrology Institute UME and the Turkish Standards Institute (TSE), the last of which is explained in more detail in the following. Because the transposition of harmonized European legislation into Turkish national legislation is nearing completion, what is needed as a last step is the establishment of a soundly functioning market surveillance system with improved administrative and technical infrastructure.

Market surveillance

The legal basis for market surveillance activities consists of Law No. 4703 of 2001 on the Preparation and Implementation of Technical Legislation on Products, the Regulation on Market Surveillance of Products of 2002, and specific product legislation and administrative legislation by public authorities in the form of circulars or communiqués. The framework law obliges producers to put on the market only safe products, and authorizes public authorities to devise and implement product-specific legislation. Even if this legislation lacks in providing for complete safety, the related authority is still bound to monitor for complete product safety with respect to its legally established competency area. The law leaves detailed procedures and principles of market surveillance to the Regulation on Market Surveillance. In addition, each competent authority may lay down detailed procedures for its market surveillance activities in a specific legislation, defining the duties and responsibilities of the inspectors and the procedures and principles for market surveillance. In 2004, a communiqué was published in order to provide for a standard form to be used by all market surveillance authorities in registering the data collected during market surveillance.

There are ten public authorities responsible for market surveillance and one coordinating body, which is the Undersecretariat for Foreign Trade. The public authorities are the Ministry of Industry and Trade, the Ministry of Health, the Ministry of Public Works and Settlement, the Ministry of Labour and Social Security, the Telecommunications Authority, the Ministry of Environment and Forestry, the Ministry of Agriculture and Rural Affairs, the Undersecretariat for Maritime Affairs, the Tobacco, Tobacco Products and Alcoholic Beverages Market Regulatory Authority and the Energy Market Regulatory Authority. An important role in the execution of market surveillance is played by the regional and provincial offices of most of the public authorities distributed all over Turkey. The provincial offices have different executive tasks, such as inspection and sampling of products and reporting of results, dealing with consumer complaints and advising the public and businesses.

The Coordination Board on Market Surveillance was established in 2002 for the coordination of market surveillance activities of the different public authorities, and is composed of members of the market surveillance authorities plus two members from the Ministry of Culture and Tourism and the Ministry of Transportation. The Board, which has no executive power, is chaired by the Undersecretariat for Foreign Trade. The current regulation relating to Market Surveillance and Inspection of the Products has been revised taking into account Regulation No. 765/2008/EC of the European Parliament and of the Council of 9 July 2008 setting out the requirements for accreditation and market surveillance relating to the marketing of products repealing Regulation (EEC) No. 339/93.

As emphasized in a report prepared for the Undersecretariat for Foreign Trade (2008a), market surveillance in Turkey faces serious problems. It is stressed that, for a large percentage of consumer products, there is no market surveillance at all; the system is fragmented and in fact invisible; there is a substantial risk of conflict of interests; the activities are mainly directed on administrative issues, not on the safety of products, and have low priority as well; in most inspections compliance with the General Product Safety Directive of the EU is absent; and enforcement by inspectors is hampered by logistic problems, lack of power and lack of experience. Thus, the report notes that the present system of market surveillance in Turkey is incomplete, ineffective and inefficient.[39]

Standardization

The Turkish foreign trade regime concerning technical regulations and standardization was originally published in 1995 by the Undersecretariat for Foreign Trade as the Ministerial Decree on the Regime Regarding Technical Regulations and Standardization for Foreign Trade and supplementary legislation.[40] This regime has been amended by Ministerial Decree No. 2005/9454 for Technical Regulations and Standardization for Foreign Trade, by a regulation and by related communiqués. The Decree covers the technical regulations, standards, conformity assessment and inspections to which import and export products are subject, the obligations of the importers and exporters, the powers and the obligations of the customs authorities and related authorities, the sanctions to apply and the notifications related to these issues. The Decree also defines the administration competent for issuing technical requirements for imports. Therefore, by force of this Decree and its implementing provisions, certain mandatory standards are still in place. The regulation and the communiqués are amended every year, except for the Communiqué on the Imports of CE Marked Products.[41] Furthermore, the regulation is related to the control of the agricultural products to be exported within the scope of the standards mandated in exports, and it determines the framework of the import controls, which are regulated by communiqués in more detail.[42]

Although, in principle, standards are voluntary in Turkey, in the absence of a proper market surveillance system, the technical ministries and the Undersecretariat for Foreign Trade have turned the process of standardization and licensing before production into a mandatory regime for both domestic and imported products, in order to protect the market and the consumers. This pre-market control system gave the TSE a great deal of power.[43] According to the European Committee for Standardization (2003), the TSE has misused its power in several cases of imports and has created TBTs. The TSE asked for the technical files of the imported products when they entered the Turkish market, and the processing of the files usually took a long time. There were also cases in which products bearing the CE mark were asked to be further inspected.

Since 2004, products covered by directives on toy safety, medical devices, active implantable medical devices, low voltage electrical equipment, electromagnetic compatibility, machinery and construction products have not been subject to mandatory controls when imported and used in the internal market. With the Communiqué on Standardization for Foreign Trade No. 2008/1, 190 commodities classified in the 12-digit harmonized system of tariff classification (HS) are, as of 2008, subject to inspection by the TSE.[44] All of these commodities refer to those in the unregulated area. The inspections are carried out in respect of minimum standards of health, safety and protection of the environment, providing adequate information to consumers.

Because of recent developments in the harmonization works, the number of standards that are mandatory for the domestic market as well as for imports has substantially decreased, and it seems that the TSE's monopoly as an active player of the mandatory standards controls is ending. Thus, Turkey has replaced all national standards with EU and international standards and significantly reduced the number of mandatory standards applied to imports; this reduction brings Turkey close to having an EU-compatible control mechanism on imports from third countries. However, as of 2008, a remarkable difference exists between the intensity of controls over imported products and domestic products in Turkey. As import control focuses on the surveillance of goods to be imported from third countries, and local products are expected to meet the same requirements as imported ones, the same directives could apply, in principle, for the surveillance of all products, whether imported or domestically produced. An obvious advantage of combining import control with the surveillance of the domestic market is that the available personnel capacity can be employed on a broader scale, and cooperation with customs can be smooth and uniform.

Conclusion

Rising exports have recently become a principal source of Turkish economic growth. In a move that benefited Turkish exporters seeking to take advantage of expanding opportunities in the world economy, Turkey chose to eliminate barriers to trade by upgrading its standards through cooperation with the EU when it formed the EU–Turkey customs union in 1995. It adopted the EU's technical legislation into Turkish legislation; took steps to establish quality infrastructure as in the EU; and tried to establish a market surveillance system as in the EU. More than 13 years have passed since the formation of the EU–Turkey customs union. However, as of 2008, TBTs between Turkey and the EU could still not be eliminated fully.[45] The establishment of the quality infrastructure was a lengthy and complex process, as Turkey, until the formation of the customs union with the EU, had neither such an infrastructure nor the required technical knowledge. Establishing public awareness of the problem, acquiring the necessary knowledge and establishing the infrastructure took quite some time. The development of a market surveillance structure as in the EU became even more challenging than establishing the quality infrastructure. Again, the reasons are various. A successful consumer product safety-related market surveillance system requires independence, visibility, a uniform surveillance policy, a uniform enforcement policy, the integration of market surveillance and import controls, stronger regions, more acting power for inspectors, and sufficient technical infrastructure.[46] Unfortunately, the Turkish system does not meet these conditions. The continuation of these problems has adversely affected the elimination of TBTs in trade with the EU.

The adjustment costs, related to the elimination of TBTs in trade with the EU, have been substantial for the Turkish public sector. These costs involve the adoption of technical legislation as in the EU; the establishment of institutions required for the efficient functioning of quality infrastructure as in the EU, such as TURKAK, the National Metrology Institute and market surveillance authorities; the training and employment of sufficient numbers of staff with suitable qualifications, experience and professional integrity; and the acquisition of the technical infrastructure (laboratories, cars, fuel) required for the efficient functioning of the system. However, the task is not complete, and additional adjustment costs will have to be incurred.

Part II
Liberalization of services

4 Liberalization of telecommunications services

(co-authored with Erkan Akdemir and Erdem Başçı)

For almost a century, telecommunications industries were organized as state monopolies, for mainly three reasons. First, there was a belief that the industry was a natural monopoly, with space for only one undertaking in the market. This view was based on the observation that the sector was subject to large economies of scale and that network infrastructures were very hard or even perhaps impossible to duplicate. Second, the monopoly was granted exclusive rights in return for the understanding that it was to provide universal service. There was thus a kind of contract between governments and the concerned monopoly, which would provide services throughout the territory, including in loss-making areas, to all customers, including unprofitable ones, with a given level of quality and without discontinuity, thereby ensuring social and geographical cohesion. The provision of universal service would certainly have a cost, but the monopoly granted to that firm would allow it to cross-subsidize profitable services with loss-making ones and still make a profit. Third, because of the importance of the industry from strategic, economic and political viewpoints governments believed that it was important to consolidate the firms into one firm, which they controlled. As the industry employed large numbers of workers and represented a significant part of the gross domestic product (GDP), and as a state monopoly was often part of the administration or had closed links with public authorities, governments felt the need to control basic infrastructures in case of war or a major crisis.

In the late 1970s, the basic tenets of the monopoly model started to be challenged because of major technological developments. It was emphasized that provision of universal service did not necessarily require the maintenance of public monopolies cross-subsidizing unprofitable market segments with profitable ones. Cross-subsidization was considered as an imprecise funding mechanism that distorted competition. Other methods of financing, such as targeted subsidies from general taxation or the creation of compensation funds, could be used to contribute to the costs of providing universal service. Second, industry organizations in sectors subject to fierce international competition argued that they were being extensively penalized by the high costs of essential production inputs of telecommunications services that were provided by public monopolies. If the sectors were to remain competitive in the face of globalization of the economy, the telecommunications services industry had to be liberalized; competition would bring lower prices and better quality of service. Third, consumers started to complain about the poor performance of public monopolies, as consumer prices tended to be high and the quality of service poor. They claimed that competition was the best way to induce better prices, improve the quality of service and stimulate innovation. Fourth, early experiences of liberalization in the United States and the United Kingdom convinced many governments that the liberalization model based on opening the telecommunications industry to competition combined with regulation through independent agencies was workable and could provide positive economic results.[1]

This chapter is structured as follows. The first section considers the distinctive features of the telecommunications industry, the second section discusses the international regulatory regime, the third section considers the regulatory regime of the European Union's (EU) telecommunications sector and the fourth section considers the regulatory regime in Turkey. Finally, the chapter ends with some concluding remarks.

Features of the telecommunications industry

The telecommunications industry is at the forefront of the information age. Whereas wireline telephone communication was once the primary service of the industry, wireless communication services and cable and satellite programme distributions today make up an increasing share of the industry. In the past, the traditional public switched telephone network (PSTN) provided a telephone for the consumer's premises, which was connected usually by a twisted copper pair to the nearest switch or concentrator, and from there to the local exchange. The local exchange was connected to the remaining local subscribers and to the rest of the network through a hierarchy of switches to other local exchanges and then to other customers and other networks.

Now almost every detail of this description has changed. The largest sector of the telecommunications industry continues to be made up of wired telecommunications carriers. Whereas voice used to be the main type of data transmitted over the wires, the wired telecommunications service now includes the transmission of all types of graphic, video and electronic data, but mainly over the internet. These new services have been made possible through the use of digital technologies that provide much more efficient use of telecommunications networks. The transmission of voice signals requires relatively small amounts of capacity on telecommunications networks. By contrast, the transmission of graphic, video and electronic data requires much higher capacity. The transmission capacity is referred to as 'bandwidth'. One way that wired carriers are expanding their bandwidth is by replacing copper wires with fibre-optic cable. Fibre-optic cable, which transmits light signals along glass strands, permits faster, higher-capacity transmissions than traditional copper wirelines. Finally, wireless telecommunications carriers transmit graphic, video and electronic data and internet access through the transmission of signals over networks of radio towers. The signal is transmitted through an antenna into the wireline network. Other wireless services include beeper and paging services. Wireless telecommunications carriers are deploying several new technologies to allow faster data transmission and better internet access that should make them competitive with wireline carriers. One technology is called third-generation (3G) wireless access. With this technology, wireless carriers plan to sell music, videos and other exclusive content that can be downloaded and played on phones designed for 3G technology.

Cable and other programme distribution is another sector of the telecommunications industry. Establishments in this sector provide television and other services on a subscription or fee basis. Some cable and satellite systems facilitate the transmission of digital television signals. Digital signals consist of simple electronic codes that can carry more information than conventional television signals. Digital transmission creates higher resolution television images and improved sound quality. Digital television also uses compression technology to expand the number of channels.

Changes in technology and regulations now allow cable television providers to compete directly with telephone companies. An important change has been the rapid increase in two-way communications capacity. As cable operators implement new technologies, some pay television systems now offer two-way telecommunications services, such as video-on-demand and high-speed internet access. Cable companies are also increasing their share of the telephone communications market through both their network of conventional phone lines in some areas and their growing ability to use high-speed internet access to provide VoIP (Voice over Internet Protocol). VoIP is sometimes called internet telephony, because it uses the internet to transmit phone calls.

Today, consumers are free to choose from a wide range of equipment such as phones, faxes, computers and video equipment to connect to the network, and they are no longer forced to rent the telephone from the phone company. In many countries the consumers have a choice of networks to which to attach, and often a choice of quality of connection. The local loop may be twisted copper pair as in the past, or a coaxial cable with a higher bandwidth, a fibre-optic connection or even a fixed radio link to a local aerial connected to a fixed network. The subscriber may also have a mobile phone that accesses the fixed network through the nearest aerial or possibly directly to a satellite.

Before the digital revolution, the local network was a classic natural monopoly. Economies of scale argued for a single network provider. After the digital revolution, the advantages of a single provider rapidly decreased. If large increases in transmission capacity and switching are needed, new entrants do not need to duplicate these facilities in order to enter, provided that they can interconnect with the existing network. The regulatory issues are primarily those of ensuring that, where competition is efficient or desirable, it can happen and, where it cannot, the natural monopoly facilities are properly regulated.

International regulatory regime

Because telecommunications is an inherently transnational technology, the development of telecommunications has required substantial cooperation and agreement between nation-states at different levels, including cooperation around adherence to certain technical and operational standards.

International Telecommunications Union

The International Telecommunications Union (ITU) grew from cooperation between European states in the 1850s on the working of the telegraph system. The ITU was concerned at first only with telegraphy, but over time it became involved with telephony and radio. The International Telegraph Union became the ITU in 1932, and the ITU became a specialized agency of the United Nations system in 1947. The basic principles for the conduct of international telecommunications services are contained in the International Telecommunications Constitution and Convention. As such, the Constitution and Convention of the ITU is an international treaty, to which member states are bound.

Complementing the Constitution and Convention are Administrative Regulations subdivided into: (1) International Telecommunications Regulations and (2) Radio Regulations. The Administrative Regulations comprise general principles to be observed when providing international telecommunications services and networks and the assignment and use of frequencies and orbital slots. The current applicable International Telecommunications Regulations are those adopted at Melbourne in 1988, comprising ten substantive articles and a series of appendices. The current applicable Radio Regulations were not signed until 1997.

One of the major issues to be settled within the ITU concerned how revenues for international traffic would be divided between participating states. The issue was resolved by the International Accounting Rate System and the principles of its operation are contained in Article 6 of the ITU's International Telecommunications Regulations. The system works as follows. When an international call is made, the call is jointly carried by the telephone company in the country where the call originates (home country) and by the telephone company in the country where the call terminates (foreign country). The collection rates are paid by consumers to the company in the home country. However, a payment is also due to the telephone company in the country where the call terminates. This payment, made by the telephone company of the home country, is based on the 'accounting rate' that is negotiated between the two countries.

Under the accounting rate system, a particular country will have a different negotiated rate with each country. If the call volume from the home country to the foreign country balances out so that incoming and outgoing minutes of calls to and from the foreign country are the same then there is no payment due to either country. On the other hand, if the minutes do not balance then a settlement payment would have to be made from the country sending more calls. The settlement payment is generally calculated by multiplying the net difference in call volume by one-half of the accounting rate. Thus, imbalances between the number of incoming and outgoing calls are then settled by the carrier with the greater traffic agreeing to pay a settlement rate to the other carrier, and collection rates are impacted by the level of accounting rates negotiated between countries. This system worked quite well when the carriers were monopolies in each country and traffic volumes were comparatively low.[2]

As emphasized by Kahai *et al.* (2006), as the United States liberalized its telecommunications sector it became increasingly dissatisfied with the ITU's accounting rates system. The deregulation of the domestic system in the United States did not help much with international tariffs, as US carriers had to negotiate mainly with monopoly public carriers in other countries. These monopoly carriers had an incentive to keep accounting rates high, thereby generating a trade surplus in telecommunications. There was no incentive for those carriers to lower their prices and they could pass on their higher prices to US consumers. As US citizens tend to make more calls than they receive, the accounting rates system began to produce large deficits for the United States. In 1996, for example, US operators were obliged to pay approximately US$6 billion to operators in other jurisdictions, of which it was estimated that 70 per cent constituted an above-cost subsidy from US consumers to foreign carriers. In recent years there has been significant pressure for the international rate system to be reformed, and it is gradually being replaced by a multitude of different arrangements reflecting the state of liberalization in member states' technological developments as well as the commercial positions of the respective parties.

World Trade Organization

The history of telecommunications has largely been a history of the ITU and the monopoly providers of telecommunications within nation-states. Under the ITU system, states and their monopolies coordinated on the development of telecommunications policy and regulation. In 1994 this system took a dramatic turn when telecommunications was brought into the trading regime of the Final Act of the Uruguay Round of trade negotiations. The shift from the ITU to the World Trade Organization (WTO) is significant because, under the General Agreement on Trade in Services (GATS), states have committed themselves to a process of trade in telecommunications-based services and the progressive liberalization of basic telecommunications.[3] The Final Act contains the GATS, which contains an Annex on Telecommunications, an Annex on Negotiations on Basic Telecommunications and a Decision of Ministers to establish a Negotiating Group on Basic Telecommunications (NGBT).

The Annex on Telecommunications establishes obligations for governments to ensure access to and use of public telecommunications transport networks and services. Once a country agrees to liberalize within the context of the WTO, the Annex requires that the public telecommunications system be accessible to foreign service providers for domestic and international service provisioning. Governments must ensure that foreign suppliers have access to and the use of private lease circuits, and that they can: (1) purchase or lease and attach terminal or other equipment interfacing with public networks, (2) interconnect private leased or owned circuits with public networks, or with circuits leased or owned by another service supplier and (3) use operating protocols of the service supplier's choice, provided that they do not disrupt the telecommunications transport networks and services to the public generally. The annex imposes obligations of transparency of conditions of access and use, including tariffs, terms and conditions and specifications of technical interfaces with the public networks and services. Access should be non-discriminatory, which embraces both the most-favoured-nation (MFN) and national treatment (NT) principles.[4] Service providers should be permitted to attach terminal equipment to the public network, interconnect private circuits and utilize any operating protocols that do not interfere with the availability of the public network. Members may only impose conditions that are necessary to safeguard the public service responsibilities of the suppliers of public networks, to protect the integrity of the network or to comply with a member's commitments in its Schedule.

At the conclusion of the Uruguay Round, ministers adopted a decision to enter into further voluntary negotiations on the liberalization of trade in the provision of basic telecommunications networks and services.[5] These negotiations were carried out under the auspices of the NGBT, which started with a group of 20 countries, with the three main players in telecommunications (the United States, Japan and Europe) all participating. The NGBT negotiations had an official deadline of 30 April 1996. On the initiative of the WTO Director-General, states agreed to plan for further negotiations in February 1997. A new body, the Group on Basic Telecommunications, assumed responsibility for the negotiations. On 15 February 1997 these negotiations closed successfully. The agreement is commonly referred to as the Basic Agreement on Telecommunications, consisting of a series of commitments and lists of exemptions from Article II concerning basic telecommunications by 69 members. These commitments supplement or modify any existing submissions made by members and are annexed to the existing schedules through a device referred to as a protocol, which becomes an integral part of the GATS. As such, these submissions constitute the Fourth Protocol. The Fourth Protocol was intended to enter into force on 1 January 1998; however, further delays meant that it became effective on 5 February 1998. The Basic Agreement has been seen as the most significant development in the global liberalization of the telecommunications market. The commitments made by members encompassed market access, foreign direct investment and, for the majority of Members, adherence to a set of pro-competitive regulatory principles.

One unique feature of the Fourth Protocol was the adoption of a Reference Paper as an additional commitment incorporated into the Schedules. The Reference Paper comprises a set of definitions and principles on the regulatory framework governing the provision of basic telecommunications. The principles address particular objectives for the establishment of a pro-competitive regulatory regime, rather than the mechanisms or processes for their achievement. As such, the Reference Paper represents an important body of international legal principles for the telecommunications sector that is of considerably greater significance than the ITU constitutional principles. However, unlike the Annex on Telecommunications, the Reference Paper holds legal status only to the extent that WTO members have incorporated it in their schedules of commitments under the GATS. For those countries, the principles are enforceable before the WTO Dispute Settlement Body.

Recognizing that the right to interconnect is the most important competition safeguard in a network industry, the Reference Paper creates a requirement for measures to permit the interconnection of competing suppliers of public telecommunications transport networks and services at any technically feasible point in the network, under non-discriminatory terms and conditions, in a timely fashion and on terms, conditions and cost-oriented rates that are transparent and reasonable, have regard to economic feasibility and are sufficiently unbundled so that the supplier need not pay for network components or facilities that it does not require for service to be provided. The Reference Paper requires the public availability of information regarding licensing criteria, the processing periods and terms and conditions, as well as reasons for denial of a licence. Furthermore, the Reference Paper requires the establishment of an independent regulator, in the sense that the regulator must be separate from and not accountable to any supplier of basic telecommunications services and that its procedures and decisions shall be impartial with respect to all market participants. In addition, the Reference Paper requires that a supplier who, alone or with others, constitutes a 'major supplier' must be subject to 'appropriate measures' to prevent anticompetitive practices, whether current or future.[6] Three specific anticompetitive practices are then listed: (1) cross-subsidization, (2) the use of 'information obtained from competitors with anticompetitive results', such as forecast traffic volumes in interconnection arrangements and (3) 'not making available to other services suppliers on a timely basis technical information about essential facilities and commercially relevant information which are necessary for them to provide services'.[7]

Although the Reference Paper addresses 'ends' rather than 'means', its influence has been considerable at both national and international level. First, as part of the schedules of commitments, the Reference Paper represents a member state's commitment, to which foreign service providers may refer. Second, over time, national legislators are likely to reflect and incorporate such principles into domestic law. Third, the Reference Paper represents a baseline from which any future multilateral negotiations will stem.

The European Union's regulatory framework

Since its inception in the mid-80s, the EU telecommunications policy has focused on two main objectives: economic efficiency and the guarantee of universal service. In 1987, the Commission issued a Green Paper that set out a Community-wide programme for action in the telecommunications sector in pursuit of these objectives. The achievement of these aims has been pursued through the application of a set of complementary principles: market liberalization and harmonization of conditions for a common regulatory framework.

Following the publication of the Green Paper, the Commission adopted the Terminal Equipment Directive 1988,[8] which obliged member states to remove special or exclusive rights relating to the importation, marketing, connection, bringing into service and maintenance of telecommunications terminal equipment. The Commission Directive 90/388/EEC (Services Directive) initiated the opening to competition of the telecommunications services market by providing for the removal of exclusive rights granted by member states to telecommunications organizations for the supply of value-added services by the end of 1990 and data services by 1 January 1993. Remaining monopolies within telecommunications services continued as 'reserved services' after the implementation of the Services Directive was lifted, through the adoption of the Satellite Directive (94/46/EC), the Cable Directive (95/51/EC) and the Mobile Directive (96/2/EC). Thereafter, the Commission adopted the Full Competition Directive (96/19/EC)[9] in February 1996, taking the final step in the liberalization of the sector. This last directive called on member states to take the necessary steps to ensure that markets would be fully open by 1 January 1998. Since 1998, the EU has fully competitive telecommunications markets in all member states but five: Portugal, Spain, Greece, Ireland and Luxembourg had derogations.

In 2002, the EU introduced the Framework, Authorization, Access and Universal Service Directives and the Local Loop Unbundling Regulation, the purposes of which are to provide a common regulatory framework and competition principles and practices for the electronic communications sector in the EU, comprising telecommunications, media and information technology services.

The Framework Directive (2002/21/EC) emphasizes the independence of the national regulatory authority (NRA) (which must be guaranteed by member states), the right of appeal against NRA decisions, mechanisms for *ex ante* regulations to be imposed on significant market powers (SMPs), market definition and market analysis procedures and the NRA's duties to resolve disputes within four months when negotiations on access and interconnections fail.[10] According to the directive the NRAs must analyze their relevant electronic communications markets in consultation with the industry and propose appropriate regulatory measures to address market failures that might be hampering competition. These findings and proposals of NRAs must be notified to the Commission and other national authorities. The Commission then assesses these findings and proposals. It may require the withdrawal of proposed regulatory measures if they are not compatible with EU law. The Framework Directive also introduces the principle of technological neutrality, that is, there shall be no separation between different means of transmission for regulatory purposes. It will apply to all telecommunications networks (fixed or wireless) as well as to broadcast networks (terrestrial, satellite and cable). In addition, the directive sets out Community consultation procedures that contribute to the development of a single market in telecommunications by ensuring a consistent and transparent application of the directives across the member states. The procedures require the NRAs in member states to conduct national and Community consultation on any regulatory measures that they intend to take, prior to their adoption.

The Authorization Directive (2002/20/EC) abolishes individual licensing and moves to a system of general authorization, according to which older licensing schemes for different telecommunications services, that is, public voice and data providers and facilities-based and resale providers, have been removed. According to the Authorization Directive, the member states may at most require a notification of the undertaking. Other than the notification no permissions or other administrative barriers to entry can be imposed, and time limits are to be observed by the administration when finalizing the applications. Although obtaining a general authorization is simple, in the event that the undertaking does not comply with the general conditions laid down by the NRAs, it may be subject to financial penalties and even be prevented from providing service. The directive also requires member states to encourage the use of standards as a means of ensuring interoperability of service. In addition, because providers of communications networks need to install infrastructure such as cables, antennas and masts, often on public buildings or land, the directive requires public authorities to consider all rights of way requests without delay and in a transparent and non-discriminatory manner.

The access to the network elements and associated facilities is regulated by the Access Directive (2002/19/EC) and the Unbundled Access to the Local Loop Regulation (No. 2887/2000). The Access Directive requires NRAs to carry out regular market analyses to determine whether one or more operators have significant power in a market and to impose obligations on any operators identified, including obligations related to cost recovery and price controls as well as obligations of transparency, non-discrimination, and good faith in negotiating access. The directive applies to all forms of communications networks carrying publicly available communications services. These include fixed and mobile telecommunications networks, networks used for terrestrial broadcasting, cable television networks, and satellite and internet networks used for voice, fax, data and image transmission. The directive also gives NRA's the power to impose accounting separation in activities relating to interconnection/access. Thus, according to the directive:

- private negotiations between undertakings for interconnections cannot be restricted by member states;
- operators, except for those having SMP, cannot be obliged to discriminate between different undertakings for equivalent service;
- operators are obliged to negotiate interconnection when others ask for it;
- NRAs can impose, when necessary, obligations on an operator to facilitate interconnections.

Likewise, the local loop unbundling regulation aims to facilitate access to the least competitive segments of the liberalized telecommunications market.[11] It is recognized that new entry to fixed-line infrastructure is very difficult and that the existing infrastructures have been financed by means of state-controlled monopolies, using public funds. In the framework of Regulation No. 2887/2000, notified operators are obliged to meet reasonable requests for unbundled access to the local loop under transparent, fair and non-discriminatory conditions. According to the regulation, the NRAs have the responsibility to identify 'notified operators'

(NOs) as those that have significant market power in fixed public telephone networks, to ask NOs to publish a reference offer for unbundled access to their local loops and related facilities, and to supervise NOs with regard to cost-based pricing and transparent, fair and non-discriminatory unbundled access provision for other operators to the local loop.

Because, according to the EU *acquis*, only firms with SMP can be regulated, the same principle applies in the case of telecommunications services. NRAs are first supposed to define the relevant markets. In each relevant market, firms with SMP are to be determined. In the case of SMP, price regulation needs to be implemented by the NRA. There are two types of price regulation, namely price-cap regulation and the rate-of-return (or cost-plus) regulation. In the case of price-cap regulation, the regulator determines a 'reasonable price' for the base year and then for the following years it follows a Consumer Price Index (CPI) inflation–x per cent adjustment on the base year's price, where x is the productivity factor, which could be positive if the sector is expected to operate more efficiently in the future or negative if efficiency declines are expected. The rate-of-return regulation has been found to have certain drawbacks. First, the NRAs are cautious about the cost figures reported by firms, and, second, it is apparent that for firms there is little incentive to improve productivity and cut costs. The trend in the EU has been towards implementing price regulation based on a long-run incremental cost approach, which reflects current costs of the facility used and creates incentives for incumbents to invest.

Universal service is defined in the 2002 *acquis* as the provision of a defined minimum set of services to all end users at affordable prices. The EU sees universal service as an obligation of its member states [Article 3.1 of the Universal Service Directive (USD)]. However, care is taken not to distort the market mechanism while safeguarding the public interest (Article 3.2 of USD). Minimum service requirements in the USD can be summarized as provision of access to a fixed telephone at every reasonable location, directory enquiry services, public payphones, special measures for disabled users, affordability of tariffs, adequate quality of services and number portability. The USD imposes obligations on all undertakings, including the competitive ones, but there are also extra obligations imposed on firms with SMP (Articles 16–19). When NRAs consider that universal service may represent an unfair burden on undertakings designated to provide this service, the net costs of its provision should be calculated (Article 11) and a mechanism introduced in order to compensate that undertaking under transparent conditions from public funds and/or to share the net cost of universal service obligations between providers of communications services (Article 12).

Liberalization in the telecoms sector in the EU, launched in the mid-80s, has been a great success. Thanks to stronger competition the price of telecoms services has fallen, on average, by around 30 per cent in the past decade. However, the European Competitive Telecommunications Association (2009) comparing the regulatory environment in 18 EU member states reports that the institutional framework as well as the application of regulation varies significantly across Europe. Key areas of divergence are described as follows:

- The power of NRAs to enforce rules under the EU telecoms framework remains limited in several significant respects.
- Independence of NRAs is not always fully guaranteed.
- Appeals remain a significant source of legal uncertainty in some countries.
- Rights of way regimes remain largely dictated by local or regional authorities and very few legislators have introduced procedures that allow one-stop shop authorizations. Charges are high or variable in many cases and delays are also of concern across a number of countries.
- Number portability for mobile and fixed services is becoming increasingly effective; however, virtually no European country would meet the proposed requirement for one-day porting under the telecoms framework proposals.
- Full compliance with the four-month legal deadline for resolving access disputes has been achieved in only a few countries.
- Accounting separation regimes in many countries suffer from a lack of transparent and timely publication of information.[12]

On the other hand, a review of the status of competition and consumer outcomes shows that:

- The United Kingdom, Sweden, Norway and the Netherlands benefit from the most competitive environments for fixed voice services generally, whereas France, Germany, Italy, Portugal and Greece have made only particular progress in achieving voice competition through local loop unbundling. Meanwhile, competition in fixed voice remains limited and prices are high in the Czech Republic and Finland, although in Finland low mobile prices may partly compensate.
- Scandinavian countries perform most strongly in mobile markets.
- France and Portugal perform most strongly on a range of broadband measures assessing existing competitive and consumer outcomes, whilst, when specifically considering current levels of infrastructure-based competition and retail outcomes, the strongest performers are Portugal, the United Kingdom and the Netherlands. Competitive weaknesses in the broadband environment are apparent in Spain and Ireland, and new member states such as Poland and the Czech Republic remain behind on a range of broadband measures.

In 2007 the European Commission noted that Europe is not reaping the full growth potential of the telecoms sector. According to the Commission there are few EU-wide communications services, most telecoms companies are active nationally, the internal market is fragmented, fragmentation is blocking or delaying the entry of new competitors to the market, and cross-border competition and pan-European services are hampered by 27 different, partly inconsistent regulatory systems. Noting that the current system risks jeopardizing the competitiveness of the telecoms sector as well as the full exploitation of the economies of scale of the single market with its 500 million consumers, the Commission proposed in November 2007 a reform of the EU telecoms rules.

The reform aims to create the right conditions so that the EU can move to a single market, by fostering pan-European markets and ensuring that EU rules are applied consistently across the EU. Therefore, the Commission proposes the creation of a European Telecom Market Authority to regulate better, more speedily and more consistently across the EU. In addition, it aims to regulate less, but more effectively, by reducing regulation where competition has already delivered results and by in turn focusing regulation on the main bottlenecks where competition problems so far cannot be tackled in a sufficiently effective way.[13]

The regulatory framework in Turkey[14]

Telecommunications services in Turkey were provided until 1994 by the state-owned company PTT, a national monopoly providing postal and telecommunications services. In 1995, Türk Telekom (TT) was legally established as a state economic enterprise, and was a national monopoly with exclusive rights to all fixed-line voice operations and all telecommunications infrastructure except that for mobile systems.[15] In addition, cable services were provided by TT, which was also responsible for radio and television transmitters. Recognizing that competition is the best way to ensure efficient operation and sufficient technological innovation to keep up with the pace of global change, and that regulation is vital, Turkey decided to liberalize the telecommunications sector during the 1990s.

In 2000, the Turkish Parliament approved the legislation to reform the telecommunications sector.[16] The new legislation initiated the process of deregulating the sector, with the goal of fixed-line liberalization to occur by the end of 2003. By that time, mobile and value-added services were also to be made truly competitive. A regulatory authority called the Telecommunications Authority (TA) was established in January 2000. Concessions and licences were to be issued by the Ministry of Transport, whereas preparation of the documents was delegated to the regulator. Pricing would be a function of the regulatory body. After the enactment of the legislation, the new regulatory board was appointed and the decree setting up the authority was published in August 2000. To open its capital to private participation the legislation further transformed TT into an independent joint-stock company, subject to all provisions of the Turkish Commercial Code. On 12 May 2001, the Turkish Parliament passed the new Telecommunications Law, which aimed to end state monopoly on land-line telecoms services by privatizing most of TT before 31 December 2003.[17] The expiry date for TT's monopoly was set as the date when the publicly owned shares of TT would fall to below 50 per cent, with the government to keep a golden share. According to the law, 99 per cent of all outstanding shares could be sold to both Turkish and foreign investors, but the share of foreigners could not exceed 45 per cent of the outstanding shares. In 2004, foreign ownership limitation was promulgated by Law No. 5189. Following the Council of Ministers' Decree dated 15 October 2004 (No. 7931), on 1 July 2005, 55 per cent of TT shares were sold to the highest bidder: Oger Telecoms Joint Venture Group.

With the latest amendments to the Telecommunications Law, concessions and licences are to be issued by the TA. The main tasks and responsibilities of the TA consist of licensing operators in the telecommunications sector, setting administrative, financial and technical regulations, performing follow-up functions of these regulations, issuing technical standards and testing the equipment in accordance with these standards, and implementing administrative and financial measures to those who break the rules and regulations. Over the last few years, the TA has issued new service licences in addition to the already-granted concessions and licences.[18] But liberalization of the telecommunications sector requires that licences are issued not only to service providers, but also to network providers. In fixed-line services TT is still a monopoly. After the privatization of TT, the new company remains a monopoly until additional licences are issued to other network providers. Finally, it should be noted that the Turkish licensing regime is still not parallel with the EU's authorization regulation, as all telecommunications services and infrastructures are subject to a licence, including services that do not need scarce resources such as frequency and numbering.

The TA published a tariff regulation in August 2001 according to which tariffs will be cost based and the price-cap formula will be applied for the services supplied by TT. In addition, TA issued two crucial regulations regarding the access regime, namely the Regulation on Access and Interconnection in May 2003 and the Regulation Regarding Local Loop Unbundling in July 2004. To implement the Ordinance on Access and Interconnection, the TA approved Principles and Procedures on Accounting Separation and Cost Accounting in February 2004 with a transition period of two years; operators having SMP can establish applicable accounting separation systems in the meantime. The communiqué regulating administrative, technical and legal issues on co-location and facility sharing was published in the *Official Gazette* on 31 December 2003. Apart from the above-mentioned regulations, the TA issued implementing regulations on the designation of SMP, numbering and personal data protection and privacy, as well as on radio and telecommunications terminal equipment. It also drafted its framework regulation on rights of way and consumer rights. A new legislation (No. 5369) was enacted in June 2005 that frames the universal services obligations. According to the current legislative framework, TT is obliged to provide payphone, emergency call and directory services as a universal service. However, there is no obligatory requirement for operators other than TT and there is no funding mechanism for the net costs of services provided by TT.

In 2008 the name of TA was altered to the Information Technologies and Communications Authority (ITCA). ITCA aims to achieve full liberalization in the telecom sector, as did the TA previously, and it is consulting the Competition Authority about decisions on the telecommunications sector. Using criteria such as control of infrastructure not easily duplicated, technological advantages or superiority, lack of countervailing buying power, easy or privileged access to capital markets/financial resources, product and/or services diversification, economies of scale, economies of scope, vertical integration, highly developed distribution and sales networks, lack of potential competition, and barriers to expansion it defines the operators and relevant markets with SMP as follows. TT has been identified as the operator with SMP in markets related to call services over the fixed network, access to the fixed telephone network market, call origination and termination markets in the fixed network, markets related to leased lines, the wholesale call termination market on fixed public telephony networks, full unbundled access to the copper network for the purpose of providing broadband and voice services, and the wholesale broadband access market including bitstream access. On the other hand, Turkcell has been identified as the operator with SMP in the market for access and call origination on mobile networks, and Turkcell, Vodafone and Avea as the operators with SMP in the market for mobile call termination. The published figures for reference and access interconnection tariffs for the incumbent and Global System for Mobile communications (GSM) operators reveal that these charges have been reduced substantially with increased competition. With the initiation of number portability in November 2008, competition among GSM operators is expected to increase further.

According to the Principles and Procedures on Accounting Separation and Cost Accounting prepared in accordance with the Access and Interconnection Ordinance, Turkcell, Vodafone and Avea are obliged to carry out accounting separation and cost accounting. Finally, it should be emphasized that a technical assistance project for the improvement of access regime in the Turkish telecommunications market funded by the EU Commission was carried out during 2008. The project aims to equip the regulatory authority with the necessary experience and competency regarding cost models and imposition of accounting separation principles to ensure cost-based access pricing in the context of the EU regulatory framework.

The European Competitive Telecommunications Association (2009) has given scores to 18 EU member states, Norway and Turkey on the basis of information provided by NRAs regarding: (1) overall institutional environment, (2) key enablers for market entry and network roll-out, (3) the NRA's regulatory processes, (4) application of regulation by the NRA and (5) regulatory and market outcomes. The analysis reveals that Turkey is the country with the weakest performance in most sections covered by the report. On institutional score Turkey ranks 16th among the 20 countries, and on regulatory score Turkey ranks last.

Conclusion

Until 1994, telecommunications services in Turkey were provided by the state-owned company PTT, a national monopoly providing postal and telecommunications services. Turkey decided to liberalize the telecommunications sector during the latter half of the 1990s. It introduced a pro-competitive regulatory regime in the telecommunications sector, and participated in progressive liberalization of its telecommunications services, first within the context of WTO negotiations and thereafter by following the EU approach to liberalization of telecommunications services. But despite the pro-competitive efforts of the Turkish regulator, the share of TT in total fixed telephone traffic is 95.98 per cent, and in broadband access measured in terms of subscriber numbers is 95 per cent. On the other hand, the share of TT in long-distance telephone services measured in terms of traffic initiated abroad and terminated in Turkey is 54.1 per cent. Thus, efforts seem to have fostered competition in the telecom sector, but much still remains to be done.

5 Electricity sector policy reform

(co-authored with Osman Sevaioğlu)

Until recently, the electricity sector was typically vertically integrated with a captive franchise market, either state-owned or under regulated private ownership. Investments in generation and transmission were chosen (in theory) to deliver the least-cost expansion plan, financed by low-cost borrowing that was underwritten by the franchise revenue base. The past decade has seen a dramatic change in views of how the electricity sector should be owned, organized and regulated. Today, many of these monopolies have been broken up, and the electricity industry in a large number of countries has been reorganized around markets.

This chapter considers the policy reforms introduced in the electricity sector and is structured as follows. The first section introduces the basic characteristics of the electricity sector, which is followed by a section studying the problems and obstacles of liberalizing the electricity sector, emphasizing the experience of the United Kingdom. The next section studies the main principles of electricity market reform in the European Union (EU), which is followed by a section describing market reform in Turkey. Finally, the chapter ends with some concluding remarks.

Basic characteristics of electricity supply

The electricity supply sector has severe operational restraints, creating certain difficulties in delivering energy. The quality of electricity measured by voltage magnitude, frequency and continuity of supply must continually be maintained within tight operational limits. Electricity is a non-storable commodity. It must be generated at the instant it is consumed, and some generation capacity must always be kept in hot and cold reserve form in order to be able to respond immediately to a sudden increase in demand or an unexpected failure of a plant. Furthermore, demand is not constant and fluctuates considerably by the time of day, season and even randomly. The supply and demand, including the technical losses and illicit utilization, must be kept in an exact balance over the whole period of operation. Severe electricity deficiencies may arise in some regions of a country during some periods, while surplus generation capacity may be available in the other regions, and it may not be possible to transfer this surplus electricity because of congestion in the transmission infrastructure.

The supply chain linking the generation of electricity and customer services has four distinct vertical stages: (1) generation, (2) transmission, (3) distribution and (4) retail and wholesaling. Electricity is generated using various fuel types, such as oil, natural gas, coal, nuclear power, hydropower, renewable fuels, wind power and solar power. The main characteristics of the electricity generation sector are its capital intensity, stranded costs and long lead times. Different generating technologies exhibit different cost structures. The main components of electricity generation costs are capital investments, fuel costs and operating and maintenance costs. The first term is generally known as the 'fixed costs', whereas the others are 'variable costs'. Costs are strongly influenced by the fuel type, age and performance of the plant. Nuclear generation has high capital costs, which result in part from long construction lead times and costs of retiring the plant at the end of its operational life. High fixed costs also result from public opposition to nuclear power plants and waste disposal. On the other hand, the contribution of fuel and operating costs on the nuclear electricity tariff is rather low, and these costs remain relatively constant over the lifetime of a nuclear plant. Generation costs of hydroelectric plants largely depend on the geography, water regime and climate. An important characteristic of hydroelectric energy generation is that its variable costs are much lower than those of other types of plants. The costs of electricity from coal-, oil- and natural gas-fired plants depend largely on fuel prices, so the variable costs of fossil fuel electricity generation are relatively higher than those of nuclear plants. However, fossil fuel generation tends to have lower fixed costs than nuclear generation, particularly in the case of gas-fired plants, which have short construction lead times. Electricity generation generally exhibits increasing returns of scale at low levels of production, and constant returns of scale otherwise; as such, it is considered competitive.

Transmission is the business of transferring electricity from generation side to customer side over a high voltage system. Transmission also involves the commitment of a large number of generators dispersed at various locations in the grid in order to maintain the system voltages and frequency at nominal levels and to prevent system breakdown. Transmission is a natural monopoly, because competition in transmission would result in duplication of the existing transmission system, which, realistically, is not needed. Power flows from generators to consumers cannot be directed and will follow every feasible route between generators and loads, according to physical laws. If too much power is forced to pass along a given line or transformer, that component of the system will have severe operational difficulties, such as temperature rise; if the necessary remedies are not implemented, it will eventually fail, leading to a contingency. Following this contingency, the power flows will be redistributed according to the resulting system configuration. In turn, any overloaded equipment in the remaining system will fail, leading to cascade contingencies and, eventually, to the collapse of the overall system. To minimize this risk, the system control centre tries to run the system in such a way that power flows will always be kept within the system's security limits. This requires leaving a certain margin of spare capacity on every part of the system, with the greatest margins on links liable to receive the additional flows after the contingencies. Hence, there must always be enough spare capacity on every line or transformer to cope with uncontrollable increases in power flows that might arise.

The distribution system is the part of the infrastructure that carries the electricity service out to customers at medium or low voltage levels. Like the transmission system, it is considered a natural monopoly, as competition would similarly entail duplication of the existing medium or low voltage system. Finally, supply of electricity is the activity of carrying electricity to the end users. In principle, supply activity is carried out both in wholesale and retail forms, which have different characteristics in terms of competition. Wholesale activity is based on full competition, whereas retail activity is partially regulated by the regulatory authority. Retail activity includes connecting/disconnecting, metering, reading, billing, toll collecting and marketing activities.[1]

The above considerations reveal that balancing supply and demand requires that generations of different plants be coordinated and scheduled, accounting for the capacity of existing lines and transformers. A certain level of hot and cold reserve must always be available in order to respond to changes in demand or supply and to withstand contingencies.

One basic result of welfare economics is that resources will be allocated efficiently as long as prices equal marginal costs in competitive markets. To explain the marginal cost of electricity, consider following the approach of Green (2005), a system with two types of plants: base-load plants and peaking plants. Base-load plants, meant to operate for most of the year, are assumed to have relatively low variable costs, consisting mainly of fuel costs, but relatively high fixed costs. On the other hand, peaking plants with higher fuel costs but lower fixed costs are committed only at periods of peak demand. The peaking plant might be an open or closed cycle gas turbine, whereas the base-load plant might be a coal-fired plant with a relatively larger capacity. The upper panel in Figure 5.1 shows the total cost per megawatt (MW) of operating two types of power plants for different periods of commitment over a year. The vertical intercepts represent the power plant's annual fixed costs FC_B and FC_P, while the slopes give the variable cost per megawatt-hour (MWh) generated, vc_B and vc_P. The figure shows that, if the plant is needed for more than a duration of t^* hours a year, it is economically more advantageous to build a base-load plant, whereas the peaking plant is cheaper with less intensive use. The ticker line segments show the lower envelope of the cost function for an efficient plant mix. Thus, peaking plants should be committed to meet the demands lasting for t^* hours or less, while base-load plants should be committed to meet longer demands.

The middle panel of Figure 5.1 shows the load duration curve, in which hours of the year are ranked in decreasing order of demand.[2] It must be noted that the load duration curve depends upon the price of electricity. The curve in Figure 5.1 is drawn on the assumption that the price of electricity is the variable cost of the marginal plant in operation. Suppose that the total generation capacity is K gigawatts (GW). In that case, it is optimal to supply K_1 GW of the load from the base-load plants and the remaining $(K-K_1)$ GW of load from the peaking

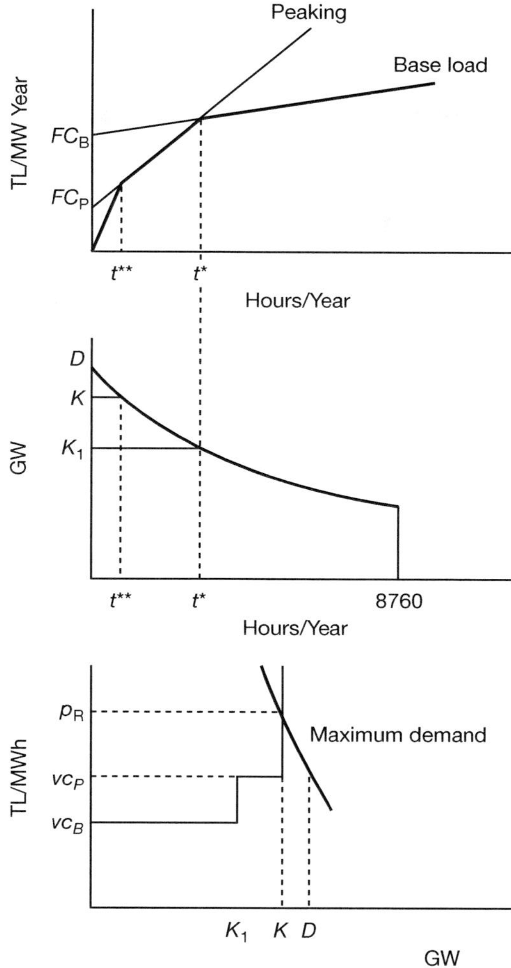

Figure 5.1   Derivation of marginal costs in electricity supply. FC_B, fixed cost of the base-load plant; FC_P, fixed cost of the peaking plant; GW, gigawatts; MW, megawatts; MWh, megawatt-hours; p_R, price charged at peak hours; TL, Turkish lira; vc_B, variable cost of the base-load plants; vc_P, variable cost of the peaking plant.

plants, as such a plant mix will yield the minimum generation cost composed of total capital and variable costs. The lower panel in Figure 5.1 shows the resulting prices, when prices are set at marginal costs.

During off-peak periods, the price becomes equal to the variable cost of the base-load plants, vc_B, which is marginal within these periods. As the demand rises, the peak plants become marginal, and the price is set at the level of their variable cost, vc_p. But, if the price were equal to vc_p, the maximum demand would be equal to D GW. However, D GW cannot be generated with the given plant capacity of K GW. The price rises to p_R as shown in the lower panel. As a result of the higher price, the price duration curve will shift downwards so that peak demand will be met by the supply. Hence, the marginal cost curve becomes vertical at K, the sector's total capacity. During peak periods, as the price rises to p_R to pay for the capacity, the maximum price p_R as shown in Figure 5.2 remains above vc_p for t^{**} hours of the year. The price equals vc_p during (t^*-t^{**}) hours of the year and vc_B during $(8,760-t^*)$ hours of the year, where 8,760 denotes the total number of hours within a year. As the price during peak hours rises above the variable cost vc_p, the amount raised above the variable cost vc_p during t^{**} hours is given by the shaded area of Figure 5.2. As long as this area equals the fixed cost of the peaking plant, FC_p, the price charged allows the peaking plant to recover its capital cost.

It is interesting to note that if the sector has the right amount and mix of capacities, all plants can recover their variable and fixed costs from market-based pricing. This is shown in the upper panel of Figure 5.1. The slope of the line at the bottom left of the panel equals the price charged at peak hours, namely p_R. By hour t^{**} if this total revenue line meets the thick line then the peaking plants break even. In that case, the total revenue for peaking plants will equal the total cost of producing electricity at peak hours, where the cost consists of capacity cost plus variable cost of generation. As the marginal revenue for each additional hour's generation up to time duration t^* is equal to the variable costs of the peaking plants, the total revenue line is superimposed on the total cost line for these plants. After t^* hours, the price drops to the variable cost of the base-load plants, and the slope of the total revenue line equals the variable cost. The base-load plants charge the price p_R for t^{**} hours, the price vc_p for (t^*-t^{**}) hours and the price vc_B for $(8760-t^*)$ hours. According to the definition of t^*, this is the point at which the two types of plants have equal total costs; thus, the base-load plants will also have total costs equal to their revenues. In terms of Figure 5.2, it can be seen that the price charged by the base-load plant equals p_R during t^{**} hours and vc_p during

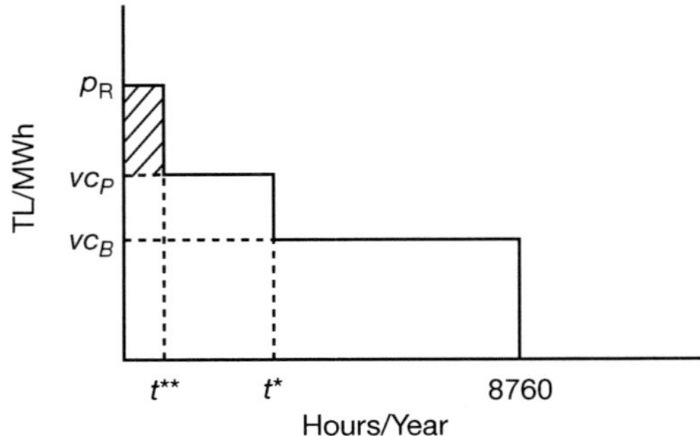

Figure 5.2 Marginal cost schedule. MWh, megawatt-hours; p_R, price charged at peak hours; TL, Turkish lira; vc_B, variable cost of the base-load plants; vc_p, variable cost of the peaking plant.

$(t^* - t^{**})$ hours; the amount raised during t^* hours is given by the shaded area plus the area that lies below the curve between prices vc_P and vc_B up to t^* hours. As long as this whole area equals the fixed cost of the base-load plant, FC_B, the prices charged allow the base plant to recover its capital cost.

The above considerations reveal that, under marginal cost pricing, all plant types can recover their costs from market-based pricing, as long as plant mix and plant capacities are correct. At off-peak hours, prices will equal the variable costs of marginal plants, and at peak hours, prices rise above the variable cost of the peaking plant. If we have too little plant capacity, prices will rise above these levels, and entry into the sector will be profitable. Investment will be attractive and, as a result, capacity will increase. On the other hand, if there is too much capacity, prices will exceed variable costs by a small amount, encouraging exit from the sector. Investment will be unattractive, and owners of high-cost, typically old plants will consider shutting down. Thus, electricity generation can be managed though competitive markets by developing new energy trading mechanisms such as energy pools, in which prices are set equal to their marginal costs.

But the efficiency gains in generation cannot be shared with customers if the transmission system suffers from inadequate transmission capacity. Sufficient transmission capacity and coordination between the generation and transmission systems is vital to ensure the integrity of the supply service. Considering the electricity network, following the approach of Crampes and Laffont (2001) with a set of final nodes (generators and consumers) and intermediary nodes (transformers) connected by lines, one can compute the optimal dispatch of the system. Each branch in the electrical system, which consists of a line or transformer, has a power transmission capacity so that power flows in each branch must be restrained to prevent the branch from exceeding this capacity. In addition, the quality of electricity at the customer nodes must be maintained within tight limits. The optimal system operation can then be seen as a problem of maximizing the net welfare obtained from electricity consumption, subject to a number of system constraints. The net welfare is considered equal to the benefit from consuming electricity minus the cost of generating it. The constraints to be satisfied are that the total generation must equal the total demand including the losses and that the power flow in each branch must be kept within the specified capacity limits. The power flows, on the other hand, depend on the power generation and loading levels of the nodes in the system. Thus, the optimum dispatch problem determines the system operating condition, in particular, power flows in each line, based on a specified system loading condition and operating constraints.

If no branch is congested, electricity is valued the same throughout the system so that there is one unique energy price at all nodes. When some branches are congested, however, differences between nodal marginal valuations arise, reflecting the shadow values of branches. Thus, if the price in each region equals the marginal cost in that region, the difference between the two prices represents the marginal cost of the transmission constraint and the economically correct charge for sending electricity between the two regions. On the other hand, in a meshed system, in which there are many possible alternative paths between any two nodes, the marginal cost at a node could be thought of as depending on the marginal cost per MWh of the constraint multiplied by the proportion of a 1-MW increase in demand at that node that would actually flow over the constraint.

Note that transmission losses also cause the marginal cost of power to differ at every node in the system. Electricity flowing in a line, transformer or any other equipment creates a loss in an amount proportional to the square of the current. As the heating losses depend on the square of current, the marginal cost is twice the average loss. This implies that the marginal cost of meeting a demand at the receiving end of a heavily loaded line can be significantly greater than at the sending end.

The above considerations reveal that market clearing must be maintained continuously at every node in the system, otherwise non-localized supply failures may be encountered. Because the transmission and distribution services in a given area are characterized by natural monopoly cost conditions, and because random variations in supply and demand conditions may happen suddenly and unexpectedly, establishing equilibrium conditions requires central control mechanisms for the transmission and distribution systems by a monopoly.

Nodal pricing is a system of marginal cost pricing, in which the differences in prices at each node reflect costs arising because of congestion and losses in the transmission system. The optimal price at node i has three components. First is the marginal cost of generation in the system plus any penalty premium needed to curtail the demand with respect to the available supply. This term is then grossed up or down by the second component, which reflects the incremental transmission losses caused by an increment in demand at node i. Finally, terms reflecting the transmission constraints are added. Even then, the resulting costs, on average, may not completely cover the overall cost incurred by the operations of the system. The part of the cost not covered by nodal pricing is collected either by Ramsey pricing or by two-part tariff.[3] Ramsey pricing is obtained as a condition of the optimal allocation of resources in a sector, in which the operators have to balance their budgets. Under such pricing, the second best efficiency requires that segments with high price elasticity should pay less for the same product than segments with low price elasticity do. On the other hand, under a two-part tariff, consumption of a quantity of energy q at node i is billed as $p_i \times q + F$, where the marginal price p_i is the nodal price at i, and F is adjusted in order to recover enough resources from all users for balancing the budget.

Electricity sector reform

Until the late 1980s, the electricity sector was largely made up of vertically integrated, typically state-owned monopolies. The reform and privatization of the electricity supply sector in the United Kingdom in 1989–90 demonstrated that it was possible to replace the state-owned vertically integrated monopolies with privately owned, unbundled and regulated companies. Over the next few years, an increasing number of developed and developing countries decided to reform and restructure their electricity supply sectors.

This section will mainly concentrate on the English model, which is becoming the reference for many countries. Before privatization, the electricity supply sector in England and Wales had two parts. The Central Electricity Generating Board (CEGB) ran the generation and transmission systems. Twelve area boards, on the other hand, distributed power to customers in their respective regions. Thus, the CEGB had a monopoly over the wholesale market, and the area boards had regional monopolies over the retail supply. On 31 March 1990, the CEGB was split both vertically and horizontally.

The CEGB was divided into four companies. About 60 per cent of the conventional generating capacity was placed in National Power, with the remaining 40 per cent mainly in PowerGen and the nuclear power plants in Nuclear Electric. The transmission system was separated from the generation system and is carried out by the newly established National Grid Company (NGC). The NGC is responsible for power generation dispatching in accordance with arrangements for the 'power tool', the new wholesale market for power. The company is owned jointly by the 12 distribution companies created from the old area boards. A total of 60 per cent of both PowerGen and National Power were subsequently sold to the public in March 1991, with the balance sold in March 1995. On the distribution side, the 12 area boards were renamed regional electricity companies (REC) and privatized in December 1990.

The Electricity Act of 1989 set out a timetable for introducing competition into the supply sector. Customers with consumptions above the 1-MW level were called 'eligible' and were free to make contracts with any supplier, but all other consumers had to buy their needs from their local REC. In 1994 the eligibility limit was lowered to 100 kW; since late 1998 the remaining consumers have had the right to make contracts with any supplier and the REC eligibilities came to an end.

The most challenging task, as emphasized by Vickers and Yarrow (1991) and Newbery (2005a), was the creation of a market for electricity. Under the old system, the grid controller would try to operate the 'merit order' dispatch of power plants on the basis of information about their operating costs. Under the new system, NGC operated merit order dispatch on the basis of the bids made by generating companies. Each day, generators informed NGC of the availability and prices at which they were willing to supply power for each of their generating units for each half-hour of the following day. On the basis of these offers, NGC ranked plants into merit order. Together with demand estimates, knowledge of constraints in the transmission system and other factors, NGC worked out a plan for the least-cost operation of the system. But demand is random, as it depends largely on weather and other conditions. Furthermore, the amount of available capacity is also random to a certain degree, as it depends on the number and capacity of plant outages, which are unpredictable. Therefore, NGC included a provision for standby reserves.

The price per kilowatt-hour (kWh) paid to the generators for electricity supplied to the pool in a given half-hour was the pool input price (PIP). This price is the sum of two terms. The first term is the system marginal price (SMP), which is the offer price of the marginal generation in that half-hour, ignoring the transmission constraints. The SMP is intended to reflect the short-run fuel and operating costs. It is the marginal cost of producing electricity, as discussed in the previous section. The second term is the capacity element. It is the probability of capacity being insufficient to meet demand, because of a random shock – the loss of load probability (LOLP) – multiplied by an amount intended to reflect the cost to consumers of a supply shock – the value of lost load (VOLL) – minus the marginal cost of power as measured by the SMP. Hence, the PIP may be written as:

$$PIP = SMP + (VOLL - SMP)LOLP$$

VOLL was set at £2 per kWh initially. On the other hand, electricity was made available from the wholesale market at the pool output price (POP). This was the same as PIP except that, at certain times of the day when demand was relatively heavy, an uplift term was added to cover the cost of transmission constraints and other factors.

The various institutions required to manage the decentralized system were codified in the Pooling and Settlement Agreement, a multilateral contractual arrangement signed by the generating companies and suppliers, which provided the wholesale market mechanism for trading electricity. It defined the rules and required almost all parties aiming to trade electricity in England to do so using the Pool's mechanisms.

In 1989, the Office of Electricity Regulation (OFFER) was set up to regulate the sector. The main instrument for regulation were the licences under which firms in the sector operated. Transmission and distribution systems were both regulated. The English solution was to ignore differences arising from nodal pricing and to adopt the single integrated market as the benchmark, with the contractual right to transmission. The amount per kilowatt (kW) charged in a given year by the NGC for the use of its transmission system was capped. The average price cap evolves over time according to an RPI–X formula. The RPI in RPI–X regulation represents the percentage change in the retail price index, and X is generally considered a productivity factor, which could be positive if the sector is expected to operate more efficiently in the future or negative if efficiency declines are expected. To explain the formula, suppose t is the base year and p_t is the transmission price in the base year. Thus, the maximum price one year hence, p_{t+1}, should equal $p_t(1 + RPI - X)$. In England, the X term was initially set equal to zero.

During the 1990s, the experience with the new rules showed that the achievement of a competitive solution in the electricity sector in England was not an easy task. The initial market structure was highly concentrated, with two fossil fuel-based generating companies setting the prices over 90 per cent of the time. Although these companies kept prices lower than might have been expected given their dominance, they clearly had exercised, as emphasized by Newberry (2005b), market power, increasing the price–cost margin steadily as vesting contracts expired. In response, the generating companies agreed with the regulator to accept a wholesale price cap in 1994, until they found an acceptable way to reduce their market power, which they did by divesting 6,000 MW of their capacities to a third company in 1996. This did not reduce the price-cost margin, but the attempt to generate companies to vertically integrate into distribution and supply (to hedge wholesale price risk) required approval from the Competition Commission. This approval was effectively conditional on further divestiture, so these generating companies traded horizontal market power for vertical integration into supply.

The failure of the price-cost margin to fall and a belief that the Pool prices were manipulable led to a detailed review of trading arrangements. In 2001, the Pool was replaced by the New Electricity Trading Arrangements (NETA). NETA replaced the Pooling and Settlement Agreement by a Balancing and Settlement Code with a well-defined method of making modifications, giving the Office of Gas and Electricity Markets (OFGEM), the successor to OFFER, more influence in the process. Electricity was now to be traded in four voluntary, overlapping and interdependent markets operating over different time scales. Bilateral contract markets covered the medium and long run, while forward markets offered standard contracts for periods up to several years ahead. A short-term 'prompt' bilateral market, operating from at least 24 hours to Gate Closure, allowed parties to adjust their portfolio of contracts to match their predicted physical positions.[4] This short-term market would yield information to construct a spot price for each half-hour.

At Gate Closure, the official end of the bilateral markets, all parties had to announce their Final Physical Notifications to the system operator. The system operator would then accept bids and offers for balancing the system. These bids and offers would be fed into the balancing mechanism to produce cash-out prices for clearing imbalances between traders' Final Physical Notifications and their actual positions.

The most obvious difference between NETA and the Pool model is that under the Pool model all generation was centrally dispatched whereas under NETA each generating company is self-dispatched. The obligation to balance output with demand was thus placed on each generating company, with the system operator's task confined to ensuring system stability. The Pool, which both acted as a wholesale market for all electricity and allowed the NGC as system operator to balance the system, was replaced by a balancing mechanism for the residual imbalances of parties that failed to self-balance. Whereas the Pool operated as a uniform single-price auction for buying and selling all power, the balancing mechanism was run as a discriminatory auction. NGC charges for balancing through the Balancing Services Use of System charge.

Elexon, the Balancing and Settlement Code Company established under the Balancing and Settlement Code, determines two cash-out prices: the weighted average of the accepted offers determines the system buy price (SBP) and that of the bids the system sell price (SSP). Any party found to be out of balance when metered amounts are compared with Final Physical Notifications is either charged the SBP if they are short, or they receive the SSP if they are long. The critical feature of the original design of the balancing mechanism is that these prices are normally different and penalize each party's imbalances, whether or not they amplify or reduce the system imbalance as a whole.

The above considerations reveal that, as emphasized by Jamasb and Pollitt (2005), liberalization requires a suitable market structure within which effective competition can be fostered. Generally, this involves restructuring the sector by unbundling vertically integrated activities and reducing their horizontal concentration. The aim of vertical unbundling is to separate potentially competitive generation and supply activities from transmission and distribution, which are mainly natural monopoly activities. The aim of horizontal separation is to create enough effective competition in generation and retail activities, where economies of scale favour competition. On the other hand, effective separation of generation and transmission activities is crucial for achieving competition in the wholesale electricity markets, as this will help prevent anticompetitive behaviour by incumbent generators and ensure non-discriminatory access to the transmission system by all market participants. Similarly, unbundling the supply and distribution activities is important for effective retail competition. Restructuring often involves the horizontal splitting of incumbent generation companies or the merging of retail companies to change market concentration to theoretically and empirically competitive levels. To facilitate competition in generation in the short term and encourage new entry in the long term, it is important to prevent high levels of concentration in the existing markets.

Establishing wholesale and retail electricity markets is essential for liberalizing the sector. Wholesale market design needs to account for various technical, economic and institutional issues associated with pricing, contracts, scheduling, balancing and system congestion, accounting for the specific conditions of the sector. Market participation and efficiency requires sufficient liquidity. Standardized contracts help liquidity and stability and facilitate investment to deliver adequate generation capacity. In the long run, new entry in generation and supply and interconnections with other systems are expected to increase competition in the market.

Establishing an initially competitive market structure requires government initiative. Regulation can be effective at policing a competitive system, but it is difficult for regulators to engineer changes in market structure following liberalization. Maintaining competitive markets requires that the incentives for new entry are correct. The regulator needs to establish clear rules for the wholesale market and to minimize regulatory uncertainty. When competitive and monopoly stages remain integrated, the regulator must ensure that there is real and non-discriminatory access to transmission and distribution systems for the generating companies and suppliers. Regulated third party access has proven the most effective and widely used approach to the provision of system access.

The main perceived effect of privatization is that the pursuit of profit by private owners will lead to efficiency improvement and cost savings. Many reforming countries have sold off public enterprises or allowed for new private entry. An increase in sector-wide ownership diversity can also facilitate direct competition in the generation and supply activities and can yardstick the regulation of systems by comparative performance. However, privatization is not a prerequisite for liberalization. In theory, competition and incentive regulation can be applied to publicly owned enterprises. However, there is significant evidence that privatization does deliver benefits, especially when combined with effective restructuring, competition and regulation.

Liberalization, through internal and cross-border competition, should lead to greater price convergence. The actual extent of convergence is, however, constrained by technological differences, interconnection capacity, the degree of cost-reflective pricing and variations in the efficiency and cost structure of transmission and distribution systems. Similarly, it is plausible that returns on investments will show signs of convergence. Also, capacity utilization should improve, while reserve margins should provide a sufficient degree of security of supply.

The above arguments refer mostly to the liberalization of electricity markets within different countries. But the economic benefits of deeper integration of electricity markets among a group of countries could also be substantial. First, cross-border power transfer for emergency support and peak demand would allow countries to lower expensive reserve margins. This would reduce investment needs and increase capacity utilization. Second, economies of scale, different load profiles and complementary energy endowments could give rise to further gains from trade. Third, private investors would be willing to invest more in large markets. Fourth, regional power markets could facilitate domestic reforms in the countries under consideration, especially the introduction of competition. But the achievement of deeper integration requires cooperation among countries. So far multilateral trade negotiations within the context of the World Trade Organization (WTO) have played a negligible role to achieve cooperation for deeper integration. Important impediments to cross-border trade in electricity and market integration arise from regulatory issues such as vertical integration, conditions of network access and state-owned monopolies. These policy issues are not yet sufficiently addressed under the General Agreement on Trade in Services (GATS) framework.[5] As geography matters a lot in the electricity sector, deeper forms of integration can only be achieved between neighbours at the regional level. Cooperation among countries has been achieved at the regional level, in particular in the EU, as well as between the neighbouring countries of the EU and the EU.

Electricity market reform in the European Union

In 1985, the European electricity sector had a highly stable market structure. In some countries, this took the form of large state-owned monopoly enterprises such as the Electricité de France (EdF) in France and the Central Electricity Generating Board (CEGB) in the United Kingdom. In others, such as Sweden and Norway, there was a mixture of state and municipal ownership, and in Germany and Spain there was substantial private sector ownership with some companies being part private and part state owned. But across Europe, electricity companies had monopoly power supported by legal protection, as in the United Kingdom, or government-supported contracts between companies, as in Germany. The companies were not subject to threat of entry, and international trade did not exist.

In 1988, the European Commission, in the context of the creation of the single market, which was to be completed by 1 January 1993, published a review of the main obstacles to the creation of a single market in energy. According to the communication entitled 'The Internal Energy Market' (Commission of the European Communities 1988) the main obstacles to the creation of an internal market were as follows:

1 National monopolies in some member states in the import and export of electricity.
2 In all member states, undertakings had been granted exclusive or special rights in connection with the transmission and/or distribution of electricity at a national and/or local level.
3 A statutory right of access to the electricity grids owned by others existed only in a few member states. The absence of these rights militated against the creation of a single market for electricity.
4 The electricity distribution monopolies contributed to the creation of captive markets.

A major aim of the Commission's programme of energy market liberalization was to secure for the large industrial consumers of electricity the right to purchase supplies of electricity from any point of sale in the European Community. The Commission therefore drew up a directive to obtain access to the necessary information on prices to final consumers. The Price Transparency Directive 90/377/EEC of 29 June 1990 was considered necessary to enable industrial end users (aluminium, steel, glass and chemical companies) to identify the most competitive producers and suppliers and thus negotiate more effectively their contracts with suppliers.

As intra-community trade in electricity has been relatively modest, the directive 90/547/EEC on the transit of electricity through transmission grids represented a first step towards changing this situation. It relates to transit of electricity between member states through the high voltage transmission grid. Its aim is to remove obstacles to the cross-border exchange of electricity through these grids. The directive requires that contracts involving electricity transit should be negotiated between the entities responsible for the relevant grids and for the quality of service provided. Conditions for transit must be non-discriminatory and fair for all parties. They should not include unfair clauses or conditions or unjustified restrictions and must endanger neither the security of supply nor the quality of service, taking fully into account the utilization of reserve generation capacity and the most efficient operation of the existing system.

The directives on price transparency and energy transit were widely seen at the time as the first steps towards the creation of an EU system of regulation, in which the Commission would play the leading role. Although the member states supported the idea of liberalization and increasing competition in energy markets, there was much less agreement on the appropriate mechanism or on the manner and timing of its introduction. In particular, the proposal to encourage access to electricity systems by third parties provoked intense opposition from both the member states and the principle utilities responsible for transmission and distribution. In 1991, the Commission came up with a proposal to allow third party access within the electricity markets of all member states. The Council of Ministers rejected that proposal. By 1993, the concept of negotiated (as opposed to full or regulated) third party access was presented as one of the options being discussed. In 1994, France introduced the single buyer model as an alternative to negotiated third party access. Eventually, in 1996, an agreement was reached on a timetable for liberalization, and each member state was given a choice between the three alternatives for access. The agreement culminated in the European Parliament's Electricity Directive.[6] Thus, it took the Commission seven years of negotiations to convince the related parties of the need for liberalization and increased competition in the electricity sector.

The Electricity Directive of 1996

The general aim of the Electricity Directive is to establish common rules for the generation, transmission and distribution of electricity. It sets out rules for the organization and functioning of the electricity sector, access to the market, criteria and procedures applicable to calls for tender, the granting of authorization and the operation of systems.[7]

On the supply side, the directive provided for two mechanisms for the development of new capacity in generation, both aiming at introducing competition: authorization and tendering. Whichever procedure is chosen, it must be carried out according to the directive in accordance with objective, transparent and non-discriminatory criteria. The difference between the two procedures is that, in the tendering procedure, the member state sets up an inventory of the need for future generating capacity, including the estimated demand for electricity. The estimates are prepared by a competent authority designated by the member state. On the other hand, in the authorization procedure, companies offer to build new power plants under an open and impartial procedure that decides whether they should go ahead.

On the demand side, the directive envisaged a minimum market opening condition on the basis of consumers being eligible, that is, being designated to have the freedom to contract their consumption of electricity. Each member state was envisaged to 'open' a given and increasing percentage of its market in three stages over the following six years. The first stage ended on 19 February 1999, the second on 19 February 2000 and the third was scheduled for 19 February 2003. The minimum market opening condition corresponding to stage one was designed as making eligible final consumers consuming more than 40 GWh per year. The second stage envisaged a reduction of this threshold to a level of 20 GWh and the third stage to a threshold level of 9 GWh. Those thresholds have been estimated to correspond to market share openings equal to 27 per cent, 28 per cent and 33 per cent respectively.[8] Each member state was to designate its own condition for being 'eligible', but consumers with more than 100-GWh consumption were to be definitely included in that designation.

In transmission, the directive rules that each member state must specify a transmission system operator (TSO). The appointment of the TSO must be for a given period of time to be determined by the member state, taking into account considerations of efficiency and economic balance. The TSO is responsible for dispatching the generating plants in its area, as well as for determining the use of interconnections with other systems. Criteria for dispatching and using interconnectors must be objective and published and be applied in a non-discriminatory manner. The system operator must be independent, at least in management, from other activities not concerned with the transmission system. It should have responsibility for the technical operation of the system, managing power flows and taking into account exchanges with other interconnected systems. It is charged with ensuring a secure, reliable and efficient electricity transmission system and the availability of all necessary ancillary services. When the system operator lacks the necessary capacity, it may refuse the access requirements to the system. The TSO should not discriminate among users.

The directive requires member states or undertakings that own or are responsible for distribution systems to designate a system operator. As in the case of the TSO, the distribution system operator (DSO) in a given area is charged with operating, maintaining and, if necessary, developing the distribution system and its interconnectors with other systems. DSOs must meet various technical requirements similar to those of TSOs. They are charged with maintaining a secure, reliable and efficient electricity distribution system in their areas, taking the environment and quality of service into account. They must not discriminate between system users or classes of system users.

For electricity to be transmitted from producers to 'eligible' customers, system access has to be provided by the system owners and operators. The directive permits three ways of organizing access to the transmission and distribution systems. Member states may choose negotiated or regulated third party access (TPA) or, if they have chosen a single buyer regime, they should follow the single buyer access procedure. Under a negotiated TPA (nTPA) procedure, producers and consumers of electricity enter into contracts for supplies with each other but must negotiate access to the system with their operators. To promote transparency and to facilitate negotiations for system access, the TSOs and DSOs must publish an indicative range of prices for the use of transmission and distribution systems. Either the TSO or DSO may refuse the access requirements in the event of a lack of necessary capacity. The burden of proof falls on the system operator, which must provide duly substantiated reasons for the refusal. Negotiations are subject to a dispute settlement procedure. Member states must ensure that negotiations are conducted in good faith by all parties and that no party abuses its negotiating position by preventing the successful outcome of negotiations.

Member states may also opt for a regulated system of access procedures, giving eligible customers a right of access on the basis of published tariffs for regulated third party access (rTPA). Access tariffs under rTPA are not negotiated, but rather are published by the regulator. Alternatively, member states may designate a legal person as a 'single buyer'. This person may be required to purchase electricity contracted by an eligible customer from a producer. Under the single buyer access procedure, eligible consumers who are not tied to a specific distributor/retailer can still contract with producers. The single buyer pays the producer its regulated sales price minus system charges. The producer can then compensate the consumer so that the consumption prices become equal to the contract price.

Historically, transmission systems have usually been owned by vertically integrated monopolies. But to bring in competition, non-discriminatory access to the system is essential, which is partly provided for by nTPA or rTPA. Non-discriminatory access also requires the effective unbundling of transmission system interests from any other interest of the vertically integrated company. To achieve this, the directive contains requirements in three areas. For internal accounts, separate accounts must be held for the generation, transmission and distribution activities and other parts of the company. The purpose of this provision is to provide maximum transparency, in particular by identifying the possible abuses of a dominant position. Furthermore, management unbundling of the TSO is required, and, to ensure non-discrimination, an independent authority for dispute settlement was also envisaged. Finally, distribution activities must be carried out under the same non-discriminatory basis as transmission.

The directive also recognizes that some objectives deemed desirable from a social point of view may not be achieved through unfettered competition. To achieve these objectives, the directive provided that member states may impose such obligations to electricity undertakings. The objectives mentioned in the directive were security (including security of supply), regularity, quality, price and environmental protection. The obligations would be defined by member states.

Progress with implementation and new measures

Various problems emerged during the phase of the transition to a single market in energy, but three stand out: (1) uneven implementation among the member states, (2) the use of discriminatory methods to manage access to systems and especially interconnection and (3) high levels of market power of incumbent electricity companies. Whereas some member countries opted for a cautious approach to market opening, other member countries preferred to go beyond the minimum requirements. The result was a patchwork of uneven implementation. On the other hand, on access issues, a negotiated form of access proved ineffective, and member states favoured a regulated approach. In general, the quality of access and tariff regulations varied among the member states as a result of the different regulatory completeness. Finally, the high levels of market power of the incumbents presented challenges that touched on the Commission's powers under competition law and on unbundling provisions in the sectoral legislation.

In March 2001, the European Commission issued a communication assessing progress in the development of the internal market for electricity and the effects of the implementation of the 1996 directive and proposed a series of amendments (Commission of the European Communities 2001a). The communication underlined the importance of the full opening of energy markets in improving Europe's competitiveness. According to the Commission, the effects of market opening were positive. However, it was also stated that, to complete the internal market, further measures were necessary. The Commission developed proposals to amend the directive as follows:

- *Market opening*. Allow all electricity customers freedom to choose their suppliers (end domestic customer franchise monopoly) by 1 January 2005.
- *Unbundling*: Strengthen unbundling to the legal and functional separation of transmission from generation in terms of both systems and activities. Hence management separation alone was no longer sufficient, and ownership separation is now appropriately promoted as a form of unbundling stronger than legal separation. Similar considerations apply for distribution. Integrated electricity undertakings are required, in their internal accounting, to keep separate accounts for their generation, distribution and supply activities and, when appropriate, consolidated accounts for other non-electricity activities.
- *Access*. TPA to transmission and distribution systems is to be based on published tariffs, applicable to all eligible customers and applied objectively and without discrimination among system users. The single buyer option is to be deleted. The proposal requires the imposition of a harmonized methodology for calculating charges for access to national systems.
- *Authorization for new capacity*. The authorization procedure for the construction of new electricity generation capacity is to be made the norm.
- *Public service obligations (PSOs)*. Explicit mention of the obligation that member states ensure universal service, defined as the 'supply of high quality of electricity to all customers in their territory', as well as the protection of vulnerable customers and final consumers' rights (Commission of the European Communities 2001a: 40).
- *Regulation*. Establish an independent regulatory authority to approve tariffs and conditions for access to transmission and distribution systems *ex ante* and to monitor and report to the Commission on the state of the electricity markets (particularly regarding supply–demand balances).
- *Security of supply*. A body must be designated by member states to monitor the security of electricity supply issues including the supply–demand balance in the national markets, the growth of future demand and envisaged additional capacity planned or under construction and the level of competition in the markets. Annual reports on these issues are to be published.

The proposals did not prescribe a specific model for the organization of wholesale activities. Some of the proposals were initially met with opposition. The principles of non-discriminatory access to the system, based on transparent and published tariffs and the establishment of independent regulators, were adopted by the Barcelona European Council in March 2002. The Council also drew attention to the need to take measures on PSOs, in particular with respect to remote areas and vulnerable groups. During the November 2002 meeting of the Energy Ministers, an agreement was reached that full market opening would be achieved in 2004 for non-household customers and by 2007 for household customers. Unbundling is intended to be achieved by July 2004 for transmission and by 2007 for distribution. The proposed amendments were finally adopted in June 2003.[9]

The EU Electricity Market Directive of 2003, while focusing on unbundling the system and on opening of national markets, promotes competition by toughening regulations on accessing systems and requiring independent regulators. The second directive aimed, as emphasized by Cameron (2005) and shown in Table 5.1, to achieve by July 2007: (1) the unbundling of the transmission and distribution system operators from each other and from the rest of the system, (2) free entry to the generation sector, (3) the monitoring of supply competition, (4) full market opening, (5) the promotion of renewable sources, (6) the strengthening of the role of the regulator and (7) a single competition-based European market.

The directive was to be implemented by all member states no later than 1 July 2004. By that time there was to be freedom of choice for non-household customers, and all consumers were to enjoy this right by 1 July 2007. Member states were required to ensure that the system of TPA that they implement is based on published tariffs, is applicable to all customers and is applied objectively and without discrimination among system users. It applies to both transmission and distribution.

In short, four types of unbundling can be listed: ownership, legal, management and accounting. Accounting separation is the weakest form, in which a company keeps different accounts for its system and for its competitive activities and must charge competitive businesses the same fees for using the system as it charges third parties. This is intended to prevent cross-subsidies between the system and the competitive activities. Management separation requires that different people are responsible for the system business and the competitive activities and that the system business cannot pass on information about rival concerns. Legal separation goes further, with a completely separate legal entity to run the system. Even in this case, however, staff working for the system business are aware of the financial interests of their parent organization and its competitive activities and may make decisions to further these. Only full ownership separation, in which the system is an independent organization rather than a subsidiary, can completely remove the incentive to favour one market participant over others. The directive emphasizes legal unbundling. No change of ownership of assets is implied, so no company will have to sell off its transmission and distribution arms.

Regarding the regulatory authority, it must be noted that member states are obliged to charge one or more competent bodies with the function of regulatory authority. Second, the directive sets out a minimum set of functions for the regulatory authority. In particular, their supervisory role over system access and setting and approving tariffs for system services has been given a basis in European law. They are charged to ensure non-discrimination, effective competition and the efficient functioning of the market. In addition, the regulatory authority is responsible for fixing or approving, prior to their entry into force, at least the methodologies used to calculate or establish the terms and conditions for connection and access to national systems, including transmission and distribution tariffs. Finally, they

Table 5.1 EU Electricity Directives

	Most common form pre-1996	1996 Directive	2003 Directive
Generation	Monopoly	Authorization and tendering	Authorization
Transmission	Monopoly	Regulated TPA, negotiated TPA, single buyer	Regulated TPA
Distribution	Monopoly	Regulated TPA, negotiated TPA, single buyer	Regulated TPA
Supply	Monopoly	Accounting separation	Legal separation from transmission and distribution
Customers	No choice	Choice for eligible customers	All non-households by 2004 and all by 2007
Unbundling transmission and distribution	None	Accounts	Legal
Cross-border trade	Monopoly	Negotiated	Regulated
Regulation	Government department	Not specified	Regulatory authority

Source: Vasconcelos (2004).

Note
TPA, third party access.

act as the dispute settlement body in cases of complaints or conflicts against a TSO or DSO.

The directive has strengthened provisions on PSOs. Electricity is to be supplied to all household customers and, if member states decide, to all small enterprises at reasonable, easily and clearly comparable and transparent prices. Furthermore, there is new emphasis on consumer protection. Where member states consider it appropriate, households and small enterprises should enjoy public service guarantees, especially with respect to security of supply and reasonable tariffs.

In addition to the Electricity Directive of 2003, a Regulation on conditions for access to the system for cross-border exchanges in electricity in the internal electricity market was published in 2003.[10] The Regulation, which entered into force on 1 July 2004, is directed at increasing cross-border trade in electricity. The increase is to be achieved by the establishment of a compensatory mechanism for transit flows of electricity, the setting of harmonized principles on cross-border transmission charges and procedures for the allocation of available interconnection capacity and the establishment of new interconnection capacities by TSOs in the event of system congestion problems.

Proposal for amending Directive 2003/54/EC

Monitoring of compliance with the Electricity Regulation of 2003 by the European Regulators' Group for Electricity and Gas (ERGEG) indicates that as of 2009 full compliance with the regulation has not been achieved. Although the electricity market in the EU has been fully opened to competition since 1 July 2007, market opening according to the European Commission (2009a) was still only 13 per cent in Estonia, 22.3 per cent in Hungary and 31.8 per cent in Cyprus. The three biggest electricity generators still control more than 70 per cent of generation capacity in 15 member states, and the market share of the three largest companies in the whole retail market was over 80 per cent in 14 member states. Although some progress was made on the unbundling of network operators, in many cases DSOs have so far been slow to implement functional unbundling effectively. Moreover, member states continue to make extensive use of derogations from unbundling at distribution level. More than half of the member states allow DSOs with fewer than 100,000 customers to be exempted from legal unbundling requirements. Furthermore, the powers of some NRAs to impose penalties and on transparency and related issues are still limited.

The European Commission (2009a) notes that some member states continued to regulate retail prices, arguing that it was a tool to protect vulnerable consumers. According to ERGEG (2007) retail prices were regulated in 15 member states. But, regulated retail energy prices are incompatible in the longer term with well-functioning, fully open markets, and hence retail price regulation should be abolished as it distorts the functioning of the market and jeopardizes both security of supply and efforts to fight climate change. Thus the ERGEG has called for member states to publish by July 2008 a plan for removing retail price regulation while protecting vulnerable customers.

In September 2007, EU officials proposed new legislation aimed at breaking open the energy market, making it more competitive and less dominated by national monopolies. The proposed measures include:

- Separation of production and supply for transmission networks. Ownership unbundling is preferred; however, an 'independent system operator' is contemplated. The path under 'independent system operator' would place control of transmission networks in independent hands, but would not affect their ownership. The harsher 'ownership unbundling' option would force companies that own both transit networks and the utilities that sell energy to consumers to split off one of those businesses.
- Establishing an Agency for the Cooperation of National Energy Regulators, with binding decision powers, to aid coordination.
- Strengthening the independence of national regulators in member states.
- Promoting cross-border collaboration and investment through a new European Network of Transmission System Operators (including developing joint market and technical codes).[11]

At its second reading on 22 April 2009, the European Parliament voted to adopt the energy reform package. The final agreement reached maintains key elements of the original proposal with some compromises made to strengthen the position of NRAs and to strengthen consumer protection and consumer rights. Some forms of vertical integration are permitted under strict rules. It is expected that the European Council will formally adopt the package in the near future.

Electricity market reform in Turkey

When Turkey introduced electricity market reform in 2001, the main drivers of the reform were neither concerns with inefficiencies of public enterprises, as in the United Kingdom, nor concerns with creating an internal market, as in the EU. The concern in Turkey was with rapid growth in demand combined with the inability of the government to meet that demand through public investments, because of the deteriorating fiscal situation in the country.

Brief history

Until recently, Turkey's electricity sector was dominated by a large, publicly-owned and vertically integrated company, the Turkish Electricity Authority (TEK), which was established in 1970 and had a statutory monopoly until 1993. Besides TEK, the privately owned Çukurova Electric Company (ÇEAŞ) supplied the regions of Adana and İçel, and KEPEZ Electric Company supplied Antalya. Before 1970, the electricity utility services were carried out largely by İller Bank, a state-owned bank responsible for rural electrification in Turkey, as well as by a number of municipalities and trade unions. All generating plants and infrastructure owned by İller Bank were transferred to TEK in 1970, and those owned by municipalities were transferred in 1982.

Following the opening of the Turkish economy at the beginning of the 1980s, TEK's statutory monopoly was abolished by the 1984 Electricity Act, and it became possible for private companies to engage in power generation, transmission and distribution. But at that time the notion of privatization based on asset sale was incompatible with Turkey's constitution. Nevertheless, the country has been keen to attract direct foreign investment in infrastructure. Therefore, alternative mechanisms were employed to allow private and foreign participation in the power sector without outright privatization, namely build–operate–transfer (BOT), build–operate–own (BOO), build–operate (BO), transferring of the operating rights (TOOR), and independent power production (IPP) or auto-production schemes.

In 1993, TEK was split into two separate state-owned companies: the Turkish Electricity Generation-Transmission Corporation (TEAŞ) and the Turkish Electricity Distribution Company (TEDAŞ). Hydroelectric plants were planned by the General Directorate of the Electric Power Resources Survey and Development Administration and were designed, constructed and operated by the Directorate-General of State Hydraulic Works. Once completed, the power-generating branches of these plants were transferred to and operated by TEAŞ. TEAŞ was responsible for the generation, operation and dispatch of all public hydroelectric plants; the construction, generation, operation and dispatch of thermal plants; and the planning, expansion and operation of the transmission system, including wholesale trading and scheduling energy import and exports.

In the 1990s, the rapid growth in electricity demand directed the government's interest to providing incentives to projects based on the BOT model. Under this model, a private investor builds the plant and transfers the legal ownership to the state with the condition that the plant is to be operated by the company for a certain period of time, typically 15–20 years, based on a certain future wholesale contract covering this period. To make the BOT model functional, the 1984 Electricity Act was complemented by the 1994 BOT Law, which contained a number of provisions designed to encourage BOT investments.[12] These incentives included exemptions from customs duties and the deferral of value added tax (VAT) duty on certain types of imported equipment. Most importantly, the law provided that the Turkish Treasury could back up the power purchase contracts between the BOT investor and the Ministry of Energy and Natural Resources (MENR) with a Treasury guarantee. Under the BOT contract, the private operators signed long-term wholesale contracts with the state, in which the latter committed to buy generated power for a certain period at a tariff in foreign currency, typically with descending time characteristics. This contract assured the investor that the project would be feasible and profitable, irrespective of the future demand for power.

However, despite all of the incentives provided to BOT projects, many investments did not materialize. The reasons for this failure can be analyzed under two headings. Under Turkish legislation, private investment in public utilities is considered a concession. According to the constitution, all concessions were based on public administrative law and not on private law, and, furthermore, these concessions were subject to review and consent of the Turkish Administrative High Court (Danıştay). All BOT projects listed in the 1994 BOT Law were automatically regarded as concessions. Under Turkish legislation, Danıştay was authorized to settle any disputes between the state and private counterparts. These legal arrangements significantly reduced enthusiasm for entrance, and the number of foreign-financed BOT projects and the number of applications by investors was significantly lower than the government's expectations. The second obstacle in establishing successful BOT projects based on foreign investment was the obvious fact that their legal classification as a concession rendered the third party arbitration under international tribunals impossible. International arbitration was a requirement for attracting foreign investment. A number of secondary issues, including disparities in 'force majeure' clauses as well as regulatory and exchange rate risks, also hindered the development of these projects.

Realizing the difficulties with the BOT projects, the government submitted to Parliament the BOO Law (Law No. 4283) enacted in July 1996. Under this model, the investor does not transfer ownership, but maintains a certain future wholesale contract for a certain period of time. Thus, the model supports the right of having ownership of the plant by the investor. In 1997, a tendering round was opened to collect bids for BOO projects.

When the government realized that the needed foreign investment in power plants would not be attracted within the existing legal context, it decided to make an amendment to the constitution towards reducing the power of Danıştay in energy projects on concession and arbitration issues. In 1999, three amendments were enacted on Turkey's constitution. A new paragraph was inserted into Article 47, establishing a legal basis for privatization for the first time in Turkish legislation. It allowed, upon enactment of an enabling law by the legislature, for public services to be performed within the context of private legislation. In addition, Article 125 allowed local or international arbitration mechanisms for disputes arising in the context of public service contracts. International arbitration was possible only if the public service contracts involved a foreign element. There was no clear definition of what a foreign element was or how international arbitration was defined, but it became clear later in the cases dealing with international arbitration that even a small percentage of foreign contribution was adequate for gaining the right for application. Finally, Article 155 had the effect of limiting Danıştay's authority of examining concession contracts to reviewing and submitting advice within two months.

Similar to these constitutional amendments, the Law Governing Danıştay and Administrative Trial Procedures was also amended.[13] As discussed by the Organization for Economic Co-operation and Development (OECD) and the International Energy Agency (IEA) (2001), these amendments restricted Danıştay's authority for dispute settlement to cases in which arbitration was not preferred or allowed by the parties. Furthermore, the BOT Law was amended so that electricity projects were no longer governed by public administrative law, but by private law. Finally, under Law No. 4501 enacted in 2000, the constitutional amendments were made applicable not only to the newly proposed BOT projects, but also retroactively to all projects that had been completed or had reached the stage of approval before the law's entry into force. However, Turkey was required to phase out the use of Treasury guarantees under its 1999 stand-by agreement with the International Monetary Fund (IMF), in order to attain sustainable fiscal policies. In January 2001, the Turkish Treasury stated that only those BOT projects that had already received approval from the State Planning Organization by the end of May 2000 would be eligible for sovereign guarantee and that no new guarantees would be granted. Moreover, the sovereign guarantee would be given only to those projects that actually began operating before 2002.

Besides BOT and BOO projects, Turkey also employed the approach based on TOOR. This scheme allows for private sector operation of the plant and/or infrastructure but does not grant ownership. The operation period envisaged by the MENR is usually 20 or 30 years. The approach has been employed for thermal generating plants and distribution/retailing services. Preparations for the transfer of operating rights of power plants had been underway since 1994, and, by 1999, tenders for eight thermal power plants had been issued, bids received and six consortia selected. However, except for one, these projects have all been cancelled without any chance for implementation. The principal objective of the TOOR model was the requirement to meet the growing refurbishment needs of these plants in order to increase operational efficiency by employing financial resources to be obtained from private investors. The MENR expected that, through the transfers, plant availability and capacity factors would increase. As it was clearly understood that transfer of ownership in the distribution sector had serious obstacles arising from the constitution, the TOOR became the only viable approach for liberalizing the distribution sector.

To allow for private and foreign participation in the power sector, Turkey employed a fourth mechanism, the IPP or auto-production scheme. Under this scheme, an investor builds, owns and produces electricity, without any obligation to transfer the ownership of the plant to the state, but can only sell a certain amount of the production, such as 20 per cent of the annual production, to other customers, the remaining part being consumed for the domestic needs of the producer. Under the rules prevailing until 2002, the state-owned distribution companies had to purchase the excess amount of electricity generated by auto-producers, including co-generators, with a price equal to 85 per cent of TEDAŞ's sale price to industrial consumers. Given that industries often need heat (steam) in addition to electricity, most of them have used the co-generation technology. Because of the favourable legal framework and governmental support to the auto-producer scheme, the installed capacity of auto-producers has increased to a significant level over time.

Although privatization can be thought of as a legal transfer of assets or operating rights from the state to a private operator, many of the benefits of privatization come with the transfer of risk. When private companies bear risk, privatization can be expected to lead to efficiency gains. Under the regulations that prevailed in Turkey until recently, the private investors in the electricity sector seemed to bear only the construction and operating cost risks. The contract, guaranteed by the Treasury, assured the investor that the project would be profitable, irrespective of variations in the future demand for power. As a result, the government retained the commercial risks. Furthermore, such an approach ensures only indirect competition and only in those cases in which contracts have been awarded on a tendering basis. In addition, there have been significant problems with these arrangements concerning the high pricing. The involved purchase costs exposed TEAŞ to extremely large losses and contingent liabilities.

Regarding the transmission facilities, we note that TEAŞ owned and operated the high voltage transmission grid. It also operated the National Load Dispatch Centre in Ankara together with regional load dispatch centres around the country. Because of the inadequacy of the equipment and the technologies deployed for load management, Turkey, during the 1990s, embarked on a programme of improving the national transmission grid with the help of a loan from the World Bank. The objectives of that project were the development of adequate transmission capability in a timely manner, the establishment of independent operation of the transmission grid system and the maintenance of financial viability of the state institution responsible for grid development and operation.

Regarding the distribution sector, we note that TEDAŞ, following the vertical unbundling of TEK in 1993, had taken responsibility for the restructuring and operation of regional districts, with the purpose of eventually transferring their operating rights to private investment on the basis of TOOR agreements. But apart from two, namely in the Anatolian side of Istanbul and in Kayseri, these projects have all been cancelled. Attempts by the government to transfer the ownership of public assets in the electricity distribution sector to the private sector have been confronted by severe opposition from political parties and non-governmental organizations. The second phase of the privatization of the distribution sector began in 1999, by restructuring TEDAŞ's distribution grid into 33 independent regions. Only 14 of these regions have had the chance to be transferred to private parties on the basis of TOOR, but the outcome of this phase has been no different to previous outcomes. Four of these projects were cancelled by Danıştay in 2000, and Danıştay cancelled the remaining ten in 2002, based on the reasoning that public interest in the projects has not been fully justified. In the case of three of these projects, in which the interested parties had international arbitration rights, those parties applied to the International Court of Arbitration, and in two of these cases the decision ruled in favour of the private parties.

Finally, it should be emphasized that TEDAŞ, after its establishment in 1993, was confronted with financial problems related to expansion, refurbishment and periodic repair and maintenance activities. It suffered from high technical losses and illicit utilization and had problems collecting electricity bills. The average ratio of losses, including technical losses and theft, to total billed and unbilled consumption was quite substantial, and the loss ratios varied significantly across distribution regions. In eastern and south-eastern Anatolia, the ratio of losses to total billed and unbilled consumption went up even further, and high variability in losses created high variability in distribution costs.

Electricity Market Law of 2001

The economic crisis of 2001 led to the crystallization and recognition of the structural deficiencies in the electricity sector. The most important of these was a build-up of public contingent liabilities as a result of the government guaranteeing debt for a substantial amount of privately financed generation capacity. These projects have imposed a heavy take-or-pay burden on the electricity system and have created difficulties in transforming to a structure in which the commercial risk can be shifted to private investors. Furthermore, the quasi-fiscal burden on the budget was rising because of high losses and illicit utilization at the distribution level. Realizing the obvious problems with the BOT, BOO and TOOR models, the government concluded that the existing financial structure was not viable and adopted the new Electricity Market Law (Law No. 4628) on 20 February 2001, laying the foundation for a competitive power market.

The new Electricity Market Law fundamentally changed the structure of the Turkish electricity sector and closed the gate to further BOT and BOO contracts. Emphasis is placed on competition. The main principles of the new regime are as follows. A new regulatory framework was put in place to allow the market to function properly. An independent regulatory authority, the Energy Market

Regulatory Authority (EMRA), was established with jurisdiction power over the electricity, petroleum and gas sectors. Regarding electricity, EMRA has the following functions:

- granting licences to market participants for market activities;
- preparing and enforcing secondary legislation concerning the regulations and performance standards on market structure and performance;
- preparing regulations for retail tariffs and end-user prices for non-eligible consumers;
- preparing regulations on transmission and distribution service charges and approving annual tariffs of the newly established Turkish Electricity Transmission Company and TEDAŞ;
- preparing secondary legislations for establishing competitive markets for wholesale activities, including energy importing and exporting;
- preparing Transmission and Distribution Grid Codes concerning the rights and responsibilities of transmission and distribution grid companies and parties who benefit from the services offered by grid companies;
- preparing customer service codes for the end users serviced by distribution companies;
- determining the minimum annual consumption level for customers to be recognized as eligible;
- acting as a tribunal for settling disputes among market participants.[14]

With the Electricity Market Act, TEAŞ was unbundled into three functional companies responsible for different complementary activities, namely the Electricity Generation Company (EÜAŞ), the Turkish Electricity Transmission Company (TEİAŞ) and the Turkish Wholesale Electricity Trading Company (TETAŞ), organized as separate legal entities. EÜAŞ is to retain all power plants not yet divested via the TOOR agreements. TEİAŞ, the sole transmission system and market operator, is responsible for planning, expanding and operating the transmission system and carrying out the balancing and settlement activity for resolving the mismatches between the supply and demand sides of bilateral contracts. TETAŞ on the other hand will carry out wholesale electricity trading activity to sell the electricity generated by EÜAŞ, BOT, BOO and TOOR companies to TEDAŞ and other eligible customers by performing a weighted average calculation on the transactions of electricity purchased, as well as act as the successor of TEAŞ in terms of maintaining the legal and financial duties and responsibilities for the existing BOT, BOO and TOOR contracts. Another and perhaps more important function of TETAŞ is to stabilize any severe price fluctuations that may be seen, particularly during the infancy period of the electricity market, as well as act as a reliable wholesale supplier in terms of the price and amount for the distribution companies during the first five-year period of the deregulation procedure.

On the supply side, the law envisages an authorization-type licensing framework.[15] The licence provides entry opportunities into the generation, wholesale trade, distribution, retail trade, import and export of electricity. The public company EÜAŞ is likely to be split into a hydro generator holding all state-owned hydropower plants and into a small number of affiliate portfolio generation companies holding the state-owned thermal plant and mobile plant contracts. EÜAŞ will also hold the physical assets associated with any TOOR (generation) contracts. Distribution companies may operate as retail sales companies in their regions by obtaining a retail sales licence, may import electricity if allowed in their licence and may establish joint ventures with generation companies or set up generation units. Transmission remains a state monopoly, but private generators can establish private direct transmission lines. The only limitation is that the EMRA's granting of generation licences is conditional on no congestion in the transmission distribution link connecting the new plant to the grid or directly to customers. The law requires a rTPA regime for access to transmission and distribution.

On the demand side, customers who consume more than the eligibility threshold are defined as eligible consumers. As a starting point, consumers consuming more than 9 GWh annually were designated 'eligible consumers', and they were able to choose their suppliers as of March 2003. Eligible customers may buy electricity from their regional distributor/retailer or TOOR distributor, but they also may buy directly from a wholesaler, from a new independent retailer or from an independent generator. Captive customers, in contrast, must buy their electricity from a distributor/retailer in their region, but they have the right to buy from any retailer carrying out the same commercial activity in the region – that is, their existing regional distributor or retailer, TOOR distributor or any other new retailer in the region.

The new regime envisages eventual direct privatization in generation and distribution. Foreign investors cannot assume sectoral controlling interest in the generation, transmission and distribution sectors. The details of licensing procedures, market operation, tariffs, vesting contracts, privatization and stranded cost mechanisms have been left to secondary legislation and decisions.

The regime is based on a bilateral contracts market in which generation companies contract with wholesale trade companies, distribution companies, any new independent retail companies and eligible customers. Bilateral contracts are agreements whose terms and duration are freely determined by parties and are subject to the provisions of private law. The actual real-time equality of demand and supply, given the bilateral contracts, will be carried out by the system operator through purchases and sales in a balancing market. For this purpose, a market system balancing and settlement centre is to be established within TEİAŞ.

However, it is clear that the balancing and settlement system, because of its complexity, cannot be fully operational in the short term. Until the new structure becomes fully operational, 'vesting contracts' have to be introduced to enable market participants to gain experience in carrying out bilateral contracts and to ensure that they will not be subject to excessive extra costs arising from system imbalances. These contracts are an initial set of bilateral contracts put into place by the government between companies it owns and between state-owned companies and private companies, such as independent retailers, in order to provide a smooth transition to competitive markets and to improve the predictability of revenues during this transition. Vesting contracts may be structured to cover different time periods within a term of one to five years into the new structure and to remain with the companies when they are privatized. The contracts are expected to amount to almost all of the energy sales made in the part of the market that is not open to competition and to a portion of the sales made in the competitive market. These shares of sales are to be reduced gradually over time and replaced by freely negotiated bilateral contracts, as the vesting contracts expire. The main objectives of the vesting contracts, as emphasized by the Energy Charter Secretariat (2007), are to avoid large physical imbalances or large financial risks to participants, to avoid chaotic prices, to ensure that distribution companies are not overexposed in the balancing market, to allow for a period of time to learn how the bilateral market works before distribution companies undertake their own contracting, to allow companies to be privatized with a set of matching purchase and sale contracts so that potential buyers can value them, to allow government to influence the portfolio mix of generation purchased by each distributor to ensure reasonable regional balance and to allow the determination of a reasonable flow of funds between companies.

Finally, the new regime allows for explicit cash subsidies to consumers. The cash refunds to consumers should not affect the price structure and the prices in cases in which consumers in certain regions and/or in line with certain objectives need to be supported. The mechanism for the allocation of these direct cash refunds has not been defined in the primary legislation, and it must be established by the Council of Ministers upon proposal by MENR.

Under the new rules, MENR retained the function of monitoring the market at the macro level, within the principles of determining the energy policy of the country, especially with respect to security of supply. The government's role will largely be confined to determining global energy policy, owning and operating the transmission system, operating the balancing and settlement mechanism and ensuring that the rules for competition are not violated and, hence, prices are competitively determined. The law and secondary legislation envisage a competitive, transparent and financially viable electricity market promoting private investment and providing sufficient, reliable and low-cost electricity to consumers without any Treasury guarantee. When the new electricity law is fully implemented, the Turkish regulatory and supervisory regime for the electricity sector will be brought to the level of international practice. As emphasized by OECD and IEA (2005), the model envisaged by the new law is mostly compatible with the European Union Electricity Directive of 2003.

Strategy Paper Concerning Electricity Market Reform and Privatization

Although the government kept the liberalization of the electricity sector on its agenda, progress could not be achieved immediately. In March 2004, the government issued a Strategy Paper Concerning Electricity Market Reform and

Privatization, drawing the map for the privatization of production and distribution sectors.[16] The strategy outlines the major steps to be taken during the period up to 2012 and addresses various issues such as privatization of distribution assets, privatization of power plants, transitional contracts and security of supply. It is stated that the primary objective is to ensure the delivery of electricity to consumers in an adequate, continuous and low-cost manner. To reach this objective, the liberalization in the electricity sector will proceed, and, following the completion of the necessary sector reforms and the restructuring of the state-owned electricity enterprises, the electricity generation and distribution assets will be privatized. The Strategy Paper considers the timely and successful privatization of electricity generation and distribution as an essential element of market liberalization. The Paper determines the primary benefits expected from the reforms as decreasing costs through the effective and efficient operation of electricity generation and distribution assets; increasing supply quality and providing supply security in the electricity sector; decreasing the technical losses in the distribution subsector to the level in OECD countries and the prevention of theft; ensuring that the required rehabilitation and expansion investments are performed by the private sector without creating any liabilities on the public institutions; and transferring to consumers the benefits obtained through competition in generation, trade of electricity and attainment of service quality.

According to the Strategy Paper, the principles by which privatization will be undertaken include the performance of privatization activities by the Privatization Administration; the encouragement of the participation of financially strong companies able to achieve the objectives and principles of the programme; the modification of legislation to accelerate and facilitate the privatization of generation and distribution; starting the privatization from the distribution sector, followed by the privatization of the generation sector; taking into account during privatization the existing public liabilities and not permitting additional state guarantees; the achievement of the competitive generation structure through appropriately grouping generation assets before their privatization; keeping the hydropower plants in government ownership; and keeping TEİAŞ as a publicly owned company.

The Strategy Paper makes the privatization of distribution assets a crucial step in the success of the overall restructuring programme. Hence, according to the document, privatization starts with distribution and is to be followed by generation. The stated reason for this sequencing was the hope that the successful privatization of distribution companies would create credible contractual counterparts for existing and especially for new entrant generation companies. In the Strategy Paper, the number of distribution regions was determined to be at most 21 throughout the country. It was stated that the licence terms would be for a maximum of 49 years,[17] there would be multiyear tariff implementation periods and the first implementation period would be five years, the tariffs applicable in the first implementation period and other issues regarding service quality targets would be determined before privatization, the distribution companies would have supply contracts with suppliers for at least the equivalent of 85 per cent of their forecasted load demand of non-eligible consumers in their regions and only distribution companies would be allowed to sell to non-eligible consumers.

The Strategy Paper envisages the restructuring of the generation sector in a set of portfolios containing a number of generating plants with various fuels. As the divestiture of the generation sector is planned to be performed after the privatization of the distribution sector is complete, the principles to be followed are mostly unclear. It is emphasized that the generation facilities to be privatized will be identified and grouped on the basis of two main criteria: (1) prevention of creating market power and (2) financial viability.

Generation, consumption, and cross-border trade

Installed power generation capacity at the end of 2007 was 40,835.7 MW, and 41.4 per cent of this capacity was owned by the private sector. During 2007, the share of EÜAŞ in total installed capacity was 49.1 per cent, affiliated partnerships of EÜAŞ 9.4 per cent, production companies 30.2 per cent, mobile plants 0.6 per cent, and auto-producers and TOORs 10.7 per cent. Hence, the single largest power generation company is the state-owned EÜAŞ. In the total installed capacity of Turkey, the share of hydroelectric plants is 32.8 per cent, thermal plants 66.8 per cent, and geothermal and wind plants 0.4 per cent. Gross electricity generation during 2007 amounted to 190 billion kWh, exhibiting a 8.7 per cent annual rate of growth during the year. During 2007, the share of EÜAŞ in total electricity generated amounted to 38.9 per cent, affiliated partnerships of EÜAŞ 9.7 per cent, production companies 41.5 per cent, mobile plants 0.4 per cent, and auto-producers and TOORs 10.3 per cent. The share of thermal plants in total energy produced during 2007 was 81 per cent, hydroelectric plants 18.7 per cent, and geothermal and wind plants 0.3 per cent.

Between 1990 and 2000, power demand in Turkey increased at an annual rate of 8.5 per cent, from 57 to 128 billion kWh. After a brief downturn during 2000–5 to 4.6 per cent, demand growth resumed. According to demand projections, electricity demand will increase from 204 billion kWh in 2008 to 440.1 billion kWh in 2020 under the low-growth scenario and to 483.6 billion kWh in 2020 under the high-growth scenario.

According to a recent Electricity Generation Company report (EÜAŞŞ 2008) the power generation capacity will have to increase to 80,000 MW in 2020 under the low-growth scenario, and to 96,000 MW under the high-growth scenario. In November 2004, TEİAŞ prepared a report entitled 'Electricity Energy Generation Planning Study for Turkey (2005–20)' (TEİAŞ 2004). The projections in the report reveal the need for utilizing nuclear energy to diversify the generation mix through zero carbon technology. According to the forecasts, nuclear power plants corresponding to a total of roughly 5,000 MW will be integrated into the Turkish electricity grid until 2020. Finally, regarding transmission facilities, we note that the high-voltage electricity transmission grid ($\geq 66\,kV$) is owned and operated by the state-run TEİAŞ. Most lines are overhead, rated at 154 kV (31,383 km) and

380 kV (14,338.4 km). There are also 85 km of 220-kV lines and about 477 km of 66-kV lines.

In Turkey, cross-border trading is allowed for licensed market participants, namely wholesale and retail licensees. Electricity can be exported to and imported from countries in which the national electricity system is operated in a manner conformable with the Electricity Market Grid Regulation and the Electricity Market Import and Export Regulation. Licences related to exports and imports of electricity are regulated under Law No. 4628, and secondary legislation has been enacted by the EMRA. Exports of electricity to countries that fulfil the international interconnection requirement are conducted by wholesale licensees, provided it is so stated in their licence. Regarding cross-border interconnections, we note connections to Azerbaijan, Georgia, Bulgaria, Iran, Syria, Armenia and Iraq. However, the connection to Armenia is currently inactive. Limited-scale exports of marginal importance are sent to Azerbaijan, Georgia and Iraq, and import power is available mostly from Bulgaria, Iran and Georgia. The cross-border interconnections are of inadequate capacity and thus provide only limited service in load management and in the improvement of the security of supply at present.

Currently, electricity import is within the level of 633.4 GWh per year from Turkmenistan through Iran, and 215.6 GWh from Georgia. Exports are 1237.2 GWh to Iraq, 962.4 GWh to Syria, 117.5 GWh to Georgia and 90.2 GWh to Greece. In the future, the Turkish Transmission Grid is to be part of the Trans-European System Program.[18] In this context, Turkey applied for UCTE (Union for the Coordination of Transmission of Electricity in Europe) membership on 21 March 2001. Since then, several studies financed by the European Commission within the framework of the Trans-European System Program have assessed different scenarios for connecting the Turkish transmission system to the UCTE system through Bulgaria and Greece. On 28 September 2005, a technical study was initiated by UCTE to complete transmission assessments including static and dynamic stability analyses to determine the technical conditions under which the Turkish power system would be synchronized with the power system of the UCTE. Turkey already has two lines to Bulgaria and will complete its linkage to Greece within the context of UCTE in the near future.

Main challenges[19]

During the period since 2001, when the new Electricity Market Law was adopted, fundamental changes have been introduced in the Turkish electricity sector. In this context, a comprehensive secondary legislation was enacted including the following: By-Law on Tariffs, By-Law on Licensing, By-Law on Distribution, By-Law on Eligible Consumers, By-Law on Customer Services, By-Law on Demand Forecast, By-Law on Grid, By-Law on Import and Export, By-Law on Balancing and Settlement, By-Law on Electricity Transmission System Supply Reliability and Quality, Communiqué Regarding the Metres to be used in the Electricity Market, Communiqué Regarding Connection to and Use of

Transmission and Distribution Systems in the Electricity Market, Communiqué Regarding Preparation of Retail Contract in the Electricity Market, Communiqué Regarding Regulation of Market Management Revenue, Communiqué Regarding the Principles and Procedures of Financial Settlement in the Electricity Market (abolished), Communiqué Regarding Regulatory Accounting Guidelines and By-Law on Principles and Procedures for Granting Guarantee of Origin for Renewable Resources.

To inform domestic and foreign investors about the market structure to be implemented in Turkey, the *Electricity Market Implementation Manual* was published in 2003.[20] The model envisaged is a bilateral contracting market completed by the Market Financial Settlement Centre under the patronage of TEİAŞ. The supply side of the market is represented by BOO, BOT and TOOR contractors, importers of electricity, EÜAŞ and its affiliates, EÜAŞ portfolio companies, auto-producers and private generation companies. It is understood that EÜAŞ will retain the large-sized, multipurpose hydroelectric plants with an installed capacity of about 7,000 MW. The remaining hydroelectric and thermal plants, both owned by EÜAŞ, will be converted into six separate portfolio companies that will be privatized following the completion of the privatization procedure for the distribution system. In reaching the goals envisaged for a competitive market, liberalization is to be realized not only on the supply side but also on the consumption side. To ensure this, the eligibility threshold was gradually reduced from 9 million kWh annually in 2003 to 7.8 million kWh in 2004, 7.7 million kWh in 2005, 6 million kWh in 2006, 3 million KWh in 2007 and 1.2 million KWh in 2008. Eligible consumers directly connected to the transmission grid have the right to choose their suppliers and sign bilateral contracts with suppliers. Non-eligible consumers purchase electricity from the regional distribution companies holding retail sale licences at the regulated retail tariffs. The purpose of the bilateral contracts, as emphasized by the Energy Market Regulatory Authority (2003), is to meet fully the electrical energy demands of customers from the supplier side. As customers' electricity demands over time may change, it is necessary to structure bilateral contracts in such a way as to match the customer's load profile as closely as possible.

Although eight years have passed since the adoption of the new Electricity Market Law, competition in the sector has not been achieved as of 2009, and the development of competition is likely to take more time, because of various challenges and difficulties, especially those related to exiting from the old system. Primary among these challenges is the fact that most generation capacity is currently either under government ownership or tied up in take-or-pay contracts. Among the main challenges on the road to full liberalization, following the Energy Charter Secretariat (2007), are the handling of stranded costs, the 'marketization' of existing contracts, the insufficient metering and communication infrastructure, the need for training market participants and for establishing attitudes compatible with a liberal market philosophy, the high losses and leakage rates in distribution systems, the lack of facility-based and cost-reflective generation prices and the full implementation of cost-reflective end-user tariffs.

As emphasized above, the state-owned electricity generation company EÜAŞ, together with the affiliated partnerships of EÜAŞ, owns 58.5 per cent of installed capacity and produces 48.6 per cent of total electricity generated in the country'. This output is sold mainly through vesting contracts. These contracts, in which at least one party is a state-owned entity, are subject to regulation by EMRA. Presently, they amount to almost all energy sales made in the market that are not open to competition. Because of commitments made in the past, private companies holding long-term BOT, BOO and TOOR contracts were granted purchasing guarantees, also named Treasury guarantees. Commitments were made to purchase all of the electricity power generated by private companies holding long-term BOT, BOO and TOOR contracts at relatively high prices for long periods of time. The holders of these contracts neither accept the cancellation of their contracts, nor the conversion of their statutes to licensed generating companies; they are not interested in conforming to competitive market conditions. Hence, TETAŞ has to purchase the power generated by these generators until the existing contracts expire. As pointed out by Özkıvrak (2005), existing BOT, BOO and TOOR contracts with 'stranded costs' pose serious problems for the liberalization process.[21] Electricity Market Law No. 4628 requires TETAŞ to be financially viable and authorizes the company to charge a wholesale price sufficient to cover its stranded cost obligations. To solve the problems with the stranded costs of existing BOT, BOO and TOOR contracts, EÜAŞ has contracted all state-owned hydropower assets to TETAŞ. With hydropower fetching a very low price per KWh, TETAŞ is thus enabled to cover a substantial part of the stranded costs by bundling the electricity purchased from EÜAŞ with electricity purchased from BOT, BOO and TOOR plants at high costs.

As shown in Table 5.2, as of 2007, the electricity distribution system, except for the Kayseri region, is owned by TEDAŞ. The system is operated by 20 regional distribution companies under TOOR contracts.[22] TEDAŞ was shifted to the privatization programme of the Privatization Administration in April 2004 and was restructured into 20 regional companies in 2005; a roadmap for privatization was then announced. The plan calls for the distribution regions to be privatized by following a TOOR approach backed by a sale of majority shares in the operating distribution company. In this approach, the investor will be the sole owner of the shares of the distribution company, which will be the unique licensee for the distribution of electricity in the designated region, but which will not have the ownership of distribution network assets and other items essential to the operation of distribution assets. The ownership of these distribution assets will remain with TEDAŞ. The investor will be granted the right to operate the distribution assets pursuant to a TOOR agreement with TEDAŞ. The distribution company will be privatized through a sale of a majority of shares on a competitive basis.[23]

In September 2006, the Privatization Administration decided to start the privatization process with the simultaneous tender of three distribution companies operating in Ankara, the Anatolian part of Istanbul and the Sakarya region. To commence privatization, legal amendments were made in the Electricity Market Law No. 4628 and other relevant laws; EMRA approved five-year tariff profiles;

and transition contracts between EÜAŞ, the portfolio generating companies, TETAŞ and the distribution companies were signed in 2006. The tenders brought considerable interest from foreign and local investors, but the process was postponed by a decision of the Privatization High Council taken on 8 January 2007.[24] Recently, the operating right of one distribution company has been transferred, tenders of four distribution companies have been completed and final privatization transactions are in progress at various stages. The privatization of 15 distribution companies remaining under the privatization portfolio will be continued in 2009. In contrast, the first privatization was successfully realized in electricity generation although it was small in terms of capacity. The transfer of nine power plants having approximately 140 MW of installed capacity to the private sector was completed.

Tariffs, according to the Strategy Paper, should be 'cost-reflective' based on predetermined operating and loss/theft improvement targets, and the system will move to a fully cost-based tariff structure in 2010. The end-user tariffs for the period after 2010 will be determined by the distribution companies in accordance with the Electricity Market Tariffs communiqué and related regulations and will be subject to the regulator's approval. The period 2006–10 will serve as the transitory period. As stated in the Strategy Paper, the 'national tariff' scheme will be maintained for the period 2006–10, rather than implementing 'regional tariffs', so that sudden price fluctuations can be avoided.[25] But the implementation of national tariffs will result in revenue imbalances. To remove such imbalances, EMRA will put in place a tariff equalization scheme to transfer revenues across the regions. The mechanism will aim to equalize across distribution companies to ensure that they recover the revenues that they require to cover eligible costs, after factoring in performance targets. It is envisaged that this equalization will be carried out through TETAŞ. Recently, a new pricing mechanism was developed to facilitate the privatization process and enhance the financial viability of the companies operating in the sector and increase competition in the market. Within this context, a cost-based pricing mechanism was put into effect on 1 August 2008 by the High Planning Council Decision. With this mechanism, final consumer sales prices will be updated automatically in a periodic manner by mainly taking into account the changes in input prices, inflation and exchange rates.

Regarding the market model, we note that the Market Financial Reconciliation Centre started operations in 2003, and the balancing mechanism was launched in August 2006. The balancing and settlement system presently covers a relatively small section of the electricity sector. On the demand side, some 80 per cent of the consumption of non-eligible customers of the distribution companies is bound with vesting contracts, and, because of the requirements of the Renewable Energy Law No. 5346, at least 8 per cent of the consumption of distribution companies is also bound.[26] On the supply side, the capacity of the power plants operating under competitive market conditions does not exceed, as emphasized by Selçuk and Erten (2007), 16 per cent of the total installed capacity, and a large amount of related generation is done by auto-producers and auto-producer groups, which are limited to selling no more than 30 per cent of the amount of their previous year's

Table 5.2 State intervention in the electricity sector, 2007

State economic enterprise	Market share	Price regulation	Other
Electricity Generation Company (EÜAŞ)	Owns 58.5 per cent of installed electricity capacity	Prices set by EÜAŞ	Private sector may participate in all segments of the market, except for transmission, by obtaining licences from EMRA. Privatization of generation is also on the agenda
Turkish Electricity Transmission Company (TEİAŞ)	Owns and operates the transmission system and also acts as market operator	Methodologies are derived and tariffs are calculated according to the Electricity Market Tariffs regulation and the related communiqués, and are submitted to EMRA for approval	TEİAŞ will remain as the sole transmission system operator and asset owner in the long run
Turkish Electricity Trading and Contracting Company (TETAŞ)	In charge of trading and wholesale of less than 50 per cent of total generation	TETAŞ submits tariff wholesale price proposals to EMRA for approval	TETAŞ took over all of the public sector purchasing obligations of the previous regime. TETAŞ may neither sell to new consumers nor sign any new Power Purchasing Agreements except for obligations as stated in the Electricity Market Law; its role is intended to diminish over time, once the cost burden is mitigated
20 state-owned, regional distribution companies formed by the restructuring of the Turkish Electricity Distribution Company (TEDAŞ), and one private regional distribution company	TEDAŞ owns the distribution system but distribution and retail sales are undertaken by regional distribution companies	Regional distribution companies submit distribution and retail tariff proposals and the methodologies to EMRA for approval	Privatization of distribution is also on the agenda

production to competitive markets.[27] The transition contracts are set at regulated prices and last for five years, except for the TETAŞ contracts. As they run out, such contracts will be replaced by market-priced bilateral contracts, which will ensure a smooth transition to the liberal market.

During the transition period, the generation of the hydropower plants that are under the possession of EÜAŞ will continue to be sold to TETAŞ as long as it is deemed necessary to achieve an average TETAŞ sales price that is not too high. In contrast, the energy purchased by TETAŞ through existing contracts and EÜAŞ generation will be allocated among the distribution companies through purchase agreements to be signed between TETAŞ and the distribution companies. Finally, the sales contracts between portfolio generation companies and distribution companies will be put in place before distribution companies are privatized, to give the generation companies/groups a track record before their privatization. The contracts should continue after privatization to ensure a predictable stream of revenues in the early years.

Recently, certain further amendments were made to legislation to improve competition in the electricity sector. The market control limit was redefined on a natural and legal persons basis. Accordingly, the total electricity installed capacity owned by any natural person or private sector legal person through production companies controlled by him/her may not exceed 20 per cent of the total previous year's published electricity installed capacity of Turkey. Similarly, the amount of electricity that may be sold by any natural person or private sector legal person through wholesale companies controlled by him/her may not exceed 10 per cent of the total amount of electrical energy consumed in the market in the previous year. Furthermore, electricity distribution companies are now obliged to legally separate their electricity production and retail sale activities until 1 January 2013. Finally, the legal infrastructure was enhanced by removing ambiguities in legislation regarding security of supply. In this context, the creation of a capacity mechanism and public sector generation investment as a last resort in case of the private sector being unable to ensure security of supply are permitted.

Conclusion

When the United Kingdom introduced electricity market reform during the 1990s the main drivers of the reform were concerns with the elimination of inefficiencies created by public enterprises in the electricity sector. In contrast, when the EU introduced electricity market reform during the 1990s the main concern was in creating an internal market. When Turkey introduced electricity market reform in 2001, the concern was with rapid growth in demand combined with the inability of the government to meet that demand through public investments, because of the deteriorating fiscal situation in the country. Eight years have passed since the introduction of the new electricity law. Although fiscal problems in the sector seem to be solved by now and considerable progress has been made toward liberalization of the electricity sector, the country is still far away from attaining efficiency and security of supply in the sector, and also from fulfilling public service obligations. With full implementation of the reform programme the country aims to achieve these goals.

6 Policy reform in the natural gas sector

(co-authored with Cenk Pala)

For a long time it was considered that natural gas lacked the prerequisites for competition to function in an open market. A key reason was the need for a grid to deliver the energy. As a result, the theory of natural monopoly in the grid-based energy industry was considered sacrosanct up until the middle of the 1980s. Competition was regarded as impractical and market thinking as superfluous. Since the mid-80s, however, one has observed a trend towards the liberalization of natural gas markets. A number of countries have launched extensive structural reforms aimed at introducing competition, which is expected to bring economic benefits to consumers. This chapter considers policy reform in the natural gas sector and is structured as follows. The first section considers the conditions for competitive gas markets and the next section analyses the regulatory framework prevailing at the global level in the natural gas sector. The third section discusses European Union (EU) regulations in the natural gas sector, which is followed by an analysis of natural gas market reform in Turkey. The final section provides some concluding remarks.

Conditions for competitive gas markets

Gas networks consist of three main segments: production, transportation and distribution. To study the conditions for competitive gas markets, consider the approaches of Cremer and Laffont (2002) and Cremer *et al.* (2003), who set out a gas network consisting of two nodes, 1 and 2, linked by a single pipeline, as shown in Figure 6.1. Assume that natural gas is supplied at node 1, and that the production cost is given by $C_1(Q_1)$ (with $C_1'>0$ and $C_1''\geq0$) where Q_1 denotes the output of natural gas. Let D_i be the demand at node $i=1, 2$; $S_i(D_i)$ (with $S_1'>0$ and $S_1''<0$) the consumer's surplus; and $p_i^d(D_i)=S_i'(D_i)$ the inverse demand function.

Natural gas flows from node 1 to node 2. Let Z_{12} denote the net flow, which implies a short-run cost of $C_{12}(Z_{12})$. The capacity of the line is given by K, which is set up at a cost (per period) of $C(K)$. The balance of flows requires that $D_1=Q_1-Z_{12}$, $D_2=Z_{12}$. Assume that natural gas at node 1 is supplied competitively with the inverse supply function given by $p_1^s(Q_1)=C_1'(Q_1)$. Social welfare is determined by the relation:

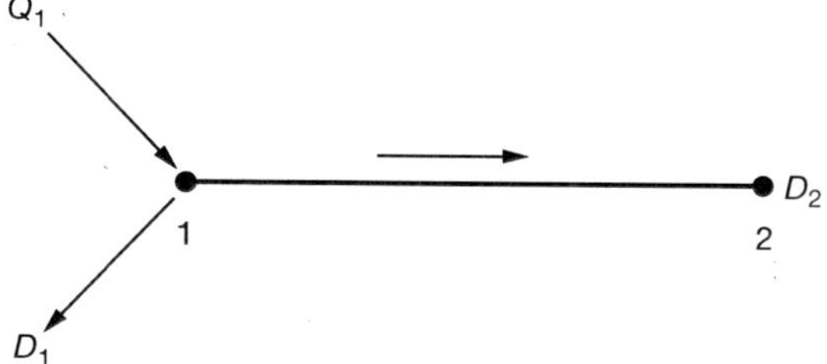

Figure 6.1 A simple network.

$$S_1(D_1)+S_2(D_2)-C_1(Q_1)-C_{12}(Z_{12})-C(K)=S_1(Q_1-Z_{12})+S_2(Q_2+Z_{12})-C_1(Q_1)-$$
$$C_{12}(Z_{12})-C(K)$$

Welfare maximization for a given level of K subject to the capacity constraint yields the marginal cost-pricing conditions at all nodes given by the relations:

$$p_1^s=C_1'(Q_1)$$

$$p_2=p_1+C_{12}'+\gamma$$

The first optimality condition states that at node 1 the price will equal the marginal production cost. The second optimality condition states that the transportation charges from nodes 1 to 2 will be given by:

$$t_{12}=p_2-p_1=C_{12}'+\gamma$$

where $\gamma\geq0$ is the multiplier of the capacity constraint, that is, the shadow price of capacity. Capacity is optimal when the shadow price of capacity equals the marginal cost of building capacity: $C'(K)=\gamma$. Thus, efficient transportation charges equal the marginal transportation costs, with a markup when a line is congested. Hence, the optimal capacity of a line is obtained by equating the per-period marginal cost of construction to the transportation markup. This optimal solution, called nodal pricing, is a system of marginal cost pricing, in which the price at node 1 equals the marginal cost of producing natural gas, and the price at node 2 equals the marginal production cost plus the short-run marginal transmission cost plus the marginal cost arising because of congestion.

The optimal solution can be obtained through decentralization under ownership unbundling. In that case, the producers of natural gas will try to maximize their profits, which are given by:

$$\text{Profit}_1=p_1Q_1-C(Q_1)$$

The optimality condition yields the best solution as long as the producer takes the price p_1 as a parameter, and the price p_1 itself equals the best solution value so that the price signal is correct. On the other hand, the operator of the transmission network will maximize the profit as:

$$\text{Profit}_2 = p_1 D_1 + p_2 D_2 - C_1(Q_1) - C_{12}(Z_{12}) - C(K)$$

subject to the capacity constraint $K - Z_{12} \geq 0$, where $D_1 = Q_1 - Z_{12}$, $D_2 = Z_{12}$. The optimality condition will yield the best solution as long as the network operator considers the prices p_1 and p_2 as given constants, and those prices equal the values at the best solution so that price signals are correct.

But prices obtained by nodal pricing on average may not cover the total cost incurred by the network operators. The part of the cost not covered by nodal pricing is to be collected through Ramsey pricing, which is obtained as a condition of optimal allocation of resources in an industry in which the operators have to balance their budgets.[1] Under such pricing, second-best efficiency requires that segments with high price elasticity should pay less for the same product than the segments with low price elasticity. Thus, optimal prices can be 'decentralized' through marginal cost pricing at the production level and through a two-part pricing scheme at the transportation level.

World Trade Organization provisions and the Energy Charter Treaty

Considerations in the previous section reveal that efficiency in the natural gas sector can be attained through:

- a market in which there is full competition in producing, wholesaling and retailing natural gas, gas can be freely traded between producers, wholesalers, retailers and consumers, and markets are liquid;
- an interconnected transmission and distribution system with clear rules for access by all prospective participants, in which pipeline capacity is in competition, capacity is tradable and transmission prices are set by reference to the market;
- arrangements in the transmission, distribution and retail sectors that provide confidence in the market and when cross-subsidizing is not occurring in vertically integrated organizations.[2]

But countries often face difficulties satisfying these optimality conditions. Consider the condition requiring full competition on the production side. This condition cannot be satisfied for the large number of countries that have limited domestic sources of gas production. In those cases, countries rely on gas imported via pipelines from other countries and/or on shipped liquefied natural gas (LNG).[3] When a country is dependent on imports from a limited number of countries, liberalization of the gas industry in the home country could conceivably leave home country gas consumers worse off, as a single buyer of gas in the importing country could conceivably exercise countervailing power against any market power exercized by gas sellers in the exporting country. As fragmenting the buying side of the market might enhance the market power of the gas sellers, there is a strong need for regulation at the global level through, for example, World Trade Organization (WTO) provisions and the Energy Charter Treaty (ECT).

World Trade Organization provisions[4]

The first question that needs to be answered within the context of the WTO provisions is whether trade in natural gas is subject to the General Agreement on Tariffs and Trade (GATT) and the associated multilateral agreements on trade in goods such as the Agreement on Subsidies and Countervailing Measures or the General Agreement on Trade in Services (GATS). Hence, we are confronted with an issue of definition and classification. Which economic activities might constitute services and might be the objects of multilateral services and trade liberalization negotiations?

Until recently, the natural gas business was dominated by vertically integrated suppliers directly engaged in the extraction, transmission and distribution of natural gas, leaving small margins for separate services activities. Then, gradually, as discussed by Musselli and Zarrilli (2005), natural gas companies went through a process of downsizing and outsourcing, and activities that were previously performed in-house were increasingly contracted to specialized service companies. The trend toward downsizing and outsourcing in the natural gas sector has contributed to the isolation of several economic activities that may constitute services and may be the object of multilateral trade liberalization negotiations. Nowadays, in a further phase of the growing reliance on service markets, natural gas companies have been outsourcing even activities that were, until recently, considered to be core functions of natural gas companies and thus were always performed by their own units. The patterns of 'vertical integration' are still present and it is interesting that the large natural gas companies were recently engaged in this process with respect to the downstream phases of the gas business. Overall, there is still great variety in the degree to which the natural gas companies either 'vertically integrate backwards' or 'outsource' services to external providers. This makes it difficult to a priori identify which activities are typically contracted to an independent services supplier as opposed to functions that are still commonly assigned to separate specialized divisions within the natural gas companies. But for practical purposes, production of energy is considered to fall within the scope of GATT, whereas transmission, distribution and related services are considered to fall within the scope of GATS.

Energy-related activities are commonly regarded as included in the scope of energy services when they are performed by an independent services supplier and not by a vertically integrated manufacturer. For GATS to apply, no title on the natural gas can be passed to the contractor, even though the contractor's remuneration might be fixed as a percentage to the profit. On the other hand, it has been maintained that the production of primary and secondary energy does not constitute services subject to GATS, but results in goods, whose trade is subject to GATT, as the production service is incorporated in the value of the goods produced.

Scope and content of GATT rules

As emphasized by the WTO (1998a) and the WTO Secretariat (2001a), energy goods have long been treated as being outside the scope of GATT rules by relying on the general exception relating to the conservation of exhaustible natural resources [Article XX(g)] and on the national security exception (Article 21). The decline in oil prices and consequent reduction in the importance of scarcity considerations in the formulation of economic policies have led countries to treat energy goods like other commodities and therefore subject them to GATT's multilateral trade rules.

The trade of natural gas encounters obstacles such as tariff and non-tariff barriers and restrictive business practices (RBPs) such as the vertical foreclosure of transmission and distribution networks in the destination country. The WTO goods agreements deal with the first types of obstacles (tariff and non-tariff barriers), whereas the second type (RBPs) falls outside the scope of WTO agreements.

In a recent paper, Selivanova (2004) considers the WTO rules on energy pricing in the context of Russia's system. She emphasizes that energy-related policies maintained by Russia were perceived to be the major element blocking the accession process of Russia to the WTO. The problem lay primarily in Russia's maintenance of different levels of internal and imported prices for gas. The EU and the United States insisted that Russia eliminate its policy of dual pricing for energy and seemed to view such a change in energy policy as a precondition to Russia's WTO accession. The prices of imported natural gas are six times higher than prices of internal natural gas. This price differential is perceived by some WTO members as constituting a subsidy favouring the production of energy-intensive products, such as fertilizers, in Russia. As Russian industrial producers do not have to pay full market price for their energy inputs, this situation has adverse implications on the ability of imported goods to compete on the Russian market. It could also lead to a displacement of members' products from third-country markets. In other words, the existing policy in Russia gives Russian producers an advantage when they compete in third markets with foreign companies that use more expensive energy inputs. Consequently, the demand to equalize energy prices corresponds primarily to the interests of industries that produce energy-consuming products.

The world's largest gas company, RAO Gazprom, holds a monopoly in the Russian gas market, accounting for 90 per cent of produced gas. Gazprom pays 25 per cent of federal tax revenues, and has complete control of the inter-regional gas pipeline network, as well as of a big part of the regional distribution systems. Gazprom also has an interest in the gas-processing conglomerate Sibur. Cross-subsidization in the gas sector is carried out through differentiated wholesale prices set by the Federal Energy Commission. The state regulates wholesale prices on gas, tariffs on gas transportation, tariffs on gas supply services for the ultimate consumers and retail consumer prices. At present, industrial producers on the domestic market can obtain gas at prices so low that Gazprom has no incentive to invest in increasing its production. Domestic sales of Gazprom are loss-making. It is apparent that Gazprom has little incentive to supply gas and invest in sales in the domestic market because of the low prices, non-payments and high taxes.

Although there are no specific WTO rules on energy, government measures restricting trade in energy are not exempt from the general rules of WTO agreements. Arguably, these general rules are not designed to address many of the practices occurring with energy exporters. Although GATT deals with export restrictions, its primary focus has been on import-restrictive practices. Russia's trading partners use three main arguments to insist that Russia's dual pricing policy is not consistent with WTO rules. First, they argue that dual pricing is an actionable subsidization of the Russian downstream industry, which obtains energy inputs at preferential rates. Second, they allege that this practice is inconsistent with the behaviour proscribed in GATT Article 27 for state trading enterprises. Finally, they contend that such dual pricing is not in line with the provision of GATT Article 3.9 on maximum price control. However, upon WTO entry, Russia refused to undertake commitments to eliminate dual pricing for gas, as it did not consider its energy policy to be inconsistent with WTO requirements.

According to Article 1 of the Agreement on Subsidies and Countervailing Measures (SCM agreement) (World Trade Organization 2002: 231) a 'subsidy' is a 'financial contribution by a government or by any public body' or 'any form of income or price support' whereby a 'benefit' is conferred. The financial contribution exists if a government provides goods or 'entrusts or directs a private body' to do so, and a 'benefit' is said to exist whenever a recipient obtains goods for 'less than adequate remuneration'. In accordance with Article 2 of the SCM agreement a subsidy is subject to its rules only if the subsidy is 'specific'. Export-contingent subsidies and subsidies contingent upon the use of domestic products over imported products are deemed to be specific. The SCM agreement prohibits such export subsidies. Furthermore, domestic subsidies, although not prohibited, can be actionable; if subsidized imports are causing injury to the domestic industry of a member, such member may impose a countervailing duty to offset the subsidy. Also, if a member believes that a subsidy results in adverse effects, it can bring a dispute settlement request before the WTO, asking for the withdrawal of the subsidy or the removal of adverse effects. But to qualify as actionable, a domestic subsidy must be specific to an enterprise or industry, or group of enterprises or industries, or regions.

Selivanova (2004) asserts that energy products at low prices are available to Russian downstream industries throughout the whole economy and are linked neither to export performance nor to specific industries or enterprises. Therefore, Russia's practice constitutes neither a prohibited nor an actionable subsidy. Moreover, WTO rules will not prohibit Russia from using domestic subsidies after its accession to the WTO. Products manufactured with the use of subsidized energy inputs could merely become subject to countervailing duties – provided that the investigation has shown that the respective imports have caused injury to domestic producers in the importing country. Alternatively, a country could challenge the Russian practice before a WTO panel, where adverse effects would have to be demonstrated.

Selivanova (2004) notes that, in Russia, the government is significantly involved in the activities of enterprises that dominate key sectors such as energy and mining. Here, the fundamental concern of many WTO members appears to be the lack of transparency in how monopolies function in Russia's energy sector, and in the relationship between such enterprises and the Russian government. It is claimed that the dual pricing policy is not consistent with the provisions of GATT Article 27, which focuses on the behaviour of state trading enterprises and aims to avoid state controls over trade that would nullify the basic principles of non-discrimination and circumvent market access commitments. As state trading enterprises are not necessarily led by market principles in making policy decisions as to pricing, availability, transport and other conditions of purchase and sale, it is stressed by WTO members that their policies might harm the competition and distort trade conditions.

In Article 27, members undertake to ensure that state trading enterprises act in a manner consistent with the general principles of non-discrimination prescribed in GATT for governmental measures affecting imports or exports by private traders. But what are the 'general principles of non-discriminatory treatment'? The issue is whether Article 27 covers incidences of national treatment as well as most favoured nation (MFN) treatment.[5] Here it is emphasized that, should the panel have the opportunity to determine the issue of coverage that Article 27 delineates, it will most likely rule that Article 27 requires state trading enterprises to accord enterprises of any member treatment that is no less favourable than that accorded to enterprises of other members, and that it is justifiable to charge different prices in different markets if this practice corresponds to commercial considerations.

Turning to investment matters, we note that foreign direct investment (FDI) in the production of natural gas is not the object of comprehensive multilateral trade rules. The Agreement on Trade-Related Investment Measures (TRIMs) applies GATT Articles 3 (national treatment) and 11 (quantitative restrictions) to trade-related investment measures such as those linking investors' rights to use imported goods as inputs to their export performance. This agreement, however, affects the cross-border trade of natural gas rather than establishment. There is also a disparity between WTO rules in the area of trade in services and WTO rules in the area of trade in goods. Under GATS, there are no restrictions on the number or types of conditions that may be attached to national treatment and quantitative restrictions. Thus, depending upon whether government measures in the natural gas sector are affecting goods or services, different regimes apply. Domestic measures relating to trade in natural gas products are subject to WTO rules on trade in goods, including the provisions of the TRIMs Agreement, whereas those affecting trade in energy services are covered by GATS rules. GATT rules are in general more stringent than GATS rules with respect to performance requirements for foreign investors. But as previously seen, the dividing line between goods and services in the natural gas sector is often difficult to draw. In addition to TRIMs there is also GATT Article 5 on freedom of transit. The Article specifies that there shall be freedom of transit through the territory of each contracting party and that all charges and regulations shall be reasonable and cost based.

Scope and content of GATS rules

As noted by the WTO Secretariat (2001a), cross-border trade in energy services encounters limited market access, national treatment, and other regulatory barriers and restrictive business practices by incumbent operators controlling transmission and distribution networks. All members are bound by the MFN unconditional obligation of GATS, while market access and national treatment barriers are dealt with by Articles XVI (market access) and Article XVII (national treatment) and by the progressive negotiation of specific commitments. Other domestic regulatory barriers are subject to the provisions of Article VI (domestic regulation), including a test of necessity linking them to the policy objectives they are meant to serve. Restrictive business practices by incumbent operators are subject to Article VIII (rules on monopolies and exclusive services suppliers) and Article IX (consultation and exchange of information between members on restricted business practices). In the case of gas transmission services, Article VIII requires members to ensure that the incumbent monopoly in a given market does not act in a manner inconsistent with MFN and with the member's specific commitments in that market, and that the monopoly supplier does not abuse its monopoly position in services markets outside the scope of its monopoly, which are the object of specific commitments under GATS. An example of this second situation would be that of a vertically integrated gas utility, active in the generation, transmission and distribution markets, that is the incumbent natural monopolist in the transmission market and which abuses this position in the liberalized generation and distribution markets.

Unlike trade in goods, trade in services is defined as including the cross-border movement of the factors of production, capital and labour. Establishment-based trade by energy service suppliers is covered by GATS (mode three). It is subject to the unconditional MFN obligation of Article II. Market access and national treatment barriers to mode three in energy services are the object of members' commitments under Article XVI and XVII. Article VI deals with other domestic regulatory barriers, whereas important aspects of restricted business practices by incumbent operators are dealt with by Article VIII (in the case of monopolies or exclusive service suppliers) or can be the object of legally binding additional commitments under Article XVIII (additional commitments).

Entities engaged in the natural gas sector are often controlled or influenced by bodies governed by public law and state enterprises combining public and private attributes. Questions might arise under GATS with respect to restrictive or limited methods such as tendering methods in the area of government procurement, tendering or auctioning used in the granting of concessions, public sale or auctioning and liquidation of debt in privatization. A tender may be restricted to contractors from certain countries. Such a measure could be challenged under GATS and be held in violation of the MFN standard. In this connection, it is worth emphasizing that the MFN treatment is a general obligation under GATS in the sense that it applies with respect to services that have not been specifically committed.

Rules applicable in the area of government procurement at the multilateral level within the WTO framework are contained, among others, in the Agreement on Government Procurement (GPA), which is a 'plurilateral agreement'. In other words, unlike the other 'multilateral agreements', whose provisions are bound to all WTO members, GPA applies only to the WTO members that have signed it. Under GPA, each party shall ensure that its procuring entities shall not give prices and other preferences to domestic products, services and suppliers and shall not discriminate between products, services and suppliers from different signatory countries. In this connection, GPA prohibits procuring entities from seeking or considering development objectives as criteria for awarding contracts. On the other hand, the current GATS framework provides countries with the greatest flexibility for applying procurement preferences in pursuing national policy goals. Pursuant to GATS Article XIII:1, laws, regulations and requirements concerning services procurement by governmental agencies are exempt from the GATS disciplines of MFN, national treatment and market access. By virtue of this carve-out, domestic measures relating to government procurement of services can discriminate in favour of domestic suppliers and providers, discriminate between foreign suppliers and providers, and inhibit foreign access to the domestic procurement market. Notwithstanding this comprehensive exemption from the most important GATS discipline, government procurement remains subject to other general GATS disciplines, notably the transparency requirements of GATS Article II.28

Within the meaning of GATS Article XIII.1, 'government procurement' involves governments or their agents acting as consumers, procuring services for ultimate consumption in governmental use and not for commercial purposes. GATS language thus clearly excludes from the scope of 'government procurement' requirements purchased by governmental agencies as intermediary inputs in commercial or industrial activities. As such, these activities in WTO language are considered a matter of 'state trading'. But because in GATS there is no equivalent of the GATT Article XVII on state trading enterprises, it can be maintained that measures affecting natural gas procurement by national companies are currently subject to general GATS disciplines such as MFN and transparency.

An important issue concerns concessions, which amount to the granting of certain exclusive rights by a government to a private party for a set period of time, in order to manage public works or resources that were under government ownership or to offer a public service that was within the exclusive competence of a government. It should be noted that concessionary schemes might be regarded as entailing title to natural gas resources, to the extent that concessionaires could be considered owners of the goods, services or works carried out during the period of concessions. Accordingly, laws, regulations and requirements relating to these types of arrangements would fall outside the scope of GATS. They could be more properly treated as a matter of investment subject to the GATT discipline. If concession agreements were regarded as public procurement, the relevant discipline would then be found in GATT Article III.8. In this respect, it is noteworthy that, whereas measures affecting procurement in services are exempted by virtue of GATS Article XIII:1 from both national treatment and MFN obligations, GATT Article III:8 exempts measures relating to public procurement of goods from the national treatment obligation only.

GATS also includes basic disciplines aimed at the promotion of competitive markets. Article VIII on monopolies and exclusive service suppliers may be relevant in cases of natural monopolies. This provision would require members to ensure that the incumbent natural monopolist does not act in a manner inconsistent with MFN and with a member's specific commitments in that market, and that the incumbent monopolist does not abuse its position in other liberalized segments of the gas market, which are the object of specific commitments under GATS.

The Energy Charter Treaty

The ECT, developed on the basis of the European Energy Charter of 1991 and signed in December 1994, entered into legal force in April 1998. The fundamental aim of the ECT is to strengthen the rule of law on energy issues by creating a level playing field of rules to be observed by all participating governments, thus minimizing the risks associated with energy-related investments and trade. The roots of the treaty date back to the early 1990s, when the end of the Cold War offered an unprecedented opportunity to overcome the earlier economic divisions on the European continent. The incentives for mutually beneficial cooperation between East and West were especially clear in the energy sector. Russia and many of its neighbours were rich in energy resources but needed major investments to ensure their development, whereas the states of Western Europe had a strategic interest in diversifying their sources of energy supplies, thus reducing their potential dependence on other areas of the world. There was therefore a recognized need to ensure that a commonly accepted foundation was established for developing energy cooperation between the states of the Eurasian continent. On the basis of these considerations, the Energy Charter process was born.

The ECT was signed by 51 states and by the European Union.[6] It provides the broadest multilateral framework of rules in existence under international law governing energy cooperation. It is a legally binding multilateral instrument.[7] It contains rules on the protection of FDI, rules on energy transit, rules on applying GATT provisions to non-WTO members in the energy sector, a mechanism for the settlement of disputes between governments and between governments and private investors, rules on transparency, and an obligation for governments to have and enforce competition laws.

The provisions on investment apply to any investment of an investor of another ECT contracting party associated with 'economic activity in the energy sector', including exploration, extraction, refining, production, storage, land transport, transmission, distribution, trade, marketing or sale of energy materials and products. Economic activities in the energy sector also include such services as construction of energy facilities, prospecting, consulting, management and design and activities aimed at improving energy efficiency. The requirements include:

1 Fulfilling any obligations that a contracting party has entered into with an investor of another contracting party.
2 Permitting investors to employ key personnel of their choice, regardless of nationality, so long as such personnel have work and residence permits.
3 Paying compensation for any losses suffered by a foreign investor in time of war or civil disturbance at least as fully as for losses suffered by the country's own nationals.
4 Prompt, adequate and effective compensation if the loss results unnecessarily from the country's own actions.
5 Paying prompt, adequate and effective compensation for any assets expropriated. The compensation has to amount to the market value immediately before the intention to expropriate it affected it.
6 Allowing a foreign investor freely to transfer out of the country, in fully convertible currency, the capital he/she invested and any associated earnings.

The ECT contains an obligation to grant to existing investments and related activities of investors of other ECT contracting parties treatment no less favourable than that accorded to domestic investors, investors of another ECT contracting party or investors of any third country. This corresponds to national treatment or an MFN standard of treatment, depending on which is more favourable.

The ECT's trade provisions, which were initially based on the trading regime of GATT, were modified by the adoption in April 1998 of a trade amendment to the treaty. The amendment brought the treaty's trade provisions into line with WTO rules and practice. The treaty's amended trade regime represents an important stepping stone for those signatory states that have not yet acceded to the WTO, such as Azerbaijan, Kazakhstan, the Russian Federation, Turkmenistan and Uzbekistan. It allows them to familiarize themselves with the practices and disciplines that WTO membership entails through application of its rules 'by reference' to trade in energy materials and products and energy-related equipment. The ECT's trade provisions are founded on the fundamental principles of non-discrimination, transparency and a commitment to the progressive liberalization of international trade. The trade amendment also expands the treaty's scope to cover trade in energy-related equipment and sets out a mechanism for the future introduction of a legally binding standstill on customs duties and charges for energy-related imports and exports.

Article V of GATT prescribes, as noted above, the principle of freedom of transit and certain rules of non-discrimination and reasonableness. It needed elaboration for the purposes of the ECT to tackle the particular problems of new or old fixed pipeline links through which more and more energy is today traded between contracting parties. In the ECT the transit provisions apply even if the energy originates outside the territory of ECT contracting parties, or is destined for outside that area. The provisions cover not only pipelines and transmission grids but also any other fixed facilities (such as marine terminals) used specifically for handling energy materials and products. The ECT requires transit traffic to be treated no less favourably than goods originating in or destined for the transit country itself, and requires governments not to impede the creation of new capacity, subject to any national legislation that is consistent with the principles of freedom of transit and non-discrimination. Furthermore, if a transit country seeks to prevent the construction of new capacity or the additional use of existing capacity on grounds that it would endanger the security or efficiency of its energy systems, it has to demonstrate that to the other parties concerned. Finally, the ECT prevents, in order to protect security of supply to consumers and security of outlet to producers, a transit country for up to 16 months from interrupting transit in order to enforce its claim in a dispute so that conciliation for which ECT provides can proceed.

The ECT includes strong international dispute settlement provisions. These provisions will reassure foreign investors of fair, consistent and predictable interpretation and application of the ECT rules by all of the contracting parties. If an investor from another contracting party considers that a government has not fulfilled its obligations under the investment protection provisions, the investor can, with the unconditional consent of the contracting party, choose to submit the dispute for resolution either to the national court or to any dispute settlement procedure previously agreed upon with the government, or to international arbitration. The contracting parties have committed themselves to carrying out arbitration decisions without delay and to ensuring that they are enforced throughout their territories. A government can refer a dispute over a non-trade provision to an arbitration tribunal, the decision of which is final and binding on the governments involved. The resolution procedure for trade disputes involving a non-WTO member is closely modelled on the dispute resolution agreement of the WTO.

European Union regulatory framework

For several decades before the 1980s, the energy sector was not considered in the EU integration process except in terms of a limited coordination of nuclear policy and coal restructuring and some measures aimed at improving the security of the oil supply. Until the mid-1980s, the natural gas industry was subject to various government regulations and controls that significantly affected all levels of the industry – extraction, production, import, transport, distribution and prices. The traditional paradigm dominated the gas industries and there was hardly any harmonization of the laws or rules in the sector across Western European countries. During the past two decades we have seen various initiatives to liberalize the natural gas industry in Europe, in which the process has been driven both by governments at the national level and by the European Commission. The Commission worked out several proposals to enhance competition at all levels in the natural gas market. The objective of the Commission has been to transform the heavily regulated national markets into an efficient European natural gas market through regulatory reforms.

In 1988 the Commission published a review of the obstacles to creating a single market in energy in a communication entitled 'The Internal Energy Market' (Commission of the European Communities 1988). The obstacles for the gas industry were: (1) exclusive national monopolies in some member states on the import and export of gas, (2) in all member states except Germany, undertakings, whether state- or privately-owned, had been granted exclusive or special rights in connection with the transmission and/or distribution of gas at a national and/ or local level, and some form of protection existed in the form of demarcation and concession areas and (3) a statuary right of access to the gas pipelines existed in only a few member states. The Working Document led to a radical reform of the EU energy sector and proposed that: (1) exclusive transmission concessions should be checked to see how to facilitate the free movement of natural gas while maintaining a high level of security of supply, (2) transmission or distribution undertakings should be allowed direct access to the resources in question and (3) the prospect of extending direct access to resources to large industrial consumers should be considered.

Although the European Community (EC) Treaty already granted the Community institutions extensive powers to deal with competition matters such as an abuse of dominant positions by the operators of energy networks, it was clear that, in practise, relying on EC competition law to deal with such cases would require many years of litigation before a body of case law could be built up that could clarify the basic legal principles to be applied. Hence, the Commission decided to tackle removing obstacles to the internal energy market by not only applying the existing law but also by submitting specific initiatives in the form of proposed directives.

The Gas Directive of 1998

The Gas Directive 98/30/EC was adopted by the Energy Council in April 1998 and entered into force on 10 August 1998 (*Official Journal of the European Communities* 1998). The aim of this directive has been to establish common rules for the transmission, distribution, supply and storage of natural gas.[8]

The directive requires accounting unbundling for vertically integrated network companies. Integrated gas companies are required to keep internal accounts for their natural gas transmission, distribution and storage activities as if they were separate businesses.[9] The aim of this requirement is to ensure non-discrimination and fair tariffs to avoid cross-subsidization and the distortion of competition.

The Gas Directive was not concerned with the provision of common rules for production operations because this had already been achieved via the Hydrocarbons Licensing Directive 94/22/EC, adopted in 1994. The principal objectives of the 1994 directive were to set up common rules to ensure that: (1) procedures for granting authorizations to prospect or explore for and produce hydrocarbons are open to all entities that possess the necessary capabilities, (2) authorizations are granted on the basis of objective, published criteria and (3) the conditions under which authorizations are granted are known in advance by all entities taking part in the procedure. The directive is based upon a careful balance between respect for the member states' rights based on sovereignty and the Community interest and the way in which those rights are exercized in order to ensure transparency and non-discrimination. Hence, member states have sovereign rights over their natural resources and can decide which areas can be opened for exploration and production. States also decide the level of taxation, royalties and other revenues, such as those arising from state participation, and they select the licensees and monitor their activities. However, these decisions must be based on objective, non-discriminatory and pre-established criteria, they must be published in advance, and all general conditions and obligations imposed on the undertakings must be established and made available to entities before applications are submitted.

A general duty is imposed by Directive 98/30/EC on transmission, storage and LNG undertakings to operate, maintain and develop secure, reliable and efficient transmission, storage and/or LNG facilities, with due regard to the environment. These undertakings must not discriminate between system users or classes of system users, especially in favour of their related undertakings. They are placed under an obligation to provide any other transmission, storage or distribution undertaking with sufficient information to ensure that the transport and storage of natural gas takes place in a manner compatible with the secure and efficient operation of the interconnected system. The confidentiality of commercially sensitive information obtained in the process of carrying out the business must be preserved such that transmission undertakings must not abuse sensitive information obtained from third parties in the context of providing or negotiating access to the system.

At the core of this directive are the provisions on system access. Member states can choose one or both of the procedures set out in Articles 15 and 16 to organize access to their gas systems (both transmission and distribution): either a negotiated or a regulated system of network access. In the former case, access is based on the 'main commercial conditions for the use of the system', whereas in the latter it is established by 'published tariffs and/or other terms and obligations for use of that system' (*Official Journal of the European Communities* 1998: 7). Both procedures must operate in accordance with objective, transparent and non-discriminatory criteria. A combination of both systems may involve the use of negotiated access at the transmission level and regulated access at the distribution level. The option of negotiated access requires member states to take measures necessary to allow natural gas producers, supply undertakings and eligible customers – either inside or outside of the territory covered by the system – to negotiate access to the system with a view to concluding supply contracts with each other. Under regulated access, member states give natural gas producers and eligible customers a right to access to the system on the basis of published tariffs and/or other terms and obligations for the use of that system. Tariffs should be objective, fair, non-discriminatory, simple, transparent and stable.[10]

Gas storage plays an important role in optimizing the operations of a pipeline network, specifically in overcoming constraints in system capacity. It helps to match gas supply and demand with seasonal and daily levels so that the utilization of capital-intensive gas production and the transport structure improves, and the unit costs of the gas supply decline. The directive includes provisions that address the issues of access to storage facilities. The provisions apply when such access is technically necessary to provide efficient access to the transmission and/or distribution of networks. Access is not granted independent of system use. Access to storage is therefore linked to system (or pipeline) access and in normal circumstances efficient system access will imply some access to storage facilities. This is an important issue because without access to storage facilities in some form or another a new market entrant will be at an immediate disadvantage vis-à-vis incumbent transmission companies that do have such access at their disposal.

The provisions for distribution and supply are almost identical to those for transmission, storage and LNG. In addition, member states may impose on distribution and/or supply undertakings an obligation to deliver to customers located in a given area. This directive also exempts member states from the obligation to grant authorizations for the construction of new distribution systems in an area where such a system has already been or is proposing to be built or if existing or proposed capacity is still available.

The directive specifies that, in the first stage, all power generators and other customers using more than 25 million cubic metres a year should qualify as 'eligible customers', who would be able to benefit from competition in the supply of gas. These customers have the legal capacity to contract for or to be sold natural gas according to the regulations on access discussed above. The initial threshold should fall to 15 million cubic metres a year after five years and to five million cubic metres a year after ten years. The definition of 'eligible customers' must result in an opening of the market equal to at least 20 per cent of the total annual gas consumption of the national gas market – increasing to 28 per cent five years after the directive has entered into force and 33 per cent 20 years after that date.

Public service obligations (PSO) that a member state may impose on a natural gas undertaking relate to: (1) security, including security of supply, (2) regularity, (3) quality of supplies, (4) price of supplies and (5) environmental protection. PSOs must be clearly defined, transparent, non-discriminatory and verifiable, and must be published and the Commission notified by member states without delay. Member states must submit a single document that identifies, lists and sets out the PSOs, their impact and/or method of funding and references to the legal provisions concerned. On receiving this document, the Commission examines its compatibility with the Gas Directive and the treaty and will 'verify whether it represents the least distortive measure necessary to achieve the objective in question' (*Official Journal of the European Communities* 1998: 5). Member states can introduce the implementation of long-term planning as a means of carrying out PSOs but only those relating to security of supply with a view to meeting the demand for natural gas of the system, diversification of sources and securing supplies to customers. Furthermore, when introducing long-term planning, a member state is required to take into account the possibility of third parties seeking access to the system. Member states may, in limited circumstances, decline to grant authorizations to distribution systems if such access is to obstruct the performance of PSOs and they may even ask for derogations that grant member states rights not to comply with its obligations under specific provisions of the directive. A member state applying for the derogation has to prove that the derogation is necessary and is based on a specific PSO.

Finally, the directive notes that the bulk of European gas supplies are under long-term contracts that contain so-called 'take-or-pay' clauses. Take-or-pay clauses generally consist of an annual contract volume, a minimum annual contract volume (typically 70–80 per cent of the annual contract quantity), a minimum daily contract volume and a seasonal and daily swing volume to allow for changes in the level of demand throughout the seasons and throughout the day. The contracts, signed for a period of 10–25 years, oblige the seller to provide defined volumes of gas and the buyer to buy the minimum volume secured by the take-or-pay obligation. The contracts use price formulae that contain a base price and escalation clause, which updates prices on a regular basis to keep them in line with price movements of competing fuels. Once the base price and escalation clause have been defined they are normally fixed for the duration of the contract. However, when market conditions change substantially over the life of the contract, the base price and escalation clause can, in principle, be re-negotiated between the parties to the contract. Thus, under take-or-pay contracts the buyer bears the market risk, while the gas producer takes the production risk. As natural gas purchased under existing contracts will not always be able to compete on price with gas that becomes available in the competitive gas market following from the Gas Directive, a transitional regime is included in the directive to mitigate the effects of the transition to a liberalized market on the performance of take-or-pay contracts entered into by transmission or distribution system companies. If a natural gas undertaking encounters, or determines it may encounter, serious economic and financial difficulties because of the take-or-pay commitments it has accepted in previous contracts, an application may be made for a temporary derogation from the access provisions discussed above. This system of derogations is important because of its potential for the delay and frustration of the objectives of the directive.

The Gas Directive of 2003

Member states implemented the 1998 Gas Directive at different speeds. Most member states elected to go beyond the minimum requirements; a few, however, did not. The result was a patchwork of uneven implementation, with more liberalized markets prey to acquisitive behaviour by entities from member states that had opted for a very cautious approach to market opening. On access issues, evidence accumulated that the access regime was not working properly in some member states, such as Germany, which has a strategic position with respect to energy trade in the EU. Germany refused to establish an independent regulatory body, relying instead on ex post action by the competition authorities, which in turn led to repeated complaints from a wide variety of parties. In many of the member states access tariffs were not well defined. Access to ancillary facilities such as storage has been highly variable, the negotiated form of access proved ineffective and the regulated approach was preferred.

To address the problems of the uneven implementation of the 1998 Gas Directive, a new Gas Directive, 2003/55/EC, was adopted by the European Parliament and Council in 2003. The new regulatory framework has repealed the first legal framework on gas, replacing it with a more detailed framework and an enhanced role for national regulatory agencies (NRAs) in its implementation and further development. The directive had two principal aims: first, to increase quantitative market opening and bring about full liberalization by July 2007; second, to enhance qualitative regulation and bring about more uniformity and coordination of national regulation. The directive was to be implemented by all member states no later than 1 July 2004. The time for implementation was half the time given to member states to transpose the preceding directive.

The provisions on unbundling represent a major step forward in the Commission's efforts to address structural constraints on the creation of an internal market in energy and barriers to competition created by corporate structure. In essence, there are four kinds of unbundling: ownership, legal, management and accounting. Under full ownership separation, when network operations are run by an independent organization rather than a subsidiary, one can completely remove the incentive to favour one market participant over others. The network operations will be completely separated from supply and generation or production activities. The transmission system operator (TSO) will be completely separate from the distribution system operator (DSO) and from other activities not related to transmission and distribution. Similarly, the DSO and the TSO will be separate from supply and generation or production activities.

In contrast, under legal unbundling, network operations are legally and functionally separated from supply and generation or production activities; however, legal unbundling does not require ownership unbundling in the sense that no change of ownership of assets is implied and so no company would have to sell off its transmission and distribution arms. But under legal unbundling, staff working for the system business will be aware of the financial interests of their parent organization and its competitive activities, and may take decisions to further these. The third kind of unbundling refers to management unbundling, which requires that different people are responsible for the TSO, DSO and competitive activities, and that the system business cannot pass on information about rival concerns. Finally, accounting separation is the weakest form of unbundling, in which a company keeps different accounts for its system and for its competitive activities, and must charge the competitive businesses the same fees for using the system as it charges third parties. This is intended to prevent cross-subsidies between the system and the competitive activities.

The idea behind the unbundling requirements is that effectively unbundled networks would have different incentives compared with vertically integrated companies. Whereas integrated companies might have incentives to restrict the flow of gas to keep the price of gas high, independent transmission and distribution networks would have incentives to maximize the amount of capacity sold because their profits would depend purely on transport incomes. The directive stipulated legal, managerial and organizational separation for the TSOs (at the latest by 1 July 2004) as well as the DSOs (at the latest by 1 July 2007) if they belong to vertically integrated undertakings. Only accounting unbundling is required for storage and LNG operators. With the legal unbundling of companies for the transport of natural gas and the sale of natural gas, which is to be complete by the middle of 2007, the EU is hoping to prevent discrimination strategies, cross-subsidies and distortion of competition by the vertically integrated suppliers.

As mentioned above, the 1998 Gas Directive was not concerned with the provision of common rules for production. On the other hand, the 2003 Gas Directive improved on the rules of the previous directive on third party access (TPA) to the transmission network. A major obstacle to the completion of the internal gas market has been the shortcomings of the regime for network access. Under the previous regime a choice was given to member states between negotiated and regulated TPA. The results from the operation of the negotiated option proved unsatisfactory. The new directive seeks to address this problem with its clear advocacy of regulated third party access. This provision is intended to promote network access to new market entrants more effectively than either the negotiated form of access or the weak form of regulatory access contained in the previous directive. The success of this provision depends largely on institutional enforcement by the NRAs, which emerged with their policing power considerably strengthened by the directive. In contrast to the previous EU legislation, the NRAs have a minimum set of competencies, with a particularly important role in the regulation of tariffs and access to conditions. Moreover, they have an advisory role on implementation and further steps through a newly established body called the European Regulators Group for Electricity and Gas (ERGEG).[11]

Third party access to transmission and distribution networks is to be provided on the basis of published and regulated tariffs, and tariffs must be cost-reflective and transparent.[12] All network operators should submit their tariffs, or at least their tariff calculation methods, to a regulator for authorization. The regulator must examine the tariffs or calculation methods to ensure that they are non-discriminatory and reasonable and alter them when necessary. This regulated TPA regime has a number of exceptions. Refusal of access by a network operator can be made: (1) when there is no available capacity, (2) if TPA would give rise to serious economic and financial difficulties with take-or-pay contracts and (3) if TPA would prevent the conclusion of long-term contracts, as long as these comply with EC competition rules. Also, for storage facilities, access is to be either on a negotiated or regulated basis or both. Access to upstream pipeline networks is also regulated and the regime continues to be separated out to give member states discretion over the arrangements adopted. Finally, exemptions from TPA may be granted for major new gas infrastructure investments such as international interconnectors, LNG and storage facilities in order to promote the new gas infrastructures for a certain period.

The 1998 Gas Directive had initiated a gradual elimination of monopolies across Europe. The underlying idea was that monopolies would first be dismantled for large customers, but that by the end of the market-opening process the monopoly conditions would be abolished for all customers, including household users. However, the directive did not decree a definitive date for total market opening and, in practise, this gradual market opening has generated serious imbalances. Some member states immediately opened their markets fully, whereas others stuck to the minimal opening specified in the directive. The resulting imbalances have quickly become evident through competition among energy suppliers and they have also had an impact on competition among energy-intensive industries. Through cross-subsidization, protected energy suppliers were able to fend off competition in the opened market segments. For energy-intensive industries, large consumers gained an advantage over smaller competitors as they benefited from competition among energy suppliers. The 2003 Gas Directive aimed to address these imbalances by its more aggressive plan for market opening for all customers.

According to the 2003 Gas Directive, the gas market was required to fully open up so that from 1 July 2004 all non-household gas customers were free to choose their energy suppliers, and household customers were to follow from 1 July 2007. Consequently, the legal monopolies remaining after the previous Gas Directive ceased to exist and distortions of competition in the energy-intensive goods markets came to an end.

The directive requires that 'member states shall designate one or more competent bodies with the function of regulatory authorities'. Thus, the EU is forcing the establishment of NRAs, which have, as a minimum, the task of ensuring non-discrimination, effective competition and the efficient functioning of the market, as well as the task of monitoring, the results of which are published in annual reports. As a fundamental governance issue, the directive specifies that the regulatory authorities must be wholly independent of the interests in the energy sector.

There are also strengthened provisions on PSOs and a raft of consumer protection measures to support requirements for handling complaints and for the protection of household consumers against misleading sales practices and unfair contract terms. The Gas Directive requires that member states ensure that, when customers are connected to the gas system, they are informed about their rights to be supplied with natural gas of a specified quality 'at reasonable prices'. The term 'reasonable' is not defined in the directive. The familiar concern about PSOs hampering competition remains and has led to some cautionary measures. Member states are now under a general obligation to notify the Commission of all measures taken to fulfil PSOs, including consumer and environmental protection, with details of their possible effects on national and international competition. In contrast to the previous directive, the provision in the new legislation is not limited to measures that relate to a request for a derogation.

The 2003 Gas Directive was later complemented by Gas Regulation No. 1775/2005. It expanded on several of the provisions in the directive, and set rules for the transmission of gas between member states. The regulation introduced qualitative minimum requirements for access to transmission systems (network tariffs, third party access services, capacity allocation, transparency, balancing and trading of capacity rights). Community legislation is supplemented by other binding and non-binding instruments, such as Community guidelines (under the Gas Regulation), voluntary guidelines developed within ERGEG and the Madrid Forum[13] (e.g. Guidelines for Good Third Party Access Practice for Storage System Operators – GGPSSO) and technical standards prepared by the European Association for the Streamlining of Energy Exchanges (EASEE)-gas.[14]

Proposal for amending Directive 2003/55/EC

Although significant improvements have taken place in the EU gas market during the last five years, the full potential of liberalization has not yet been realized. According to the European Commission (2009a) there are still a number of areas in which the Gas Directive of 2003 has not yet been properly implemented. In the gas market the three biggest operators still control a market share of 90 per cent or more in 12 member states. Similar considerations apply also to the retail market. Although some progress was made on the unbundling of network operators and functional unbundling became compulsory in all member states as of 1 July 2007 at the distribution level, in many cases DSOs have been slow to implement functional unbundling effectively, and member states continue to make extensive use of derogations from unbundling at distribution level. Furthermore, common standards and approaches for cross-border trade could not be developed.

The achievement of real competition in the natural gas market requires a liquid market. But a liquid market for natural gas has so far developed only in North America and to a lesser extent in the United Kingdom. As noted by the European Commission (2006c), gas hubs and spot markets have a key role to play in market liberalization because they provide a direct outlet for new gas resources not supplied under long-term contracts. Liquid hubs provide a price formation mechanism that reflects supply and demand, and therefore creates price signals for investment. They enable traders to take advantage of short-term price differentials, and this arbitrage keeps the market efficient. Arbitrage between hubs also helps integrate geographical markets. The absence of liquid hubs creates significant entry barriers, hindering the development of competition. A lack of liquidity increases the risk of trading, as it reduces the chances of finding an acceptable counter-party when a trader needs to close a position. It also facilitates price manipulation and therefore makes it more difficult to analyze and manage risk. Low liquidity therefore deters entrants, and tends to mean liquidity stays low. Thus, the establishment of a European grid network with gas hubs at key nodal points could boost the fluidity of cross-border exchanges and accelerate market opening by facilitating swaps. According to the European Commission (2009a) gas hubs in Europe are developing. The volumes traded at the gas hubs rose by 33 per cent in 2007 after the 44 per cent increase in 2006. But, the physical volumes delivered at most of the hubs are still relatively low compared with the total consumption in their markets.

Turning to TPA conditions, we note that the main issue regarding TPA relates to allocation of capacity. As discussed by the European Commission (2006c), many TSOs in the EU operate in a first-come, first-served system, which effectively denies access to capacity to new entrants. Transit is generally treated separately from domestic transportation. The capacity of transit lines is frequently booked up under long-term contracts and there are cross-subsidies between transit and domestic charges. Cross-border capacity is generally underutilized, except maybe into Italy, and there are also large discrepancies among transmission tariffs within EU countries for transporting similar loads similar distances. Although relatively high tariffs may be justifiable in growth markets in which there is an intensive capital requirement, there is less justification for differences among more mature and well-established gas markets in which costs should be broadly similar. It is to be noted that tariffs are lower where regulators have taken an active role in forcing out inefficiency and economic rent than in countries where independent regulators have been less forceful in regulating tariffs. Furthermore, despite the increased obligations in the second directive, difficulties in accessing the transmission infrastructure remain a competition concern. Potential entrants into the gas market complain about lack of transparency of the exact obligations of network operators and state that lack of transparency is conducive to a discriminatory environment.

On 17 September 2007, EU officials proposed new legislation with the purpose of breaking open the EU's energy market, making it more competitive and less dominated by national monopolies. The Commission's aim is to separate production and supply from transmission networks. The Commission would prefer ownership unbundling to meet this goal, but it also proposed a second option – the 'independent system operator' – which makes it possible for existing vertically integrated companies to retain network ownership provided that the assets are operated by a company or body completely independent from it. Furthermore, the Commission requires the effective unbundling of TSOs and supply and production activities not only at national level but also throughout the EU. The package contains safeguards to ensure that, in the event that companies from third countries wish to acquire a significant interest in or even control of an EU network, they will have to demonstrably and unequivocally comply with the same unbundling requirements as EU companies. The Commission proposed the requirement that third party individuals and countries cannot acquire control over a Community transmission system or TSO unless this is permitted by an agreement between the EU and the third party.

In addition to the above regulations, the Commission proposed measures to strengthen and guarantee the independence of national regulators in member states. The Commission suggested that the Agency for the Cooperation of National Energy Regulators be established, with binding decision powers, to complement national regulators. This agency enables the EU to develop a real European network, working as one single grid, promoting diversity and security of supply. The Commission also proposed the European Network for Transmission System Operators. EU grid operators would cooperate and develop common commercial and technical codes and security standards, as well as plan and coordinate the investments needed at EU level. Finally, the Commission aimed to improve the legislative framework to facilitate third party access to key infrastructures, increase transparency of the market, enhance market integration and improve access to retail customers.[15]

Under the EU plan, utilities that extract natural gas will have to sell their transmission networks or lease them to an independent operator. However, the Russian natural gas monopoly Gazprom and other energy suppliers outside the EU will not have that choice. The new rules force these companies to follow the EU's unbundling plan, making it all but impossible for a supplier such as Gazprom, the EU's single largest energy supplier, to control downstream network assets.

The natural gas sector reform in Turkey

Natural gas consumption in Turkey began in 1987 and increased rapidly thereafter, particularly since the mid-1990s. It reached 35.1 billion cubic metres (bcm) in 2007 and 36 bcm in 2008. The annual growth rate of natural gas consumption between 1987 and 2008 amounted to 16.2 per cent; demand is expected to increase further but at a lower growth rate. Currently, 55.8 per cent of total natural gas demand is used for electricity generation, 22.2 per cent for residential gas consumption, and 21.9 per cent for industrial consumption. Turkey's indigenous gas production corresponds to 2.8 per cent of its total gas demand, making the country almost fully dependent on gas imports. It has long-term sales and purchase contracts with different supply sources. The Russian Federation's share in contracted total volume during 2008 amounted to 61.8 per cent, Azerbaijan's share 12.3 per cent, Iran's share 11.1 per cent, Algeria's share 11.2 per cent and Nigeria's share 2.7 per cent.

Until recently, the Turkish natural gas sector was dominated by government-owned entities. The Turkish Pipeline Corporation (BOTAŞ) owned pipeline infrastructure for oil and gas transmission, LNG terminals and gas distribution. BOTAŞ had monopoly rights for gas imports and exports, wholesale trading and also transmission and storage.[16] With the passing of a new gas market law (2 May 2001), the government aimed to establish a competitive market as in the EU and encourage private sector participation through a phasing-in policy. The main features of the new law (No. 4646) are the following:

1   All legal entities can carry out import, export, wholesale trade, transportation, distribution, compressed natural gas and storage activities under licence from the Energy Market Regulatory Authority (EMRA).
2   The natural gas activities of BOTAŞ are to be unbundled. BOTAŞ is to be split into three state economic enterprises after 2009, with the first enterprise responsible for trading, the second for storage and the third for transmission. The storage and trade companies will be privatized in 2011, and the transmission company will come under control of BOTAŞ.
3   No importer will be allowed to import more than 20 per cent of Turkey's gas consumption during any one year. BOTAŞ will be required to sell part of its

gas import contracts to comply with this provision. This will be accomplished through a series of annual competitive tenders to sell existing import contracts to new importers for no fewer than 10 per cent of total imports each year. No new natural gas purchase agreement can be executed by any import company with countries that have existing contracts with BOTAŞ. This limitation shall apply for the duration of the agreement.

4　No legal entity is allowed to sell more than 20 per cent of annual gas consumption. Only national gas producers may sell more than 20 per cent of annual gas consumption in the domestic market, provided that the amount sold directly to eligible consumers does not exceed 20 per cent. The remaining gas could be sold through importers, distributors or wholesalers.

5　To ensure security of supply, gas importers must inform EMRA about the source and security of their gas imports, and they must store 10 per cent of the gas they import. Importers shall also prove that they can contribute to the improvement and security of the national transmission system.

6　Transportation companies owning transportation networks, as well as owners and operators of LNG and storage facilities, are to offer services in transparent and non-discriminatory conditions.

7　Third parties will be allowed to build pipelines. Investments by BOTAŞ and other potential grid operators are subject to EMRA's approval. The regulatory authority is to control these investments, as well as their service quality. Existing and planned national transmission networks, as well as transmission networks under construction, remain under the ownership of BOTAŞ.

8　TPA is regulated. Access to the transmission and distribution systems is a right for all parties. However, a connection request may be turned down in case of insufficient system capacity, failure in performing obligations upon entry into the system, and financial difficulties arising from existing contracts. System entry cannot be rejected if the user requesting system entry undertakes the necessary expenses to eliminate the lack of capacity or connection.

9　Eligible consumers will be free to select a supplier of their choice. Eligibility is to be determined by the regulator. Consumers purchasing more than 1 million cubic metres of natural gas per year, and users' unions, power generators and co-generators are considered eligible.

10　Distribution rights for cities and municipalities must be awarded under a tender. Prequalification will be based on the financial strength and experience of the companies. Once a distributor has won a tender, he applies the unit service and depreciation charge as specified in the tender announcement. After this period, its prices and conditions will be reviewed by the regulator every year. Distributors must construct, operate and extend distribution equipment as specified in the licence and tender documents. Once the licence for a distribution area has been awarded, the selected operator must allow the local government to invest up to 20 per cent in the company's capital. A total of 10 per cent of the local government's share in the total capital could consist of unpaid capital and up to 10 per cent could consist of paid capital. The size of the public's share, to be remunerated at the nominal share price, is to be determined by the regulator. Distribution companies may hold a licence for no more than five cities in Turkey.

11 EMRA must develop five different categories of gas prices: price for connection, price for transmission and supervision of conveyance, price for storage, price for wholesale and price for retail sales. Prices for connection will be determined between the regulator and the distribution companies. Network tariffs will be based mainly on distance and volume. Storage tariffs will be freely determined between storage companies and users. Transmission and storage companies will have an obligation to prove to the regulator that their services are economical and safe. Wholesale prices are to be negotiated by the trading parties, but the regulator maintains some control over wholesale prices. The distribution companies must prove that they provide gas from the cheapest source and they must operate efficiently and safely during their licence period. Distributors' retail sales prices for captive consumers are subject to rate-of-return regulation. All tariffs are subject to EMRA's approval.

12 EMRA is empowered to settle disputes regarding access and connection to the transmission and distribution system and must approve investment plans by transmission and distribution companies. EMRA also has responsibility for certain safety elements of the gas sector, including the construction and service of gas facilities.[17]

Under the 2001 law, the objective of harmonizing Turkish natural gas legislation with the EU's energy *acquis* is, as shown in Table 6.1, almost fully achieved. The basic concepts of Directive 2003/55/EC are all incorporated into the 2001 law, including unbundling, market opening, establishing an independent regulatory body and third party access.

Turning to consideration of the natural gas transmission and distribution network we note that the system in Turkey is well developed. As of the end of 2008 the network is 11,130 km long. The existing international gas pipeline system is composed of the Russia–Turkey natural gas pipeline, Eastern Anatolia pipeline, Blue Stream pipeline, Turkey–Greece pipeline and Azerbaijan–Turkey pipeline.

The Russia–Turkey pipeline running from Russia through Ukraine, Romania and Bulgaria into Turkey has been in operation since 1988 and within Turkey it is 842 km long. The pipeline system transports up to 14 bcm of natural gas annually. The Eastern Anatolia pipeline bringing gas from Iran has been in operation since 2001 and is 1,491 km long. It extends as far west as Ankara and transports up to 10 bcm of gas annually.

The Blue Stream pipeline, which transports up to 16 bcm of natural gas per year from Russia to Turkey, was completed in October 2002. The pipeline starts at Izobilnoye, near Krasnodar in southern Russia, and runs overland on the Black Sea coast 370 km to Dzhubga. The undersea portion consists of twin pipelines running under the Black Sea from Dzhubga to the Turkish port of Samsun. From Samsun, the pipeline then continues overland to provide gas to Ankara.

The Turkey–Greece pipeline completed in 2007 forms the first stage of the South European Gas Ring. Connecting this pipeline to Italy by a pipeline under the

Table 6.1 Harmonization of natural gas legislation with the EU's natural gas *acquis*

Issue	EU Natural Gas Directive	Natural gas market legislation
Eligible customers and market opening	Non-household customers by July 2004 All customers by July 2007	Until all consumers become eligible, the threshold value is set by the board
Third-party access	Regulated Regulated/negotiated for storage	Regulated Regulated/negotiated for storage
Unbundling	Separation of activities and accounts	Separation of activities and accounts
Authorisation	Objective and non-discriminatory	Objective and non-discriminatory
Dispute resolution	An independent authority (two months)	EMRA (one month)
Technical rules	Transparent and interoperability	Transparent and interoperability (ISO, EN)
Cross-subsidy	Prohibition of cross-subsidy	Prohibition of cross-subsidy
System operation	Secure, reliable, non-discriminatory and efficient	Secure, reliable, non-discriminatory and efficient

Source: Özkoç (2004)

Adriatic will be the second stage of the South European Gas Ring. The feasibility study for the connection to Italy has been completed and the engineering and environmental impact studies started in 2007. The Italian connection is planned for completion in 2012. The transportation volume will start with 0.75 bcm per annum and is expected to reach nearly 12 bcm per annum in 2014, of which 3.6 bcm per annum and 8 bcm per annum will be delivered to Greece and Italy respectively.

The Azerbaijan–Turkey pipeline (SCP) transports gas from Azerbaijan to Turkey. According to the contract, natural gas delivery started at 2 bcm annually in 2006 and will reach 6.6 bcm per annum by 2010. The project consists of three phases. The first two phases of the project have already been completed, and natural gas is provided to Kars in Eastern Turkey. Eventually, the capacity of the pipeline will be increased up to 18–20 bcm annually.

In the EU the share of imports in total domestic demand is expected to grow over time to about 80 per cent in 2030. To increase competition in the natural gas market the EU realizes that it must increase the number of suppliers to its gas market. Since New Year's Day 2006, when Russia turned off the natural gas taps to Ukraine and customers in the EU felt the impact, 'supply security' has been the buzz phrase in the EU.[18] Similar considerations applied also after the Russia–Ukraine gas dispute in January 2009.[19] Because of its advantageous geographical location, Turkey is determined to play an active role in bridging Europe's and Asia's gas markets, especially by transporting Caspian, Central Asian and Middle East gas to Europe. It is the only country other than the Russian Federation that connects Eastern Europe with Central Asia by land, and its outlet to the Mediterranean at Ceyhan offers stability and proximity to more gas-producing regions than any country other than Russia. With full awareness of this fact, Turkey has been developing safe transportation alternatives for Western markets for the last 10 years. BOTAŞ has been carrying out various pipeline projects developed to align with pronounced European strategies and priorities.[20] Turkey, undertaking all responsible and necessary steps to function as a real hub in the region and effectively assuming the role of strengthening Europe's energy supply security, assigns utmost importance to the realization of the following cross-border gas pipeline projects: (1) Turkey–Bulgaria–Romania–Hungary–Austria (Nabucco) Natural Gas Pipeline Project, (2) Turkmenistan–Turkey–Europe Natural Gas Pipeline Project, (3) Iraq–Turkey Natural Gas Pipeline Project and (4) Egypt–Turkey Natural Gas Pipeline Project

The Turkey–Bulgaria–Romania–Hungary–Austria (Nabucco) Natural Gas Pipeline Project, aiming to transport Caspian and Middle Eastern gas supplies to Central and Eastern European gas markets, is being carried out on schedule. In June 2006, the EU Commissioner for Energy and the Energy Ministers of the stakeholder countries of Nabucco agreed at a ministerial conference in Vienna to accelerate the commercial, regulatory and legal work in order to build the Nabucco gas pipeline in the shortest possible time. The EU presented a scenario in which 10–15 per cent of its gas demand would come from Nabucco by 2025, and at the end of the conference the ministers and the EU signed a joint declaration. The intergovernmental agreement among the participating countries laying down the political and legal foundation for the project was signed in July 2009 in Ankara. The pipeline, slated to begin operations in 2012, would transport 25–31 bcm of natural gas per year. Thus, over the next 20–25 years one-third of the EU's gas demand is expected to be supplied through Turkey.

The Azerbaijan–Turkey pipeline (SCP) mentioned above is quite important for the Nabucco and Turkey–Greece pipelines. As the SCP contracts do not have destination clauses and restrictions on re-exports, SCP will act as a feeder line for the pipelines linking Turkey and Europe. On the other hand, studies on the transportation of Turkmen gas to Turkey and Europe by a convenient route and without any restrictions have been underway since 1991. A frame agreement was signed by the presidents of Turkmenistan and Turkey in Ankara on 29 October 1998 to supply from Turkmenistan to Turkey natural gas up to 16 bcm annually, and through the pipeline 14 bcm annually to Europe. In 2006, several feasibility studies were performed regarding both the Kazakhstan–Azerbaijan and the Turkmenistan–Azerbaijan connections for exporting Caspian/Central Asian gas to Europe via the Turkey–Azerbaijan and Nabucco pipelines.

BOTAŞ has a long-standing project to take 10 bcm of gas from Iraq per year. The Energy Ministers of Iraq and Turkey signed a frame agreement in 1996, but the project's implementation was stalled for many years because of the imposition of UN sanctions on Saddam Hussein's regime in Iraq. With the emergence of a new Iraqi government, the parties declared their intention in 2007 with new plans for connecting to Europe. A protocol for cooperation regarding oil and gas issues was signed between Turkey and Egypt in 2000. In 2004, a frame agreement was signed by the respective ministers. The agreement foresees natural gas imports by BOTAŞ from the Egypt Natural Gas Company (EGAS) and the transit of Egyptian natural gas across Turkey to Europe. The agreement foresees the transport of gas amounting to 2–4 bcm per annum from Egypt to Turkey and 2–6 bcm from Egypt to Europe via Turkey.

Regarding LNG facilities we note that the LNG import terminal was built in Marmara Ereğli not far from Istanbul in 1994 for diversifying natural gas supply sources and increasing the supply security. Currently, the terminal's permanent output capacity has reached 685,000 cubic metres per hour. Turkey has one major domestic gas storage facility, namely the Northern Marmara – Değirmenköy facility. The facility, with a capacity of 1.6 bcm, started operation in 2007. The Tuz Gölü storage project is under development.[21] Upon completion, the storage facility will have the ability to store almost 4 per cent of Turkey's annual gas consumption.

Regarding the distribution of natural gas we note that the distribution activities in Turkish cities are carried out by private companies and municipalities. Before the enactment of the 2001 law there were seven companies established in six cities. At the beginning of 2004, the two distribution companies owned by BOTAŞ were privatized, thus removing BOTAŞ from the distribution sector. With the tenders for new distribution regions, the total number of distribution regions has reached 54 and the number is expected to increase. In some of the tenders, the bids were so competitive that companies accepted terms that have them operating with zero profits for the first eight years, in addition to paying an initial lump sum payment to EMRA. As noted by the Energy Sector Management Assistance Program (2007a), the gas distribution tenders, preceding other measures aimed at liberalizing Turkey's gas wholesale and import business, created strong interest in favour of a liberalized gas market.

Although the 2001 law theoretically opened the Turkish gas market to competition, no actual competition has yet developed. Trading has been hampered by BOTAŞ's ongoing import dominance, which has been preserved by some restrictive provisions of the 2001 law.[22] As noted by the World Bank (2004a) and the OECD and IEA (2005), BOTAŞ continues to have monopoly status in selling gas (wholesaling) and buying gas (importing), and in its transit function.

To increase competition Turkey has to develop wholesale gas competition, which requires that BOTAŞ's wholesale monopoly be broken up. Such a move will provide choice to eligible buyers, move market risk away from BOTAŞ to private economic units, initiate commercialization of the sector and attract the interest of multinationals. Furthermore, new investors could emerge as importers, paving the way towards import competition. The law, calling for a process of contract release, intends to reduce BOTAŞ's shares of the market to 20 per cent by 2009. But reducing BOTAŞ's shares to this level in such a short period of time has been impossible, mainly because of possible resistance from foreign suppliers and reluctance of new private players to take on the liabilities associated with BOTAŞ's different contracts. It is also not clear how such a system will work in practice. One possibility would be a tendering procedure based on objective criteria.[23]

To ensure competition, BOTAŞ's monopoly in imports needs also to be abandoned. This can only be realized, however, when Turkey's demand for gas outstrips the minimum 'take-or-pay' obligations on the current contracts. In that case, financial liabilities will also no longer be carried by BOTAŞ (i.e. by the government of Turkey) but by new private players. The new law prohibits BOTAŞ from entering into new contracts until its market share has fallen substantially. Furthermore, the law requires that gas importers must store 10 per cent of the gas they import.[24]

In addition, BOTAŞ is the sole owner of pipeline infrastructure for gas transmission, LNG terminals and gas distribution. BOTAŞ was mandated to implement accounting unbundling by 2005. But as emphasized by the OECD and IEA (2005), this is insufficient to create a level playing field in the market. Legal unbundling and operating as a private enterprise does would be required, and this will happen only gradually.

A major problem facing the sector is whether the present regulatory framework will lead to efficient allocation of resources under competition as specified in the first section of this chapter. After 2010 all transactions in Turkey will be open to competition. By that time BOTAŞ will be unbundled into State Gas Import Corporation, BOTAŞ Wholesale and BOTAŞ Transmission and Storage, and BOTAŞ will retain monopoly rights in transmission only. After 2010 new importers will join BOTAŞ in primary supply to the market, new wholesalers will be able to purchase from those importers or from BOTAŞ State Gas Import Corporation, market risk will be shared across the system by operating contracts, and the Turkish government's contingent liabilities will be proportionately reduced. Regulation is needed to support the opening of transmission with the development of regulations on third party access, network codes and balancing agreements and transmission tariff regulation. Probably because of Turkey's unfavourable geology gas storage will likely remain in the hands of one company, in a natural monopoly, in which prices will be regulated through EMRA.

Conclusion

Efficiency in a natural gas market requires that: (1) there is full competition in the production, wholesaling and retailing of natural gas, in which gas can be freely traded between producers, wholesalers, retailers and consumers, and markets are liquid, (2) the interconnected transmission and distribution system has clear rules for access for all prospective participants, and the pipeline capacity is in competition, capacity is tradable and transmission prices are set by reference to the market and (3) the arrangements in the transmission, distribution and retail sectors provide confidence in the market and cross-subsidizing is not occurring in vertically integrated organizations. Most countries in the world cannot satisfy these conditions; some exceptions are the United States and the United Kingdom.

In the case of Turkey, a crucial impediment for efficient functioning of the natural gas market is the fact that much of the commodity must be imported via pipelines from Russia and through the state-controlled company Gazprom. To satisfy the efficiency conditions Turkey needs to increase the natural gas supply from alternative sources. It needs to create a level playing field of rules to be observed by all participating governments. Achieving cooperation in future through, for example, WTO negotiations would be a big step in the right direction. Although Turkey faces difficulties satisfying the efficiency conditions on the production side, it tries to satisfy the remaining efficiency conditions by adopting the EU's natural gas sector *acquis* and liberal FDI policies in the sector.

7 Liberalization of banking services

(co-authored with Hakan Berument and Hasan Ersel)

In a large number of low- and middle-income countries, entry into the banking sector was for a long time tightly controlled by regulatory boards that limited the ability of providers to offer a full range of banking services and limited market access. In those countries, banks were the main source of domestic financing for governments. Many developing countries had high reserve, liquidity and portfolio requirements that necessitated significant holdings of cash and government bonds. Banks were used to finance government expenditures directly and to direct credit to preferred ends, which often included the political supporters of government circles. Lately, objectives such as boosting economic development, preventing and mitigating costly crises and protecting consumers became important policy goals, and the liberalization of banking services is considered an essential tool to achieve these objectives. We emphasize that an efficient and well-regulated banking sector leads to the efficient transformation of savings to investment, ensuring that resources are deployed wherever they have the highest returns, and facilitates better risk sharing in the economy. It also enhances efficient capital reallocation, bringing tremendous benefits to consumers.

Complete liberalization of banking services entails domestic financial liberalization, internationalization of financial services and capital account liberalization. Domestic financial liberalization allows market forces to work both by eliminating controls on lending and deposit rates and on credit allocation and, more generally, by reducing the role of the state in the domestic financial system. The internationalization of financial services eliminates discrimination in treatment between foreign and domestic financial services providers, removing barriers to the provision of cross-border financial services. Finally, capital account liberalization removes controls on the movement of capital in and out of a country and facilitates the convertibility of currency.

Internationalization and domestic deregulation are said to be mutually reinforcing. Increased foreign entry from countries with no gaps in regulation and supervision bolsters the financial sector framework by creating a constituency for improved regulation and supervision, better disclosure rules and improvements in the legal and regulatory framework for the provision of financial services. It also adds to the credibility of rules. Although the two reform processes are mutually reinforcing, they need to be supported by an appropriate regulatory and supervisory framework. Having a supportive institutional framework is more important in the case of capital account liberalization. Experiences in the past have shown that achieving the potential gains and avoiding the risks of capital account liberalization depend largely on whether domestic institutions and prudential authorities have developed sufficiently to ensure that foreign finance is channelled in productive directions.

The chapter is structured as follows. The first section considers bank regulations and the second section studies global regulation of the banking sector within the framework of the Basel Committee and negotiations under the World Trade Organization (WTO). The next section discusses bank regulations in the European Union (EU), which is followed by a study of bank regulations in Turkey. Finally, the chapter ends with some concluding remarks.

Bank regulation

The banking system is critical for the sound functioning of a market economy as it performs the function of channelling funds from savings to those individuals and firms that have productive investment opportunities.[1] If the banking system does not perform this function well then the economy cannot operate efficiently, and economic growth will be hampered. A crucial impediment to the efficient functioning of the banking system is asymmetric information, a situation in which one party to a financial contract has much less accurate information than the other party. It is well known that asymmetric information leads to adverse selection and moral hazard.[2]

Banks have particular advantages over other financial intermediaries in solving asymmetric information problems. Banks' natural advantages in collecting information and reducing moral hazard explain why banks have such an important role in financial markets throughout the world. When the quality of information about firms is worse, asymmetric information problems will be more severe, and it will be harder for firms to issue securities. Thus the smaller role of securities markets in emerging economies leaves a greater role for financial intermediaries such as banks.

Because, in general, depositors in banks lack information about the quality of loans made by the banks we end up with another asymmetric information problem leading to two reasons why the banking system might not function well. First, in the absence of government intervention, a bank failure means that depositors have to wait to get their deposit funds until the bank is liquidated and its assets turned into cash, and at that time they will be paid only a fraction of the value of their deposits. Unable to learn if bank managers are taking too much risk or are crooks, depositors may be reluctant to put money in the bank.[3] Second, depositors' lack of information about the quality of banks' assets can lead to bank panics, which can have serious harmful consequences for the economy. Such panics may reduce the amount of financial intermediation and so lead to a decline in investment and aggregate economic activity.

A government safety net can short circuit runs on banks and bank panics. This can be achieved through deposit insurance, by providing funds to troubled institutions through the central bank acting as the lender of last resort, and/or by taking over the troubled institutions and guaranteeing that depositors will receive their money in full. But there are serious drawbacks of government safety nets, the most serious of which stems from moral hazard. Banks with a government safety net have an incentive to take on greater risks then they otherwise would. A further problem with the government safety nets arises because of adverse selection. Because depositors who are protected by a government safety net have little reason to impose discipline on the bank, risk-loving entrepreneurs might find the banking industry a particularly attractive one to enter.

When banks are large, governments are in general reluctant to allow them to fail. But this kind of behaviour on the part of government, in turn, increases the moral hazard incentives As a result of the too-big-to-fail policy big banks might take on even greater risks, thereby making bank failures more likely.

Because of the above reasons governments establish regulations to reduce risk taking and to reduce the risk of bank failures. In other words, governments are expected to take proactive measures to prevent such problems. Supervisors monitor banks to see that they are complying with these regulations and not taking excessive risk. Hence supervision is required to ensure the safety and soundness of the banking system. Regulation and supervision, therefore, are considered necessary to control and contain systemic risk in the banking system.

Banking regulations can be analyzed under nine headings:[4]

1 *Restrictions on banks, and on links to commerce.* Banks may engage in financial activities such as securities underwriting, insurance or real estate, which may involve more risk than traditional banking activities; however, governments may restrict banks from entering into these businesses.

2 *Entry restrictions and exit rules.* By screening bank entry, governments can try to promote bank stability and protect the economy from the negative effects of bank failure. Thus, overseeing who operates banks is an important method for reducing the adverse selection problem created by the government safety net. Furthermore, governments may also protect banks from increased competition through entry restrictions on domestic and foreign banks, restrictions on branching, and ceilings on rates charged on loans and on deposits.

   Thus, licensing, transfer of ownership and bankruptcy rules are vital in keeping unfit companies out of the financial sector. If banks are not licensed properly or if they cannot go out of business, unsound institutions are likely to emerge. This can create a moral hazard problem. If banks or other financial institutions are in difficulty, corrective measures or, in the worst case, liquidation must be regulated.

3 *Reserve requirements.* Reserve requirements force banks to hold a portion of their assets in liquid form that is easily mobilized to meet sudden deposit outflows.

4   *Capital requirements.* It is widely accepted that banks can be discouraged to undertake undue risks by requiring them to hold an appropriate amount of capital. Governments, therefore, may require banks to have sufficient capital. Prudential rules help financial institutions to measure and manage their exposure to risk.

5   *Supervisory powers.* Typically, regulators focus on assessment of the quality of the bank's balance sheet and loans at a point in time and determine whether the bank complies with capital requirements and restrictions on asset holdings. They evaluate the quality of a bank's loans and classify them into problem categories whenever loans are unlikely to be repaid. This information is crucial to limiting the moral hazard created by the government safety net. Recently, there has been a major shift in thinking about the bank supervision process. In the new approach, there is more emphasis on the soundness of a bank's management practices with regard to controlling risk.

An important element of prudential regulation is the assessment of and provision for non-performing loans. Once non-performing loans are discovered, adequate reserves to cover them must be established. In addition, excessive exposure to single borrowers can also cause difficulties for financial institutions. If exposure to one particular borrower is large and if this borrower becomes insolvent, a domino effect can occur, causing insolvency of the bank itself. Lending to related parties such as bank managers or employees is often restricted as well. Furthermore, the supervision of multinational institutions poses particular challenges in both the home and the host countries of such institutions. Normally the 'home country rule' should be applied, in which the country of registration supervises all operations worldwide. Global consolidated supervision, therefore, requires the application of prudential norms to the domestic and foreign operations of financial institutions. In the host country, foreign operations should also be subject to similar prudential inspection and reporting requirements as domestic institutions, recognizing obvious differences such as branches not being separately incorporated. Contact and exchange of information between the supervisory authorities in home and host countries is crucial to successful cross-border supervision.

6   *Safety net support.* Failure of financial institutions can occur despite adequate rules and effective supervision. If one bank fails, depositors may lose confidence in other banks as well. This can result in a chain reaction and even affect institutions that are healthy under normal conditions. A deposit insurance scheme can help prevent such a chain reaction. However, deposit insurance can also cause, as emphasized above, moral hazard problems. Depositors may be less likely to scrutinize their banks, and banks could take on excessive risks if monitoring by customers weakens. 'Co-insurance' schemes, which still leave some risk with depositors, could limit this problem. Thus, governments provide a safety net for the purpose of lender of last resort and as an explicit deposit insurance scheme.

7   *Lender of last resort.* Because the central banks have the ability to create currency they can lend it to banks facing massive deposit outflows to satisfy

their depositors' claims. When a central bank acts in this way it is acting as a 'lender of last resort' to the bank. But if banks think that the central bank will always bail them out they may take excessive risks.

8   *Market monitoring.* Market-based monitoring of banks can increase their stability and complement government supervision. If, for example, private rating agencies regularly rate banks, this provides valuable information to customers and regulators on their soundness. Banks then have an incentive to improve their performance to maintain business. Thus, regulators can require banks to obtain and publish certified audits or ratings from international rating firms. International monitoring and assistance are also beneficial. For example, International Monetary Fund (IMF) surveillance of member countries' macroeconomic and financial positions and the recent introduction of data dissemination standards increase transparency. These mechanisms facilitate the 'early warning' of financial sector problems.

   To insure that there is better information for depositors and the marketplace, regulators can require that banks adhere to certain standard accounting principles and disclose a wide range of information that helps the market assess the quality of a bank's portfolio and the amount of the bank's exposure to risk.

9   *Government ownership.* The most complete form of government control of banks is outright ownership.

In general, each country has a different set of regulations and supervisory practices in place, and countries often have little interest in each other's regulatory regimes or have little confidence in the quality of such regimes. If each country has different regulations in place and does not recognize qualifications in a foreign bank's home country then the national qualification costs become cumulative costs, as banks intending to establish abroad incur costs to comply with the qualification criteria of each country. We now consider how these qualification costs could be lessened if countries would accept some international norms as regulations.

Global regulation of the banking system and regulatory convergence

Turning to the role of international forces for achieving regulatory convergence, we first consider the Basel Committee and thereafter the negotiations under the WTO.

The Basel Committee

The Basel Committee was established at the end of 1974 by the central bank governors of the Group of Ten countries. The Committee formulates broad supervisory standards and guidelines and recommends statements of best practice in the expectation that individual authorities will take steps to implement them. Its initial focus was primarily on the gaps in international regulation and supervision, specifically how branches and subsidiaries of foreign banks should be regulated and supervised. Over time, its area of responsibility and influence expanded with the increase in foreign bank entry and as the goal of establishing a level playing field became accepted.[5]

Basel I

In 1988, the Committee introduced a capital measurement system commonly referred to as the Basel Capital Accord (Basel I). Basel I primarily focused on credit risk, the risk of loss due to a debtor's non-payment of a loan or other line of credit, and required banks with international presence to hold capital equal to 8 per cent of the risk-weighted assets.

The purpose of having the minimum capital adequacy ratio is to ensure that banks can absorb a reasonable level of losses before becoming insolvent, and before depositors' funds are lost.[6] Thus, applying minimum capital adequacy ratios serves the purpose of promoting the stability and efficiency of the financial system by reducing the likelihood of banks becoming insolvent. It also gives some protection to depositors. In the event of a winding up, depositors' funds rank in priority before capital, so depositors would lose money only if the bank makes a loss that exceeds the amount of capital it has. The higher the capital adequacy ratio, the higher is the level of protection available to depositors.

Basel I defines a standard methodology for calculating the capital to assets ratio. The ratio consists of a numerator that represents the amount of capital in a financial institution and a denominator that represents the asset classes, by various risk categories, that a financial institution holds. The calculation of the capital adequacy ratio requires first the calculation of capital, which is defined as the sum of tier 1 and tier 2 capital. Tier 1 capital consists of the types of financial capital considered the most reliable and liquid, primarily shareholders' equity. It is the part of capital that is permanently and freely available to absorb losses without the bank being obliged to cease trading. The economic meaning of tier 2 capital was made more explicit when its name was changed to 'supplementary capital' under Basel II. It is that portion of capital that generally absorbs losses only in the event of a winding up of a bank, and so it provides a lower level of protection for depositors and other creditors. Tier 2 capital consists of undisclosed reserves, asset revaluation funds, general provisions/general loan loss reserves, hybrid (debt/equity) capital instruments and subordinated debt. Tier 2 capital is further subdivided into upper and lower tier 2 type of capital. Upper tier 2 capital has no fixed maturity, whereas lower tier 2 capital has a limited life span, which makes it less effective in providing a buffer against losses by the bank.

A credit exposure arises when a bank lends money to a customer, buys a financial asset or has any other arrangement with another party that requires that party to pay money to the bank under, for example, a foreign exchange contract. A credit risk is a risk that the bank will not be able to recover the money it is owed. The calculation of credit exposures adjusts for two factors: on-balance sheet and off-balance sheet exposures. On-balance sheet credit exposures differ in their degree of riskiness. In Basel I, countries have been divided into two groups. The first group, referred to as the Organization for Economic Co-operation and Development (OECD), consists of full members of the OECD and countries that have concluded special lending arrangements with the IMF associated with the Fund's General Arrangement to Borrow. All other countries are called 'countries outside the OECD'. Claims on the central government within the OECD are assigned a zero weight. A 20 per cent weight is applied to claims on all banks, wherever they are incorporated, with a residual maturity of up to and including one year. Longer-term claims on OECD incorporated banks are weighted at the rate of 20 per cent and longer-term claims on banks incorporated outside the OECD are weighted at the rate of 100 per cent. Loans fully secured by mortgage on occupied residential property are weighted at 50 per cent, and all claims on private sector and claims on central government outside the OECD are weighted at 100 per cent.

As off-balance sheet contracts such as loan commitments, letters of credit, interest rate swaps and trading positions in futures and options also carry credit risks, off-balance sheet credit exposures are first converted to a 'credit equivalent amount'. This is achieved by multiplying the nominal principal amount by a factor that recognizes the amount of risk inherent in particular types of off-balance sheet credit exposures. After deriving credit equivalent amounts for off-balance sheet credit exposures, these are weighted according to the riskiness of the counterparty, in the same way as on-balance sheet credit exposures.

The minimum capital adequacy ratios set by the Basel Capital Accord are as follows: (1) tier 1 capital to total risk-weighted credit exposures to be not less than 4 per cent, (2) total capital (i.e. tier 1 plus tier 2 less certain deductions) to total risk-weighted credit exposures to be not less than 8 per cent, (3) tier 2 capital to not exceed 100 per cent of tier 1 capital and (4) lower tier 2 capital to not exceed 50 per cent of tier 1 capital.

Although Basel I was intended for internationally active banks, it quickly became a de facto standard around the world. Developing country regulators, who were actively attempting to move away from direct controls to a more modern system of prudential regulation, began to follow the evident best practice in industrial countries embodied in Basel I.

Market risk

In 1996, an important amendment to the framework took place, when an additional capital charge was introduced to cover market risk in banks' trading books.[7] To calculate regulatory capital requirements, banks classify their assets and off-balance sheet items under one of the two following categories: banking book and trading book. Most medium- and long-term transactions are held in the banking book, and it is subject to regulatory capital requirements for the credit risk arising from these transactions. On the other hand, the trading book consists of positions in financial instruments and commodities held either with the intent to trade or in order to hedge other elements of the trading book. The trading book includes most derivatives such as financial futures, interest rate and currency swaps and options on securities, and it is subject to capital requirements for market risk.

With the 1996 amendment to the Capital Accord, banks were required to measure and apply capital charges with respect to their market risks in addition to their credit risks, and market risk was defined as the risk of losses in on- and off-balance sheet positions arising from movements in market prices. The risks subject to this requirement are those pertaining to interest rate-related instruments and equities in the trading book and to foreign exchange risk and commodities risk throughout the bank. The capital charges for interest rate-related instruments and equities apply to the current market value of items in banks' trading books.

Banks must therefore back the following risks in their trading book with regulatory capital: (1) interest rate risk, (2) equity position risk, (3) foreign exchange risk and (4) commodities risk. In addition, capital charges are applied on options of all kinds. Here, interest rate risk refers to the risk of holding or taking positions in debt securities and other interest rate-related instruments in the trading book. The instruments covered include all fixed rate and floating rate debt securities and instruments that behave like them, including non-convertible preference shares. Equity position risk refers to the risk of holding or taking positions in equities in the trading book. It applies to long and short positions in all instruments that exhibit market behaviour similar to equities, but not to non-convertible preference shares. The instruments covered include common stocks, whether voting or non-voting, convertible securities that behave like equities and commitments to buy or sell equity securities. Foreign exchange risk refers to the risk of suffering losses due to adverse exchange rate movements. Finally, commodities risk refers to the risk of holding or taking positions in commodities, including precious metals, but excluding gold, which is treated as a foreign currency.[8]

According to the 1996 amendment, banks are permitted to use either the standardized approach or the model approach to calculate their market risks. In the standardized approach, as in the case of credit risk calculations, fixed risk weights are used. Therefore the outcome is sensitive to the assumptions made concerning these weights and not to the variations in markets. The internal model approach, on the other hand, calculates market risk-based capital requirements on the basis of their value-at-risk figure. The value at risk, or VaR, is a measure used to estimate how the value of an asset or of a portfolio of assets could decrease over a certain time period (usually over one day or ten days) under usual conditions.[9] VaR is not only a risk measurement tool, but also facilitates risk management. Banks are also required to conduct a regular stress testing programme.[10] Whether a bank can use the model approach is determined by compliance with the qualitative and quantitative criteria defined in the regulation.

The principal form of eligible capital to cover market risks consists of tier 1 and tier 2 types of capital. However, banks may also, at the discretion of their national authority, employ a third tier of capital called tier 3 capital, consisting of short-term subordinated debt.[11] To be called tier 3 capital, the short-term subordinated debt must meet the following criteria: it must be unsecured, subordinated and fully paid up; have an original maturity of at least two years; not be repayable before the agreed repayment date unless the supervisory authority agrees; and be subject to a lock-in clause that stipulates that neither interest nor principal may be paid (even at maturity) if such payment means that the bank falls below or remains below its minimum capital requirement. Banks are entitled to use tier 3 capital solely to support market risks, and tier 3 capital is limited to 250 per cent of a bank's tier 1 capital that is required to support market risks.

To ensure consistency in the calculation of the capital requirements for credit and market risks, an explicit numerical link is created by multiplying the measure of market risk by 12.5 (i.e. the reciprocal of the minimum capital ratio of 8 per cent) and adding the resulting figure to the sum of risk-weighted assets compiled for credit risk purposes. The ratio is then calculated in relation to the sum of the two, using as the numerator only eligible capital. In calculating eligible capital, it is necessary first to calculate the bank's minimum capital requirement for credit risk, and only afterwards its market risk requirement, to establish how much tier 1 and tier 2 capital is available to support market risk. Eligible capital will be the sum of the bank's entire tier 1 capital and its entire tier 2 capital under the limits imposed in the 1988 Accord. Tier 3 capital will be regarded as eligible only if it can be used to support market risks under the conditions stated above.[12]

Basel Core Principles

In the wake of the Mexican crisis of 1994, it was realized that capital requirements alone were not sufficient to ensure safe and sound banking. As a result, the Basel Committee issued its Core Principles for Bank Supervision in 1997, summarized in Appendix Table A7.1. Over time, the Basel Core Principles (BCP) became accepted as best practice for bank supervision around the world. The core principles, 25 in total, are grouped under the following headings: (1) preconditions for effective banking supervision (principle 1), (2) licensing and structure (2–5), (3) prudential regulations and requirements (6–15), (4) methods of ongoing supervision (16–20), (5) information requirements (21), (6) formal powers of supervisors (22) and (7) cross-border banking (23–25). The principles, regarded as minimum requirements, are to be supplemented when necessary by other measures and should be applied with respect to the supervision of all banks. The core principles propose minimum standards for licensing, ownership transfer and liquidation. They also suggest prudential rules and requirements, supervision methods, and information and disclosure requirements for both domestic and cross-border activities.

To facilitate implementation and assessment, the Basel Committee developed the Core Principles Methodology in October 1999. In June 1999, the Committee issued a proposal for a revised capital adequacy framework. The proposed capital framework consists of three pillars: minimum capital requirements, supervisory review of an institution's internal assessment process, and effective use of disclosure to strengthen market discipline as a complement to supervisory efforts. The Core Principles and the Methodology were revised and released in October

2006. The crises in East Asia led to the creation by the IMF and the World Bank in May 1999 of the Financial Sector Assessment Program (FSAP), whose goal is to assess the primary stability and developmental issues in countries' financial sectors. Virtually all FSAPs have included an assessment of countries' compliance with the BCP.

Basel II

Notwithstanding consensus among regulators, shortly after its completion, Basel I began to be criticized because of its narrow focus. First, it was emphasized that Basel I focused on arbitrary assignment of risk weights. Moreover, the risk weights did not differentiate between loans to small, risky firms and those to large, highly rated multinationals. In Basel I the requirement on credit exposure is the same whether the borrower's credit rating is triple-A or triple-C. Thus, the degrees of risk exposure are not sufficiently calibrated to differentiate adequately between borrowers' differing default risks. Furthermore, Basel I originally dealt only with credit risk, the risk that loans might become non-performing, and, later, with market risk; however, banks are also confronted with operational risks. A third set of critiques addressed the approach more broadly. Rather than setting minimum capital requirements on a loan, by loan criterion, what matters for the riskiness of a bank is its diversification or the covariation in its portfolio – yet Basel I made no adjustment for these factors, as the risk buckets were completely independent. Finally, a fourth set of critiques concerned the inappropriate treatment of sovereign risk. It was emphasized that Basel I's capital treatment for sovereign exposures made little economic sense and that the mechanical application of Basel I rules often created perverse incentives and led to the mispricing of risks. For example, lending to OECD governments became more attractive because it incurred no regulatory capital charge, even though this group included countries with substantially different credit ratings such as Turkey, Mexico and South Korea. Claims to the national central government also enjoyed a zero risk weight, encouraging many banks to ignore basic diversification principles and lend heavily to their sovereigns, thereby reducing financial intermediation. Both in response to these critiques, and in recognition of the changing financial markets, the Basel Committee devoted several years to revising the Capital Accord, announced Basel II in June 2004 and stipulated its implementation by the end of 2006 in G10 countries. Basel II consists of three pillars: (1) minimum capital requirements, (2) supervisory review process and (3) market discipline.

Basel II assumes that consolidated supervision is performed. Although consolidated supervision is included in the BCP, data on principle 20 and principle 23 indicate that many countries fail in this area, as shown by the IMF (2002). Indeed, principle 20 has the highest percentage of countries in either non-compliance or material non-compliance compared with any other principle.

Basel II, pillar 2 (Supervisory Review) is largely encompassed by the BCP and, hence, there is little new in pillar 2. It starts with four key principles, which commence with the responsibilities of the banks and then the responsibilities of the supervisor. Next, pillar 2 states that supervisors should normally 'expect' banks to operate with capital above the regulatory minimum and should have the ability to require banks to have more than any standard minimum amount. Lastly, it states that supervisors should seek to intervene at an early stage in the case of problem institutions. Following the four key principles, pillar 2 lists a set of 'other risks' that banks and supervisors need to consider (that did not make it into pillar 1) regarding actual quantitative requirements. Here, emphasis is to be placed on interest rate risk, credit concentration risk and liquidity risk. To a large extent these 'other risks' are what banks need to monitor carefully, but there is not yet agreement on whether or how quantitative requirements can be developed. Pillar 2 is particularly relevant for two main reasons. First, many countries fall short of complying with the key principles of supervision and, second, 'other risks' turn out to be particularly important for developing countries.

Basel II, pillar 3 (Market Discipline) focuses largely on the appropriate disclosure of bank capital and capital adequacy. While Basel I and the BCPs did not specifically refer to what banks must disclose to the public, the focus of pillar 3 is on reporting rather than disclosure to the market. Thus, it is a novel approach. First, it dictates how a banking group should disclose figures, depending on how that group is consolidated. Second, pillar 3 includes disclosure requirements on capital structure and on capital adequacy, in the aggregate, by portfolio and by type of risk, thus reflecting the different portfolios and 'risks' as defined in pillar 1. There are also disclosure requirements for credit risk, the risk of equity investments, credit risk mitigation techniques, securitization risks, market risks, operational risk and interest rate risk in the banking book.

Most of the innovation of Basel II lies in pillar 1 (Minimum Capital Requirements). In Basel II, the minimum capital to risk-weighted asset requirement of 8 per cent remains unchanged. The numerator that defines the acceptable types of regulatory capital (i.e. tier 1 and tier 2 capital) is also largely unchanged. The core modifications in Basel II are to the denominator, which defines risk-weighted assets. The credit risk measurement methods are more elaborate than in Basel I. The new framework proposes, for the first time, a measure for operational risk, while the market risk measure remains unchanged. When all of these are taken into account it can be safely argued that Basel II has a much more risk-sensitive framework than Basel I.

Basel II provides different approaches that can be used to obtain a risk weighting of assets. The menu of approaches to measure the associated risks include the standardized approach (SA), foundation internal rating-based (IRB) approach and advanced IRB approach.

The SA uses both private credit rating agencies and export credit agencies to establish credit risk assessments and feed those into capital requirements. As credit rating agencies rate corporations and banks as well as sovereigns, this approach adds the possibility of using these assessments to link the capital to risk more finely. For credit risk, the SA is similar to the approach of Basel I in that it requires fixed risk weightings to be applied to different types of assets. It prescribes, as in Basel I, specific risk weights for certain types of credit exposures, such as 0 per cent, 20 per cent, 50 per cent or 100 per cent of the 8 per cent standard, and there is now a weight of 150 per cent for borrowers with poor credit ratings. The risk assessments under the SA depend heavily on the ratings assigned by external rating agencies in the individual risk groups, as shown in Table 7.1.

Most pages of the pillar 1 proposals are devoted to the more advanced IRB methodologies. IRB gives a significant degree of autonomy to banks to define their own rating scales and to use those scales in determining the default probabilities.[13]

Basel II contains a new capital requirement for operational risk, defined as the risk of loss from fraud, computer failures and poor documentation. As operational risk differs greatly from credit risk and market risk, it is far more difficult to capture because it is inherent in many activities. Banks usually set aside one-fifth of their internal capital for operational risks, as concepts for delineating, quantifying and controlling operational risk are not as well developed as in the other risk categories. As operational risks can be significant, and the resulting losses can even threaten a bank's existence, the Basel Committee on Banking Supervision decided to introduce capital requirements for operational risk and to offer three levels of approach in this context. First is the basic indicator approach, in which a bank's operational risk is estimated as a percentage (alpha factor) of a single indicator. Next is the standardized approach, which uses a set of indicators and factors (betas), based on the bank's business lines. Hence, this approach can be seen as a basic indicator approach applied to each business line. Finally, the internal measurement approach requires banks to utilize their internal loss data and a model-based approach in the estimation of required capital. These data always form a matrix of business lines and loss events, based on which banks, depending on the detailed approach chosen, are to determine the probability of event and loss given event for potential operational losses. Based on work to date, the Committee expects operational risk to constitute approximately 20 per cent, on average, of the overall capital requirements under the new framework.

Basel II no doubt constitutes a major achievement towards harmonizing bank regulation on the global scale. However, as can be expected, it is far from perfect. First of all, although pillars 1 and 3 of Basel II, in principle, imply homogeneous practices for all countries, pillar 2 does not. In fact, by keeping a sufficiently broad playground for national supervisory authorities, Basel II implicitly accepted the continuation of differences in implementation among countries. This is more a logical requirement than a choice. The Basel II approach is based on the idea of developing criteria for banks to deal with risks that they face. By requiring banks to comply with these criteria, the Basel II approach also aims to enhance risk management practices and competitiveness. It is well known that, although this is a necessary condition for the stability and soundness of a financial system, it is by no means sufficient. In the Basel II framework, such measures to deal with systemic risk are left to the discretion of the national authorities. Basel II, therefore, by design, was not aiming to provide a completely homogenized system for all. It confines itself to the broad acceptance of the minimum requirements of risk management and competitiveness.

Table 7.1 Risk weights under Basel II standardized approach (%)

	AAA to AA–	A+ to A–	BBB+ to BBB–	BB+ to B–	Below B–	Unrated
Claims on sovereigns	0	20	50	100	150	100
Claims on banks option 1 (rating refers to sovereign)	20	50	100	100	150	100
Claims on banks option 2 (rating refers to bank)	20	50	50	100	150	50
Claims on banks option 3 (preferential treatment for short-term claims)	20	20	20	50	150	20
	AAA to AA–	A+ to A–	BBB+ to BB–	Below BB–	Unrated	
Claims on corporations	20	50	100	150	100	

Source: Basel Committee on Banking Supervision (2006).

Second, the Basel II approach itself is not immune from criticism. Therefore, it is natural to observe a cautious or, occasionally, even overcautious approach on behalf of national authorities at the implementation stage. It is universally recognized that Basel II indeed increased the risk sensitivity of minimum capital requirements and enhanced risk management of banks. However, these visible improvements at the micro level may still create problems for the system as a whole. There are concerns that market-sensitive risk systems may amplify shocks and lead to macroeconomic instability.[14] On the other hand, as pointed out by Tarullo (2008), the rather complex structure of the Basel II rules can hardly prevent and in fact may even encourage regulatory arbitrage. Finally, the cost of administrating Basel II rules may also be prohibitive for some countries. These factors may explain the slowness of the implementation of the Basel II process and the reluctance of national authorities to go beyond accepting the core points.

Recent Developments

During 2007–8 a worldwide financial crisis of enormous magnitude rooted in industrial countries' financial systems unfolded. Defaults on securitized subprime mortgages as a real estate market bubble burst led to failures or near failures of several large financial institutions. First, they sought new capital to support their strained balance sheets. But with the crisis accelerating, and most providers of capital retreating to the sidelines, banks had to sell assets and/or dispose of businesses. However, this accelerated the downturn. To deal with financial strains, public authorities had to act. They reduced the benchmark lending rates, injected massive amounts of government money into the financial sector, and in some cases they even adopted full-scale nationalization to restore the failing solvency of banks and insurance companies.

The financial crisis has exposed major weaknesses in the current regulatory and supervisory frameworks, and has generated a growing debate about the role that these weaknesses may have played in causing and propagating the crisis. As emphasized by the Financial Stability Board (2009) the Basel Committee has been working to build stronger buffers into the financial system. In this context it has been agreed that: (1) the level and quality of minimum capital requirements will increase substantially over time, (2) capital requirements will operate counter-cyclically, so that financial institutions will be required to build capital buffers above the minimum requirements during good times that can be drawn down during more difficult periods, (3) significantly higher capital requirements for risks in banks' trading books will be implemented, with average capital requirements for the largest banks' trading books at least doubling by the end of 2010, (4) the quality, consistency and transparency of the tier 1 capital base will be raised and (5) a leverage ratio will be introduced as a supplement to the Basel II risk-based framework with a view to migrating to a pillar 1 treatment based on appropriate review and calibration.

World Trade Organization

The WTO General Agreement on Trade in Services (GATS) is the first multilateral trade agreement to promote the liberalization of services in countries around the world. After an exhausting negotiation process that failed to reach full agreement at the end of the Uruguay Round in 1993, negotiations on financial services were extended, and WTO members reached an interim agreement in 1995 and a final permanent agreement on services at the end of 1997.[15]

The GATS contains certain obligations, the most important of which is the most favoured nation (MFN) principle. The MFN imposes the obligation on member countries not to discriminate among foreign services and service suppliers.[16] However, an exception to this general principle is that members have the right to enter into economic integration agreements, such as the EU, and accord preferences to other participants without extending those preferences to the entire WTO membership. The other two key principles are market access and national treatment, which are negotiable principles, meaning that WTO members can decide voluntarily to what extent they will allow foreign participation in their markets and under what conditions, with respect to the four modes of supply: (1) cross-border, (2) consumption abroad, (3) commercial presence and (4) temporary movement of natural persons. Agreements to eliminate or reduce limitations to market access or to provide national treatment are voluntary, applying only to those banking services included in a member country's schedule and to the extent specified therein.

The national treatment principle imposes the obligation not to discriminate between foreign services and service suppliers and national services and service suppliers. Subject to any conditions or qualifications that are negotiated and become part of a schedule of commitments, it requires that host regulators treat foreign banks no less favourably than domestic banks. This means that member countries cannot erect barriers to entry or operation that discriminate against foreign banks. In contrast, market access is not defined in GATS. Instead, a list of six measures restricting free access to domestic banking markets is provided. A country that does not impose any of these restrictions is regarded as providing full market access. The list includes numerical quotas on the number of foreign banks or their total assets, limitations on the type of foreign bank entry, limitations on the percentage of ownership in domestic banks and limitations on the total number of natural persons that may be employed in the host country's banking sector or which the foreign bank itself may employ.

Like any other trade agreement, GATS contains exception provisions, which allow WTO members to depart from their obligations or commitments under the agreement in specific circumstances. One of those exception-type provisions is the so-called 'prudential carve-out', which allows WTO members to take measures for prudential reasons, including the protection of investors and depositors and preserving the integrity and stability of the financial system.

Under GATS, prudential regulations are dealt with in paragraph two of the Annex on Financial Services, and non-prudential regulations to pursue various public policy objectives other than those falling under trade restrictions concerning market access or national treatment are dealt with in Article VI. Trade restrictions concerning market access or national treatment are dealt with in Articles XVI and XVII. Thus, GATS allows members to take measures for prudential reasons. Under GATS, members can take their own measures regarding capital adequacy ratios, limits on risk concentration and the risk management system, liquidity requirements, prohibitions on insider trading and transactions giving rise to conflicts of interest, rules on the classification of and provisions for non-performing assets, and 'fit and proper' tests for directors and managers, as well as transparency and disclosure requirements. Furthermore, non-prudential regulatory measures such as lending requirements to certain sectors or geographical regions, restrictions on interest rates or fees and commissions, and requirements to provide certain services may also exist. Services related to the issuance of public debt are often subject to special rules and standards. Some of these measures may be subject to scheduling under GATS as limitations on market access or as limitations on national treatment, particularly when they are applied in a discriminatory manner. They may also necessitate MFN exemptions if applied in a discriminatory manner between trading partners.

Regulatory regime in the European Union

In the EU, progress in harmonization came in 1973 with the adoption of the directive on the abolition of restrictions on freedom of establishment and freedom to provide services for self-employed activities of banks and other financial institutions. This document contributed to establishing a single banking market. It required member countries to comply with the national treatment principle. This means that member states are to provide equal regulatory and supervisory treatment for all banks, both domestic and foreign. However, despite this effort toward harmonization, the existence of capital controls and a lack of coordination among the different bank regulatory and supervisory authorities meant that banks operating in different member countries remained subject to different rules. This situation led to further attempts to achieve greater harmonization of bank regulations and supervisory practices among member countries. In 1997, the first directive on the coordination of laws, regulation and administrative provisions relating to the taking up and pursuit of credit institutions was adopted. Essentially, this directive set the rules for expansion across national boundaries within the European Community (EC) by adopting the concept of 'host country rule'. Under host country rule, expansion is possible. However, a foreign bank or branch is required to have permission from the supervisory authorities in the host country before they are allowed to operate in the host state. According to the First Banking Directive, banks and branches were typically regulated by each host country's regulatory agency. Under this regime, banks involved in cross-border expansions were required to operate under multiple regulatory and capital standards, that is, one for their home country and another for each host country in which they operate. Furthermore, in most countries, branches had to be provided with earmarked endowment capital as if they were new banks, and the supply of cross-border services was impaired by the restrictions on capital flows.

In April 1983, a White Policy Paper on financial integration called for further work to achieve a better allocation of savings and investment in the EC. Following various European Councils, the Commission (1985) proposed its White Paper on the completion of the internal market. The Paper called for the removal of physical, technical and fiscal barriers in all industries by 1 January 1993. The content of the White Paper was incorporated into the 1986 Single European Act, which called for the effective integration of markets. In the context of banking, the White Paper called for a single banking licence, home country control and mutual recognition. To establish the single market in banking services, the EU introduced a series of key directives, which can be considered under five headings: barriers to trade and establishment, capital adequacy, deposit protection, consolidated accounts and supervision, liberalization of capital movements and interest rate deregulation.

Barriers to trade and establishment

The cornerstone of the single market programme is the Second Banking Directive, which was adopted in 1989 by Council Directive 89/646/EEC. The Second Banking Directive has three major features. First, it defined exactly what is meant by 'banking'. The banking activities permitted in the EU cover all major commercial and investment banking activities, requiring the endorsement of universal banking. Thus, according to the Second Banking Directive, besides the traditional commercial banking activities, credit institutions can engage in all forms of transactions in securities, including transactions for their own account or for the account of customers in all types of security, participation in share issues and portfolio management and advice.

The second component of the directive is the principle of home country control, or mutual recognition. According to this principle, each country acknowledges the regulation of its partners and accepts service provision by foreign institutions as if they were domestic entities.[17] Hence, banks are governed by and conform to the regulations and legislation of their home country. If a bank does business in another EU nation, the regulatory authorities of the host nation must recognize the primacy of the home nation.

The third component of the Second Banking Directive is the concept of a 'single passport'. Mutual recognition of the single banking 'licence' eliminates the need for EU banks to get a local banking charter from the host country for branches and/or bank products that are permitted by their home country bank regulations. A bank licensed to do business in any EU nation is allowed to do business in any other EU nation on whatever basis it considers most advantageous. The host nation is not allowed to impose any barriers to such action.

To ensure that the single passport does not lead to a situation in which the regulations and supervisory practices in a member country are so lax as to undermine the safety and soundness of the entire banking system in the EU, the Second Banking Directive also limits the scope for regulatory competition among countries. Therefore, the Second Banking Directive introduces essential supervisory requirements related to sound administrative and accounting procedures, the initial capital necessary for authorization and for the execution of activities, and the supervision of holdings of banks in sectors outside the banking business. Under this principle, banks operating in more than one EU member state are entitled to comply to a great extent with a set of uniform standards and capital requirements. However, for gold-plating cases or in cases of breaches of the law by operating institutions, possible risks can be eliminated via close cooperation of the supervisory authorities.

Concerning the banks' holdings in non-banking institutions, we note that the Second Banking Directive introduces two limits. First, a credit institution may not have a qualifying holding in excess of 15 per cent of its own funds in such an undertaking. Second, the amount of all holdings in such undertakings may not exceed 60 per cent of the funds of the credit institution. However, member states need not apply these limits to holdings in insurance companies.

Directive 2000/12/EC relating to the taking up and pursuit of the business of credit institutions consolidated various directives, including the Second Banking Directive, with the aim of compiling them under a single publication. According to the directive, these are the essential requirements for authorization (subject to exceptions set out in the directive): (1) the existence of separate own funds, (2) the existence of initial capital of at least €5 million, (3) the presence of at least two persons who effectively direct the business of the credit institution (and who are of sufficiently good repute and experience to perform such duties) and (4) notification to the competent authorities of the identities of the shareholders or members that have qualifying holdings and of the amounts of those holdings. Applicants must be notified whenever an authorization is refused, and the reasons for refusal must be given. The competent authorities may withdraw an authorization, subject to the conditions set out in the directive, in particular when the above conditions are no longer fulfilled. The parties concerned and the Commission must be notified when authorization is withdrawn, and the reasons for withdrawal must be given. The competent authorities of the home member state must require that all credit institutions have sound administrative and accounting procedures and adequate internal control mechanisms. Furthermore, the directive states that supervision, in principle, is carried out by the home member state, while the competent authorities of the member states concerned cooperate closely. In particular, they supply each other with any information necessary for effective supervision. Such information exchanges are protected by professional secrecy.

Capital adequacy

Because of the crucial role of capital in banking, the EU promulgated a series of directives intended to ensure that all banks in the EU had the same capital standards. The Own Funds Directive (89/299/EEC) harmonized the definitions of own funds for all credit institutions in the EU to ensure the comparability of prudential ratios of EU banking organizations, and the Solvency Ratio Directive (89/647/

EEC) harmonizing minimum solvency requirements for credit institutions in the EU addressed the issues related to credit risk. The requirements of Directive 2000/12/EC, which has replaced, among others, the Own Funds Directive, are consistent with those of the 1988 Basel Committee Capital Accord (Basel I) on international banking capital adequacy.

The directive on the capital adequacy of investment firms and credit institutions, called the Capital Adequacy Directive (CAD) (93/6/EEC), sets out the minimum capital requirements for credit institutions and investment firms for the market and the risks associated with their trading activities. CAD was amended by Directive 98/31/EEC (CAD2), extending the concept of 'trading book' to positions in commodities and commodity derivatives that are held for trading purposes and are subject mainly to market risks. With CAD2, there has been no change in the CAD regime. But parallel to CAD2 principles, the communiqué on capital adequacy was amended in February 2001 to cover market risks, and further amendments were made in January 2002 to include options and to address specific issues such as the inclusion of tier three capital and structural positions. Recently, the directive was amended by the Capital Requirements Directive, comprising Directive 2006/48/EC and Directive 2006/49/EC, translating Basel II into EU legislation. It applies Basel-type provisions to investment firms and domestic credit institutions as well as to international banks. The directive took effect in 2007, with the most sophisticated approaches being available from 2008.

An unacceptable concentration of risk can occur if a bank has what is deemed to be an excessive degree of exposure with a client or group of connected clients. The Directive on Monitoring and Controlling Large Exposures of Credit Institutions (92/121/EEC) regulates the supervision of large exposures of credit institutions, sets limits on exposures of credit institutions and sets limits on exposures as a large percentage of reserve funds. It requires that the maximum lending exposure to a single client or to a group of connected clients not exceed 25 per cent of a bank's own funds; a bank must report to its supervisor any exposure greater than 10 per cent of capital, as it is defined as a 'large exposure'; and the total of large exposures extended by a credit institution not exceed 800 per cent of its own funds.

Deposit insurance

With Council Directive 94/19/EC, the EU issued a Deposit Guarantee Scheme Directive, effective 1 July 1995. The directive, designed to increase the confidence and stability of the financial system, made it compulsory for every EU member state to establish a deposit insurance fund and for credit institutions to join this insurance plan. In this context, the deposit insurance scheme was regarded as being as essential as the prudential rules for the completion of the single banking market. The directive set the coverage of the aggregate deposits of each depositor, in the event of deposits being unavailable, up to ECU 20,000. The directive explicitly allowed the member states to provide a higher cover for deposits over this determined amount. Although no indication is given as to which public (or private) authority would be responsible for the guarantee scheme, the spirit of the directive ensures the public character of the whole scheme. On the other hand, the opening paragraphs indicate that the cost of financing the scheme falls to the credit institutions. The directive also indicated that depositors should be paid within a short period following the unavailability of the deposit. Furthermore, the directive allowed a bank with a low-coverage home country scheme to enter a high-coverage market and join the host country scheme for the difference. According to the directive, the host country scheme provides deposit protection coverage in excess of what the home country provides.

Consolidated accounts and supervision

The harmonization of legislation governing companies that are members of the bodies of undertakings was necessary both to ensure that consolidated accounts are drawn up so that the financial information concerning such bodies is conveyed to members and third parties and to achieve comparability and equivalence in the information that companies must publish within the EC.

The Council Directive on the supervision of credit institutions on a consolidated basis (92/30/EEC), which replaced the previous Directive 83/349/EEC and was integrated into the text of Directive 2000/12/EC of the European Parliament and of the Council on 20 March 2000, provided a framework for the supervision of the consolidated financial situation of a credit institution, the parent undertaking of which is a financial holding company. The consolidated accounts must give a true and fair view of the assets and liabilities, the financial position and the profit and loss of all undertakings consolidated, taken as a whole.

The Council Directive on the annual accounts and consolidated accounts of banks and other financial institutions (86/635/EEC) provided special accounting rules for the financial sector. It described the standardized form of balance sheet and profit-and-loss accounting as well as rules for the valuation of certain assets.

According to the capital adequacy directives integrated into Directive 2000/12/EC, credit institutions are subject to prudential requirements with respect to supervision of solvency, adequacy of their own funds to cover market risks and large exposures calculated on a consolidated basis, where the relevant company has a credit institution subsidiary or an interest in such a company, or if the parent group is a financial holding company. Generally, the supervisory authority of the member country that authorized the parent company of this group is responsible for the consolidated supervision of the group, although CAD permits delegation to other competent authorities in certain circumstances. Other provisions permit the offsetting of requirements that would otherwise apply individually to each group company.

The Council Directive 2000/12/EC was lately amended by the Council Directive 2002/87/EC, which introduced specific prudential legislation for financial conglomerates so as to amplify the sectoral prudential legislation for credit institutions, insurance companies and investment firms.

Liberalization of capital movements and interest rate deregulation

Freedom of movement of capital was seen as one of the essential elements of a fully integrated European single market. With regard to legislation on the liberalization of the movement of capital, a final directive was adopted in 1988. This directive stipulated that freedom of capital movement should exist, in principle, by 1 July 1990. Only Greece, Ireland, Spain and Portugal could apply derogation provisions until 1 January 1993. This deadline was extended to 1 January 1994, which was the start of the second phase of the European Economic and Monetary Union (EMU) as implied by the Treaty of Maastricht of 1992.

From the early 1970s onwards, government regulation of the financial sector shifted from the restriction of market forces to more market-oriented systems. Although there is no specific EU legislation relating to deregulation of interest rates, interest rate controls were gradually disbanded. By 1993 interest rate determination was fully deregulated in the EU.

Later developments

A further step towards a single market in financial services was taken on 1 January 1999 with the launch of the third stage of the EMU. Since the irrevocable fixing of exchange rates and the introduction of the euro, the 12 current member states of the EMU have enjoyed cross-border access to the euro zone's financial markets without the risks and costs caused by exchange rates. Thus, measured in terms of criteria such as the free movement of capital and payments, the freedom of establishment, the free movement of services and facilitation of cross-border transactions as a result of the principles of home country control, minimum standards at the EU level and the single European passport with mutual recognition, the single market in banking seemed a reality at the end of the twentieth century. But despite this progress, there are still barriers to cross-border financial transactions within the EU. Although the EU has managed to create single submarkets in banking, insurance and investments, it does not yet have a single market in financial services as of the beginning of the twenty-first century.

Just before the introduction of the euro, the European Council in June 1998 asked the European Commission to prepare a report on financial services. Upon this mandate, the Commission proposed a framework for action by means of a report entitled 'Financial Services: Commission proposes Framework for Action', which included suggestions on the need for the effective enforcement of financial services legislation without radical surgery, the adaptation of new and flexible methods vis-à-vis changing market conditions and the introduction of new legislation especially in the fields of pension funds and consumers (Commission of the European Communities 1998b). In May 1999, the Commission, furthering the previous year's work on financial services, published a comprehensive document called the 'Financial Sector Action Plan', which has since functioned as a basic framework for new political initiatives concerning.[18] The Financial Sector Action Plan distinguishes between strategic objectives concerning a single EU wholesale market, open and secure retail markets, prudential rules and supervision and general objectives concerning wider conditions for an optimal single financial market. The aim was to provide guidelines for financial services policy at the EU level and to set out a framework for an integrated capital market by 2005, while the target date for the integration of the securities and the risk capital markets was pronounced to be the end of 2003.

To attain the first strategic objective concerning a single EU wholesale market, according to the Financial Sector Action Plan, it is necessary to take action, among other things, to enable companies to raise capital on an EU-wide basis, to establish a common legal framework for integrated securities and derivatives markets and to enhance the comparability of financial reports issued by listed companies. To attain the second strategic objective concerning retail markets, the Financial Sector Action Plan proposes actions to bring about the convergence of rules on business-to-consumer marketing and sales techniques for financial services, to facilitate the free provision of services by insurance intermediaries and to improve the quality of information for consumers of financial services. With respect to the third strategic objective, prudential rules and supervision, the plan contains proposed actions concerning the winding up and liquidation of financial institutions, disclosure of financial instruments, the capital framework for banks and investment firms, solvency requirements for insurance companies and prudential rules for financial conglomerates. Proposed actions concerning wider conditions for an optimal single financial market comprise a directive on savings tax, a review of the taxation of financial service products, proposals for coordinating the tax arrangements governing supplementary pensions and a review of EU corporate governance practices.

Over the past few years the EU has been very active, and the Financial Sector Action Plan has strongly boosted the integration of the financial markets. Moreover, the EU has made considerable progress in giving the single market for financial services a more efficient institutional framework. The 'Lamfalussy process' helped make the legislative process more flexible so that regulatory authorities could respond more quickly to events in the rapidly changing markets. According to the Financial Sector Action Plan evaluation of 24 January 2007 prepared by the European Commission, 39 of the 42 Financial Sector Action Plan measures proposed have been adopted (Commission of the European Communities 2007f). The list of adopted directives, amendments and regulations cover areas such as fair value accounting, the application of international accounting standards, financial collateral arrangements, the European Company Statute, the undertaking of collective investment in transferable securities (UCITS), the distance marketing of financial services, insurance intermediaries, the winding up and liquidation of insurance undertakings and banks, electronic money, money laundering and solvency requirements for insurance companies.

The Financial Sector Action Plan, as emphasized above, has strongly boosted the integration of financial markets in the EU. However, a number of issues exist. In its 'White Paper on Financial Services 2005–10', the Commission set out its objectives in the area of financial services policy for the period up to 2010

(Commission of the European Communities 1999). These objectives aim to build on the Financial Sector Action Plan to achieve an integrated, open, inclusive, competitive and economically efficient EU financial market by: (1) implementing, enforcing and continuously evaluating existing legislation and ensuring future initiatives are backed up by rigorous impact assessment and thorough consultation, (2) removing remaining barriers so that financial services can be provided and capital can circulate freely throughout the EU at the lowest possible cost, resulting in high levels of financial stability, consumer benefits and consumer protection and (3) enhancing supervisory cooperation and convergence in the EU, deepening relations with other global financial marketplaces and strengthening European influence globally.

The above considerations reveal that a substantial degree of harmonization has been achieved in the banking sector through the adoption of the various banking directives and the Financial Sector Action Plan. The European Commission, moreover, established the Committee of European Banking Supervisors (CEBS) in 2004. Its role is to contribute to the consistent implementation of Community directives and to the convergence of member states' supervisory practices throughout the Community.

The 2007–8 financial crisis revealed the weaknesses in the current regulatory and supervisory frameworks of the EU. How to improve regulation was central to the discussions. As a result of these considerations the EU has adopted a comprehensive set of new rules for the financial sector to avoid the repetition of the crisis: control over credit rating agencies, stronger capital requirements on complex products such as securitization, and strengthened deposit guarantee schemes. The EU has agreed on a more efficient system for supervision of the financial sector within Europe to better monitor systemic risks, to ensure that EU regulation is applied consistently, to settle disagreement between national supervisors and to deal with crisis situations. Banks must now hold sufficient capital, ensure liquidity, and reward only genuine value creation and not short-term risk-taking (see Brown and Sarkozy 2009).

Regulatory regime in Turkey

During the 1990s, Turkey lacked competent supervisory authorities, a regulatory framework and legal and institutional infrastructure; in addition, the prevailing prudential regulations were poorly enforced. In February 2001, the country faced a financial crisis. The loss of income and wealth and the associated social and political stresses created in the country were unprecedented. The gross domestic product (GDP) contracted in 2001 by 5.7 per cent, and the loss in employment was put at more than 1.4 million. The cost of the crisis in the banking sector alone has been estimated as US$53.2 billion by Steinherr *et al.* (2004), that is, 33.3 per cent of Turkish GDP. The restructuring cost to the Treasury of state banks and of banks taken over by the Savings and Deposit Insurance Fund (SDIF) made up the lion's share of the costs of the crisis.

After the crisis, the Banking Regulation and Supervision Agency (BRSA) announced the Banking Sector Restructuring Program. The main objectives of the programme were the elimination of distortions in the financial sector and the adoption of regulations to promote an efficient, globally competitive, sound Turkish banking sector. The restructuring programme was based on four main pillars: (1) restructuring the state banks, (2) seeking prompt resolution of the intervened banks, (3) strengthening the private banks and (4) strengthening the regulatory and supervisory framework.[19]

In the aftermath of the banking crisis, efforts were directed to introduce a new legal framework for the banking system. Turkey passed a new banking law, Law No. 5411, on 1 November 2005. The purpose of the new law was to bring the regulatory framework closer to international and in particular to EU standards. Law No. 5472 of 8 March 2006, which amended Law No. 5411, was aimed at clarifying certain articles, rather than changing its structure and vision. Recent changes in the regulations are studied below within a comparative framework, the comparator being the EU banking *acquis*.

Barriers to trade and establishment

The new banking law brings the scope of the permitted banking activities in Turkey in line with those in the EU.[20] Although the EU definitions are more general, the Turkish legislation, on the other hand, prefers to define the activities in more detail. However, in order to have room for initiative for further actions, an open end was introduced by allowing activities determined by BRSA. Two additional types of activity expressed in the Turkish law are the insurance and private pension scheme agencyship and banks' activities pertaining to interbank transactions and market making.

Regarding home country control, we note that, in the EU, actions and applications to be taken by the banking institutions in other member states are initiated through the competent authority of the home country. However, in Turkey such actions are initiated and completed through the BRSA. Similarly, regarding the single passport issue, we note that, in the EU, after a bank acquires a licence of operation in a member state, the bank is free to establish a branch in another member state unless the related authority of the host state gives a refusal notice to any communication by the home member state. However, in Turkey such a request is subject to licensing procedures by the BRSA.

In Turkey, banks are not allowed to hold more than 15 per cent of their own funds as shares in non-credit and financial institutions, and the total amount of shares held in such institutions may not exceed 60 per cent of their own funds (Article 56/1 of Law No. 5411). Thus, Turkish regulations on holding shares in non-credit and financial institutions conform to the regulations in the EU.

Capital adequacy

Article 43/1 of the new banking law states that the BRSA is:

authorized to make the necessary regulations and to take any measure regarding banks in order to specify, analyze, monitor, measure and evaluate the relationship and balance between the assets, receivables, own funds, debts, liabilities, commitments of banks, revenues and expenses of banks, all other factors affecting their financial structures, and the risks encountered, by setting limitations and standard ratios as well.

(Banks Association of Turkey 2008: 23)

Banks are required to maintain and keep an 8 per cent capital adequacy standard ratio on a consolidated (applicable for banks and their financial subsidiaries combined) and unconsolidated basis, in order to ensure that banks maintain an adequate amount of capital to cover losses that may result from existing and potential risks. The consolidated financial reporting requirements allow quarterly verification of a bank's compliance with the consolidated capital adequacy requirement. When evaluating the capital adequacy ratio, banks are required to take capital charges for market risks such as foreign exchange risk, interest rate risk and securities price fluctuation risk.

Although Turkish regulations satisfy Basel I standards, this is not the case with Basel II standards. Complete adoption of the Basel II framework within Turkish legislation needs extensive work. Regarding the solvency ratio, the constituents of own funds, and risk weighting applications, we note that the rules in the EU and Turkey are essentially similar. However, the writing technique and technical approach show differences in the main directives of the two legislations. The EU directive prefers defining every instrument in more detail. On the other hand, the Turkish case prefers to define the whole calculation procedure as a continuous process and defines the instruments in a more general sense. Regarding the credit risk, market risk and operational risk, we note that they are defined in detail in the EU legislation, whereas the Turkish regulation gives only a concise definition of them. In fact, the detailed regulations for each of them must be published following the document on the road map of Basel II published by BRSA (Banking Regulation and Supervisory Board 2005). In the Turkish legislation, risks on foreign exchange positions and open position limits are elaborated in depth. Similarly, specific reserves to be put aside against credits in accordance with their performance classifications are defined in detail in the Turkish case. These concerns reflect the bitter experiences of the latest Turkish banking crisis. Regarding the derivative instruments, we note that they are not covered extensively in the Turkish legislation. As the use of these derivative instruments will become more widespread, the definitions and procedures will be covered extensively in the future.

Deposit insurance

In 1994, the government took drastic measures to save the economic system from collapse during the banking crisis. The most controversial of these was the introduction of a full (100 per cent) state guarantee on deposits. Introduction of a full guarantee on deposits was effective in ending bank rush and the drastic shifts in deposits from private banks to state-owned banks. However, fear of the renewal of the banking crisis prevented the authorities from abandoning this supposedly temporary measure in favour of a reasonable deposit insurance scheme. The decision by the government to provide full guarantee on deposits led the banks to take higher risks and stimulated moral hazard. After experiencing the 2001 financial crisis the country removed the state guarantee on deposits only in 2003. According to the new scheme, all depositors and creditors are totally protected in the case of intervened banks, whereas only individual depositors, but not commercial deposits, are fully protected in the case of banks being liquidated without intervention. A limited savings deposit insurance system replaced the previous guarantee scheme on 5 July 2004. Simultaneously, the savings deposit insurance was limited to TL50,000 (around €28,300). With these amendments, the Turkish scheme converged with that of the EU.

Consolidated accounts and supervision

According to Article 66 of the new banking law, the parent undertakings are subject to limitations and standard ratios on a consolidated basis. Their domestic and foreign subsidiaries, their jointly controlled undertakings and their branches and representative offices are also subject to consolidated supervision. These institutions shall keep their information and documents regarding their internal control, risk management and internal audit systems, accounting and financial reporting units, and financial statements and reports, as well as loans extended to risk groups, ready for consolidated supervision. The consolidated supervision of subsidiaries and jointly controlled undertakings shall be performed together by the officials of the BRSA and other authorities who are legally authorized for the regulation and supervision of institutions subject to consolidated supervision. Thus, full convergence has been realized between Turkish and EU legislations regarding consolidation of accounts and supervision. Although it is the responsibility of the home member state's competent authority to supervise in the EU, as emphasized above, supervision is carried out by the BRSA in Turkey.

Liberalization of capital movements and interest rate deregulation

Capital movements were liberalized in Turkey in 1989, and the Turkish lira became convertible in 1990. The coverage of the term 'capital' is the same in both the Turkish legislation and the EU *acquis*, and the maximum amount of money transfers allowed without any need for notification is US$50,000 in Turkey and €50,000 in the EU. In contrast, deregulation of the interest rates was realized in Turkey in the 1980s, after successive efforts. By the launch of Decision No. 32 on liberalization of capital movements in 1989, this issue was settled.

Finally, we note that internal control and the internal audit system are elaborated more in the Turkish law than in the Banking Directive of the EU. This parallels the detailed approach of the Turkish code. Aside from this, the Turkish code necessitates banks to follow accounts according to international standards. In the EU legislation, no such statements exist, as the EU has a dominant say at the international standard setting bodies. Basically, it is the responsibility of banks to establish sound accounting procedures and adequate internal control mechanisms. In addition, the Turkish law mandates the creation of two control divisions: internal control and risk management. In both legislations, competent authorities are allowed to supervise the financial reports. In Turkey, if the BRSA detects a failure in the accounts, it is authorized to take necessary measures. In the EU legislation, this responsibility lies with the home country's competent authority.

Epilogue

Although Turkey introduced major changes in banking law with the intention of bringing the regulatory framework closer to EU standards, and tried to implement these changes, it is still far from satisfying the international standards specified by the BCP. Recently, the Turkish financial system was assessed within the context of the FSAP of the IMF and the World Bank. According to the IMF (2007), Turkey fails to satisfy compliance with the BCP for effective banking supervision in a number of cases, analyzed below.

According to BCP 1, an effective system of banking supervision has clear responsibilities and objectives for each agency involved in the supervision of banking organizations. Each agency will possess operational independence and adequate resources. A suitable legal framework for banking supervision is necessary, including provisions relating to the authorization of banking organizations and their ongoing supervision, powers to address compliance with laws and safety and soundness concerns, and legal protection for supervisors. Arrangements for sharing information between supervisors and protecting the confidentiality of such information should also be in place. The IMF (2007) states that the BRSA lacks full operational independence in regulatory and budgetary matters. BRSA has difficulty recruiting and retaining staff with expertise in areas of banking supervision, information technology, stress testing, the assessment of banks' contingency planning and the evaluation of financial models. Furthermore, cooperation among regulators needs to be further strengthened. Thus, preconditions for effective banking supervision are generally not satisfied.

BCP 5 states that banking supervisors must have the authority to establish criteria for reviewing major acquisitions or investments by a bank and ensuring that corporate affiliations or structures do not expose the bank to undue risks or hinder effective supervision. According to the IMF (2007), the banking law or subregulations need to be amended to empower the BRSA to require prior permission if a bank wants to establish or acquire a financial institution such as an insurance company or an institution operating in capital markets as a subsidiary. The BRSA should continue to assess whether the bank has the financial and managerial capabilities to handle the new subsidiary. It should also continue to ensure that the new structure would not impede effective supervision.

BCP 7 states that an essential part of any supervisory system is the evaluation of a bank's policies, practices and procedures related to the granting of loans and making of investments and the ongoing management of the loan and investment portfolios. The IMF (2007) stresses that BRSA should rigorously assess a bank's credit policies and the implementation of them. Furthermore, BRSA should ensure that banks have appropriate standards and credit information when lending to the household sector and to small and medium-sized enterprises and conglomerates and should require them to act appropriately to correct deficiencies in this area.

According to BCP 8, banking supervisors must be satisfied that banks establish and adhere to adequate policies, practices and procedures for evaluating the quality of assets and the adequacy of loan loss provisions and loan loss reserves. The IMF (2007), on the other hand, states that the subregulation on loan classification and provisioning of loans should be amended to provide for specific provisioning for loans in the special category mentioned. The BRSA should encourage its supervisory staff to further the use of 'forward looking' criteria for classifying loans, and more internal guidance on the use of such criteria should be developed to support on-site inspectors' efforts. The BRSA should also continue to ensure that supervisory staff retain up-to-date skills on loan evaluation techniques.

BCP 9 states that banking supervisors must be satisfied that banks have management information systems that enable management to identify concentrations within the portfolio, and supervisors must set prudential limits to restrict bank exposures to single borrowers or groups of related borrowers. The IMF (2007) highlights potential weaknesses in the capacity of banks and supervisors to identify the full extent of any excessive concentration of credits. BRSA should ensure that banks implement risk management procedures to identify all beneficial owners and effectively monitor concentrations of credit and adherence to prudential risk limits.

According to BCP 10, banking supervisors, to prevent abuses arising from connected lending, must have in place requirements that banks lend to related companies and individuals on an arm's-length basis, that such extensions of credit are effectively monitored, and that other appropriate steps are taken to control or mitigate risks. The IMF (2007) maintains that the BRSA should ensure that banks implement risk management procedures to identify all beneficial owners of other financial and non-financial companies and to monitor concentrations of credit and adherence to prudential risk limits. To meet the additional criteria for this BCP, the banking law should be amended to ensure that the aggregate limit for exposures to a bank's insiders should not be higher than the 25 per cent limit set for exposures to other groups of connected borrowers. The recently enacted sublimit of 20 per cent for exposures to large shareholders and other connected parties should be maintained.

Regarding country risk, market risk and other risks, BCP 11 states that banking supervisors must be satisfied that banks have adequate policies and procedures for identifying, monitoring and controlling country risk and transfer risk in their international lending and investment activities and for maintaining appropriate reserves against such risks. According to BCP 12, banking supervisors must be satisfied that banks have systems in place that accurately measure, monitor and adequately control market risks; supervisors should have powers to impose specific limits and/or a specific capital charge on market risk exposures, if warranted. Finally, BCP 13 states that banking supervisors must be satisfied that banks have in place a comprehensive risk management process to identify, measure, monitor and control all other material risks and, when appropriate, to hold capital against these risks. The IMF (2007) notes that the effectiveness of prudential regulation is limited by the absence of certain subregulations on country and transfer risk and on interest risk in the banks' books. It states that the BRSA should issue explicit regulations and guidelines that address gaps in the supervisory framework for country risk and fully implement them. Furthermore, the BRSA should continue to improve its capacity to monitor the complex market activities of banks through additional training opportunities for supervisors in assessing market risks and validating banks' VaR models. The BRSA should proceed to inspect the implementation by banks of the new market risk subregulations. It should introduce computer-assisted supervision tools and train personnel accordingly. Finally, the BRSA should issue specific subregulations for legal risks and interest rate risks in the banking book.[21]

BCP 15 states that banking supervisors must determine that banks have adequate policies, practices and procedures in place, including strict 'know-your-customer' rules, which promote high ethical and professional standards in the financial sector and prevent the bank from being used, intentionally or unintentionally, by criminal elements. According to the IMF (2007), the BRSA should ensure that its regular activities address anti-money laundering-related risks as a major element of operational risk on a systemic basis. Bank reports on suspicious activities of material amounts concerning the safety, soundness or reputation of the bank should always be submitted not only to the Financial Crime Investigation Board (MASAK) but also to the BRSA.

BCP 16 states that an effective banking supervisory system should consist of some form of both on-site and off-site supervision. According to the IMF (2007), the main inspection report should contain the findings of other examinations of the same bank conducted during the same supervisory cycle. This is necessary in order to present a complete picture of a bank's soundness. The off-site analysis should be fully integrated with the on-site process. The enforcement of supervisory orders and recommendations should also be fully integrated with the on-site process.

BCP 18 states that banking supervisors must have a means of collecting, reviewing and analyzing prudential reports and statistical returns from banks on a solo and consolidated basis. The IMF (2007) maintains that the BRSA should advance its recent work to enhance off-site supervision. This would include expanding its information base to collect, review and analyze unconsolidated information on non-bank financial subsidiaries and affiliates. The BRSA should also periodically collect and analyze information on banks' parents and, when relevant, their affiliates. The BRSA should begin planning for the collection and analysis of additional information of, for instance, banks' off-balance sheet operations, as new markets develop, and market-based indicators of financial soundness.

BCP 19 states that banking supervisors must have a means of independently validating supervisory information through either on-site examinations or external auditors. The IMF (2007) states that the BRSA should fully implement ongoing efforts to enhance the information technology inspections of banks and should improve staff capacity in this area. Over the next one or two years, the BRSA should consider adopting a work standard that requires a report to be issued within 60 days of the completion of an examination visit and following the exit review at the end of on-site exercises.

BCP 20 states that an essential element of banking supervision is the ability of supervisors to supervise the banking group on a consolidated basis. The IMF (2007) maintains that the BRSA should adopt a general practice to conduct an 'integrated' supervision inspection of the entire group, assessing the potential effects on the bank emanating from the other entities, financial and non-financial. When securities firms, mortgage finance companies or insurance firms are regulated by other supervisory agencies, the BRSA should always proactively request to see inspection reports and other relevant documents. The BRSA is encouraged to plan and conduct simultaneous on-site inspections of such groups in concert with other domestic regulators. The BRSA should issue specific subregulations requiring banks to adopt appropriate risk management procedures to ensure the proper identification of beneficial owners and cross-holdings of other financial and non-financial companies. Such powers would also contribute to compliance with large exposure and connected lending principles. The BRSA should also be prepared to conduct on-site visits of banks' parent companies, be they financial or non-financial, focusing on the relationship between the parent and the bank and, when relevant, the parent's affiliates.

The discussion on methods of ongoing banking supervision as summarized by BCP 16–20 indicates that compliance with the principles needs to improve over time. In the authorities' response to the assessment in the IMF report (2007), supervision is emphasized as one of the main functions of BRSA, and BRSA gives significant importance to strengthening its supervision capabilities.

BCP 21 states that banking supervisors must be satisfied that each bank maintains adequate records, prepared in accordance with consistent accounting policies and practices, enabling the supervisor to obtain a true and fair view of the financial condition of the bank and the profitability of its business, and that the bank regularly publishes financial statements that fairly reflect its condition. The IMF (2007) maintains that the BRSA should proceed with its plans to assess a bank's implementation of the updated Turkish accounting standards.

BCP 22 states that banking supervisors must have at their disposal adequate supervisory measures to bring about timely corrective action when banks fail to meet prudential requirements, when there are regulatory violations or when depositors are threatened in any other way. In extreme circumstances, this should include the ability to revoke the banking licence or recommend its revocation. The IMF (2007) maintains that the BRSA's enforcement process should not reassess nor reprioritize the recommendations of the supervisors, unless it finds material evidence of mistakes or if the BRSA Board makes such a decision. The inspection reports should clearly spell out the recommendations, in priority order, and measures for taking corrective actions. The BRSA review processes should be accelerated both in the first internal review phase by the supervision departments and in the enforcement phase. A formal 'exit meeting' involving on-site and off-site supervisors as well as the Enforcement Department, at the end of a supervisory cycle for an individual bank, could assist in ensuring timely and comprehensive follow-up of supervisory inspection findings. Over the next one or two years, the authorities should adopt guidelines that activate a progression to more severe supervisory and enforcement measures, according to objective and consistent criteria. This does not exclude taking additional action if the situation warrants.

BCP 23 states that banking supervisors must practice global consolidated supervision over their internationally active banking organizations, adequately monitoring and applying appropriate prudential norms to all aspects of the business conducted by these banking organizations worldwide, primarily at their foreign branches, joint ventures and subsidiaries. The IMF (2007) maintains that the BRSA should include in the supervision of a bank group its foreign affiliates of supervised entities on a fully consolidated basis, including assessing the potential risks, such as reputational and legal risks, on the parent bank emanating from the foreign operations.

BCP 24 states that a key component of consolidated supervision is establishing contact and information exchange with the various other supervisors involved, primarily host country supervisory authorities. According to the IMF (2007), the BRSA should develop informal or formal arrangements with foreign supervisors to ensure ongoing cooperation and information sharing.[22]

In short, the IMF (2007) indicates that vulnerabilities remain in the Turkish financial sector. The main risk factors relate to macroeconomic volatility, especially because of large current account deficits; risks from rapid credit expansion into new activities, such as housing, lending and credit cards; banks bearing large interest rate risk; banks bearing large sovereign risk; and lending in foreign currency, which still accounts for almost one-third of bank loans, exposing banks to foreign currency risk indirectly via credit risk. Thus, effective regulation, supervision and supporting infrastructure are needed to reduce the systemic impact of any shock that may impinge upon the financial system. We stress that supervision must keep up with rapid advances in banking practice, such as in risk modelling, and cover new forms of business, such as that of mortgage companies. The growing international connections of banks operating in Turkey may increase the need for domestic supervisors to cooperate intensively with counterparts abroad. As a result, the IMF (2007) recommends implementing all of the regulations of the new banking law; developing and implementing a comprehensive plan for the BRSA to supervise banks in line with the new legal and regulatory framework, including their risk management; reviewing and amending procedures for handling failing banks and ensuring active involvement of all relevant agencies, to guarantee timely and cost-effective action; and ensuring that foreign currency-linked domestic currency loans are subject to similar constraints as foreign currency loans.

During the 2008 crisis, Turkish banks seemed rather robust to unfavourable external shocks. This is neither surprising nor contradicts the validity of the points raised in the IMF report (2007). It should be pointed out that both the BRSA and the banks followed rather conservative strategies in the aftermath of the 2001 crisis. Banks were quite reluctant to take risks by broadening their corporate credit customer base, and securing conforming capital to risk-weighted assets ratios became their major concern. This behaviour was in line with the BRSA's intentions. As can be expected, when this 'recovery from crisis' attitude of the banking system was coupled with a rather positive global financial environment, the Turkish corporate sector increased its external borrowing considerably, notably after 2005. Banks responded to the 2008 crisis by further curbing their credits to the private sector, which may have contributed to the rather dramatic decline in Turkey's GDP in the first half of 2009. The sharp increase in the budget deficit coupled with central bank's policy of reducing interest rates, on the other hand, helped banks to sustain their profitability.

Conclusion

A crucial impediment to the efficient functioning of the banking sector is asymmetric information, which leads to adverse selection and moral hazard. The sector needs to be regulated. But, in general, each country has a different set of regulations and supervisory practices in place, and the countries often have little interest in each other's regulatory regimes or have little confidence in their quality. Thus, banks intending to establish abroad in different countries will have to incur the costs of complying with the various regulatory regimes of those countries. Because international norms can help reduce the costs of compliance, the Basel Core Principles for effective banking supervision were developed. Thus, countries intending to liberalize their banking sectors should give priority to achieving compliance with the Basel Core Principles for effective banking supervision. After achieving such compliance, a country could adopt at a later stage the EU banking legislation. The main reason is that this part of the *acquis* is highly complex and geared towards sophisticated financial markets.

In the case of Turkey, the analysis reveals that there is tremendous scope for the country to benefit from adopting and implementing first the Basel Core Principles for effective banking supervision and thereafter the legislative, regulatory and institutional framework of the EU banking system. If Turkey had adopted the Basel Core Principles for effective banking supervision after 1997 and had enforced these rules, the cost of the banking crisis faced in 2001 would have been much smaller than the estimated US$53.2 billion.

The 2008 crisis on the other hand led to the questioning of not only the ability of the supervisory authorities, especially in financially advanced economies as in the EU, but also the adequacy of the existing regulations and the theoretical ideas behind them. Although there is widespread agreement on the questions being asked along these lines, at this point of time the interested parties are far from coming to an agreement on a new regulatory framework and a new set of principles for coordinating the supervisory activities on the global scale.[23]

Appendix

Table A7.1 Basel Core Principles

Preconditions for effective banking supervision

1   An effective system of banking supervision will have clear responsibilities and objectives for each agency involved in the supervision of banking organizations. Each such agency should possess operational independence and adequate resources. A suitable legal framework for banking supervision is also necessary, including provisions relating to authorization of banking organizations and their ongoing supervision; powers to address compliance with laws and safety and soundness concerns; and legal protection for supervisors. Arrangements for sharing information between supervisors and protecting the confidentiality of such information should be in place

Licensing and structure

2   The permissible activities of institutions that are licensed and subject to supervision as banks must be clearly defined, and the use of the word 'bank' in names should be controlled as far as possible

3   The licensing authority must have the right to set criteria and reject applications for establishments that do not meet the standards set. The licensing process, at a minimum, should consist of an assessment of the banking organization's ownership structure, directors and senior management, its operating plan and internal controls, and its projected financial condition, including its capital base; where the proposed owner or parent organization is a foreign bank, the prior consent of its home country supervisor should be obtained

4   Banking supervisors must have the authority to review and reject any proposals to transfer significant ownership or controlling interests in existing banks to other parties

5   Banking supervisors must have the authority to establish criteria for reviewing major acquisitions or investments by a bank and ensuring that corporate affiliations or structures do not expose the bank to undue risks or hinder effective supervision

Prudential regulations and requirements

6   Banking supervisors must set prudent and appropriate minimum capital adequacy requirements for all banks. Such requirements should reflect the risks that the banks undertake, and must define the components of capital, bearing in mind their ability to absorb losses. At least for internationally active banks, these requirements must not be less than those established in the Basle Capital Accord and its amendments

7   An essential part of any supervisory system is the evaluation of a bank's policies, practices and procedures related to the granting of loans and making of investments and the ongoing management of the loan and investment portfolios

Continued on next page.

8   Banking supervisors must be satisfied that banks establish and adhere to adequate policies, practices and procedures for evaluating the quality of assets and the adequacy of loan loss provisions and loan loss reserves

9   Banking supervisors must be satisfied that banks have management information systems that enable management to identify concentrations within the portfolio and supervisors must set prudential limits to restrict bank exposures to single borrowers or groups of related borrowers

10   In order to prevent abuses arising from connected lending, banking supervisors must have in place requirements that banks lend to related companies and individuals on an arm's-length basis, that such extensions of credit are effectively monitored, and that other appropriate steps are taken to control or mitigate the risks

11   Banking supervisors must be satisfied that banks have adequate policies and procedures for identifying, monitoring and controlling country risk and transfer risk in their international lending and investment activities, and for maintaining appropriate reserves against such risks

12   Banking supervisors must be satisfied that banks have in place systems that accurately measure, monitor and adequately control market risks; supervisors should have powers to impose specific limits and/or a specific capital charge on market risk exposures, if warranted

13   Banking supervisors must be satisfied that banks have in place a comprehensive risk management process (including appropriate board and senior management oversight) to identify, measure, monitor and control all other material risks and, where appropriate, to hold capital against these risks

14   Banking supervisors must determine that banks have in place internal controls that are adequate for the nature and scale of their business. These should include clear arrangements for delegating authority and responsibility; separation of the functions that involve committing the bank, paying away its funds, and accounting for its assets and liabilities; reconciliation of these processes; safeguarding its assets; and appropriate independent internal or external audit and compliance functions to test adherence to these controls and to applicable laws and regulations

15   Banking supervisors must determine that banks have adequate policies, practices and procedures in place, including strict 'know-your-customer' rules that promote high ethical and professional standards in the financial sector and prevent the bank being used, intentionally or unintentionally, by criminal elements

Methods of ongoing banking supervision

16   An effective banking supervisory system should consist of some form of both on-site and off-site supervision

17   Banking supervisors must have regular contact with bank management and thorough understanding of the institution's operations

18   Banking supervisors must have a means of collecting, reviewing and analyzing prudential reports and statistical returns from banks on a solo and consolidated basis

19   Banking supervisors must have a means of independent validation of supervisory information either through on-site examinations or use of external auditors

20   An essential element of banking supervision is the ability of the supervisors to supervise the banking group on a consolidated basis

Information requirements

21   Banking supervisors must be satisfied that each bank maintains adequate records, drawn up in accordance with consistent accounting policies and practices that enable the supervisor to obtain a true and fair view of the financial condition of the bank and the profitability of its business, and that the bank publishes on a regular basis financial statements that fairly reflect its condition.

Formal powers of supervisors

22   Banking supervisors must have at their disposal adequate supervisory measures to bring about timely corrective action when banks fail to meet prudential requirements (such as minimum capital adequacy ratios), when there are regulatory violations, or where depositors are threatened in any other way. In extreme circumstances, this should include the ability to revoke the banking licence or recommend its revocation

Cross-border banking

23   Banking supervisors must practice global consolidated supervision over their internationally active banking organizations, adequately monitoring and applying appropriate prudential norms to all aspects of the business conducted by these banking organizations worldwide, primarily at their foreign branches, joint ventures and subsidiaries

24   A key component of consolidated supervision is establishing contact and information exchange with the various other supervisors involved, primarily host country supervisory authorities

25   Banking supervisors must require the local operations of foreign banks to be conducted to the same high standards as are required of domestic institutions and must have powers to share information needed by the home country supervisors of those banks for the purpose of carrying out consolidated supervision

---

Source: Basel Committee on Banking Supervision (1997).

8 Maritime freight transport sector policy reform[1]

High transport costs resulting from inefficiencies in transport services and poor transportation conditions are an obstacle to trade, and they impede the realization of gains from trade liberalization. On the other hand, efficient transportation services contribute to a country's ability to participate in global trade and enhance the economic development of the country. As the elimination of inefficiencies in transport services and the improvement of transportation infrastructure can be achieved to a large extent by liberalizing the sector, countries try to implement the required policy reforms in the sector.

In this chapter, the maritime freight transport sector is considered. Observing that barriers to trade in this sector are regulatory in nature, that countries often have little interest in each other's regulatory regimes or little confidence in their quality, and that countries are generally reluctant to modify their own regulatory regimes, it is noted that the achievement of liberalization faces difficulties. As maritime transport is inherently international in character, and vessels on most voyages must operate under the regulatory requirements of many jurisdictions, there is an inherent need for harmonization across countries. Thus, to liberalize the sector, countries need to adopt not only international norms, but, in the case of regional integrations, also the rules and regulations of countries with stricter policies. Furthermore, liberalization requires the removal of any legal or administrative provisions restricting market access in maritime transport services.

The chapter is structured as follows. The international regulatory regime is studied in the first section, followed by a study of the regulatory regime in the European Union (EU). Here, it is noted that the EU has adopted most of the international rules and regulations and that the EU rules and regulations are much stricter than the international ones. Next, we discuss Turkish maritime rules and regulations, and, finally, the chapter ends with some concluding remarks.

Maritime transport services

Maritime transport services consist of three types of activities: (1) international maritime transport, that is, the actual transportation service performed from the time that a commodity is on board a ship in one country until the moment that the vessel reaches the destination port of a different state, (2) maritime auxiliary services, that is, any activities related to cargo manipulation in ports and on ships and (3) port services, that is, activities related solely to ship management in ports (Fink *et al.* 2002).

Because of differences in commodity types and technological improvements in the shipping industry, international maritime freight transport has developed specialized branches. For instance, a clear distinction must be drawn between liner shipping and bulk shipping. Liner shipping is regular shipping with set schedules in different harbours published in advance. The liner fleet includes container ships, reefers (refrigerated vessels), roll-on/roll-off ('ro-ro', where trucks and trailers are driven onto ships) and multipurpose vessels and cargoes, which are transported for several shippers simultaneously. The capital-intensive character of liner shipping, particularly container shipping, has led to a substantial degree of concentration. As emphasized by the United Nations Conference on Trade and Development (UNCTAD 2006), the top 20 liner operators, 11 of which are based in Asia, accounted for 67 per cent of the capacity in 2004. In contrast, non-liner shipping is performed irregularly and is provided on a demand basis, predominantly by specialized bulk carriers. Vessels carry unpacked dry carriages (iron, grain) or liquid cargoes (oil, gas), and bulk shipping operations are carried out for individual shippers. Compared with liner shipping, there is less concentration in bulk shipping, and there are many small owners with fleets of one or two vessels. Although non-liner tankers and bulk carriers dominate in terms of trade volume, liner vessels are far more significant in value terms, as they tend to carry relatively high-value and low-volume cargoes (Kang and Findlay 2000; WTO 1998b, 2001b).

A principal organizational feature of the liner sector is the ability of operators to enter into cooperative arrangements and agreements with the organization of 'conferences'. According to the Organization for Economic Co-operation and Development (OECD 2001), there are over 300 liner conferences worldwide. As one of the oldest in the world, shipping cartels commonly involve collusion to set prices and limit competition among members. Closed conferences not only set freight rates, which apply to all members, but also allocate cargo quotas and restrict membership, whereas open conferences merely set the freight rates on a specific route.[2] A recent development in the sector has been the supplementation of conferences with verbal agreements and similar arrangements. Compared with independent shipping operations, conferences are expected to determine the fleet capacity, create scale economies, prevent unexpected fluctuations in freight rates, limit competition between members and generate higher profits. However, it is usually argued that, even if conferences create cost savings, the savings are not always passed on to shippers, consumers or producers of shipped commodities. Conferences usually cause increased shipping rates and establish market power for their members, thereby restricting the entry of newcomers and delaying improvement in the quality of shipping services.

The prevalence of conferences flows directly from the exemption they enjoy under the anti-trust laws of the United States, the EU and many countries.[3] Under these systems, shipping conferences are considered necessary to ensure stability and certainty in the movement of freight. But, in recent years, the power of conferences has eroded. Containerization has made it possible for outsiders to supply the same services as conferences at a lower cost to consumers. Non-conference lines offering independent, semi- or full container services at a frequency varying between weekly and fortnightly have emerged and are based mainly in the newly industrializing economies of East Asia. The WTO (2001b) reports that the share of non-conference lines in the world liner shipping market is about 50 per cent.

Nevertheless, the bulk traffic is organized as a spot market, and contracts are allocated on an extremely competitive basis. As pointed out by the WTO (2001b), business is won on the basis of freight rates a few cents per tonne lower than the competitor. Hence, bulk shipping services and related freight rates respond to market developments and to supply and demand pressures. Bulk shipping pools are occasionally created, but they fail to survive for long periods.[4] In addition, these pools are not generally exempted from competition policy laws and, therefore, are dealt with by competition agencies in the same way as other commercial activities.

Another organizational feature of the maritime transport sector is the existence of classification societies. Classification societies make rules for ship construction and maintenance and issue a 'class certificate' to reflect compliance. They arose from the efforts of insurers to establish that the vessels for which they were writing insurance were sound.[5] Classification societies have no legal authority. Today, they mainly aim to enhance the safety of life and property at sea by securing high technical standards of design, manufacture, construction and maintenance of mercantile and non-mercantile ships. More than 50 organizations worldwide define their activities as providing marine classification. Ten of those organizations form the International Association of Classification Societies (IACS).[6] It is estimated that these ten societies, together with the additional society that was accorded associate status by IACS, collectively class the ships dealing with more than 90 per cent of all commercial tonnage involved in international trade worldwide.[7] The voluntary nature of classification implies that classification societies compete with each other to offer attractive classification services to ship owners. In general, the services offered fall into two major categories, namely developing rules and implementing them. The societies continuously update the rules to reflect changes in maritime technology, and they are responsible for the application of the rules, including a technical inspection of the plans of the ship, surveys during construction and periodic surveys for the maintenance of class.

Turning to the consideration of maritime auxiliary and port services, it is noted that seaports offer many different services. According to Trujillo and Nombela (1999), seaport activities can be divided into: (1) infrastructure, (2) services provided by ports, which require the use of infrastructure, and (3) coordination between different activities performed at ports. Infrastructure consists of the infrastructure within ports (berths, quays, docks and storage yards) and the superstructure (sheds, fuel tanks, office buildings, cranes, van carriers and transtainers). Besides the provision of basic infrastructure for the transfer of goods between sea and land, ports provide numerous services to ships, such as pilotage, towing, tying, cargo handling, freezing, administrative paperwork, permits, cleaning, refuse collection and repair facilities. As many different activities are performed simultaneously within the limited space of port areas, there is a need for an agent to act as coordinator to ensure the proper use of common facilities and to oversee the safety of port facilities. In most seaports, these functions are performed by the port authority, which is usually a public organization.

There are three main organizational modes for seaports. Under the so-called 'landlord ports' system, the port authority owns and manages port infrastructure, and private firms provide the rest of the port and maritime auxiliary services. Private firms are able to own superstructures and operate assets pertaining to infrastructure by concession or licensing. Under a 'tool ports' system, the port authority owns both the infrastructure and superstructure, but private firms provide services by renting port assets through concessions or licences. Finally, under the 'service ports' regime, the port authority owns assets and supplies services by directly hiring employees.

International maritime laws are developed by the participation of flag and port states in treaties or conventions. International conventions set out agreed objectives for legislation on particular issues, such as maritime safety, pollution control and the conditions of seafarers' employment. They provide internationally accepted templates from which individual flag states can develop their own national maritime legislation. By so doing, it is hoped that most countries will have the same laws on key maritime transport issues, so that major inconsistencies between national maritime legislations are avoided. Consultation, drafting, the adoption of drafts, the opening for signature by governments and ratification by countries were the major steps in creating a maritime convention in which several United Nations (UN) agencies and the OECD are involved. At the global level, the maritime industry is principally regulated by the International Maritime Organization (IMO), which is a small UN agency responsible for the safety of life at sea and the protection of the marine environment.[8] The International Labour Organization (ILO) is responsible for the development of labour standards applicable to seafarers worldwide.[9] The third UN agency that deals with international shipping conventions is the Shipping Committee of UNCTAD. Finally, the WTO's General Agreement on Tariffs and Trade (GATT) commitments, the ongoing services negotiations at the WTO, and the Maritime Transport Committee (MTC) of the OECD provide important forums for the liberalization of maritime services.[10]

The shipping industry is controlled by a web of national and international regulations and practices. Overall, these regulations and practices can be classified, following the approach of the OECD (2001), under two broad headings: (1) regulations related to commercial operations and practices and (2) regulations related to the rights and obligations of states and to safety and environmental regulations.

Regulations related to commercial operations and practices

Regulations related to commercial operations and practices include shipping-specific economic policy regulations, ship registration conditions, cargo reservation/cargo sharing provisions, cabotage laws, cargo liability regimes, national security measures, competition legislation and seaport industry. These regulations reflect a more pragmatic rationale, aimed at giving effect to government policies, achieving economic or national objectives and ensuring national participation or simply regulating commercial activities. Although some regulations (such as competition or anti-trust laws) are intended to free up the market, the majority probably distort or interfere with the market to some degree.

In the case of liner shipping, the basic regulatory framework among OECD countries consists of the Code of Liberalization of Current Invisible Operations (the Code) and the Common Shipping Principles (OECD 2000, 2009a). The Code was formally adopted by the Council of the OECD in 1961. Under the Code, members are obliged to eliminate restrictions on current invisible transactions and transfers relating to maritime transport operations, such as harbour services, repair and chartering. According to Note 1 to Annex A of the Code, the provisions of maritime freights are intended to give residents of a member state the unrestricted opportunity to avail themselves of and pay for all services in connection with international maritime transport that are offered by residents of any other member state. These provisions include chartering, harbour expenses, disbursements for fishing vessels, all means of maritime transport including harbour services (bunkering and provisioning, maintenance, repairs, expenses for crews) and other items that have a direct or indirect bearing on international maritime transport. As the shipping policy of the governments of the members is based on the principle of free circulation of shipping in international trade in free and fair competition, it follows that the freedom of transactions and transfers in connection with maritime transport should not be hampered by measures in exchange control, by legislative provisions in favour of the national flag, by arrangements made by governmental or semi-governmental organizations giving preferential treatment to national flag ships, by preferential shipping clauses in trade agreements, by the operation of import and export licensing systems so as to influence the flag of the carrying ship, or by discriminatory port regulations or taxation measures. The aim is to ensure that liberal and competitive commercial and shipping practices and procedures are followed in international trade and that normal commercial considerations alone determine the method and flag of shipment. Thus, the Code generally obliges OECD members to refrain from introducing and maintaining legislation or other measures in favour of national flag vessels within the OECD; the OECD member states, by having subscribed to the Code, are generally obliged to eliminate barriers to free trade in maritime transport services.

The Common Shipping Principles, adopted by the Council of the OECD in 1987, lay down a common approach to international shipping policy and practices among OECD members based on the following principles: (1) the maintenance of open trade and free competitive access to international shipping operations,

(2) a coordinated response to external pressure based on full consultations among member countries, (3) the role and recognition of governmental involvement by member countries to preserve free competitive access and the provision of choice to shippers and (4) a common approach to the application of competition policy to the liner shipping sector. These principles were reviewed in the late 1990s, and a modified version extending and adding to the 13 principles was formally adopted by the OECD Council in September 2000.[11] Principle 14 deals with maritime auxiliary services and provides that access to and use of these services shall be non-discriminatory. Principle 15 acknowledges the importance of international multimodal transport services involving a sea leg and stipulates non-discriminatory treatment in access to and use of those services as well as a free and fair competitive environment with regard to their provision. Finally, Principle 16 deals with measures related to safety, the environment and the prevention of substandard shipping.

The OECD is also involved in the liberalization of maritime services on a regional basis. OECD members signed an 'understanding on common shipping policy principles' in 1993 with the republics of the former Soviet Union and Central and Eastern Europe, largely modelled on the common shipping policy principles discussed above. OECD members have begun a dialogue with the Dynamic Non-Member Economies (DNME): Argentina, Brazil, Chile, Hong Kong China, the Republic of Korea, Malaysia, Singapore and Chinese Taipei. This dialogue is aimed at the promotion of free access to international maritime trade, respectful of the principle of free and fair competition on a commercial basis, the promotion of maritime safety, the protection of the marine environment, the need to prevent the operation of substandard vessels and to improve the training of seagoing personnel, and the promotion of modern business technologies such as electronic data interchange.

An important category of barriers that have been applied to international maritime transport is the various cargo reservation schemes. These require that part of the cargo carried in trade with other states must be transported only by ships carrying the national flag or interpreted as national by other criteria. These policies have typically been justified by either security or economic concerns. Cargo reservation can be imposed unilaterally, if ships flying national flags are given the exclusive right to transport a specified share of the cargo passing through the country's ports, through cargo sharing with trade partner countries on the basis of bilateral or multilateral agreements, or through a specific form of cargo reservation scheme. In the last case, the governments of two or more countries may decide to distribute cargo arising from their common trade, so that each national flag fleet is granted a significant share. Ships belonging to other countries are allowed access to a small share or, in some cases, no share at all.

It was mentioned above that a principle feature of the liner sector is the ability of operators to enter into cooperative arrangements and agreements. To counteract the anti-competitive actions of liner conferences at the multilateral level, the UN Convention on a Code of Conduct for Liner Conferences was adopted in 1974 (United Nations 1974). The so-called UN Liner Code, which entered into force in

1983 by its ratification by more than 70 countries, applies only to liner conferences in trades between contracting states and embraces a self-regulatory philosophy for 'closed' conference shipping operations. The Code establishes a framework within which conferences should operate in trades between contracting states and grants certain rights to those conferences, but at the same time it imposes certain obligations upon them, thereby protecting shipper interests. The Liner Code is best known for its cargo-sharing formula of 40:40:20, which suggests that cargo between member countries be divided, with 40 per cent of cargo being carried by vessels of the country of origin, 40 per cent by vessels of the country of destination and 20 per cent by cross-trading vessels. It should be noted that the 20 per cent figure, and therefore the '40:40', is recommended only. However, two important qualifications need to be made about this provision. First, the provisions concern conference trades only, not the totality of the liner trade. Second, it is for conferences themselves, not governments, to determine the allocation of the cargo shares between conference members. Governments have no part to play in that allocation. Countries opposing the convention do so for a variety of reasons. Some reasons are that cargo sharing leads to inefficiencies, reduced competition, reduction in shipper choice and, ultimately, higher freight rates. It is contended that shipper protection could be provided more efficiently through national legislation and that ratification of this convention would be inconsistent with OECD obligations and would run counter to existing competition legislation. Despite having been in force for more than 25 years, the convention is of limited economic relevance, as numerous countries have not complied with it.

The primary legal authority governing the activities of merchant ships is the state in which the ship is registered, the flag state. It is responsible for regulating all aspects of the commercial and operational performance of the ship. By registering in a particular country, the ship and its owner become subject to the laws of this flag state. That is, registration makes the ship an extension of national territory while it is at sea. Therefore, for ship owners, the choice of register is a major issue that may have important consequences in terms of: (1) tax, applicable company law and financial law, (2) compliance with maritime safety conventions, (3) crewing and terms of employment and (4) naval protection. Besides national registers, however, there are also open, or international, registers. International registers aim to offer terms that are favourable to an international ship owner.[12] Furthermore, in some cases, it is also possible for a ship owner to register a ship under two different flags. All of these alternatives – to register a ship in one or two national registers or simply in an open register – force ship owners to carefully weigh the relative advantages and disadvantages of each possibility. In general, the restrictions that apply to ship registration set maximum allowable stakes in a ship permitted for foreign nationals/corporate bodies, or minimum levels that must be owned by domestic interest. Many also require that the person or organization owning that ship should have their principle place of business located within their own country or that certain senior management posts within the owning company be filled by nationals.

In an effort to reserve the largest possible share of the country's seaborne trade, foreign firms are sometimes restricted from entering or operating in the domestic market. Ships engaged in cabotage, referring to the transportation of commodities between ports of the same country, have been required to be manned by the country's own citizens, either wholly or majority owned by domestic nationals, and built at domestic shipyards or registered under the national flag. In return, owners operating ships on cabotage routes have not had to compete with foreign flag vessels.

Finally, it should be noted that relevant negotiations at the WTO in Geneva with respect to the opening of maritime transport service markets are, as emphasized by the WTO Secretariat (2001b), of significant relevance to the fortunes of shipping. These negotiations proved difficult because of the complex and diverse nature of the sector. The first issue negotiators had to deal with during the Uruguay Round was to decide which subsectors and activities could be covered in the schedule for maritime transport services. It was decided that negotiations should cover the three pillars international maritime transport, maritime auxiliary services, and access to and use of port services. The first pillar, international maritime transport, was recognized as being relatively liberal, although important aspects still needed to be addressed, such as national cargo reservation and unilateral retaliatory measures. During the Uruguay Round, considerable attention was given to the second pillar, maritime auxiliary services, including cargo handling and storage services and providing services to ships while in their berths. It was recognized that this was a sector with considerable scope for liberalization. The third pillar, access to and use of port services, covered all other services provided to ships while accessing and berthing in ports, for example towage.

During the Uruguay Round of multilateral trade negotiations, there was considerable discussion as to whether multimodal transport should be added to the negotiations as a fourth pillar. During negotiations in the specialized Negotiating Group on Maritime Transport Services, it was stressed that door-to-door services would play an increasing role in international shipping. The aim was to ensure that a multimodal transport operator should be able to rent or lease lorries, railway trucks, barges and related equipment for inland cargo transport, and operators should have access to, and use of, these facilities on reasonable and non-discriminatory terms and conditions. Hence, it was argued that multimodal transport should be considered a fourth pillar to the schedule. Other countries have pointed out, however, that multimodal transport involves regulatory regimes (such as road and rail transport) that go beyond the maritime transport sector and that, as such, it should not be incorporated into the schedules.

Negotiations on maritime transport services at the WTO aimed to improve commitments in international shipping, auxiliary services and access to and use of port facilities through eliminating restrictions within a fixed time scale. Although negotiations were scheduled to end in 1996, little progress has been achieved until now. Participants failed to agree on a package of commitments. Lately, talks have resumed. As of 2009, some commitments exist in certain countries' schedules covering the three main areas of maritime services.[13]

In the case of seaports, public budgets have been used until recently to finance the construction of most large infrastructure. Generally, public port authorities have financed the costs of maintenance and repairs for infrastructure, and the port authority itself has been financed with a combination of public funds and tariffs and fees exacted from private firms operating in the port. With the increase in private participation in the operation of seaports, the landlord port became the most desirable category for the operation of seaports from an efficiency standpoint, as it allows private enterprises and market forces to play a role in the supply of services while preventing the monopolization of essential assets by private firms. Trujillo and Nombela (1999) and Clark *et al.* (2001) maintain that the type of economic regulation changes with the size of seaport. For small and large local ports that do not require more than a general cargo terminal, it is possible to consider the introduction of some form of competition among those firms that are willing to operate in the port. Once a single operator is chosen, it is necessary to have some regulation over the charges that this firm imposes on port users as, otherwise, it would enjoy a monopoly position. The regulatory authority could mainly use price-cap systems or a rate-of-return type of regulation. On the other hand, in cases of larger seaports, one could introduce competition within the port. If a large port is divided into several independent terminals, it is possible to induce competition between operators for the traffic that calls at the port. In such a case, regulation of prices is less of an issue. However, some form of supervision would be needed, as the parties could collude because of their small numbers.[14]

Regulations related to safety and environment

The regulations on safety and environmental protection are generally based on UN conventions such as the UN Convention of the Law of the Sea of 1982 (UNCLOS) (United Nations 1982). According to this convention, the flag state has primary legal responsibility for the ship in terms of regulating safety and environment, while the coastal state also has limited legal rights over any ship sailing in its waters. The limits of the rights of the coastal states to enforce their own laws are defined by dividing the sea into four 'zones', each of which is treated differently from a legal point of view: (1) the territorial sea, which is the strip of water closest to the shore, (2) the contiguous zone, which is a strip of water to the seaward of the territorial sea, (3) the exclusive economic zone, which is a belt of sea extending up to 200 miles from the legally defined shoreline and (4) the high sea, which nobody owns. On the high seas, all vessels enjoy, in principle, freedom of navigation under the exclusive jurisdiction of their flag state (UNCLOS Articles 87, 89 and 92). Although the high seas are free from sovereignty claims by individual nations, the intensity of state control over the waters increases landwards. In the exclusive economic zone, the coastal state enjoys considerable sovereign exploration, exploitation, conservation and management rights, as stipulated in UNCLOS Articles 56 and 60. Despite the existence of sovereign exploitation and related jurisdictional rights of the coastal state in the exclusive economic zone, the freedom of navigation under Article 58 applies in this zone, albeit with a number of explicit and implicit restrictions. Article 3 stipulates that coastal states have the right to enforce international laws and their own laws on safe navigation and pollution in a territorial area with a maximum width of 12 nautical miles. The coastal states have limited powers to enforce customs, fiscal and immigration laws in the contiguous zone, and in the exclusive economic zone they have the power to enforce only oil pollution regulations.

As an international maritime transport service involves the movement of goods by vessel from the port of one country to the port of another country, access to ports is an indispensable element of any international shipping service. Access includes the loading and unloading of cargo, the embarking and disembarking of passengers, the taking on board of fuel and supplies and even the possibility of conducting trade. As emphasized by Parameswaran (2004), it is a basic condition for the smooth operation of the international maritime transport industry that merchant vessels from all nations are permitted unhampered access to and the efficient use of ports. The 1923 Geneva Ports Convention and the Statute annexed thereto secures freedom of communication by guaranteeing in the maritime ports, under the sovereignty and authority of the parties and for purposes of international trade, equality of treatment among the ships of all contracting states, their cargoes and their passengers (League of Nations 1923).

The 1982 Paris Memorandum of Understanding (MOU) on Port State Control aims to eliminate the operation of substandard ships through a harmonized system of port state control (Secretariat of the Paris Memorandum on Port State Control 1982). Ships are selected for inspection according to the Paris MOU targeting system. Only internationally accepted conventions are enforced during port state control inspections. When serious deficiencies are found, the ship is detained. The captain is instructed to rectify the deficiencies before departure. Flag states that are not a party to conventions receive no more favourable treatment. The results of each inspection are recorded in the central database, located in Saint-Malo, France. Their periodically updated black-grey-white lists, which show the degree of riskiness of individual ships from different flag states, have become one of the major indicators of the safeness and environmental friendliness of national shipping fleets within the last decade.

The IMO has adopted a comprehensive framework of detailed technical regulations in the form of international conventions that govern the safety of ships and the protection of the marine environment. National governments, which form the membership of IMO, are required to implement and enforce these international rules and to ensure that the ships registered under their national flags comply. The majority of IMO conventions fall into three main categories. The first group is concerned with maritime safety, the second with the prevention of marine pollution and the third with liability and compensation, especially in relation to damage caused by pollution. Outside these major groupings are a number of other conventions dealing with facilitation, tonnage measurement, unlawful acts against shipping and salvage.

The level of ratification and enforcement of the IMO conventions is generally high, in comparison with international rules adopted for shore-based industries.

The principal responsibility for enforcing IMO regulations concerning ship safety and environmental protection rests with the flag states. Flag states enforce IMO requirements through inspections of ships conducted by a network of international surveyors. Much of this work is delegated to classification societies. However, flag state enforcement is supplemented by what is known as Port State Control, whereby officials in any country that a ship may visit can inspect foreign flag ships to ensure that they comply with international requirements.

Among the IMO conventions, the International Convention for the Safety of Life at Sea (SOLAS), which entered into force in 1980, covers a wide range of measures to improve the safety of shipping (International Maritime Organization 1974). The provisions of the convention cover the design and stability of passenger and cargo ships, machinery and electrical installations, life protection, life-saving appliances, navigational safety and the carriage of dangerous goods. In 1990, the International Safety Management Code was incorporated into the SOLAS regulations (International Maritime Organization 1993a). The Code requires shipping companies to develop, implement and maintain a Safety Management System, which includes company safety, environmental policy and written procedures to ensure the safe operation of ships and the protection of the environment. The Code has been effectively enforced as its violation could result in detention of the vessel by port authorities and denial of permission for the ship to enter its intended port of call, as well as fines.

The IMO recently adopted comprehensive maritime security measures at the Conference of Contracting Governments to the International Convention for the Safety of Life at Sea. The Conference, held at the end of 2002, adopted a number of amendments to the 1974 SOLAS, the most far-reaching of which enshrines the new International Ship and Port Facility Security Code (ISPS Code) (International Maritime Organization 2002). The Code contains detailed security-related requirements for governments, port authorities and shipping companies in a mandatory section, together with a series of guidelines about how to meet these requirements in a second, non-mandatory section. The Conference also adopted a series of resolutions designed to add weight to the amendments, to encourage the application of the measures to ships and port facilities not covered by the Code and to pave the way for future work on the subject.

The International Convention for the Prevention of Pollution from Ships (MARPOL), adopted in 1973, deals with all forms of marine pollution except the disposal of land-generated waste (International Maritime Organization 1973). It covers such matters as the definition of violations, special rules on the inspection of ships, enforcement and reports on incidents involving harmful substances. It should be noted that most oil tankers are currently of 'single hull' design. In such vessels, oil in the cargo tanks is separated from the seawater only by a bottom and a side plate. Should this plate be damaged as a result of collision or stranding, the contents of the cargo tanks risk spilling into the sea and causing serious pollution. An effective way to avoid this risk is to surround the cargo tanks with a second internal plate at a sufficient distance from the external plate. This design, known as a 'double hull', protects cargo tanks against damage and thus reduces the risk of pollution. Following the *Exxon Valdez* accident in 1989, the United States unilaterally imposed double hull requirements on both new and existing oil tankers according to vessel age limits and deadlines for the phasing out of single hull oil tankers. Faced with this unilateral action on the part of the United States to impose double hull requirements on both new and existing oil tankers during the 1990s, the IMO established double hull standards in 1992 through MARPOL. This convention requires all oil tankers with a deadweight tonnage (DWT) of 600 tonnes or more, as delivered from July 1996, to be constructed with a double hull or an equivalent design. Therefore, no single hull tankers of this size have been constructed since this date. It also requires that single hull tankers with a deadweight tonnage of 20,000 tonnes or more, and delivered before 6 July 1996, comply with the double hull standards at the latest by the time that they are 25 or 30 years old, depending on whether or not they have segregated ballast tanks.

It has long been recognized that limitations on the draught to which a ship may be loaded make a significant contribution to its safety. These limits are set in the form of freeboards. In the 1966 International Convention on Load Lines, adopted by the IMO in 1996, provisions are made determining the freeboard of tankers by subdivision and damage stability calculations (International Maritime Organization 1966). The regulations account for the potential hazards present in different zones and different seasons. The technical annex contains several additional safety measures concerning doors, freeing ports, hatchways and other items. The main purpose of these measures is to ensure the watertight integrity of a ship's hull below the freeboard deck. All assigned load lines must be marked midship on each side of the ship, together with the deck line.

The 1978 International Convention on Standards of Training, Certification and Watchkeeping for Seafarers was the first to establish basic requirements on an international level (International Maritime Organization 1978). The convention prescribes minimum standards relating to training, certification and watchkeeping for seafarers that countries are obliged to meet or exceed.

Because of the unique character of seafaring, most maritime countries have special laws and regulations for seafarers. In addition, the ILO has adopted over 60 maritime labour standards during the past 75 years. The standards adopted specifically for seafarers cover a multitude of questions: minimum age of entry to employment, recruitment and replacement, medical examination, articles of agreement, repatriation, holidays with pay, social security, hours of work and rest periods, crew accommodation, identity documents, occupational safety and health, welfare at sea and in ports, continuity of employment, vocational training and certificates of competency. Among the ILO conventions, one of the most important international labour agreements is ILO Convention No. 147, which sets minimal acceptable standards of safety and health, social security and living and working conditions of seafarers (International Labour Office 1976). Additionally, ILO Convention No. 180, adopted in 1996, aims to promote the health and safety of workers, improve maritime safety and protect the marine environment (International Labour Office 1996). The convention establishes limits on seafarers' hours of work or rest on board ship, requiring a maximum of 14 hours work per day and 72 hours per week for seafarers on board ship, with minimum rest periods of ten hours daily and 77 hours weekly.

EU rules and regulations on the maritime sector

Europe, with thousands of kilometres of coastline, is surrounded by a number of islands, including island-states. The EU, surrounded by five seas and one ocean, has the world's largest maritime territory, while, today, the maritime regions of Europe account for nearly half of the EU's population and GDP. In total, 22 out of 27 EU members are coastal states. After Romania and Bulgaria joined the EU, EU borders extended to the Black Sea. Within the enlarged EU there are now more than 1,000 ports situated near industrial and population centres, representing the largest concentration of ports in the world. Because over 90 per cent of EU external trade travels by sea, and more than 1 billion tonnes of freight a year are loaded and unloaded in EU ports, maritime transport is of fundamental importance to Europe. Shipping is the most important mode of transport in terms of volume.

EU maritime transport legislation aims to apply the EC Treaty's principle of free movement of services to the EU's sea transport industry and its compliance with competition rules. Thus, it aims to improve the functioning of the internal market in maritime services by promoting safe, efficient, environmentally sound and user-friendly maritime transport services. The maritime transport *acquis* relates to market liberalization, technical and safety standards, security, social standards and state aid control in the context of the internal maritime transport market.

The main international rules that regulate commercial operations and practices and safety at sea have been transposed into Community law, which ensures that they have legal force and uniform application throughout the member states.[15] In this context, it is noted that almost all of the EU-15 member states subscribe to the OECD's Code of Liberalization of Current Invisible Operations and the Common Shipping Principles.[16] Regarding the UN Convention on a Code of Conduct for Liner Conferences, it is noted that the Community is not a party to the Code, as, by providing for the allotment of freight on the basis of national shares, the Code was held to be contrary to the Treaty of Rome. In 1979, Regulation (EEC) No. 954/79 was adopted, requiring member states to enter a reservation while ratifying the convention, according to which member states had to open the national share granted under the Code to all ship owners established in the Community. On 25 September 2006, the Council adopted Regulation (EC) No. 1419/2006 repealing Regulation (EEC) No. 4056/86, which detailed rules for the application of Articles 85 and 86 of the EC Treaty to maritime transport. With the adoption of this regulation, shipping conferences would become unlawful on trades to/from ports of the Community at the end of a transitional period that expired on 18 October 2008. This implies that member states that were party to the Code would no longer be able to fulfil their obligations thereof, namely to ensure that their national shipping lines have the right to be members of conferences serving their foreign trade. Those member states would therefore have to withdraw from the Code of Conduct, and member states that are not party to the Code would no longer be able to ratify or accede to it. Furthermore, it is noted that the EU countries have ratified UNCLOS and joined the 1973 MARPOL convention amended in 1978, the 1974 SOLAS convention and the Load Lines conventions. The EU-15 countries have also subscribed to the Paris MOU, the International Convention on Standards of Training, Certification and Watchkeeping for Seafarers and the ILO conventions including Convention No. 147 and Convention No. 180. Finally, it should be emphasized that most of the EU-15 countries are party to the 1923 Geneva Ports Convention and the Statute annexed thereto.

When considering the EU rules and regulations on maritime transport services, it is noted that real progress towards the realization of a common maritime transport services market free of restrictions was achieved in the EU during the 1980s and 1990s. The 1986 maritime package consisting of a bundle of four EC regulations enabled the freedom to provide services to the maritime transport sector. These four regulations are basic regulations related to commercial operations and practices in the EU. Council Regulation (EEC) No. 4055/86 gives member state nationals (and non-Community shipping companies using ships registered in a member state and controlled by member state nationals) the right to carry passengers or goods by sea between any port of a member state and any port or offshore installation of another member state or of a non-Community country. Regulation No. 4056/86, which was repealed by Regulation (EC) No. 1419/2006, implements the EC competition rules within certain fields of maritime transport. Regulation (EEC) No. 4057/86, which entered into force on 1 June 1987, enables the EC to apply compensatory duties in order to protect ship owners in member states from unfair pricing practices on the part of non-Community ship owners. Concerned with anti-dumping in maritime transport, Regulation No. 4057/86 was adopted in order to respond to unfair pricing practices by non-member state ship owners engaged in international cargo liner shipping. Finally, it is noted that in cases in which a non-member state seeks to impose cargo-sharing arrangements on member states in liquid or dry bulk trades, the Council shall take the appropriate action, in accordance with Regulation (EEC) No. 4058/86, to safeguard free access to cargoes in ocean trades for shipping companies of member states or by ships registered in a member state.

It has been common practice in the majority of nations around the world to reserve a major part of the transport of goods and passengers between national ports to domestic fleets. In the EC, the southern member states have been reluctant to open up this sector to service suppliers from other EC member states. On the other hand, northern member states have insisted on easing national cabotage laws. A milestone in the process of liberalizing cabotage trades within EC member states has been achieved through the adoption of Council Regulation (EEC) No. 3577/92. It implements the freedom to provide services to the national maritime transport of EU member states, and provides for the progressive liberalization of cabotage restrictions. The regulation liberalizes maritime cabotage in countries in which that economic sector was reserved for nationals. Accordingly, freedom to operate between two ports in the same member state is offered to all Community ship owners, not only to national ship owners.

Regarding ship registration conditions, note that conditions vary among the EU countries. In Germany, registration in the German Ship Register is reserved to vessels owned by nationals of an EU member state or by companies having their place of business in an EU member state, and registration is a precondition for the right to fly the German flag. In Sweden, however, a ship is entitled to fly the Swedish flag if it is more than half-owned by a Swedish national or a Swedish legal entity. The Swedish national maritime administration may grant the right to fly the Swedish flag to other ships whose operation is essentially under Swedish control and whose owner has their permanent residence in Sweden.

It is noteworthy that the Commission has also taken steps regarding port policy. In 2001, the Commission adopted the communication 'Reinforcing Quality Service in Sea Ports: A Key for European Transport'.[17] The cornerstone of this communication was a proposal for a directive concerning market access to port services, the principles and objectives of which were confirmed by the White Paper on transport.[18] After almost three years of inter-institutional legislative process, at the end of the conciliation procedure, the European Parliament rejected the compromise text. The Commission, believing it necessary in the interests of operators, authorities and consumers to introduce specific and clear rules on access to the port services market, decided to bring forward a new proposal. The objective of the proposal is to ensure freedom to provide port services or carry out 'self-handling' at sea ports for EU providers of port services, subject to certain objective and relevant constraints, such as space or capacity available at the ports, the development policy of the port, maritime traffic security or safety requirements at certain ports, protection of the environment and 'public service requirements'.[19]

Turning to EU regulations on safety at sea, it is noted that the EU authorized 12 classification societies to carry out the inspection, survey and certification of ships via Commission Decision No. 2002/221/EC. In addition, Council Directive 95/21/EC passed in June 1995 aims to improve maritime safety in Community waters by banning substandard shipping. The directive applies to all merchant shipping and crews using a seaport of a member state or an offshore terminal or anchored off such a port or installation. Member states are obliged to establish and maintain national maritime administrations for the inspection of ships in their ports and in the waters under their jurisdiction. Each member state is obliged to inspect at least 25 per cent of the ships flying other countries' flags that enter its ports. Vessels inspected within the previous six months are exempt. Additionally, enhanced controls must be carried out on all oil tankers scheduled for phasing out within five years, all bulk carriers older than 12 years of age and all passenger ships and gas and chemical tankers over ten years old (counting from the date of construction represented on the ship's safety certificates). An obligation is placed on the member states to ensure that any deficiencies revealed in the course of the inspection are rectified and that conditions warranting detention of the ship are laid down.

Council Directive 93/75/EEC, signed on 13 September 1993, establishes minimum requirements for vessels bound for or leaving Community ports and carrying dangerous or polluting goods. Carriers must declare the loading of such goods in accordance with international regulations. This directive defines the information that the operator must supply to the relevant authorities of the member states to which the vessel is bound or from which it is leaving and the action to be taken in the event of an accident. That directive was repealed, however, by Directive 2002/59/EC, which establishes a Community vessel traffic monitoring and information system. The main objective of the new system is to enhance the safety and efficiency of maritime traffic; to improve the response of authorities to incidents, accidents or potentially dangerous situations at sea, including search and rescue operations; and to contribute to better prevention and detection of pollution by ships. Applicable to ships of 300 gross tonnage and upwards, the directive lists the information to be provided by operators, agents or masters of ship seeking to use Community ports. It also requires that all ships calling at a member state port be fitted, in accordance with a set timetable, with an AIS (identification of ships system) meeting IMO standards and a voyage data recorder system. In addition, the directive sets out rules for the notification of dangerous or polluting goods onboard ships, for the monitoring of hazardous ships and for intervention in the event of incidents and accidents at sea. When conducting any marine casualty or incident investigation, member states are required to comply with the provisions of the relevant IMO code.

Regarding the regulations on the environment, it is noted that Council Regulation (EC) No. 2978/94 of November 1994 governs the implementation of IMO Resolution A.747(18) on the application of tonnage measurement of ballast spaces in segregated ballast oil tankers (International Maritime Organization 1993b). The regulation aims to encourage the use of oil tankers fitted with segregated ballast capacity by requiring the community's port and pilotage authorities either to apply the recommendations of Resolution A.747(18) or to permit a system of rebates on dues, such as that provided for therein. Resolution A.747(18) invites governments to advise port authorities to apply to all tankers with segregated ballast tanks the recommendation of deducting the segregated ballast tank tonnage from the gross tonnage, whenever their dues are based on the latter, and to advise pilotage authorities to act in accordance with the same recommendation. Recent environmental catastrophes caused by oil spills in European waters have put the oil tanker sector under intense scrutiny. After the November 2002 sinking of the single hull oil tanker *Prestige*, the EU adopted straightforward measures. For example, it banned from entry into EU ports and offshore terminals under the jurisdiction of the EU member states single hull tankers carrying heavy grades of oil, and it accelerated the phasing out of single hull oil tankers calling at EU ports. Regulation (EC) No. 417/2002 aims to reduce the risk of accidental oil pollution in European waters by speeding up the phasing in of double hulls. The regulation applies to all tankers of 5,000 tonnes deadweight or above entering or leaving a port or offshore terminal or anchoring in an area under the jurisdiction of a member state, irrespective of their flag.

Directive 2000/59/EC on port reception facilities for ship-generated waste and cargo residues seeks to reduce the discharges from ships using ports in the Community of ship-generated waste and cargo residues into the sea, especially illegal discharges. By improving the availability and use of port reception facilities for ship-generated waste and cargo residues, the Community hopes to enhance the protection of the marine environment. Member states must ensure the availability of port reception facilities adequate to meet the needs of ships using the port. Costs will be borne by ships, and the system must provide no incentive for ships to discharge at sea. The purpose of Directive 2005/35/EC on ship-source pollution and on the introduction of penalties for infringements is to incorporate international standards for ship-source pollution into Community law and to ensure that persons responsible for discharges are subject to adequate penalties, in order to improve maritime safety and to enhance protection of the marine environment from pollution by ships.

Regulation (EC) No. 782/2003 prohibits organotin compounds on ships flying the flag or operating under the authority of a member state and on ships sailing to or from member state ports.[20] The purpose of the regulation is to reduce or eliminate the adverse effects of organotin compounds on the marine environment and on human health in general.

Finally, it is noted that Council Directive 1999/63/EC of June 1999 concerning the agreement on the organization of working time for seafarers was largely inspired by ILO Convention No. 180. The current directive is intended to enforce the European Agreement concluded in 1998 between the trade union and employers' organizations of the maritime transport sector concerning the working time of seafarers. The agreement, comprised in an annex to the directive, applies to seafarers on board every seagoing ship, whether publicly or privately owned, that is registered in the territory of a member state and is ordinarily engaged in commercial maritime operations. Hours of work and rest are laid down as follows: (1) the maximum hours of work must not exceed 14 hours in any 24-hour period or 72 hours in any seven-day period, and (2) the minimum hours of rest must not be fewer than ten hours in any 24-hour period or 77 hours in any seven-day period. Hours of rest may not be divided into more than two periods, one of which must be at least six hours in length, and the interval between consecutive periods of rest must not exceed 14 hours. Musters, firefighting and lifeboat drills and drills prescribed by national laws and international instruments must be conducted in a manner that minimizes the disturbance of rest periods. Provision is to be made for a compensatory rest period if a seafarer's normal period of rest is disturbed by call-outs. Seafarers are entitled to paid annual leave of at least four weeks, or a proportion thereof for periods of employment of less than one year. The minimum period of paid leave may not be replaced by an allowance in lieu. Seafarers under the age of 18 years are not permitted to work at night. In addition, no person under 16 years of age is allowed to work on a ship. All seafarers must possess a certificate attesting to their fitness for the work for which they are employed and have regular health assessments.

In 2007 the EU ratified the ILO 2006 Maritime Labour Convention (MLC), which consolidates and updates more than 65 international labour standards related to seafarers adopted over the last 80 years (International Labour Office 2006). The convention sets out seafarers' rights to decent conditions of work on a wide range of subjects, and aims to be globally applicable, easily understandable, readily updatable and uniformly enforced.

To guarantee the safe, secure and clean transport of maritime goods the EU set up in June 2002 the European Maritime Safety Agency with Regulation (EC) No. 1406/2002. Its main objective is to provide technical and scientific assistance to the European Commission and member states for the proper development and implementation of EU legislation on maritime safety, pollution by ships and security on board ships. On 11 March 2009 the European Parliament adopted the third maritime safety package. With the adoption of this package the EU delivered the message that substandard shipping would no longer be tolerated.

In October 2007 the European Commission adopted a communication setting out its vision for an Integrated Maritime Policy for the EU, together with a detailed action plan setting out a work programme for the years ahead.[21] In January 2009 the Commission presented its strategic objectives for the European maritime transport system up to 2018.[22] The communication identifies the key areas for action whereby action by the EU will strengthen the competitiveness of the sector while enhancing its environmental performance.

Turkish maritime rules and regulations

Turkey is a peninsula country surrounded by the Black Sea in the north, the Aegean Sea in the west and the Mediterranean in the south. It sits on important transport routes through the strategic waterways of the Istanbul (Bosporus) and Çanakkale (Dardanelles) Straits connecting the Black Sea and other northern countries to southern seas. Turkey's coastline is 8,300 km long, and the country's major industrial centres are on or near the sea. It is thus not surprising that 86 per cent of the quantity and more than 50 per cent of the value of goods traded by Turkey are transported over water. In 2005, the total freight handled in Turkish ports (excluding transit and cabotage cargo) was 182 million tonnes (55 million tonnes of exports and 127 million tonnes of imports). According to the WTO (2008), total loading and unloading in the maritime subsector including transit and cabotage cargo rose from 206 million tonnes to over 232 million tonnes in 2006, and, in 2006, container handling reached 3.9 million teu.[23] The share of Turkish flag vessels in total freight handled amounted to only 24 per cent, and Turkey's maritime fleet has been shrinking, mainly because of problems of financing and flag avoidance. Finally, it should be emphasized that the large public fleet was recently privatized.

In Turkey, all maritime-related decision- and policy-making activities, including signing international maritime conventions, are carried out by the Undersecretariat for Maritime Affairs. Maritime activities in Turkey are mainly subject to Turkish Commercial Law No. 6762, Cabotage Law No. 815, Law on Turkish International Ship Registry No. 4490 and Ports Law No. 618.

Regarding regulations on commercial operations and practices, it is noted that Turkey does not associate itself with the OECD Common Shipping Principles and has a reservation on Note 1 of the OECD Code of Liberalization of Current Invisible Operations. Turkey has signed the UN Liner Code but has not ratified it yet. Turkey has no laws and regulations governing the operation of liner conferences.

Until 1983, Turkish regulations required that all imports of public enterprises and public entities be transported by Turkish flag vessels. This restrictive policy was liberalized in 1983 by Decree 152, which stipulates that all imports for the account of public entities are to be carried on board Turkish flag vessels if the freight rate is not more than 10 per cent higher than that quoted by foreign operators. In contrast, according to the Cabotage Act, cabotage is reserved to national flag carriers, and maritime transport among Turkish ports is assigned to Turkish ships only. Furthermore, towage, pilotage and other services related to ports are executed only by Turkish ships.

According to the Law on Turkish International Flag Registration enacted in 2000, there are two different types of ships registry: the National Ship Registry (NSR) and the Turkish International Ship Registry (TISR). To fly the Turkish flag on the NSR, shipping companies must be 51 per cent owned by Turkish nationals, and first mates and masters of ships must be of Turkish nationality, while up to 40 per cent of the officers of ships engaged in international seaborne transportation, excluding cabotage, can be foreign nationals. Ships registered in the NSR benefit from cabotage rights. Ships that belong to legal persons, such as bodies, institutions, associations and foundations set up in accordance with Turkish law, the majority of whose boards of directors are of Turkish nationality, and ships that belong to trading companies, the majority of whose managerial staff and representatives are of Turkish nationality and are registered on the Turkish Trade Register, are considered Turkish. On the other hand, the TISR is open to foreign ships with foreign seafarers for seaborne transport, excluding cabotage. On Turkish flagged ships registered to the TISR, 49 per cent of the crew can be made up of foreign seafarers, provided that the first captain is a Turkish citizen. Ships registered to the TISR benefit from cabotage rights if the ship owner is a Turkish citizen, the majority of shares belong to Turkish citizens and the majority of partners are Turkish citizens. Finally, vessels rented by foreigners cannot operate inside Turkish coastal waters, and vessels rented by Turkish nationals are considered foreign vessels and may not fly the Turkish flag.

Regarding regulations on safety and the environment, Turkey is one of 38 states that have not signed UNCLOS. The Turkish flag is on the grey list of the Secretariat of the Paris MOU on Port State Control. According to the Commission of the European Communities, the percentage of Turkish flag vessels detained following Port State Control has decreased from 24.59 per cent in 2001 to 7.85 per cent in 2005.[24] Turkey is a signatory to many of the IMO rules and regulations. Although Turkey has ratified the MARPOL (mandatory Annexes I and II, and also Annex V) and SOLAS conventions and acceded some of the amending protocols, it has not ratified SOLAS Protocol 78, SOLAS Protocol 88 (International Convention for the Safety of Life at Sea), MARPOL Annexes III and IV (International Convention for the Prevention of Pollution from Ships), and Load Line 88. According to the Law on Environment No. 2872, discharge of pollutants from ships, ports and other coastal installations is prohibited, and fines for discharge from ships depend on the kind of pollutant. The law regulates obligations to establish port reception facilities and imposes penalties for violating these obligations. Furthermore, Part A and parts of Part B of the International Ship and Port Facility Security Code (ISPS Code) are applicable in Turkey, and technical studies to prepare a By-Law on Implementation of ISPS Code are underway. Finally, it should be emphasized that Turkey has fulfilled its international obligations under the SOLAS Convention/Chapter XI/2.

Turkey signed only 12 of the ILO conventions concerning seafarers and dockworkers. According to the Law on Maritime Labour No. 854, the working time of seafarers is eight hours in a day and 48 hours in a week. Working time is the time of work and watchkeeping. By-Law on Seafarers No. 24832 requires that minimum hours of rest shall not be fewer than ten hours in a day and 72 hours in a week. Daily hours of rest may be shortened because of musters and emergency cases. In that case, rest time shall not be fewer than six hours and this implementation shall not continue for more than two days. Turkey has ratified the 1978 International Convention on Standards of Training, Certification and Watchkeeping for Seafarers, and the Code is applicable. Finally, it is noted that Turkey has authorized ten classification societies (nine IACS members together with the Turkish Lloyd) to carry out the inspection, survey and certification of ships. But Turkish Lloyd has not been recognized by the EC. As a result, ships classed by Turkish Lloyd are subject to further inspection in Paris MOU ports because of targeting factors.[25]

In December 2003, Turkey adopted an ambitious five-year Maritime Transport Action Plan for the enhancement of maritime safety. This action plan sets out a road map for legislative alignment with the *acquis* on maritime safety, measures aimed at strengthening administrative structures (in the area of flag state and port state control) and training and equipment needs. Since January 2004, the Turkish Undersecretariat for Maritime Affairs has been conducting a broad legal and institutional harmonization project with the participation of Spain as an EU partner country (the 'twinning project'), to strengthen the Turkish institutional infrastructure on maritime transport in advance of Turkey's accession into the EU.

Turkey's major ports are owned by two state institutions: the Turkish State Railways (TCDD) and the Turkish Maritime Organization (TDI). TCDD owns and operates seven ports that have direct railway connections. The capacity of these ports is around 30 million tonnes per year, and about 90 per cent of all cargo passing through state-owned ports is handled by TCDD. Three ports operated by TCDD (Haydarpasa/Istanbul, Izmir and Mersin) can also handle container cargo (total container capacity of about 750,000 teu per year). Whereas the port of Haydarpasa is focused on import cargo, the ports of Izmir and Mersin are export oriented. The TDI owns 20 ports all around Turkey. TCDD ports offer a full range of services (pilotage and towage, stevedoring services, water supply, waste removal, handling services, equipment rental, etc.). TCDD sets tariffs, which may differ slightly among various ports. Akarsu and Kumar (2002: 6) mention that:

> the bulk of the income of TCDD ports is generated through stevedoring and storage services. Turkish ports are relatively expensive with close to 60 percent of the cost of port operation being attributable to port labour while the world average is only 30 percent.

According to the WTO (2008), the cost for a 20-foot container unit during 2004 in Turkey was, on average, 370 euros compared with 70 euros in Alexandria, Egypt and 210 euros in Rades, Tunisia. The Turkish ports suffer from insufficiency of port equipment, infrastructure and lack of computerization, causing delays in tracing cargo.

TCDD is one of the largest public sector enterprises in Turkey. In addition to the seven largest ports in Turkey, it manages rail transport and operates locomotive, wagon and coach manufacturing plants and repair workshops. Many researchers claim that TCDD cross-subsidizes its main activity, rail transport, by the revenue it generates from port operations. As stated by the World Bank (2004b):

> cross-subsidization of the railways by the ports' excess profits within TCCD suggests pervasive overcharging by the Port Authorities, or inadequate depreciation and maintenance schedules, or maybe both. Whatever the case, it is more than likely to result in non-optimal cost-efficiency in the delivery of port services. If overpricing is a reality, then it is at the expense of the country's external trade competitiveness and increased costs of imports. If inadequate depreciation and maintenance is occurring, then it will shortly result in decreasing service quality because of infrastructure wear and tear, which in turn will translate into additional costs for port customers in time, cargo losses, etc.

According to Turkish Ports Law No. 618, dated 20 April 1925, only Turkish citizens, and companies that are majority owned, managed and controlled by Turkish citizens, may exercise the rights related to the ports. Again, foreign ownership in companies involved in port undertakings is restricted to 49 per cent. All services, access to ports, pilotage, towing, tug assistance, provisioning, fuelling, watering and navigation aids are available to all users of port services. However, pilotage and all other port services can be provided only by Turkish flag ships. In the last few years, 13 public ports operated by the General Directorate of the TDI were privatised, but, until recently, the main ports were operated by the TCDD. Recently, the Mersin and Izmir ports, two of the main ports in Turkey, were also privatized. The privatizations were carried out by granting concessions for the operating rights for up to 30 years. Thus, in the market for port operations and services (pilotage, towage, cargo handling, container handling, etc.) the public sector was heavily involved in the past. Currently, the situation is advancing rapidly, as ports under the control of TCDD are subject to an ongoing liberalization process.

According to EuroMed (2005), container terminals are operating at relatively low levels of efficiency because of insufficient availability of handling equipment, the suboptimal use of stacking areas and the long dwell times of containers, where dwell times refer to the time that container units/cargoes remain in the port between vessel discharge and leaving or between entering and vessel loading. In Istanbul, dwell times are about 12 days, which is a relatively high figure. It is a result of not only infrastructure deficiency, but also the suboptimal statutory, regulatory, procedural and documentation frameworks used within the ports. It is clear that there is a need to improve this situation and to reduce container dwell times. These terminals would operate much more efficiently within their existing configuration provided that investments were made in equipment, improvements were introduced to stacking and handling procedures, and dwell times were shortened.

The international experiences suggest several approaches through which port reform can be undertaken: (1) decentralization of port management, (2) commercialization of ports and (3) introduction of private management in ports. The first approach, as stressed by EuroMed (2005), is decentralization of port management, which includes separating the task of port regulation from the task of port management and encouraging the decentralization of the task of port management from the national level to the local level. The second approach of reform, the commercialization of ports, includes injecting momentum into the competitive spirit of the port by allowing/increasing the participation of the private sector in the provision of port services and operations. Finally, the third approach, the introduction of private management in ports, includes seeking an advanced and sophisticated degree of private sector involvement in ports, with even a transfer of accountability from the public sector to the private sector. The international experience reveals that the landlord model, the third approach, should be sought as the primary consideration or option, given that it is widely common at the international level and has been hugely successful.

Conclusion

Because maritime transport is inherently international in character, and vessels on most voyages must operate under the regulatory requirements of many jurisdictions, there is an inherent need for harmonization across countries. Countries need to harmonize their own rules and regulations to international rules and regulations, which are classified as: (1) regulations related to commercial operations and practices and (2) regulations related to rights and obligations of states and to safety and environmental regulations. From the first set of rules and regulations, countries should, at a minimum, adopt the international rules and regulations that will enhance competition in the sector. In addition, the second set of international rules and regulations must be observed at any cost. As the EU rules and regulations in the maritime sector are generally much stricter than those at the international level, priority should be given by Turkey to achieve convergence with the international rules and regulations on safety and environment as well as on those on commercial operations and practices that will increase competition in the sector. Active convergence with the EU maritime freight transport sector *acquis* could be achieved at a later stage during the accession process, as immediate convergence with the EU *acquis* would be extremely costly for Turkey.

9 Policy reform in the road freight transport sector

(co-authored with Sare Arıcanlı)

Road freight transportation represents between 2 per cent and 6 per cent of countries' gross domestic product (GDP) and employment, depending on the structure of the transport networks and the geography. Studies show that road is the principal mode of freight transport for a large number of countries. In the European Union (EU-27) road accounted for 45.6 per cent of total freight transport during 2007 and the share has been steadily increasing. While road freight transport activity in the EU has increased at the annual rate of 3.4 per cent during 1995–2007, air freight transportation has increased at the annual rate of 3.7 per cent, maritime freight transportation by 2.7 per cent, and rail freight transportation by 1.3 per cent during the same period.[1]

The road freight industry is geared to distribution, logistics and basic physical transport. As emphasized by Boylaud (2000) it is a key sector of the economy, playing a major role in market integration and having a direct impact on transaction costs for economic agents. The World Trade Organization (WTO) Secretariat (2001c) emphasizes that, because of the downstream nature of road transport activity, the steadily increasing complexity of production methods and the widespread use of just-in-time production, road transport has a considerable impact on GDP and employment. Transport benefits the economy as a whole and, if it is paralyzed, it is the economy as a whole that suffers. It is also a secondary activity in the sense that an increase in GDP results in a more than proportional increase in the demand for transport.

In the 1980s many countries liberalized their road freight transport sectors to improve the safety, security and efficiency of transport operations and to ensure development of efficient transport networks. Liberalization requires first the removal of legal or administrative provisions restricting market access and commercial presence, and second the harmonization of rules and regulations between the major trading partners in the sector.

This chapter on the liberalization of road freight transportation services is structured as follows. The first section considers international rules and regulations in the road freight transportation sector, the second section analyzes EU rules and regulations, and the third section discusses Turkish rules and regulations. Finally, the last section provides some concluding remarks.

Road freight transportation services

The road freight transportation industry is divided into two segments. The first segment consists of a large number of small firms providing basic transport services to destinations within a limited distance and the second segment incorporates a limited number of major hauliers providing more sophisticated logistics services. Firms in the first segment compete mainly on price, and barriers to entry into the sector are low because, in general, little start-up capital is needed. This segment of the sector has small economies of scale with low entry and exit costs, and is therefore competitive. Firms in the second segment compete both on price and range and quality of services. Here, economies of scale are important, and increasing use is being made of information and communications technologies such as electronic data transfer and tracking systems that, because of improved productivity, enable hauliers to provide better-quality services to a much wider range of destinations.

The regulation of issues such as market access and prices has been motivated in a large number of countries by concerns that competition could cause instability and lead to bankruptcies in the sector. Furthermore, according to the European Conference of Ministers of Transport (ECMT 2001) and Boylaud (2000), the main rationales for regulating the road freight business relate to road safety, the environment and infrastructure congestion. There are two broad categories of regulations: regulations regarding traffic and vehicles and regulations regarding the operation of the market. The first category includes vehicle standards, highway codes, labour, social conditions, carriage of hazardous substances and traffic restrictions. The second category mainly covers market access conditions and prices.

Vehicle regulations relate to how motor vehicles should be manufactured. These rules are numerous and apply to a great many technical points such as fittings, roadworthiness tests and specific characteristics of the vehicles. According to RAND Science and Technology (2004), the world market is roughly divided into two major geographical regions in terms of technical regulations and standards affecting motor vehicles. In North America, the United States and Canada have adopted similar technical regulations on safety and emissions, and the US, Canadian and Mexican motor vehicle industries are extremely integrated; with some minor exceptions, standards are virtually identical. On the other side of the Atlantic, Europe has developed a regulatory system that is generally applicable across the European continent and is becoming increasingly accepted in other regions of the world as well. In 1949, the Convention on Road Traffic was adopted in Geneva. In 1952, the Working Party on Construction of Vehicles [Working Party 29 (WP29)] was set up by the Inland Transport Committee under this convention. Initiatives by the Working Party to harmonize regulations on vehicle construction affecting safety led to negotiations on a treaty to harmonize regulations on motor vehicles. In 1958, a treaty was signed under the auspices of the United Nations Economic Commission for Europe (UNECE), entitled 'Agreement Concerning the Adoption of Uniform Technical Prescriptions for

Wheeled Vehicles, Equipment and Parts, which can be Fitted and/or be Used on Wheeled Vehicles and the Conditions for Reciprocal Recognition of Approvals Granted on the Basis of These Prescriptions'. This treaty has become the basis for creating common motor vehicle and component regulations in Europe and, now, beyond, for mutual recognition of certification. As emphasized by Braithwaite and Drahos (2000), the scheme was such that if, for example, a German factory received approval from the German government to manufacture vehicles of a certain type, other European states would recognise that approval. The job of WP29 was to ensure that the grounds for type approvals in different states converged sufficiently to make mutual recognition acceptable. Since 1958, the agreement has been revised twice, most recently in 1995. In 1998, Japan became a signatory to the UNECE agreement, and Japanese technical regulations are now being modified to correspond with UNECE regulations. Australia, New Zealand and South Africa signed in 2000. Recently, the European Commission helped to develop new standards. Once the Commission decides on a standard that can be agreed upon among the experts in its member states, a member state is delegated to take it to WP29. In this way the European Commission uses WP29 to attempt to globalize a direction for standards.[2] Because of these moves, regulations agreed to under the UNECE treaty are the most commonly adopted, both inside and outside Europe.

Historically, the transport sector has had many regulations with respect to entering and exiting the market, as in the case of Mexico prior to 1989. During that period, the country had extremely rigid regulations in the road freight transportation sector, with a high degree of government involvement. As noted by Dutz *et al.* (2000), important government-imposed barriers to competition included entry restrictions to operate on federal highways, discretionary allocations of freight among truckers, and strong restrictions on moving cargo outside the established transport corridors. Official tariffs applied to all cargo and a semi-public company held a monopoly in handling containers. Regulations did not allow companies to charge higher rates for better service and hence there was no incentive to offer better services. Neither did they allow them to compete with one another by offering lower rates. As a result, the trucking industry was characterized by a limited number of firms operating with minimal competition. Moreover, to maintain this highly inefficient and archaic system, the government employed a sizeable bureaucracy. Thus, the effect of restrictions on itineraries or distances, the need to pass through freight centres and the impossibility of transporting a load on the return journey was to diminish the productivity of the undertakings. These undertakings were protected from the full effects of competition, and as a result they could enjoy higher returns. Hence, the consequence of quantitative regulations was to limit gains in productivity and technical and organizational innovations, thereby preventing a downwards trend in transport prices, whether in relative or in absolute terms. With liberalization, all these restrictions were eliminated.

The ECMT (an inter-governmental organization established by a protocol signed in 1953) is a forum in which ministers responsible for transport, and more specifically the transport sector, can cooperate on policy.[3] The ECMT's role primarily consists of: (1) helping to create an integrated transport system through-out the enlarged Europe that is economically and technically efficient, that meets the highest possible safety and environmental standards and which takes full account of the social dimension and (2) helping to build a bridge between the EU and the rest of the continent at a political level.[4] Over the last 50 years, the ECMT has developed a set of agreements and resolutions on general transport policy, market integration, trade facilitation, road freight transport, intermodal transport and logistics, infrastructure and road safety to which countries can subscribe to. According to the rules accepted by the international community, individual trans-port operations may be undertaken without authorization in any ECMT member country,[5] but the vast bulk of European international transport, that is, outside the EU, is still subject to authorization. Transport operations other than individual ones, to or from countries that do not belong to the EU, require an international transport licence of which there are two distinct types: (1) the 'bilateral' licence, which may be used both for transport 'on own account' and for transport 'for hire or reward' and (2) the ECMT multilateral licence, only available for transport for hire or reward.[6] Currently, a licence or permit is also required in most countries to set up a new road freight company, as well as registration. When deciding on the entry of new operators, requirements such as financial soundness, moral sound-ness and public safety requirements are taken into consideration, and decisions are made on a transparent basis.

The purpose of bilateral agreements is to ensure the right balance of traffic between transport operators from the concerned countries. The agreements estab-lish the authorized annual number of journeys. The contracting states exchange blank licences, which each issues to its transporters on behalf of the other. Bilateral licences cover the activity of both own-account transport operations and public transport operations. Moreover, these licences are the only ones to which own-account operators are entitled to for carriage outside the EU. Bilateral licences cover the major part of transport between two countries when one of them is not an EU member. Bilateral licences can be valid for one journey and the return journey undertaken within a maximum of three months from the date of issue, or for a period of one year and an indeterminate number of journeys. Moreover, some countries make licences valid for transit only, whereas others make them valid for both the return journey and transit-only journeys. The bilateral licences, granted according to the principle of reciprocity, present the apparent advantage for the issuing countries of enabling them to control the flow of traffic and, in principle, of producing a certain balance of national operators.

A quota for multilateral permits was put in place in 1974 between ECMT member states. The licences entitle their holders to engage in the international carriage of goods for hire or reward, using a single vehicle or coupled combina-tion of vehicles, where the points of loading and unloading are located on the territories of different member countries, and also to engage in empty runs on the territory of member countries that require a licence for such journeys. These licences are valid for one year but each country is entitled to transform part of its quota into short-term licences valid for 30 days. The ECMT licences, when they do not contain qualifications, may be used for all public road haulage operations, including transit but excluding carriage within a country, on all infrastructures connecting ECMT member countries that subscribe to the system. Over time changes were made to the licence system to accommodate environmental standards. By introducing standards on noise and exhaust emissions, the multilateral quota promotes the use of environmentally friendly and safe vehicles. The number of total licences per member country is allocated by specifying the percentage allocation by vehicle type in line with environmental standards. Since 1 January 1999, states have been able to exchange a traditional licence for two 'green' lorry licences or four 'greener and safe' licences.[7]

Although the ECMT licences play an essential role, especially with respect to crossing certain countries, because of their limited number they cover only a small part of the trade between the countries concerned, which is a serious limitation to bilateral quotas. Finally, it should be emphasized that ECMT licences since 1 January 2006 can be used only for transport operations after a laden trip between the country of registration and another ECMT country, and vehicles can only make three laden trips before they must return to the country of registration, either laden or unladen.

According to the 'Final Resolution of the XXVIth Congress of the International Road Transport Union' held at Marrakesh on 20 March 1998, there are different types of barriers to cross-border trade (International Road Transport Union 1998). The first of these barriers is blocked roads and motorways as a result of political conflicts.[8] These problems are generally very complex and their resolution is important as a prerequisite for enabling any kind of border crossing.

The second type of barrier to border crossings includes standardization of documents required at customs, customs declaration and clearance procedures and infrastructure and equipment at border points. Regarding the level of standardization of documents, it is noted that the use by customs of the single administrative document (SAD) facilitates trade. This document constitutes a standard form that can be shared by all involved border authorities, thereby enabling significant time savings in crossing borders and clearing cargo.[9] Many countries use information technology (IT) packages to automate and computerize customs declaration and clearance procedures, but many packages do not support the implementation of modern risk management techniques and therefore are not linked to the overall port management systems, disallowing electronic data interchange (EDI) with the services providers and economic operators, such as the freight forwarders and customs. The rate of inspections at customs without these linkages continues to be much higher than the rate in countries where these linkages are used.[10] If different parties involved in the process of clearing cargo were connected through IT and EDI, full automation of customs declarations, cargo manifests, drawings illustrating cargo distribution on ships, cargo invoices, certificates for payment of taxes and duties and certificates issued by the monitoring authorities could be achieved.

In addition to the lack of technology, the infrastructure and equipment at border points may often be insufficient or in need of upgrading. The main issues here are the lack or underdevelopment of inspection and control agents' offices, laboratories, warehouses, road approaches to the border, border gates, vehicle parking areas, reliable electricity and power sources and reliable telecommunications services. Elimination of these shortfalls would improve the efficiency of customs services and procedures and decrease barriers to trade in road freight services. According to the WTO Secretariat (2001c), the annual cost of these barriers has amounted to between 1 per cent and 7 per cent of the total transport costs in Western Europe, and between 8 per cent and 29 per cent of the total transport costs in Central and Eastern Europe.

Because hauliers move internationally, there is a strong need to standardise those aspects of national road freight transportation rules and regulations related to the international operation of hauliers. In addition to those from the ECMT, these rules and regulations are developed through the European Neighbourhood Policy (ENP) and the UNECE. Finally, WTO commitments, and the services negotiations at WTO provide an important forum for the discussion of liberalization of road transport services.

The ENP identifies priorities such as transport and customs, and works on action plans with partner countries in order to improve issues such as international transport. Action plans in transport focus on improving competition, efficiency, security and safety, promoting changes in the structure of policy, developing modern regulatory structures and promoting interoperability. This includes: (1) institutional reform, removing non-physical barriers such as convoluted customs procedures, and promoting interoperable satellite radio navigation systems, (2) issues specific to road transport including designing and implementing a Regional Road Safety Master Plan on licensing, infrastructure, safety checks, upgrading road networks, and replacing bilateral agreements with comprehensive multilateral agreements and (3) that the application of relevant safety and environmental issues is taken into consideration while implementing transport regulations.

Since its creation in 1947, the UNECE Inland Transport Committee has been working towards facilitating international transport while improving its safety and environmental performance. There are over 50 international agreements and conventions that provide the international legal and technical framework for developing international transport in the UNECE region. These international legal instruments, some of which are also applied by countries outside the UNECE, address a wide array of transport issues that fall under government responsibility and which have an impact on international transport. Such instruments include coherent international infrastructure networks, uniform and simplified border-crossing procedures and rules and regulations aimed at ensuring a high level of efficiency and safety and environmental protection in transport. Some of the important international conventions that have an impact on facilitating border crossings include the Customs Convention on Containers, the Convention on Harmonizing the Frontier Control of Goods, the Convention on Customs Treatment of Pool Containers used in International Transport, the Convention on the International Carriage of Dangerous Goods by Road, and the Agreement on the International Carriage of Perishable Foodstuffs.[11]

The UNECE also produced the Transports Internationaux Routiers (TIR) Convention, the most recent provisions of which entered into force on 17 February 1999.[12] The TIR customs transit procedure permits the international carriage of goods, as long as a road leg is involved, in international journeys from a customs office of departure to a customs office of arrival, through as many countries as necessary, without any intermediate frontier control of the goods carried. This facilitation of international goods transport requires a number of measures to be fulfilled and applied by customs authorities and transport operators. These include the use of customs-approved vehicles and containers, the use of the TIR Carnet as an international customs document, the provision of an international TIR guarantee and the mutual recognition of customs control measures in the countries involved.

Finally, it should be noted that negotiations at the WTO in Geneva are of significant relevance to road freight transport's fortunes. Although the WTO document W/120 identifies five subcategories under road services (passenger, freight, rental, maintenance and supporting services), many countries have given commitments using the United Nation's more detailed Central Product Classification (CPC), which distinguishes between 25 types of road transportation services. Road freight transportation is divided into seven types: transport services by refrigerator vehicles, transport services by tanker trucks or semi-trailers, transport services of containerized freight by trucks equipped with a container chassis, transport services by man- or animal-drawn vehicles, moving services of household and office furniture and other goods, transport services of letters and parcels, and other road transport services of freight.

According to the WTO Secretariat (2001c), 25 countries have given commitments within the context of WTO multilateral negotiations regarding freight transportation. Table 9.1 shows the market-access commitments by modes of supply. Mode 1, or cross-border supply, applies when service suppliers resident in one country provide services in another country without either supplier or buyer/consumer moving to the physical location of the other. Mode 2, consumption abroad, refers to a consumer resident in one country moving to the location of the supplier(s) to consume a service. Mode 3, commercial presence, refers to legal persons (firms) moving to the location of consumers to sell services locally through the establishment of a foreign affiliate or branch. Mode 4, or movement of natural persons, refers to a process through which individuals (temporarily) move to the country of the consumer to provide a service.

The table reveals that for freight transportation the most liberalized mode is mode 2, where full commitments have been given in four-fifths of the cases. In the case of mode 4, all countries preferred to remain unbound except as indicated in the horizontal commitments. In more than three-quarters of the cases there are no commitments for mode 1. Only five members have taken full commitments for mode 1 and there are two cases of partial commitments. Mode 3 is evenly split between full commitments and partial commitments. Reasons listed against committing are typically economic-need tests, foreign ownership restrictions, incorporation requirements, nationality of the board of directors, citizenship

Table 9.1 Analysis of commitments made by members on road transport services (number of full, partial and non-commitments by subsector and by mode of supply)

Market access	Cross-border supply			Consumption abroad			Commercial presence			Presence of natural persons		
	F	P	N	F	P	N	F	P	N	F	P	N
Transportation of frozen or refriger-ated goods (CPC 71231)	5	2	20	22	0	5	14	12	2	0	27	0
Transportation of bulk liquids and gases (CPC 71232)	5	2	17	20	0	4	12	11	2	0	24	0
Transportation of containerized freight (CPC 71233)	5	2	19	21	0	5	12	13	2	0	27	0
Transportation of furniture (CPC 71234)	5	2	19	21	0	5	14	11	2	0	26	0
Mail transportation (CPC 71235)	4	1	15	16	0	4	10	9	2	0	20	0
Freight transportation by human- or animal- drawn vehicle (CPC 71236)	5	1	15	17	0	4	9	10	2	0	21	0
Transportation of other freight (CPC 71239)	5	1	17	19	0	4	11	10	3	0	23	0
Rental services of commercial freight vehicles with operator (CPC 7124)	7	1	1	9	0	0	8	0	1	0	9	0

Source: World Trade Organization Secretariat (2001c)

Note
F, full commitment (indicated by 'none' in the market access column); P, partial commitment (limitation recorded in the market access column of the schedule), N, non-commitment (indicated by 'unbound' in the market access column).

requirements, authorization requirement not extended to foreign-registered vehicles, emergency safeguards on the number of services suppliers, services operations and services output, and limitations on the use of leased vehicles. Only two members have undertaken no commitments for mode 3.

In the case of national treatment few specific restrictions have been listed: requirement of establishment in the country concerned to provide cabotage services; prior approval; and obligation for entities established under mode 3 to use vehicles with national registration.[13] Finally, the most-favoured nation (MFN) exemptions have an important bearing on the extent of the commitments undertaken.[14] Out of the 25 countries that have given commitments on freight transportation, ten also have one or more MFN exemptions regarding cargoes. Five members, including the EU, have felt it necessary to lodge separate exemptions for preferential fiscal treatment on value added tax (VAT), vehicle tax and income tax. In other instances, the preferential tax treatment has been combined with cargo-sharing provisions in a single derogation, either by mentioning the preferential tax treatment specifically or by referring more generally to the operating conditions. The cargo-sharing provisions are mainly bilateral, although there are cases in which they are regional or both bilateral and regional. In six cases they are unilateral and in five of those cases they are based on reciprocity. In nearly all cases they cover all countries and existing and future agreements, although sometimes accompanied by a detailed list of beneficiaries.

As far as auxiliary road transport activities are concerned, rental services of commercial freight vehicles with operators have been offered by only a few members, but with nearly no restrictions. Finally, supporting services for road transport, covering bus station services and highways, bridges and tunnel operation services and parking services have attracted very few commitments.

EU regulatory framework

In Europe, liberalization of the sector became possible only through the single market reform of 1993. As the main objective of the EU is to create a single open market through liberalization, with freedom of establishment and freedom to provide services, the main concerns were market access, competition and the harmonization of legislation. Therefore, EU regulations aim to ease entry into the market and to liberalize the prices and supply of transport. There is movement towards a functionally homogeneous transportation system that can take safety, efficiency, social conditions and environmental factors into account. In the EU, however, non-EU firms generally do not have the same rights as the EU firms, and a number of limitations apply. For example, cabotage in the EU was fully liberalized in July 1998, but excludes non-member countries. Finally, it is noted that, although state ownership is becoming a relatively minor occurrence, there are nevertheless several countries with state-controlled companies operating in the road freight haulage sector. Often, they are subsidiaries of state-owned companies in other sectors, such as the railways or the post office, and they concentrate on only a few activities.

The main international rules that regulate safety and commercial operations and practices have been transposed into the Community law, ensuring that they have legal force and uniform application throughout the member states. EU countries have been founding members of the UNECE and the ECMT. It is party to the rules and regulations developed by the ECMT as well as to various UNECE conventions and agreements. In this context it should be noted that the EU is party to the Convention on Harmonizing the Frontier Control of Goods, the Convention on Customs Treatment of Pool Containers, the European Agreement on the International Carriage of Dangerous Goods by Road, the Agreement on the International Carriage of Perishable Foodstuffs, and the TIR Convention.

Turning to WTO services commitments made by the EU shown in Table 9.2, it is noted that for 'cross-border supply' (mode 1) no commitments have been made to passenger transportation, freight transportation, storage and warehouse services and other transport services; and no limitations have been placed on maintenance and repair of road transport equipment, freight transport agency/ freight forwarding services and pre-shipment inspection. Although no limitations have been placed on 'consumption abroad' (mode 2), different restrictions

Table 9.2 Specific commitments by European Communities in road transportation services

Mode of supply	Market access				National treatment			
Cross border	1				1			
Consumption abroad		2				2		
Commercial presence			3				3	
Presence of natural persons				4				4
Road transport services	*Commitments*							
Passenger transportation (CPC 71213 + 7122)	■	□	◨	■	■	□	■	■
Freight transportation (CPC 7123)	■	□	◨	■	■	□	■	■
Maintenance and repair of road transport equipment (CPC 6112)	□	□	□	■	□	□	□	■
Services auxiliary to all modes of transport								
Storage and warehouse services (CPC 742) (other than in ports)	■	□	□	■	■	□	□	■
Freight transport agency/freight-forwarding services (CPC 748)	□	□	□	■	□	□	□	■
Pre-shipment inspection (CPC 749)	□	□	□	■	□	□	□	■
Other transport services								
Land transport, provision of combined transport service	■	□	□	■	■	□	□	■

Source: http://tsdb.wto.org/default.aspx.

Note
Commitments: ■ full; ◨ partial; □ none.

have been placed on 'commercial presence' (mode 3) and on 'market access' in the cases of passenger transportation and freight transportation. No limitations for commercial presence have been placed on maintenance and repair of road transport equipment, services auxiliary to all modes of transport or other transport services. Finally, mode 4 (movement of personnel) for all cases does not diverge from the pattern 'unbound except as indicated in the horizontal commitments'.

Market access and competition

Market access for goods and passengers is based on Article 71 of the Treaty. Historically, the liberalization of the road transport sector in the EU started with the 1985 White Paper, which stressed the importance of freedom to provide services and outlined the Community Common Transport Policy. Three important guidelines were accepted: having a free market by 1992, increasing bilateral as well as Community quotas and eliminating distortions to competition. Infrastructure development, decreasing border controls and bureaucracy and improving safety by the end of 1992 were also outlined as goals in this White Paper. A regulation was adopted in 1988 which stated that all quantitative restrictions and Community and bilateral quotas would be abolished starting 1 January 1993. The international transport of goods between member states was liberalized with Council Regulation 881/92. According to the regulation, a road transport operator that works among at least two member states must obtain a Community licence; this gives the operator the right to access the whole EU market with no quantitative restrictions. The conditions to obtaining this licence are set forth in the same regulation. But own-account transport and small vehicles under 3.5 tonnes do not require such a licence.[15] Thus, within the EU, simply holding a Community licence, issued under the authority of the country of establishment, is sufficient to authorize the holder to carry out transport between any two member states: there is therefore free access to the market.

The process of liberalization took even longer for road cabotage, in which a non-resident carrier holding a Community licence can transport goods, on 'a temporary basis', from two points within a member state. Liberalization on 'a temporary basis' means that such transport is not continuously carried out. Cabotage was liberalized for freight transport in 1993, with Council Regulation 3118/93. However, Greece, the United Kingdom, Italy and France tried several times to restrict cabotage.[16] The Commission is expected to issue a regulation restricting cabotage to three operations in seven days. Thus, the new rule will be a backwards step in terms of market liberalization.

Council Regulation 3916/90 put forth measures that are to be taken for the carriage of goods by road in the event of a crisis in the market. With the implementation of deregulation measures, the road haulage market in the EU has become very competitive, integrated and efficient. The cabotage regime was extended to the European Free Trade Association (EFTA) countries on 1 July 1994 with the exception of Austria, which joined on 1 January 1997, and Switzerland. Following the accession of Cyprus, Malta and Slovenia to the EU on 1 May 2004, restrictions have been lifted for hauliers from those countries as well. Other new member states will be able to enjoy the right to cabotage services after a transitional period.[17] Lately, Directive 2006/1/EC has laid down two conditions for hiring vehicles for international road transport: the vehicle must be registered in the same member state as the road haulage transportation company that is hiring it and the driver must be an employee of the company.

It should be noted that access to the transport market not only requires looking at services and access to infrastructure, but also involves the development of traffic control systems. Only by establishing non-discriminatory access to infrastructure can the goal of increasing efficiency and competition be met, and non-discriminatory access must be applicable to all current and potential service providers, as grandfathered rights used by incumbents can severely decrease competition. Traffic control systems are not just a safety aspect but are integral to properly allocating infrastructure capacity, and also play a crucial role in the relationship between operation and infrastructure. Finally, it is noted that the EU countries have been using the SAD for almost two decades. Furthermore, the IT packages in use in the EU support the implementation of modern risk management techniques, they are linked to the overall port management systems, and they allow EDI interaction to be made with the service providers and economic operators such as the freight forwarders and customs. In addition, the infrastructure and equipment at border points are on the whole sufficient.

Prices and fiscal conditions

Road transportation is projected to continue to increase, and there is universal recognition that it is not possible to improve road infrastructure in proportion to the forecasted increases in traffic unless financing issues are solved. Most countries with high-performance and access-controlled highway systems have financed their expressways either by general tax revenues and/or through toll receipts. In almost every country that uses tolls, however, regulations require that a parallel untolled route be available to motorists, even though the alternative is usually not built to expressway standards.

The Common Transport Policy is based on the principle of 'sustainable mobility', which refers to maximizing efficiency in terms of energy, time and distance while internalizing external costs of infrastructure, environment, operation, upkeep, congestion and accidents. This system required the development of a new approach to fiscal issues, and the Green Paper of December 1995 put forth taxation as one of the important solutions to this problem.[18] The Green Paper stated that internalizing costs would improve traffic, safety and environment and would remove distortions in competition. On the other hand, the White Paper of 1998 emphasized a range of issues contributing to the problem of keeping up with the infrastructure, including the need to manage transport capacity more efficiently, to finance transport infrastructure and to improve the efficiency of the transport sector by means of institutional reform involving deregulation and privatization.[19]

According to the objective of sustainable mobility outlined in the Common Transport Policy, the EU maintains that charges for infrastructure should reflect the marginal social cost.[20] Hence, users should incur both the internal costs such as fuel, driver time and wear and tear, as well as the external costs of operation, infrastructure, congestion, environment and accidents. Table 9.3 shows that the environmental external cost of road transport as a percentage of GDP is much higher than that of other modes. Charging vehicles for external costs will discourage them from taking trips when the benefits do not exceed the total social cost. This would decrease congestion and increase efficiency.

It is emphasized that transport is the cause of 50 per cent of nitrogen oxide emissions, which forms nitric acid and leads to acid rain. Internalizing the above costs not only aids in improving traffic conditions, but also is environmentally helpful, as it will reduce emissions. When considering external costs, we must also look at the combination of noise, air pollution, congestion delays and aesthetic factors. Estimates show that, if the external costs of road transport were internalized, operating costs would increase (as noted by Button 1990) by between 20 per cent and 33 per cent. The 1998 White Paper sets out to internalize the externalized costs with a step-by-step approach, with the objective to harmonize transport charges across all member states, whereby individuals would participate in funding the road systems and cover the marginal social costs. The aim here is that harmonization due to liberalization would also be in accord with social aspects, safety measures and environmental concerns. Furthermore, it should be noted that the aim of internalizing costs is not to increase the cost of transport, but to ensure that costs are apportioned properly, with external costs incurred across all transport modes to avoid distortion of competition. It is also important to state that, although internalization is based on marginal social cost, a multi-tier charging system should be designed to incorporate taxes based on factors such as emissions. Given the projected continued dominance of road transport, one should consider options in addition to pricing, such as less-harmful fuels and cleaner technologies.

Table 9.3 Estimates of costs of selected environmental damage due to land transport, expressed as a percentage of gross domestic product (GDP)

	Cost as a percentage of GDP	
Environmental problem	*Road*	*Other modes*
Noise	0.10	0.01
Pollution	0.40	
Accidents	2.00	
Time	6.80	0.07
Use expenditure[a]	9.00	0.30
Total	18.30	4.71

Source: Button (1990).

Note
a Includes such items as infrastructure management.

Directive 1999/62/EC, based on Articles 71 and 93 of the EC Treaty, sets forth the rules for harmonizing the requirements for the taxes on heavy goods vehicles to be used on infrastructure. The directive covers vehicle taxes, tolls and user charges imposed on vehicles intended for the carriage of goods by road and having a maximum permissible gross laden weight of not fewer than 12 tonnes. According to the 2006 revision, this threshold will fall to 3.5 tonnes by the year 2012. The directive states that tolls should be levied according to the distance travelled and type of vehicle and user charges should relate to the duration of the usage of the infrastructure. Tolls and user charges may vary according to congestion and vehicle emission class. As a general rule, distance-based tolls and time-based user charges shall not be applied on the same stretch of road. Tolls and user charges can be imposed only on users of motorways (or multi-lane roads similar to motorways), bridges, tunnels and mountain passes. National tolls and charges should be non-discriminatory, and should be easy for the motorist to understand, to avoid unnecessary hold-ups and problems at toll booths. Mandatory checks at the EU's internal borders should also be avoided. Directive 2006/38/EC, amending Directive 1999/62/EC, establishes a new Community framework for charging for the use of road infrastructure. The directive lays down rules regarding how member states apply tolls or user charges on roads, including roads on the trans-European road network and roads in mountainous regions, and the directive will apply from 2012 onwards to vehicles weighing between 3.5 and 12 tonnes. According to the directive, member states are able to levy tolls according to a vehicle's emission category ('EURO' classification) and the level of damage it causes to roads, as well as the place, time and amount of congestion.[21] This tackles the problems of traffic congestion, including damage to the environment, through 'user pays' and 'polluter pays' principles.[22]

It should be noted that the level of government at which taxes are levied is important (Vaillancourt and Wingender 2006). Modal and regional differences can be addressed while designing an efficient system to internalize the external costs. Some of the revenues from congested regions could be allocated to financing deficit regions, as stressed by Sikow-Magny (2006). Two-part tariffs are also a way to encourage users to show their willingness to pay, and can be helpful in allocating infrastructure capacity while also taking welfare effects into consideration.

Employment and working conditions

With liberalization and the creation of a free market in the EU, certain social conditions need to be harmonized in order to achieve sustainable mobility. Regulation 561/2006 harmonizes certain social legislation with respect to road transport. Its aims are to improve road safety by limiting driving times, improving working conditions and standardizing the conditions across member countries. It sets out rules for maximum daily and fortnightly driving times and daily and weekly minimum rest periods for road haulage as well as for passenger transport vehicles.[23] It also stipulates that, as of 1 May 2006, a digital tachograph be fitted in all new service vehicles.[24] This regulation includes national and international transport,

transport for long and short distances, own-account and for-hire transport and employees and self-employers.

Regulation 3821/85 concerns the recording equipment in road transport, primarily the analogue tachograph that records driving time, breaks and rests. Council Regulation (EC) 2135/98, amending the regulation, requires the use of the fully digital tachograph, which is more reliable and which includes a printer for roadside inspections. Directive 2006/22/EC lays down the minimum conditions for implementation of Regulation 3821/85 regarding the amount of roadside inspections of driving time, rest periods, breaks and checks at the premises of undertakings. Finally, Directive 2002/15 regarding the working time of those persons performing road transport activities sets forth the minimum requirements for working time in order to improve road safety as well as the health of workers, and Directive 2002/15 defines working time, place of work, night work, and maximum working week.[25]

The harmonization of the rules regarding access to the profession is outlined in Directive 96/26/EC, which is based on Article 75 of the Treaty. Being a road haulage operator requires, according to the directive, good repute in the exercise of business, a certain minimum financial standing and professional competence. This involves a policy that replaces quantitative licensing with qualitative criteria for allowing access to the road transport market. Given that road haulage undertakings are subject to numerous rules that affect the safety of other road users, an operative who is certified as professionally competent is one who is familiar with all these rules and is also able to manage a company. Good repute means that entrepreneurs who have few scruples about disregarding the law may be excluded from the occupation, while the financial standing requirement ensures that they have the capital necessary to continue managing the undertaking and maintenance of the vehicles, so that any practice that might endanger safety is prevented. The directive requires that each member state must accept the documents issued by another member state stating that these conditions are fulfilled. The scope of this directive excludes the operators of vehicles with a laden weight below 3.5 tonnes. Regular checks (at least every five years) ensure that these three criteria continue to be satisfied. The criteria are justified; they halt the proliferation of unscrupulous firms seeking to gain market share by skimping on safety, they achieve greater harmonization of standards between member states, particularly regarding levels of financial standing required and the standard of professional competence expected, they facilitate establishment in other member states and the mutual recognition of professional status and they improve the overall professional standing and quality of road transport. Directive 96/26/EC was later amended by Directive 98/76/EC.

According to Regulation (EC) No. 484/2002, amending Council Regulation No. 881/92 and No. 3118/93, every driver from a non-EU country driving an EU operator's vehicle while carrying out cross-border haulage activities within the EU must carry the correct driver attestation. This is a uniform document certifying that the driver of a vehicle carrying out road haulage operations between member states is lawfully employed by the Community transport operator concerned, in the member state in which the operator is established, or lawfully placed at the disposal of that operator. This document enables inspecting officers in all member states to check the employment status of drivers carrying out transport operations between member states in Community vehicles and with a Community licence, thereby helping the authorities to combat effectively the use of irregularly employed drivers and the resulting distortions of competition.

Improving traffic safety is an important objective in the EU. Directive 91/439/EEC introduced the mutual recognition of driver's licences along with the harmonization of many aspects of driver's licences including categories, issuing conditions and requirements. A review in some member states showed that 30 per cent of service-vehicle drivers had never received driver training. This situation was remedied with Directive 2003/59/EC regarding qualifications and periodic training of drivers of certain road vehicles for the carriage of goods or passengers. Drivers would be trained in road safety, technical aspects of the vehicle, fuel consumption, loading, accidents and physical risk, criminality, emergencies and the economic image of the company. Since the end of 2008 it has been required that all new drivers receive training. Training leads to better skills, improved and higher-quality service, improved road safety, reduced fuel consumption and reduced costs. The Directive 2006/126/EC recasts the existing legislation harmonizing the conditions for issuing national driving licences with the aim of enabling reciprocal recognition of licences to make it easier for people to move within the Community.

Road safety

Harmonizing technical conditions concerns interoperability, safety and environmental issues such as tread depth of tyres, installing speed limitation devices, maximum authorized weights and dimensions, roadworthiness tests, technical roadside inspection and registration documents. With respect to the tread depth of tyres in certain categories of motor vehicles and their trailers, Directive 89/459 states that the minimum tread depth in main grooves must be 1.6 mm in vehicle categories M1, N1, O1 and O2.[26] Directive 92/6, on environmental and safety concerns in relation to heavy goods vehicles and buses, puts forth the necessity of installing and using speed limitation devices in M2, M3, N2 and N3 categories of vehicles. The directive further stipulates that M2 and M3 vehicles can have a maximum speed of 100 km/hour and N2 and N3 vehicles can have a speed limit of 90 km/hour. This directive was later amended by Directive 2002/85/EC.[27] Directive 96/53/EC puts forth the maximum dimensions that are authorized for M2, M3, N2 and N3 categories of vehicles in national and international traffic, as well as the maximum authorized weights in international traffic.[28] Directive 96/96/EC states that member states must conduct periodic roadworthiness tests for vehicles and trailers registered in the state, and that the test will be mutually recognized by other member states. These inspections should be carried out once a year for heavy vehicles, and at least every other year for light vehicles and passenger cars.[29]

Council Regulation 4060/89 is on eliminating controls at the frontier. It states that controls on weights and dimensions be carried out on a sample basis. Council Regulation 3912/92 extends the scope of Regulation 4060/89 to those vehicles and vessels registered in third countries. Controls on vehicles registered in third countries must be carried out at the external frontier of the Community.

An increase in the number of vehicles also leads to an increase in the number of accidents. Regarding road safety and environmental concerns, Directive 2000/30/EC puts forth that commercial vehicles in EU territory will be subject to unannounced technical roadside inspections. These inspections will be non-discriminatory, and will try to minimize the costs and delays to the operators involved. The inspector shall draw up a report and give it to the driver of the commercial vehicle. Directive 2003/127/EC (previously Directive 1999/37) deals with registration documents for vehicles and aims to harmonize some codes and contents.

Seatbelts are another important aspect of road transport safety. Council Directive 91/671/EEC on the approximation of the laws of the member states relating to compulsory use of safety belts in vehicles of less than 3.5 tonnes applied only to cars and vans and did not require the use of child restraints in vehicles. Directive 2003/20/EC extends the scope of Directive 91/671 and requires the use of seatbelts, where provided, in all motor vehicles. It further states that children must be restrained by an appropriate child restraint system conforming to the latest UNECE standards when travelling in M1 and N1 vehicles.

Traffic accidents in the EU result in more than 40,000 fatalities and 1.7 million injuries per year and cost an estimated 160 billion euros annually.[30] The objective of the CARE database (Community database on Accidents on the Roads in Europe) set up in 1993 by Decision 93/704/EC is to provide a powerful tool to make it possible to identify and quantify road safety problems throughout European roads. The plan to reduce the disastrous effects of accidents includes disseminating accident prevention information and introducing accident prevention measures to do with vehicles, people and infrastructure.

Directive 2004/54/EC concerns the minimum safety requirements for tunnels in the Trans-European Transport Network (TEN). Many tunnels are aging, many lives have been lost in tunnels in recent years and the costs related to closing a tunnel are great. The objectives of this directive are to prevent those situations that endanger the lives of people using the tunnels and to protect the tunnels and the environment.

Another issue of importance for safety is the transportation of dangerous goods. International transport of dangerous goods has long been governed by established agreements, and the EU, through its directives, tries to apply such guidelines to national traffic. Directive 94/55/EC concerns the laws regarding the transport of dangerous goods by road within or between member states. The rules are based on the European Agreement concerning the International Carriage of Dangerous Goods by Road. Directive 94/55/EC was later amended by Directive 2000/61/EC. Directive 95/50/EC relates to uniform procedures for random checks on dangerous goods transported by road. In 1999, Directive 1999/36/EC, often referred to as the Transportable Pressure Equipment Directive, was introduced. This directive, aiming to increase safety in transporting pressure equipment by setting technical requirements, was later amended by Directives 2001/2/EC and 2002/50/EC. Directive 96/35/EC concerns appointing safety advisors for the transportation of dangerous goods by road, rail and inland waterway, and their qualifications. The directive stipulates that all operations involved in the transportation, loading or unloading of dangerous goods must appoint a safety advisor who has gone through the necessary training, passed an examination and received a certificate. Directive 2000/18/EC sets out the examination requirements for safety advisors for the transportation of dangerous goods. Recently, the Directives 94/55/EC and 96/35/EC were repealed by the Directive 2008/68/EC establishing a common regime for all aspects of the inland transport of dangerous goods, by road, rail and inland waterway. Noting that international transport of dangerous goods is regulated by the European Agreement concerning the International Carriage of Dangerous Goods by Road, the Regulations concerning the International Carriage of Dangerous Goods by Rail and the European Agreement concerning the International Carriage of Dangerous Goods by Inland Waterways, the Directive 2008/68/EC extends such rules to national transport in order to harmonize the conditions under which dangerous goods are transported.

Road transport in Turkey

The transport sector, which is vital for the economic development and integration of Turkey, accounted together with the communication sector for 14.2 per cent of GDP in 2008. The modal share of the transport sector is greatly skewed towards road transport, taking up 95.4 per cent of national passenger transport and 91.6 per cent of national freight transport during 2007. As of 2009, Turkey had 13 million registered vehicles, and the road network, excluding rural roads, had 2,010 km of motorways, 31,311 km of state roads and 30,712 km of provincial roads, amounting to a total of 64,033 km. Of this total, 14,523 km consisted of divided roads, and the total length of roads having hot-mix asphalt pavements capable of handling heavy axle loads stood at 9,393 km. While the share of road transport in total exports was 38.5 per cent during 2008, the share of road transport in total imports amounted to 20.4 per cent.

As modes of freight transport other than road are largely underdeveloped in Turkey, a great amount of pressure is put on the road infrastructure, which is in need of serious improvement. In 1993, 80 per cent of the roads were rated as good, 15 per cent as fair and 5 per cent as poor, but the situation has seriously deteriorated since. In 2003, 19.4 per cent of the roads were in good, 33 per cent in fair and 47.6 per cent in poor condition. Having 52 per cent of roads in good or fair condition is extremely low compared with the 95 per cent in good or fair condition in Western European countries. Infrastructure development remains one of the key issues affecting Turkey's growth, and significant investment is needed. Recently, the Eastern Black Sea Coastal Highway project of 561 km and the Bolu Mountain Crossing project of 25 km were completed and opened to traffic.

Turkey's East–West Traceca (transport corridor Europe–Caucasus–Asia) corridor provides an efficient road connection between Europe and Asia. Major traffic is carried along the Trans-European Motorway, an extension of Pan-European Corridor IV from Bulgaria to Ankara. In 2002, the Turkish government set a target of 15,000 km of multi-lane highway networks; up to now, 13,929 km of multi-lane highways have been completed. Furthermore, the construction of the main body of the Gaziantep–Şanlıurfa motorway was completed in 2008, while the main body of the Kemerhisar–Pozantı motorway, located on the Ankara–Habur corridor, is to be completed in 2009.

The European Commission's January 2007 communication 'Extension of the Major Trans-European Transport Axes to the Neighbouring Countries – Guidelines for Transport in Europe and Neighbouring Countries' to the Council and the European Parliament focuses on linking the major axes of the trans-European networks with the transport networks of neighbouring countries (Commission of the European Communities 2007h). The Commission identified five major transnational transport axes and one of those concerns road transportation in Turkey. The South-Eastern Axis will link the EU with the Balkans and Turkey and further – with the Southern Caucasus and the Caspian Sea as well as with the Middle East up to Egypt and the Red Sea. The continuation of the Trans-European Transport Network roads to Iran (the Istanbul–Amasya–Erzurum–Iranian borders) and south to Arab countries (Istanbul–Ankara–Adana–Iskenderun, then to the Syrian or Iraqi borders) is under study. The Transport Infrastructure Needs Assessment Study, which aims to identify transport axes that will connect the Turkish transport network to the Trans-European Transport Network, has recently been completed.

To increase access to foreign markets Turkey has signed 32 bilateral agreements with various countries. These agreements are cooperative in the fields of passenger and freight transport, and usually have capacity clauses imposed on foreign carriers, with some of the agreements including tariff clauses. In addition, it is noted that Turkey is a founding member of the ECMT and UNECE. It has ratified various ECMT and UNECE resolutions, agreements and conventions. In particular, Turkey has ratified the Customs Convention on Containers, the Convention on Harmonizing the Frontier Control of Goods, and the TIR Convention. But Turkey has not yet signed the Convention on Customs Treatment of Pool Containers 1994, the European Agreement on the International Carriage of Dangerous Goods by Road, and the Agreement on the International Carriage of Perishable Foodstuffs. Recently, by introducing major reform in the sector, Turkey tried to close the gap between legislation pertaining to the internal and international markets.

Table 9.4, showing WTO commitments made by Turkey, reveals that no passenger transportation and freight transportation commitments for market access and national treatment have been made regarding 'cross-border supply' (mode 1) and no limitations have been placed on 'consumption abroad' (mode 2) and movement of personnel (mode 4) for market access and national treatment. In the case of 'commercial presence' (mode 3), limitations have been placed on market access and no limitations have been placed on national treatment.

Table 9.4 Specific commitments by Turkey in road transportation services

Mode of supply	Market access				National treatment			
Cross border	*1*				*1*			
Consumption abroad		*2*				*2*		
Commercial presence			*3*				*3*	
Presence of natural persons				*4*				*4*
Road transport services	*Commitments*							
Passenger transportation (CPC 7121 + 7122)	■	□	◨	□	■	□	□	□
Freight transportation (CPC 7123)	■	□	◨	□	■	□	□	□

Source: http://tsdb.wto.org/default.aspx.

Note
Commitments: ■ full; ◨ partial; □ none.

Market access

The responsibilities of the Turkish Ministry of Transport include, among other things, regulating access to the market and the profession, regulating and issuing operating licences, and inspecting and monitoring market conditions. The Ministry of Public Works and Settlements has been responsible for the development and maintenance of state and provincial roads, as the General Directorate of Highways (KGM) has been part of the Ministry. In addition, the Ministry has been responsible for regulating and collecting tolls, as well as data regarding traffic on toll roads. The Ministry of Interior is responsible for roadside inspections, the Ministry of Industry and Trade regulates technical standards, including tachographs and speed limiters, and the Ministry of Labour and Social Security regulates social conditions such as driving times, working times and rest periods. After the abolition of the General Directorate of Rural Affairs of the Ministry of Agriculture, the construction and maintenance of rural roads was decentralized and given to rural authorities. Recently, the institutional capacity has been further strengthened. The KGM has been transferred from the Ministry of Public Works and Settlement to the Ministry of Transport, leading to improved coordination between transport authorities.

The regulatory framework in the transport sector is comprised of one general law regarding the duties of the Ministry of Transportation and a number of other laws specific to the subsectors. The main legislation in the road transport sector is the Law on Road Transport No. 4925, which gives the framework for access to the market and the profession, and the By-Law on Road Transport, which puts forth the secondary legislation. Related laws include the By-Law on Training for Professional Competence in Road Transport Operations, the Foreign Direct Investment Law No. 4875, and the Turkish Commercial Code No. 6762.[31] These regulations put forth conditions for admission to the profession and market access;

licensing systems for transport operations and auxiliary transport categories; rights and responsibilities of carriers, undertakings and consumers; conditions for vehicles; competition in the sector; rules regarding inspections, rights, responsibilities of personnel; and rules and procedures for training and obtaining the Professional Competence Certificate.

Turkey has recently introduced a licensing system, in line with conditions set by the EU, which resulted in the registration of 90 per cent of the commercial vehicles in domestic freight transport and almost all of the commercial vehicles in international freight transport. According to the licensing system, natural as well as legal persons registered in the Turkish commercial registry can apply for a licence as long as they meet the following conditions: (1) they are of good repute, (2) they are registered at relevant chambers of trade and industry or chambers of tradesmen and craftsmen, (3) at least one mid- or high-level manager in the organization has the Professional Competence Certificate or is in the employment of a person who has such a certificate and (4) they have sufficient financial resources as well as sound management and operational skills. Furthermore, natural and legal persons who are not Turkish nationals can also obtain the licence, as long as applications are in accordance with the requirements of the Foreign Direct Investment Law and satisfy the conditions specified in the Law on Road Transport and the related by-law.

In Turkey foreign vehicles may not conduct transport operations between any two points within the country. Foreign vehicles transporting goods to and from, or through, Turkey require a permit unless specified otherwise in bilateral agreements. Moreover, goods coming to Turkey by sea, rail or air and carried to a third country can be transported only by Turkish hauliers, and special permission for registered foreign vehicles is required from the Ministry of Transport by the Law on Road Transport. International freight transport licences are valid for five years, are not transferable and may be suspended in case of loss of good repute or financial standing. According to Article 7 of the law, fire brigades, ambulances, funeral transport, transport of medicine/medical equipment, postal services and transport related to accidents are exempt from the authorization of permits. However, the Ministry of Transport may institute further restrictions and make new arrangements in the event of a crisis.

The By-Law on Training for Professional Competence in Road Transport Operations outlines regulations regarding training and examining professional competence, qualifications of institutions in charge of giving such training, authorization given to those institutions, and the regulations regarding the Professional Competence Certificate.

The new law and series of by-laws issued under this law helped to bring Turkish national legislation in line with international standards, and in particular in line with those of the EU road freight transport *acquis*. These legal regulations allow the creation and development of strong and efficient enterprises having financial and professional competence and solid reputations.

Fees and fiscal conditions

There are a number of administrative units in charge of road fees. The Ministry of Finance is responsible for vehicle tax and the Ministry of Transport is responsible for transit passage fees determining and implementing the Transit Passage Fee By-Law on Road Transport, Article 16.[32] The transit passage fee is charged to foreign vehicles at borders, but vehicles can be exempt from it within the context of bilateral agreements. The fee is calculated according to the gross weight of the truck, measured in tonnes, and the distance that the truck is travelling, measured in kilometres.

As per Article 15 of the Law on Establishment of General Directorate of Highways No. 5539, the Ministry of Public Works and Settlements is responsible for tolls. Tolling is done on high-performance motorways and bridges over the Bosporus in Istanbul. Article 21 of the law outlines consequences for toll evaders.[33] The legislation on tolling is outlined in the By-Law on Istanbul Strait Bridge Operation, the By-Law on Motorway Operation, and Ministerial Approvals.[34] For open tolled motorways, the rate varies according to the class of vehicle, and, for closed tolled motorways, it depends on the vehicle class and distance travelled.[35] Turning to issues related to state aid, it is noted that, according to Decree No. 2002/4367, investment in the transportation sector is encouraged when the objectives are to support and orient investment in line with international commitments, create new employment opportunities and add value in order to achieve international competitiveness.[36] The programme covers investment in trailer/truck renewal for international land transport, public transportation, heavy construction equipment, bus terminal construction and combined container transport. In the above cases, imports of machinery and equipment are exempted from customs duty, and VAT is exempt from imported and domestically purchased equipment. Foreign financing is provided for transport sector projects that include the construction of highways and toll roads if the project is part of the Annual Investment Program prepared by the State Planning Organization.[37] Finally, it is noted that the construction of roads is the responsibility of the KGM. KGM uses either budgetary resources or foreign financing for its road construction.

Although Turkey has road and vehicle charges in place, it is doubtful whether these charges reflect the marginal social costs, as outlined by the European Commission (1998c). According to the Commission, users should bear the internal and external costs, which include infrastructure damage, congestion, scarcity, environment and accident costs. As emphasized by Goodwin (2002), the decision of one person to make a trip during a peak traffic period imposes a delay on others (and hence him/herself), which results in a trip of longer duration than that person expected. It is clear that the increase in car ownership and road transport is due to the fact that road transport has not internalized its full cost. Internalizing these costs would prevent excessive use of road transport, and would be a way to equalize the conditions of competition across different modes of transport. To increase internalization of costs, Turkey should introduce mechanisms to secure short-term road maintenance financing and implement willingness-to-pay tolling principles. Increasing the differentiation in toll structures would be an additional way of achieving the above objective. Turkey realizes that there is a need to rebalance modes of transport, and to improve linkages between intermodal transport.

Social conditions, technical conditions and safety

Aspects of social conditions such as setting the rules on working time, rest periods and driving time are the responsibility of the Ministry of Labour and Social Security. The Ministry of Interior is responsible for enforcing rules regarding driving times and rest periods of vehicles on the road, and the Ministry of Industry and Trade is responsible for determining the technical specifications for recording equipment. The related laws are the Labour Law No. 4857, By-Law on Working Time that Cannot be Divided into Weekly Working Days, and the By-Law on Road Traffic.[38]

The objective of the Labour Law is to regulate the rights and obligations regarding working conditions, and the work environment of employers and workers who have a labour contract (the law does not apply to those who are self-employed). The By-Law on Working Time that Cannot be Divided into Weekly Working Days outlines the methods and principles that are applied to working time and periods of work that cannot be divided into weekly working days.[39] Again, the law does not apply to the self-employed. On the other hand, the By-Law on Road Traffic applies to all drivers, including the self-employed, and pertains to vehicles carrying goods for commercial purposes where the weight limit exceeds 3.5 tonnes, and to those that carry passengers for commercial purposes where the capacity exceeds nine people, including the driver.[40]

According to the regulations a driver needs a Professional Competence Certificate, and buses and trucks have to install mechanical, electronic or electromechanical tachographs. Tachograph records must be kept in the vehicle for one month and in the office for five years. Turkey has also issued a decree setting out the principles of a fleet renewal scheme and for phasing out old vehicles. Each year checks must be performed on at least 1 per cent of the days worked by a driver of a vehicle, in which at least 15 per cent of the checks are at the roadside and 25 per cent are at the undertakings themselves. Checks at the undertakings concern weekly and fortnightly driving times and rest periods, compensation for reduced weekly rest periods and record sheets and driver card data. The Labour Inspection Board, one of the organizational bodies in the Ministry of Labour and Social Security, is responsible for premises checks, enforcing the rules at the undertakings, and has units in ten regions. According to the ILO Convention Concerning Labour Inspection in Industry and Commerce No. 81 and other relevant legislation, collection of statistical data is of prime importance (ILO 1947). The data are published in the 'General Report of Labour Inspection' and submitted to the ILO annually. The General Directorate for Labour is the other half of the Labour Ministry, and is responsible for preparing draft legislations. The General Directorate of Security at the Ministry of Interior is responsible for checks at roadsides and terminals. During 2005, the ministry checked 2.3 million drivers, and 13,500 drivers and operators were fined for not obeying rules regarding working hours. Regarding employment and working conditions, note that Turkey has ratified the European Agreement on the Work of Crews of Vehicles Engaged in International Road Transport (AETR Agreement) and the ILO Convention concerning Hours of Work and Rest Periods in Road Transport.[41]

Legislation regarding technical conditions includes the By-Law on Establishment and Management of Vehicle Technical Inspection Stations and Vehicle Inspection.[42] The Ministry of Transport is responsible for conducting roadworthiness tests. A consortium was recently authorized for a 20-year contract to build and operate technical inspection stations. The consortium set up fixed and mobile stations, which are to be supervised by the Ministry of Transport. Weights and dimensions of freight are regulated mainly by the By-Law on Road Traffic.[43] Freight weight is planned to be controlled through the fixed and mobile control systems. Other related legislation includes the By-Law on Type Approval of Speed Limitation Devices of Motor Vehicles and their Installation, the Law on the Amendment of Law on Road Traffic No. 5495 and the Fundamental Principles of International Passenger and Freight Transport by Road No. 8/984.[44] According to the By-law on Amending By-Law on Road Traffic, installation of speed limitation devices for category N3 trucks and tractors and M3 buses, when the mass exceeds 10 tonnes, is mandatory.[45,46]

Road safety is another issue of concern in Turkey. Although there has been some improvement over the past ten years, road accidents remain a serious problem. The 2 per cent annual growth in the number of accidents is in line with the growth rate of traffic. While fatalities are decreasing, injuries are increasing at the rate of 1.3 per cent annually. However, the current rate of eight fatalities/10,000 vehicles is four times higher than the EU's average rate, which is two fatalities/10,000 vehicles. The General Directorate of the Security of the Ministry of Interior is responsible for regulating road safety on all motorways and state and provincial roads, and the Gendarmerie is responsible for the remaining roads. The Ministry of Transport is responsible for regulating and monitoring the transport of dangerous goods by road, the Ministry of Education for training drivers, the Ministry of Health for drivers' health conditions and the Ministry of Trade and Industry for type approvals of transportable pressure equipment.

The carriage of dangerous goods is regulated by the By-Law on Transport of Dangerous Goods by Road and the By-Law on Training for Professional Competence in Road Transport Operations.[47] Recently, the Directorate-General for Land Transport (DGLT) has established a new unit for the implementation of the regulation on dangerous goods. However, the DGLT has not reached the necessary monitoring and control standards and a precondition for the regulation implementation has not been fulfilled as Turkey has not yet become a party to the European Agreement on the International Carriage of Dangerous Goods by Road.

With regard to administrative capacity, it is noted that new staff have been recruited, a new Department for Professional Competence has been set up within the Ministry of Transport, and the Department for Transport of Dangerous Goods has been established. Furthermore, the institutional capacity of the DGLT has increased. According to the European Commission (2007i), an IT system was put into operation to establish an information infrastructure with regional transport directorates and enables all licensing of road transport activities to be conducted electronically. The DGLT also established a new unit for roadside checks on the weights and measures of vehicles. The DGLT signed protocols with the governors of 80 provinces to devolve authority regarding weight and measure inspections. However, the number of weighing stations in Turkey is limited compared with the travel frequency and the number of heavy vehicles in traffic. Insufficient inspection of overloaded vehicles exacerbates damage to transport infrastructure and high accident rates.

Thus, legislative studies are in progress on the harmonization of driving licences in Turkey with those in the EU, installing speed-limiting devices into certain vehicle types, regulating the working and rest hours of drivers, building a database compatible with EU standards for traffic accidents and ensuring driver training in Turkey is equivalent to that in EU member states. Furthermore, Turkey aims to increase road traffic safety by conducting effective and sound mechanical inspections, and ensuring correct vehicle weight and dimension controls. In this context, the process of delegating the opening and operation of vehicle inspection stations to the private sector has largely been completed. By now, all operations and transactions in the road transport sector are conducted electronically in real time by means of the recently developed Land Transportation Automation System. However, according to the European Commission (2008) the implementation capacity in Turkey is lagging behind and continued efforts are required to ensure due enforcement of road safety.

Conclusion

The development of Turkey's road infrastructure remains one of the most important issues affecting its economic growth. The existing infrastructure needs replacing and expanding because of the high growth rate of road transportation. Recent achievements include the completion of the country's longest running road project – the highway between Istanbul and Ankara – and the opening of the Turkish section of the Black Sea ring road, from Samsun to the border with Georgia. Current plans envisage an increase in the motorway network to 15,000 km, and much of this capacity is expected to be built and operated by the private sector. The bulk of investment is foreseen to occur in the overcrowded western provinces.

Turkey relies heavily on road transport, and as 48 per cent of roads are in poor condition and as the road transport sector serves as an important intermediate input both nationally and internationally, changes in the regulatory regime of the sector can have important economic effects. Currently Turkey is in the process of adopting and implementing the legislative, regulatory and institutional framework of the EU's road freight transport sector. By changing the regulatory regime, the country aims to increase competition in the sector, improve infrastructure and lower the cost of road freight transport services.

Part III

Quantifying the impact of economic liberalization

10 Impact of economic liberalization

(co-authored with Hakan Berument and Jan Michalek)

To design successful reform strategies it is crucial that the effects of economic liberalization be analyzed thoroughly. To do that, we first need to quantify the barriers to trade in services, and then using these measures of trade barriers assess quantitatively the effects of liberalizing services.

The chapter is structured as follows. The first section considers the various problems faced in the quantification of barriers to trade in services and network industries. The next section assesses the tariff equivalents of barriers to trade in the Turkish telecommunications, electricity, natural gas, banking, maritime freight transport and road freight transport services sectors. The third section studies the effects of liberalization in goods and services within the context of Turkey's accession to the European Union (EU) on the Turkish economy. The final section concludes this study of economic liberalization.

Quantifying barriers to trade in services and network industries

First, we discuss the simplest and most common approach to measuring the barriers to trade in services, which involves frequency measures developed by Hoekman (1995). Next, we consider the approach adopted by the Australian Productivity Commission (APC) discussed by Findlay and Warren (2000). Finally, we consider the gravity approach developed by Francois (1999).[1]

Hoekman's approach to estimating tariff equivalents in services

Hoekman (1995) constructs frequency ratios on the basis of commitments scheduled in the World Trade Organization's (WTO) General Agreement on Trade in Services (GATS). He considers the four modes of supply of GATS: (1) cross-border supply, (2) consumption abroad, (3) commercial presence and (4) movement of natural persons. According to the WTO's Services Sectoral Classification List (MTN.GNS/W/120) there are 155 non-overlapping service sectors (WTO 1991). As there are four possible modes of supply for each sector, 620 such openness/binding factors (commitments) exist for each member country.

As commitments scheduled in GATS apply to national treatment and market access separately, there are potentially 1,240 data cells for each member (620 × 2).[2,3] Commitments were then classified into three categories and each category was assigned a numerical score as follows:

- if no restrictions were applied for a given mode of supply in a given sector ('none' in GATS jargon), a value of 1 was assigned;
- if no national treatment or market access liberalization policies were bound for a given mode of supply in a given sector ('unbound'), a value of 0 was assigned;
- if restrictions or limitations were listed for a given mode of supply in a given sector ('bound'), a value of 0.5 was assigned.

The value of these indicators was chosen to allow aggregation across sectors and countries. The higher the number, the greater the implied extent of openness-cum-binding. Using these scores, Hoekman calculated three indicators: (1) the number of sector/mode-of-supply combinations (cells) in which a commitment was made (as a share of the maximum possible – 620 for market access and 620 for national treatment), (2) the 'average coverage' of each schedule of commitments, defined as the arithmetic weighted mean of the scale factors allocated to each cell and (3) the share of 'no restriction' commitments in (a) a member's total commitments and (b) relative to the 155 possible sectors of the classification list. The higher the number, the more 'liberal' the service regime in the country.[4]

Although the original purpose of these coverage indicators was to quantify GATS commitments, Hoekman argued that they could also be used to generate information on the relative restrictiveness of policy regimes pertaining to service industries by assuming that the coverage of each country's schedule is an indicator of its policy stance. He used the frequency ratios as a starting point for estimating country-specific 'tariff equivalents' of the relative degree of discrimination of foreign service providers across countries and sectors. Here, he somewhat arbitrarily defined a set of benchmark 'guesstimates' of tariff equivalents for each sector. These are a subjective set of benchmark tariff equivalents for individual sectors to reflect the degree to which market access to these sectors is restricted. A value of 200 per cent was chosen for the sectors in which access tended to be prohibited by most countries, and which did not appear in most schedules, such as maritime cabotage and basic telecommunications; values between 20 per cent and 50 per cent were assigned to sectors in which access was less constrained (e.g. hotels and restaurants or wholesale services). Each country and sector was then assigned a value related to that benchmark. For example, the financial services sector (excluding insurance) was assigned a benchmark tariff equivalent of 50 per cent. The tariff equivalent of barriers to trade in a particular sector of a given country was then obtained by multiplying the guesstimated subjective tariff rate in the sector by one minus the coverage ratio of the sector in the country. Thus, if the subjective benchmark tariff rate is 200 per cent and coverage ratio is 10 per cent, then the country would have a tariff equivalent of 180 per cent (i.e. 0.9 × 200).

Hoekman (1995), when reporting the results of calculations for 26 sectors and 49 countries, used the information on market access commitments and not that on national treatment.

The importance of Hoekman's contribution is acknowledged in the literature, and the indices have been used in many empirical studies. There are certainly some clear advantages of Hoekman indices. First, they cover all sectors and a very large group of countries. Second, it is fairly easy to apply the Hoekman approach to the new WTO member states undertaking new GATS commitments. His approach requires no specific country and sectoral field studies.

The Australian Productivity Commission's approach to estimating tariff equivalents in services

A more elaborate restrictiveness measure than that of Hoekman has been constructed for different service industries by the APC in collaboration with the University of Adelaide and the Australian National University. To develop these indices, the actual restrictions on trade in a service industry are compiled from specifically designed questionnaires using a number of different sources. These restrictions are then assigned scores and grouped into categories, each of which is assigned a numerical weight. These scores and weights are based on subjective assessments of the costs of restrictions to economic efficiency. Finally, the sectoral tariff equivalents are computed using these scores and econometrically estimated relations between restrictiveness values and performance indicators such as the price of the service under consideration.[5]

The gravity approach to estimating tariff equivalents in services

The basic method for estimating services barriers by the gravity approach involves the estimation of sector-specific gravity equations, which relate the bilateral trade flow from country i to country j to the exporting and importing countries' gross domestic product (GDP) per capita, the populations in the two countries, the distance between the two countries, the trade barriers and a set of country dummies such as adjacency, common language and regional trading arrangements (e.g. EU membership). Using the econometrically estimated gravity equation and a measure of the elasticity of substitution for the service sector under consideration we obtain the tariff equivalent of barriers to trade in the service sector under consideration.[6]

Barriers to trade in different service sectors

When trying to estimate the tariff equivalents in services in Turkey it is noted that Hoekman's approach reveals certain weaknesses. First, the indices do not assign weights to entry barriers based on their differential impacts on the economy. As all limitations receive the same weighting (0.5), minor impediments are treated exactly the same as almost complete refusal of foreign entry into a domestic market. Second, the indices are constructed on the basis of the GATS schedules of commitments, many of which do not provide an accurate description of the actual barriers. The indices reflect the level of commitments made by the member countries some time ago and, as a result, they do not in general show the present level of restrictions in particular service sectors. In several sectors the current level of liberalization exceeds the level of liberalization when the schedules of WTO commitments were undertaken in 2004. Thus, current average levels of tariff equivalents can be quite different from Hoekman's guesstimates, even assuming that they were initially correct. Third, considering an unscheduled sector as being completely closed to new entry does not give a clear picture of the situation either. It may well be the case that actual practices are more liberal than commitments, and therefore the indices may be overstating the degree of protection. Finally, the absolute level of indices depends very much on benchmark guesstimates of tariff equivalents of the most protectionist countries. For example, the guesstimate for non-life insurance financial services is 50 per cent, whereas that for life insurance services is 200 per cent. In consequence, the average sectoral level of all countries depends mainly on the level of the guesstimate. Thus, they reflect relative restrictiveness among countries rather than the absolute level of sectoral tariff equivalents; such estimates cannot be directly used in liberalization simulations when information about the absolute level of protection is required.

The main issue with the gravity model is related to the non-availability of data on bilateral sectoral trade flows in services for a large number of countries. Essentially, there are three sources of data for bilateral trade flows in services. The Global Trade Analysis Project (GTAP) database provides a cross-section dataset of world bilateral service trade flows for 2001. Second, the Organization for Economic Co-operation and Development (OECD) provides data on bilateral trade flows in services among the OECD countries.[7] Finally, EU EUROSTAT provides data on EU members' trade in services.[8] The bilateral GTAP data is constructed using various data sources and balanced against the input–output tables and balance-of-payments data. This dataset is aimed at computable general equilibrium (CGE) analysis and is not meant to be used in econometric studies, as many missing data points are estimated using various techniques and do not necessarily resemble real service flows. Moreover, GTAP data refer to one period only, which rules out their use for panel analysis.

On the other hand, the APC's approach is more appropriate for estimating tariff equivalents, as will be explained in some detail later on. As a result, when quantifying the barriers to trade in the Turkish telecommunications, electricity, natural gas, banking, maritime freight transport and road freight transport service sectors we consider the APC's approach, and in cases in which this approach cannot be used we consider the gravity approach or a related approach.

Telecommunications

To estimate the ad valorem equivalent of the prevailing barriers to the telecommunications services sector in Turkey we calculate first the restrictiveness index values, following an approach similar to that of Warren (2000a) and Kimura *et al.* (2003a). Appendix Tables A10.1–A10.3 show – for fixed-line, mobile and internet services, respectively – the restriction categories, weights for them and the scoring for each category. The weights show the importance of the category in terms of how significantly the restriction of the category would limit service suppliers from entering or operating in the market. The sum of weights for all categories is 1. A score with a range from 0 (least restrictive) to 1 (most restrictive) is assigned for each category according to the degree of restrictiveness, and so the score reflects the type of restriction imposed by the economy.

In Appendix Tables A10.1–A10.3 the restriction categories are classified into 'restrictions on commercial presence' and 'other restrictions'. In the case of fixed-line, mobile and internet services the 'restrictions on commercial presence' include 'licensing of fixed-line services', 'form of commercial presence', 'direct investment: equity participation permitted', 'direct investment: restrictions on certain types of services', 'joint venture arrangements' and 'permanent movement of people'. 'Other restrictions' in the case of fixed-line services include 'third party resale of lease line', 'end-user tariff', 'regulation of network interconnection', 'market structure', 'composition of board of directors' and 'temporary movement of people'. In the case of mobile services, 'other restrictions' includes 'allocation of radio spectrum' instead of 'third party resale of lease line', and in the case of internet services 'other restrictions' includes 'infrastructure' instead of 'third party resale' and 'end-user tariff'. Among restrictions, 'licensing of fixed-line services' and 'direct investment: equity participation permitted' have a weight of 20 per cent each. These weights indicate that these barriers are the most important ones.

The Appendix tables reveal that in Turkey there are no restrictions on direct investments or on the permanent movement of people. Comparing the restrictions of fixed-line, mobile and internet services, it is noted that there are fewer restrictions of mobile and internet services than of fixed-line services.[9]

Appendix Table A10.4 shows the foreign restrictiveness (FR) index values for Turkish fixed-line, mobile and internet services. The FR value equals 0.193 in the case of fixed-line, 0.165 in the case of mobile and 0.12 in the case of internet services. To convert these index values into tariff equivalents, we use the coefficients estimated by Warren (2000a). The regression results obtained by Warren (2000a) for fixed-line services and mobile services are reported in Table 10.1. In the table, the penetration rate of fixed-line networks (main lines per 100 inhabitants denoted by q_f) is regressed on GDP per capita (y), household density (number of households per square km denoted by I), per cent of main lines connected to the digital exchange (*dshare*), waiting list as a per cent of the total demand for main lines (*wait*), population density (number of persons per square km denoted by *pd*) and measure of trade policy (p_f). On the other hand, the penetration rate of the mobile network (cellular phones per 100 inhabitants denoted by I) is regressed on y, *pd* and measure of trade policy (p_m).

Denoting the value of the trade policy variable under the full liberalized policy approach by p_i^*, the associated value of the dependent variable by q_i^* and the price elasticity of demand by η_i, ($i = f, m$), we note that:

Table 10.1 The estimated results for the fixed-line and mobile penetration models

	The fixed penetration model		The mobile penetration model	
	Coefficient	Standard error	Coefficient	Standard error
Constant	12.26	2.66	−1.3	0.7
GDP per capita (y)	0.004	0.0003	0.0008	0.00005
y^2	−6.30E–08	0.0	−1.90E–09	0.0
y^3	1.30E–13	0.0		
Household density (hd)	0.003	0.003		
Waiting list ($wait$)	−0.08	0.05		
Digitized network share ($dshare$)	−0.13	0.03		
Population density (pd)			0.001	0.0006
Policy variable (1 − FR index)	5.26	3.11		
Adjusted R-squared	0.89		0.78	

Source: Warren (2000a) (Model 5 in Table 6.5 and Model 7 in Table 6.6).

Note
Dependent variable for the fixed penetration model: mainlines per 100 inhabitants. Dependent variable for the mobile penetration model: cellular mobile subscribers per 100 inhabitants.

$$\frac{q_f^* - q_f}{q_f} = \eta_f \left[\frac{p_f^* - p_f}{p_f} \right] \quad \text{and} \quad \frac{q_m^* - q_m}{q_m} = \eta_m \left[\frac{p_m^* - p_m}{p_m} \right]$$

where subscripts f and m refer to fixed-line and mobile services respectively. Hence, the tariff equivalents (TE_i) are obtained as:

$$\left[\frac{p_f^* - p_f}{p_f} \right] 100 = TE_f \quad \text{and} \quad \left[\frac{p_m^* - p_m}{p_m} \right] 100 = TE_m^{10}$$

Based on these equations, we calculate the ad valorem tariff equivalents of restrictions on the fixed-line services during 2005 as 2.7 per cent, on mobile services as 3.43 per cent and on internet services as 1.64 per cent.[11] The tariff equivalent of restrictions in the telecommunications sector obtained as a weighted average of the tariff equivalents of restrictions in fixed-line, mobile and internet services weighted by sectoral employment levels is then 2.74 per cent. The calculations reveal that the Turkish telecommunications sector as of 2005 was quite liberal but that further efforts are needed for complete liberalization.

The tariff equivalents in the Turkish telecommunications sector during the 1990s were estimated by Warren (2000a) using index values derived from an international survey undertaken by the International Telecommunications Union (1998) for 136 countries. Warren (2000a,b) estimated first the restrictiveness indices to trade in telecommunications and thereafter the price impact. The results are shown in Appendix Table A10.5. From the table, we note that the ad valorem tariff equivalents of restrictions in the telecommunications sector during the 1990s were 33.53 per cent in Turkey and zero per cent in Finland and the United Kingdom. These figures reveal that, as a result of restrictions in the telecommunications sector, the price of telecommunications services in Turkey during the 1990s was 33.53 per cent higher than the average price of telecommunications services in Finland and the United Kingdom.

Electricity

One of the first studies to develop indices of regulatory indicators in the electricity sector was that by Steiner (2000), who uses them to empirically investigate the linkages between regulatory regimes, market environments and performance. The author uses as indicators of performance industrial electricity prices, the ratio of industrial to residential electricity prices, utilization rates (an efficiency measure for generation) and reserve plant margins (an alternative efficiency measure for generation). Steiner concludes that the unbundling of generation and transmission, the expansion of third party access (TPA) and the introduction of electricity markets reduce industrial end-user prices.[12] The results obtained by Steiner were later extended by Doove *et al.* (2001) by increasing the number of countries under consideration from 19 to 50.[13] The data in their analysis refer to the year 1996. Concentrating on the econometric model of the effects of regulation on industrial electricity prices, Steiner's model can be written as follows:

$$p_e = \alpha + \beta R + \gamma NR + \varepsilon$$

where p_e denotes the industrial electricity prices, R the regulatory variables and NR the non-regulatory variables; α, β and γ are vectors of coefficients that were estimated and ε is the residual term. The author considers six regulatory and three non-regulatory variables, as shown in Table 10.2.

Although industrial electricity prices vary with the type and size of business, the electricity demand, the time of day, the time of year, the conditions of supply and the available generating capacity, Steiner (2000) considers the annual average electricity prices per kilowatt-hour (kWh) actually faced by 'industrial' customers, as determined by the International Energy Agency (IEA), as the dependent variable. All prices are converted from units of local currency to US dollars using the OECD's purchasing power parities. It must be noted that the IEA adjusts its electricity prices for the direct effect of taxes and subsidies. The regulatory variables focus on the key economic regulations needed to establish a competitive generation sector – vertical unbundling of the generation system from the transmission system, whether third parties can access the transmission grid and whether a wholesale environment (electricity market) exists. Dummy variables are used to indicate the three key economic regulations needed to establish a competitive generation sector. The unbundling of generation from transmission

Table 10.2 Steiner's model of industrial electricity prices

Variable	How measured
Dependent variable	
Industrial electricity price	Pre-tax industrial price (expressed in US PPP$ per kWh)
Independent regulatory variables	
Unbundling of generation from transmission	Dummy variable (1 = accounting separation or separate companies; 0 = otherwise)
Third-party access	Dummy variable (1 = regulated or negotiated third-party access; 0 = otherwise)
Wholesale pool	Dummy variable (1 = presence of a wholesale electricity market; 0 = otherwise)
Ownership	Discrete variable (4 = private ownership; 3 = mostly private ownership; 2 = mixed; 1 = mostly public; 0 = public)
Time to liberalization	Negative of the number of years to liberalisation (ranges from −11 to 0)
Time to privatization	Negative of the number of years to privatisation (ranges from −11 to 0)
Independent non-regulatory environmental variables	
Hydropower share	Share of electricity generated from hydropower sources
Nuclear share	Share of electricity generated from nuclear sources
Gross domestic product	Gross domestic product (expressed in US PPP$ billion)

Source: Steiner (2000).

Note
US PPP$, value in US dollars at purchasing power parity rates.

variable takes on a value of 1 if separate companies are involved in the generation and transmission sectors or if both sectors are managed by a single entity, but separate accounts are kept for each sector (accounting separation); otherwise it takes on a value of 0. The TPA variable takes on a value of 1 if generators and eligible customers have a legal right to access the transmission grid on certain prespecified terms and conditions (regulated TPA) or can negotiate the terms and conditions under which grid access can occur directly with the operator of the transmission grid (negotiated TPA); otherwise it takes on a value of 0. The wholesale environment variable takes on a value of 1 if generators can voluntarily sell or are obliged to sell their electricity into a wholesale electricity market; otherwise it takes on a value of 0.

In addition to the above three regulatory variables needed to establish a competitive generation sector, Steiner (2000) included three market structure variables in the model: ownership, the time to liberalization and the time to privatization. The ownership variable takes on different discrete values ranging from 0 to 4, depending on the mix of public and private ownership, as shown in Table 10.2. The time to liberalization and time to privatization variables measure the (negative) number of years to liberalization and privatization respectively. Indicators of the time remaining to liberalization and privatization are included as a proxy for the impact of expectations of liberalization and privatization on prices. They are forward-looking indicators in that they assess the effect of regulation on prices before liberalization or privatization. Here, 'time to liberalization' is interpreted as being the time until the year in which key legislative changes are enacted, and 'time to privatization' is deemed to be the time until the year in which the first sale of a publicly owned generator occurs.

The model also included three non-regulatory environmental variables – the share of electricity generated from hydroelectric resources, the share of electricity generated from nuclear fuel and the GDP. The two share variables reflect differences in generating technologies across economies, which affect the marginal cost and hence the price of generating electricity. Finally, the inclusion of GDP adjusts for differences in the size of economies and is also an overall measure of national income.

As emphasized by Doove *et al.* (2001), Steiner's econometric results, summarized in Table 10.3, indicate the impact of *each* economic regulation parameter on price. From these individual effects it is possible to gauge the overall impact of all economic regulations (regulatory regime) on price. As Steiner's study includes only a subset of economic regulations affecting the generation sector, the impact

Table 10.3 Effects of regulation on electricity prices: random effects model

Variable	Estimated coefficient	Z-statistic	Value under the benchmark regime
Constant	0.0667[a]	7.104	0.0667
Regulatory and industry variables			
Unbundling of generation from transmission	−0.0011	−0.659	Separate
Private ownership	0.0029[a]	2.7	[c]
Third-party access	−0.0027	−1.357	Third-party access
Wholesale pool	−0.0052[a]	−2.306	Yes
Time to liberalization	0.0008[a]	2.814	[c]
Time to privatization	0.0006[b]	1.51	[c]
Non-regulatory environmental variables			
Hydropower share in generation	−0.0341	−3.252	[d]
Nuclear share in generation	0.0023	0.132	[d]
Gross domestic product	0	1.011	[d]

Source: Steiner (2000).

Notes
a Statistically significant at the 5 per cent level.
b Statistically significant at the 20 per cent level.
c Not included in the calculation of the price impacts because sign of estimated coefficient was counterintuitive.
d Takes actual value in benchmark regime.

measures calculated here are unlikely to measure the full extent to which economic regulations impact industrial electricity prices.

The price impacts estimated for each economy measure the percentage increase in price attributable to inappropriate regulation. Here, we need an appropriate benchmark against which the effect of regulatory regimes can be measured. This benchmark corresponds to the optimal level of regulation, namely the socially least costly way of achieving the desired objectives. Doove *et al.* (2001) emphasize that one practical option is to use the combination of regulations that minimize the prices implied by the estimated equation. Noting that, for regulation i, the effect of inappropriate regulation on price (dp^i_e) is the extent of inappropriate regulation (dR_i) multiplied by the estimated coefficient corresponding to regulation i (β_i), $dp^i_e = \beta_i dR_i$, the impact of the entire regulatory regime on price (dp_e) is obtained by adding the individual effects of all of the n regulations, irrespective of whether or not the coefficients are statistically significant:

$$dp_e = \sum_{i=1}^{n} \beta_i \, dR_i$$

If inappropriate regulation increases prices by dp_e, the notional price expected to exist under the benchmark regime (p^0) can be estimated as the actual price less the change in price attributable to inappropriate regulation, or

$$p^0 = p_e - dp_e = p_e - \sum_{i=1}^{n} \beta_i \, dR_i$$

Expressing this change in price as a percentage of the implied price under the benchmark regime gives:

$$\text{Price impact} = \frac{dp_e}{p^0} = \frac{p_e - p^0}{p^0} = \frac{\sum_{i=1}^{n} \beta_i \, dR_i}{p_e - \sum_{i=1}^{n} \beta_i \, dR_i}$$

When using this approach we note that three of the six regulatory coefficients have the expected sign. Separating generation from transmission, allowing TPA to the transmission grid and allowing for a wholesale electricity market are all found to lead to lower prices. The coefficients on the three remaining variables – private ownership, time to liberalization and time to privatization – are less intuitive. As the coefficients are counterintuitive, Doove *et al.* (2001) decide not to include them in the calculation of the price impacts.

Using the methodology outlined above, price impacts were estimated for industrial electricity prices for each of the 50 economies during 1996. The price impact for the EU countries and Turkey are shown in Table 10.4. From the table, we note that the ad valorem tariff equivalent of restrictions in the Turkish electricity sector during the 1990s was 20.7 per cent. This figure reveals that, as a result of the regulatory regime implemented in Turkey in the electricity sector during

Table 10.4 Price impact of regulation in electricity supply

Country	Price impact (%)
Austria	13.2
Belgium	15.4
Denmark	8.5
Finland	0.0
France	16.0
Germany	8.3
Greece	16.6
Ireland	13.9
Italy	17.1
Luxembourg	13.8
Netherlands	15.5
Portugal	17.9
Spain	9.5
Sweden	0.0
United Kingdom	0.0
Turkey	20.7

Source: Doove *et al.* (2001).

this time, the price of electricity services was 20.7 per cent higher than the price of electricity services in the United Kingdom and Sweden.

Natural gas

To estimate the ad valorem equivalent of barriers to trade in natural gas, we make use of a study by the Department of Trade and Industry (2005). This study, developing a model of the natural gas market for the EU, considers three scenarios. The first scenario, which is called the 'constrained case', takes a fairly pessimistic view of what competition in the gas market will be like by 2015. Here, although the second gas directive has been transposed into national law by all member states of the EU, there has been little real enthusiasm for competition and the European gas market continues to be characterized as a series of national markets. The second case, called the 'most competitive case', represents the most positive outcome from the point of view of competition in the gas market that can reasonably be expected over the next ten years. Long-term contracts continue to play an important part in the market but pricing terms move away from oil-price indexation to market-related pricing. Liberalization within the EU itself is substantially complete but there remain problems beyond the EU's borders. Although some reform has been attempted in Russia, who, in this outcome, has signed the Energy Charter Treaty, Gazprom remains dominant over Russian production and effectively manages to exclude gas from the Caspian area from direct access to the European market. The third case, called the 'fully competitive case', represents the best possible case from the point of view of competition in the gas market. It depicts a fully competitive gas market in the EU and globally by 2015–16. Within the EU, the liberalization process has been completed and there has been substantial reform in the gas market in Russia and other gas-producing countries. The liquid natural gas (LNG) market becomes fully commoditized with extensive spot trade.

Using the Energy Markets' European Gas Model, the Department of Trade and Industry (2005) calculates the spot price for each of the 25 countries considered in the study to be the marginal cost of supply, including gas costs, transportation costs and storage costs. The marginal cost is calculated as the increase in total costs in the entire model that result from increasing the demand in a particular country in a particular quarter by a small increment (1 million cubic metres) while holding all other assumptions and constraints unchanged. The results are reported in Table 10.5. Considering the constrained case as the base case, we note

Table 10.5 Gas price by scenario (price per unit of therm, real 2004 prices)

Country	Constraint case	Most competitive	Fully competitive
Austria	18.9	21.1	14.6
Belgium	31.0	19.5	15.3
Bulgaria	17.1	10.8	11.6
Croatia	19.9	12.3	16.3
Czech Republic	20.3	10.9	14.0
Denmark	17.7	13.8	13.8
Finland	11.6	8.2	9.1
France	37.4	20.6	16.1
Germany	22.8	14.6	14.2
Greece	18.6	11.9	12.9
Hungary	18.0	21.1	12.1
Ireland	36.6	24.6	18.2
Italy	19.7	10.0	14.1
Luxembourg	24.6	16.9	17.4
Netherlands	26.1	16.1	12.7
Poland	11.5	9.8	9.2
Portugal	12.7	20.5	17.6
Romania	16.5	20.0	11.2
Slovak Republic	15.8	8.6	11.7
Slovenia	20.5	13.2	16.2
Spain	30.6	13.6	15.0
Sweden	18.8	14.1	12.7
Switzerland	32.8	20.5	15.2
Turkey	34.9	14.1	11.2
UK	31.5	20.4	16.6

Source: Department of Trade and Industry (2005).

by comparing the most competitive case with the base case that liberalization of natural gas markets will lead to a 59.6 per cent reduction in the spot price of natural gas in Turkey.

Banking

McGuire and Schuele (2000), extending the work of McGuire (1998), develop index values of restrictiveness in financial services for a number of countries. The authors base their analysis on 1997 data and distinguish between prudential and non-prudential requirements. They note that prudential requirements aimed at ensuring the stability of the banking system by preserving solvency, limiting risks and protecting bank deposits are generally similar across economies. Therefore they remove from consideration prudential requirements and concentrate on non-prudential requirements. The index values of the non-prudential variables considered by McGuire and Schuele are shown in Appendix Table A10.6, in which scores range from 0 (least restrictive) to 1 (most restrictive). In the table, the restrictions have been divided into two groupings: those affecting 'commercial presence' and other restrictions called 'restrictions on ongoing operations'. Whereas the first group indicates restrictions on the movement of capital, the latter group is modelled as restrictions on trade in banking services. The commercial presence restriction grouping covers restrictions on licensing, direct investment, joint venture arrangements and the permanent movement of people. The other restrictions grouping covers restrictions on raising funds, lending funds, providing other lines of business, expanding banking outlets, the composition of the board of directors and the temporary movement of people. Given the scores shown in Appendix Table A10.6 for each variable considered, the authors assign weights to the variables and first obtain restrictiveness index values for the two categories and then the overall restrictiveness index values for the economies considered.

The scores shown in the second column of Appendix Table A10.7 reveal that the foreign restrictiveness index (FR index) for Turkish banking services is 0.05. The foreign discriminatory restrictiveness index (FDR index) is a subset of the FR index and covers discriminatory restrictions imposed only on foreign services providers. When estimating the FDR index, we regard 'licensing of banks', 'other business of banks – insurance and securities' and 'expanding the number of banking outlets' as aspects that partially restrict the activities of both domestic and foreign services suppliers, that is, as possible non-discriminatory restrictions. As such restrictions could still be imposed on foreign suppliers more discriminatorily but could be removed at the same time for both domestic and foreign suppliers, half of their weights are assigned for these restriction categories in calculating the FDR index. Calculations reveal that the FDR index for the Turkish banking sector is 0.025.[14]

To convert the index values into tax equivalents, we use the coefficients estimated by Kalirajan *et al.* (2000) that quantify the impact of restrictions on trade in banking services on the net interest margins (NIM) of banks.[15] The ad valorem equivalent of restrictions is then calculated from the formula:

$$100*\left[\frac{NIM_1 - NIM_0}{NIM_0}\right] = 100*(e^{0.732*TRI} - 1)$$

where NIM_1 denotes the net interest margin under restrictions, NIM_0 the net interest margin under free trade and *TRI* the value of the trade restrictiveness index. Based on this equation, we calculate the ad valorem tariff equivalent of restrictions in the banking sector measured by the FR index as 3.73 per cent. On the other hand, the tariff equivalent of restrictions in the banking sector measured by the FDR index is 1.85 per cent. These calculations reveal that the Turkish banking sector as of 2005 was quite liberal.

Using the methodology outlined above, tariff equivalents of barriers to trade in banking services were estimated by Kalirajan *et al.* (2000) for a large number of countries using 1997 data. The results of these calculations for EU countries and Turkey are shown in Appendix Table A10.8. From the table, we note that the ad valorem tariff equivalents of restrictions in the banking sector during the 1990s were 31.54 per cent in Turkey and 5.32 per cent in the EU countries. This figure reveals that, as a result of restrictions in the banking sector, the price of banking services in Turkey during the 1990s was 26.22 per cent higher than the average price of banking services in the EU.

Maritime freight transportation

To assess the tariff equivalents of barriers to trade in the maritime freight transport sector, we first calculate restrictiveness index values following the approach of McGuire *et al.* (2000) and Kimura *et al.* (2004). Appendix Table A10.9 shows for maritime transportation services the restriction categories, weights for them and scoring for each category.[16] The weights again show the importance of the category in terms of how significantly the restriction of the category would limit service suppliers from entering or operating in the market.[17] In the table the restriction categories are classified into 'restrictions on commercial presence and cross-border trade' and 'other restrictions'. The 'restrictions on commercial presence and cross-border trade' include 'conditions on the right to fly the national flag', 'form of commercial presence', 'direct investment in shipping service suppliers', 'direct investment in onshore maritime service suppliers', 'permanent movement of people', 'cabotage' and 'transportation of non-commercial cargoes'. On the other hand, 'other restrictions' include 'port services', 'discretionary imposition of restrictions, including for retaliatory purposes', 'United Nations Liner Code', 'government permits conferences', 'bilateral maritime services agreements on cargo sharing', 'composition of board of directors' and 'temporary movement of people'.

Appendix Table A10.10 reveals that the FR index value for Turkish maritime transportation services equals 0.5667. The corresponding restrictiveness index values for the EU countries estimated by McGuire *et al.* (2000) for the period 1994–8 are shown in Appendix Table A10.11. To convert these index values into tariff equivalents, we use the method employed by Kang (2000). He uses shipping margins as a proxy for shipping price and defines shipping margins from country i (exporter) to country j (importer), M_{ij}, as:

$$M_{ij} = \frac{IM_{ji}}{EX_{ij}},$$

where IM_{ji} represents the value of imports inclusive of cost, insurance and freight (CIF) of country j, which are imported from country i, and EX_{ij} represents the observed free on board (FOB) value of exports of country i, which are exported to country j. Shipping margins, M_{ij}, are assumed to be a function of bilateral restrictions (R_{ij}), distance between countries (D_{ij}) and the scale of bilateral trade (SC_{ij}). As R_{ij} includes the information on restrictions on both sides, that is, exporter's and importer's, the equation determining shipping margins can be rewritten as follows:

$$\ln(M_{ij}) = C + \alpha_{11}\ln(R_{io}) + \alpha_{12}\ln(R_{ic}) + \alpha_{21}\ln(R_{jo}) + \alpha_{22}\ln(R_{jc}) + \beta\ln(D_{ij}) + \gamma\ln(SC_{ij}),$$

where R_i and R_j, the restrictiveness indices in countries i and j, respectively, are divided into restrictions on commercial presence $(R_{ic}$ and $R_{jc})$ and other restrictions $(R_{io}$ and $R_{jo})$. Based on this equation, Kang (2000) estimates the price impact of restrictions on shipping margins for the case of developing economies as follows:

$$\ln(M_{ij}) = 0.3388 + 0.1416\ln(R_{ic}) + 0.0443\ln(R_{jo}) + 0.0011\ln(D_{ij}) - 0.0049\ln(SC_{ij}).$$

To study the effects of EU integration, we consider the case in which the degree of existing restrictions in Turkey is lowered to the level of the EU average calculated from data provided by McGuire *et al.* (2000). To obtain ad valorem equivalents of restrictions in Turkey, shipping margins with existing restrictions, M_{Turkey}, and shipping margins with restrictions at the average EU levels, M^*_{Turkey}, are first calculated based on the following equations:

$$\ln(M_{Turkey}) = \ln(M_{Average}) - 0.1416[\ln R^c_{Average} - \ln R^c_{Turkey}] - 0.0443[\ln R^o_{Average} - \ln R^o_{Turkey}]$$

$$\ln(M^*_{Turkey}) = \ln(M_{Turkey}) - 0.1416[\ln R^c_{Turkey} - \ln R^c_{EU}] - 0.0443[\ln R^o_{Turkey} - \ln R^o_{EU}]$$

where $M_{Average}$, $R^c_{Average}$ and $R^o_{Average}$ denote the average of the shipping margins, the average value of the restrictiveness index on commercial presence and the average value of the restrictiveness index on other restrictions, respectively, over the countries reported in McGuire *et al.* (2000). Similarly, R^c_{Turkey}, R^o_{Turkey}, R^c_{EU} and R^o_{EU} denote restrictiveness index values on commercial presence and other restrictions in Turkey and the EU. The ad valorem equivalent is then calculated by the formula:

$$\left[\frac{(M_{\text{Turkey}} - 1) - (M^*_{\text{Turkey}} - 1)}{(M^*_{\text{Turkey}} - 1)} \right] 100$$

Based on this equation, we calculate ad valorem tariff equivalents of restrictions in the maritime transportation sector, measured by the FR index, as 193.5 per cent, taking as the benchmark the prices in Germany. Thus, the price of maritime services in Turkey decreases by 193.5 per cent if Turkey adopts and implements the EU rules and regulations on maritime transport services.

Road freight transportation

To estimate the ad valorem equivalent of barriers to trade in road freight services we make use of the gravity model. We consider the approach developed by Francois *et al.* (2007). They use data on services trade that come from the OECD supplemented with published International Monetary Fund (IMF) balance of payments statistics. These data cover 178 countries for 10 years (1994–2004), and they show trade with the world. Other country data (GDP, country populations) are from the World Bank's World Development Indicators database. The authors employ a two-step procedure. In the first stage they regress transport service imports on the usual gravity variables: GDP per capita, population and distance. As transport service data do not refer to bilateral trade data the authors construct a measure of GDP-weighted distance to a hypothetical centre of the world. This index of 'centrality' is then used as the distance variable in the first stage. In the second stage they regress the residuals from the first stage on individual country dummies. This second stage gives an indication of how protected individual markets are, and the authors then use the resulting coefficients to calculate the trade costs in percentages of delivered prices. These costs are seen as relative protection benchmarked against Hong Kong and Singapore, which the authors consider to be the closest they have in the sample to free trade countries. The calculations reveal that the ad valorem equivalent of barriers to trade in transport services is 41.05 per cent, which we in the following consider as the ad valorem equivalent of barriers to trade in road freight transport services.

Effects of liberalization

We predict that liberalization of trade in goods and services will remove the distortions in the price system, which in turn will boost the economy's allocative efficiency. As a side effect, this heightened efficiency will improve the country's investment climate. Investments will increase as well as foreign direct investment (FDI) inflows. Consequently, the allocative efficiency gains from liberalization will be boosted by induced capital formation. While investment increases above its normal level the economy will experience a growth effect. All of these possible developments are salutary for the material well-being of people in the long term. To quantitatively assess these effects we study first the implications of liberalization on the telecommunications, electricity, natural gas, banking, maritime freight transport and road freight transport sectors of the Turkish economy, and thereafter concentrate on an analysis of the trade effects of economic liberalization.

Estimated benefits of liberalization through harmonization

To estimate the benefits of liberalization through harmonizing rules and regulations we consider the case of a particular sector, namely electricity, in some detail.[18] This approach is then applied to other sectors in a similar way.

In the case of electricity, we compare the Turkish economy in a base case with the case when Turkey liberalizes completely in the sector. As the base case we consider the Turkish economy with the rules and regulations as they prevailed during the 1990s, when Turkey's electricity sector was not liberalized. Next we consider the case when Turkey liberalizes the electricity sector by adopting and implementing all of the rules and regulations of the most liberal countries in the EU.[19] Here we refrain from explicit consideration of the problems of implementation over time, and assume that, once the electricity sector *acquis* is adopted, liberalization of the sector is achieved. This is a grand simplification, but it permits the analysis to be performed rather easily.

From the section on barriers to trade in different service sectors we know that the tariff equivalent of barriers to trade in electricity services in Turkey during the 1990s was 20.7 per cent. On the other hand, the tariff equivalent of barriers to trade in electricity services in the United Kingdom and Sweden, the benchmark countries, was zero per cent during the 1990s. One could thus infer that, as a result of the regulatory regime implemented in Turkey during the 1990s in the electricity sector, the price of electricity services during the 1990s was 20.7 per cent higher than the price of electricity services in the United Kingdom and Sweden. A change in the Turkish regulatory regime to that of the United Kingdom or Sweden would thus decrease the price of electricity services by 20.7 per cent. Given this change in the price of electricity services resulting from the change in Turkey's regulatory regime, one could then compute the change in Turkish consumer surplus as a measure of the welfare effect of liberalization from information on the consumers' electricity demand schedule.[20] However, electricity services are intermediate commodities that are used in the production of other commodities. Therefore, prices of other commodities in the economy will change as a result of the change in the price of electricity services. To study the welfare effects of liberalization, one has to consider not only the change in consumer surplus due to changes in the price of electricity services but also the changes in consumer surpluses due to changes in the prices of other commodities.

To analyze the effect of the change in the price of electricity services on the prices of other commodities we consider the 1998 input–output table for Turkey, which consists of 97 sectors and in which electricity is sector 69. Let **A** be the 97×97 matrix of input coefficients. Given **A**, form the 96×96 input matrix **B** by deleting the sixty-ninth column and the sixty-ninth row referring to the electricity sector. Denote the sixty-ninth row of **A** where the sixty-ninth column element has been deleted by e. Let p be the 1×96 price vector of the 96 commodities, excluding the electricity services sector, and va the corresponding 1×96 unit gross value added vector. The price equations in the economy can be written as $p = pB + p_e e + va$, where p_e denotes the price of the electricity services. Hence we have $p = p_e e (\mathbf{I} - \mathbf{B})^{-1} + va(\mathbf{I} - \mathbf{B})^{-1}$. Note that base year domestic prices of all commodities equal unity in the input–output table. Given the tariff equivalent of barriers to trade in electricity services denoted by t we can write the price equation in the electricity sector as $1 = p_e(1 + t)$. Thus we have $p_e = 1/(1 + t)$. Hence, given the new price of electricity services that will prevail in Turkey after it adopts and implements rules and regulations similar to those in the United Kingdom and Sweden, p_e, we can determine the equilibrium prices of the other 96 commodities from the above relation.

Given the new equilibrium price vector p, form the 1×97 price vector as $\pi = (p \ p_e)$. Let CON be the 96×1 consumption expenditure vector obtained from the 1998 input–output table by deleting the value of the consumption of the electricity services sector, and con_e be the value of the consumption of electricity services. Form the 97×1 consumption vector as:

$$CONS = \begin{bmatrix} CON \\ con_e \end{bmatrix}$$

Letting u denote the 1×97 unit vector, we can express the value of total consumption expenditure evaluated at base prices as $C = u\text{CONS}$. The value of total consumption expenditure evaluated at the prices that will prevail after Turkey adopts and implements the EU rules and regulations in the banking services sector can be computed by the relation $C^* = \pi\text{CONS}$. The effect on consumer welfare can now be calculated as:

$$(C - C^*)100/C^*$$

Hence, with the new price of electricity services, we observe that the welfare of Turkish society will increase by 0.6458 per cent. Given that consumption formed 80.834 per cent of the 1998 Turkish GDP, the percentage change in the welfare of society is equivalent to a 0.522 per cent increase in real GDP.

Table 10.6 shows the tariff equivalents of barriers to trade in various service sectors and network industries prevailing in the latter half of the 1990s in Turkey, as well as the tariff equivalents for the year 2005. The table also shows the tariff equivalents in the EU or in some benchmark countries of the EU during the latter half of the 1990s. Finally, the last column shows the tariff equivalents used in the present study when evaluating the effects of the liberalization of services and network industries within the context of economic liberalization.

Using the approach adopted for analyzing the effects of the liberalization of electricity services on other sectors, we note the percentage change in GDP as a result of the liberalization of banking, telecommunications, maritime transport, road freight transport, electricity and natural gas services will be as reported in Table 10.7.

Table 10.6 Tariff equivalents of barriers to trade in services and network industries in Turkey and the EU (%)

	Turkey end of 1990s	*EU end of 1990s*	*Net effect end of 1990s*	*Turkey 2005*	*EU 2005*	*Tariff equivalent in trade with the EU used in this study*
Banking	31.54	5.32	26.22	3.73	–	26.22
Telecommunications	33.53	0.00	33.53	2.74	–	33.53
Maritime transportation services	–	–	–	193.50	–	193.50
Road transportation services	–	–	–	–	–	41.05
Electricity	20.70	0.00	20.70	–	–	20.70
Natural gas	–	–	–	–	–	59.60

Sources: Own calculations, Findlay and Warren (2000) and Francois *et al.* (2007).

Note
Tariff equivalents for the EU at the end of the 1990s in telecommunications and electricity refer to those of Finland and the United Kingdom. Tariff equivalents for road transport services are obtained from Francois *et al.* (2007).

Estimated benefits of liberalization via increased trade exposure

To study the trade effects of economic liberalization within the context of the possible accession of Turkey to the EU, we consider the gravity equation:

$$[(\ln X_{ij} + \ln X_{ji})/2] = \beta_0 + \beta_1 \ln[Y_i Y_j] + \beta_2 \ln[Y_i^{pc} Y_j^{pc}] + \beta_3 \ln GD + \beta_4 Z + \varepsilon$$

where X_{ij} are the exports from country i to country j, Y_i is the GDP of country i, Y_i^{pc} is the GDP per capita in country i, GD is the geographical distance, Z refers to the additional vector of variables and ε stands for the error term.

Estimates of the various gravity specifications based on data for the EU-15 countries and Turkey are presented in Table 10.8, which suggests that the gravity equation explains at least 90 per cent of the variation in 1989–2004 data.[21] Panel income elasticity of average trade flow is positive and statistically significant as expected, ranging between 0.82 and 0.96. GDP per capita also contributes positively to trade. Geographical distance between countries has a significant negative coefficient estimate in all specifications. Existence of a common border implies higher trade between countries.

Among the specifications presented in Table 10.8, ordinary least squares (OLS) forms a good basis to generate forecasts of trade flow between Turkey and the EU-15 countries because it includes practically all conventional constituents of a gravity equation, with the expected impact coefficients and adequate statistical significance. Moreover, this specification includes country-specific controls for Turkey.

Table 10.7   Effect of liberalization of services and network industries on gross domestic product (GDP) in Turkey

Service	Change in GDP (%)
Banking	2.402
Telecommunications	0.448
Maritime transportation	0.514
Road freight transportation	2.489
Electricity	0.522
Natural gas	0.067

Source: Own calculations.

The estimate of the gravity equation obtained above is used to make forecasts of bilateral trade for Turkey with the EU-15. We compute the bilateral flows for Turkey with each of the EU-15 countries and aggregate the individual flows to obtain the aggregate view of trade between Turkey and the EU-15. This specification includes all explanatory variables except for the common border dummy. This omission is not vital as Turkey has no common border with any EU-15 country except Greece. The forecasts are presented for the period 1996–2005 in Table 10.9.

While computing the forecasts, the only estimated coefficient that was tailored was the coefficient for the Turkey dummy. No other prior judgements were imposed on the overall setup. One can recall that the coefficient sign of the Turkey dummy is negative in the OLS (2) specification. This indicates that trade values of country pairs including Turkey are lower than those excluding Turkey. Accession of Turkey to the EU can be expected to address this disadvantaged situation and improve Turkey's trade with the union. Consequently, the coefficient of the Turkey dummy is taken as zero in computing forecasts. In this way, the assumption that Turkey's trade with the EU economy will reach the current intensity of intra-EU trade flows is facilitated.

Focusing on the 2002–5 time period, the hypothesized accession of Turkey to the EU yields an extra volume of trade, which is equivalent on average to 3.59 per cent of Turkey's GDP. Following Frankel and Rose (2002), this is at least equivalent to a 1.2 per cent increase in the Turkish per capita income.

Epilogue

The ten chapters of this book cover issues related to liberalization of foreign trade, liberalization of FDI and the role of regulatory institutions in trade liberalization. This book shows that economic liberalization, whether pursued unilaterally, multilaterally or regionally, has beneficial effects for the country under consideration. To provide a partial cross-check on the results, consider the OECD (2005b) study, which quantifies the benefits that arise from significant reductions of the barriers that inhibit product market entry, FDI and trade in OECD countries.

Table 10.8 Gravity equation estimates

	OLS (A1)	OLS (A2)	*Random effects GLS (A1)*[a]	*Random effects GLS (A2)*[a]
Constant	−9.488522 [−13.12622][b]	−12.32887 [−16.54704]	−11.52878 [−5.511467]	−12.41714 [−6.111803]
Log real product GDP	0.837095 [87.04632]	0.818938 [86.76206]	0.961756 [21.23487]	0.93844 [20.77914]
Log real product GDP per capita	0.104796 [3.136588]	0.21013 [6.237921]	0.029293 [0.333312]	0.061381 [0.700540]
Log distance	−0.943771 [-38.65429]	−0.761815 [−26.40042]	−0.870832 [−7.801302]	−0.758538 [−6.786132]
Common border		0.485018 [10.95026]		0.361623 [4.312924]
Time trend[c]	0.017455 [5.529738]	0.013852 [4.515573]	0.013862 [3.511735]	0.013697 [3.511987]
Turkey[d]	−0.532389 [−7.492635]	−0.390682 [−5.591877]	−0.650494 [−0.913367]	−0.626695 [−0.904461]
Turkey 0204 (2002–4 period)[e]	0.469746 [5.192272]	0.476349 [5.449031]	0.500977 [6.731960]	0.50392 [6.712375]
Sample (time dimension)	1989–2004	1989–2004	1989–2004	1989–2004
Sample (number of cross-sections)	105	105	105	105
R-squared	0.907655	0.913834	0.898355	0.905318

Source: Own calculations.

Notes

GLS, generalized least squares; OLS, ordinary least squares.

a Component variances have been obtained through Swamy and Arora estimator. For the cross-section standard errors and variances, the White procedure, with degrees of freedom correction, was used.

b *t*-statistics are displayed in square brackets.

c Time trend is defined over each cross-section such that it has a unit increment each year.

d Turkey dummy controls the trade pairs involving Turkey.

e This controls the post-2001 episode for the trade pairs involving Turkey.

Table 10.9 Forecast of Turkish trade with EU-15 (1996–2005)

	Actual trade *(million US$)*	*Forecast trade[a]* *(million US$)*	*GDP* *(million US$)*
1996	15,843.16	16,900.20	181,051.10
1997	17,148.11	17,496.82	189,164.60
1998	17,904.72	18,217.73	199,633.80
1999	17,314.40	17,742.43	183,823.40
2000	19,570.38	18,862.05	199,267.30
2001	16,938.80	17,591.24	145,243.60
2002	20,339.64	31,315.30	183,888.30
2003	27,623.67	37,717.66	240,375.80
2004	37,424.88	46,216.75	302,785.80
2005	40,630.98	49,962.69	363,299.90

Note
a   The forecast figures have been obtained by using the OLS (A1) specification in Table 10.8. No calibrations were made to the estimated coefficients.

The study identifies across the OECD the countries with a regulatory framework most supportive of good economic performance and evaluates what economic benefits would materialize if other countries aligned their frameworks with 'best practices'. The relaxed barriers include competition-restraining product market regulations, obstacles to FDI and tariffs. It turns out that the benefits from such liberalization are substantial. On average, reducing barriers to trade, investment and competition could increase the level of GDP per head over the medium term by some 3 per cent in each of the main OECD regions, and for the OECD as a whole GDP per capita would increase by 2–5 per cent. In particular for Turkey, the effect of bilateral tariff reductions is 1 per cent, the effect of relaxing obstacles to FDI 0.3 per cent and the effect of regulatory reforms 3.1 per cent. Thus the overall effect of liberalization for Turkey according to the OECD (2005b) amounts to a 4.7 per cent increase in GDP per capita.

Although economic liberalization is beneficial for countries, it also imposes costs, which may vary depending on the type of economic liberalization adopted (unilateral, multilateral or regional). The costs for Turkey have been particularly high in the case of the elimination of technical barriers to trade (TBT), discussed in Chapter 3, and they will be considerably high in the cases of adjusting to EU's banking, maritime freight transportation and road freight transportation *acquis*.

Trying to eliminate the TBTs following the EU approach, the Turkish public sector incurred considerable adjustment costs associated with adopting the EU's technical legislation; establishing institutions required for the efficient functioning of quality infrastructure such as the Turkish Accreditation Agency (TURKAK), the National Metrology Institute, and market surveillance authorities; training and employing a sufficient number of qualified and experienced staff with the necessary professional integrity to be employed in those institutions; and acquiring the technical infrastructure (laboratories, cars, fuel) required for efficient functioning of the system. Although substantial progress has been achieved by Turkey between 1995 and 2009, the task is still not complete. Additional adjustment costs must be incurred. Turkey has incurred these costs with the hope of becoming a full member of the EU, and they were considered the unavoidable costs of EU accession. But as the chances of EU membership have decreased over time, doubts have arisen in Turkey as to whether the strategy adopted to eliminate TBTs by following the EU approach has in fact been the right strategy. Similar considerations apply also to the costs of adopting and implementing the maritime freight transportation *acquis* discussed in Chapter 8 and the road freight transportation *acquis* discussed in Chapter 9.

From the point of view of a neighbouring country of the EU with no hope of EU accession the optimal economic liberalization strategy is to acquire the institutions for running a successful market economy and to follow the 'universal' principles of sound economic policy discussed in Chapter 1. The neighbouring country of the EU could achieve these goals by adopting and implementing that part of the *acquis* which may be considered as pro-growth – all of the directives and regulations that will help the neighbouring country to acquire the high-quality institutions for running a successful market economy and to follow the 'universal' principles of sound economic policy.[22] On the other hand, the current Turkish EU policy of carrying on with accession negotiations, however long the negotiations might take, remains as the best strategy for Turkey, as long as Turkish policy makers perceive the chances of the country's eventual EU membership as quite high. But during the period when accession negotiations take place, Turkey could still concentrate its efforts on adopting and implementing the pro-growth part of the *acquis* and leave the adoption and implementation of the other part of the *acquis* for later periods when the prospects of EU accession improve. This kind of policy would provide a plan B in case the accession negotiations fail at some point in the future.

Appendix

Table A10.1 The foreign restrictiveness index: restrictions on the fixed-line sector in Turkey, 2005

Weight	Scoring	Score	Category
			Restrictions on commercial presence
0.20			*Licensing of fixed-line services*
			(a) Regional line service
	1.00	1.00	No new licence allowed
	0.75		Licences are issued through complicated (discriminately) and costly procedures
	0.20		Licences are generally issued with application fee and several requirements
	0.10		Licences are generally issued with application fee
	0.00		Licences are automatically issued upon application without any cost
			(b) Domestic long-distance line service
	1.00		No new licence allowed
	0.75		Licences are issued through complicated (discriminately) and costly procedures
	0.20	0.20	Licences are generally issued with application fee and several requirements
	0.10		Licences are generally issued with application fee
	0.00		Licences are automatically issued upon application without any cost
			(c) International line service
	1.00		No new licence allowed
	0.75		Licences are issued through complicated (discriminately) and costly procedures
	0.20	0.20	Licences are generally issued with application fee and several requirements
	0.10		Licences are generally issued with application fee
	0.00		Licences are automatically issued upon application without any cost
0.10			*Form of commercial presence*
			(a) Regional line service
	1.00	1.00	Measures that restrict or require a specific type of establishment
	0.00		No restriction on establishment
			(b) Domestic long-distance line service
	1.00		Measures that restrict or require a specific type of establishment
	0.00	0.00	No restriction on establishment
			(c) International line service
	1.00		Measures that restrict or require a specific type of establishment
	0.00	0.00	No restriction on establishment

Weight	Scoring	Score	Category
0.20			*Direct investment: equity participation permitted*
		0.00	The score is inversely proportional to the maximum equity participation permitted in an existing domestic company
0.10			*Direct investment: restrictions on certain types of services*
	1.00		Restrictions on providing some types of telephone service
	0.00	0.00	No restrictions on providing any type of telephone service
0.10			*Joint venture arrangements*
	1.00		Issues no new licence and no entry is allowed through a joint venture with a domestic company
	0.50		Foreign company can enter only through a joint venture with a domestic company
	0.00	0.00	No requirement for foreign companies to enter through a joint venture with a domestic company
0.02			*Permanent movement of people*
	1.00		No entry of executives, senior managers and/or specialists
	0.80		Executives, specialists and/or senior managers can stay for up to 1 year
	0.60		Executives, specialists and/or senior managers can stay for up to 2 years
	0.40		Executives, specialists and/or senior managers can stay for up to 3 years
	0.20		Executives, specialists and/or senior managers can stay for up to 4 years
	0.00	0.00	Executives, specialists and/or senior managers can stay for a period of 5 years or more

Other restrictions

Weight	Scoring	Score	Category
0.10			*Third-party resale of lease line*
	1.00		Resale is not permitted
	0.00	0.00	Resale is permitted in any market
0.05			*End-user tariff*
	1.00		End-user tariff is determined by rate of return regulation
	0.50	0.50	End-user tariff is determined by price cap established by the authority
	0.00		End-user tariff is determined by market force (no regulation)
0.05			*Regulation of network interconnection*
	1.00		Interconnection is completely regulated by the authority
	0.50	0.50	Interconnection is determined by private negotiations in general, but general terms are determined by the authority
	0.00		Interconnection is completely determined by private negotiations (no regulation)

Continued on next page.

Weight	Scoring	Score	Category
0.05			*Market structure*
			(a) Regional line service
	1.00	1.00	Monopoly
	0.00		Competition among plural providers
			(b) Domestic long-distance line service
	1.00		Monopoly
	0.00	0.00	Competition among plural providers
			(c) International line service
	1.00		Monopoly
	0.00	0.00	Competition among plural providers
0.02			*Composition of board of directors*
		0.00	The score is inversely proportional to the percentage of the board that can comprise foreigners
0.01			*Temporary movement of people*
	1.00		No temporary entry of executives, senior managers and/or specialists
	0.75		Temporary entry of executives, specialists and/or senior managers for up to 30 days
	0.50		Temporary entry of executives, specialists and/or senior managers for up to 60 days
	0.25		Temporary entry of executives, specialists and/or senior managers for up to 90 days
	0.00	0.00	Temporary entry of executives, specialists and/or senior managers for over 90 days

Source: Kimura *et al.* (2003a).

Table A10.2 The foreign restrictiveness index: restrictions on mobile services in Turkey, 2005

Weight	Scoring	Score	Category
			Restrictions on commercial presence
0.20			*Licensing of mobile phone services*
	1.00		No new licence allowed
	0.75		Licences are issued through complicated (discriminately) and costly procedures
	0.20	0.20	Licences are generally issued with application fee and several requirements
	0.10		Licences are generally issued with application fee
	0.00		Licences are automatically issued upon applicatin without any cost
0.10			*Form of commercial presence*
	1.00		Measures that restrict or require a specific type of establishment
	0.00	0.00	No restriction on establishment
0.20			*Direct investment: equity participation permitted*
		0.00	The score is inversely proportional to the maximum equity participation permitted in an existing domestic company
0.10			*Direct investment: restrictions on certain types of services*
	1.00		Restrictions on providing some types of telephone service
	0.00	0.00	No restrictions on providing any type of telephone service
0.10			*Joint venture arrangements*
	1.00		Issues no new licence and no entry is allowed through a joint venture with a domestic company
	0.50		Foreign company can enter only through a joint venture with a domestic company
	0.00	0.00	No requirement for foreign companies to enter through a joint venture with a domestic company
0.02			*Permanent movement of people*
	1.00		No entry of executives, senior managers and/or specialists
	0.80		Executives, specialists and/or senior managers can stay for up to 1 year
	0.60		Executives, specialists and/or senior managers can stay for up to 2 years
	0.40		Executives, specialists and/or senior managers can stay for up to 3 years
	0.20		Executives, specialists and/or senior managers can stay for up to 4 years
	0.00	0.00	Executives, specialists and/or senior managers can stay for a period of 5 years or more

Continued on next page.

Weight	Scoring	Score	Category
			Other restrictions
0.05			*Regulation of interconnection between fixed-line and mobile or between mobiles*
	1.00		Interconnection is completely regulated by the authority
	0.50	0.50	Interconnection is determined by private negotiations in general, but general terms are determined by the authority
	0.00		Interconnection is completely determined by private negotiations (no regulation)
0.10			*End-user tariff*
	1.00		End-user tariff is determined by rate of return regulation
	0.50		End-user tariff is determined by price cap established by the authority
	0.00	0.00	End-user tariff is determined by market force (no regulation)
0.05			*Allocation of radio spectrum*
	1.00		Allocation is discriminately decided by the authority
	0.20		Allocated by auction with application fee
	0.10		Allocated by auction without application fee
	0.00	0.00	Radio frequencies are obtained with mobile services
0.05			*Market structure*
	1.00		Monopoly
	0.00	0.00	Competition among plural providers
0.02			*Composition of board of directors*
		0.00	The score is inversely proportional to the percentage of the board that can comprise foreigners
0.01			*Temporary movement of people*
	1.00		No temporary entry of executives, senior managers and/or specialists
	0.75		Temporary entry of executives, specialists and/or senior managers for up to 30 days
	0.50		Temporary entry of executives, specialists and/or senior managers for up to 60 days
	0.25		Temporary entry of executives, specialists and/or senior managers for up to 90 days
	0.00	0.00	Temporary entry of executives, specialists and/or senior managers for over 90 days

Source: Kimura *et al.* (2003).

Table A10.3 The foreign restrictiveness index: restrictions on internet services in Turkey, 2005

Weight	Scoring	Score	Category
			Restrictions on commercial presence
0.20			*Licensing of internet services*
	1.00		No new licence allowed
	0.75		Licences are issued through complicated (discriminately) and costly procedures
	0.20		Licences are generally issued with application fee and several requirements
	0.10	0.10	Licences are generally issued with application fee
	0.00		Licences are automatically issued upon application without any cost
0.10			*Form of commercial presence*
	1.00		Measures that restrict or require a specific type of establishment
	0.00	0.00	No restriction on establishment
0.20			*Direct investment: equity participation permitted*
		0.00	The score is inversely proportional to the maximum equity participation permitted in an existing domestic company
0.10			*Direct investment: restrictions on certain types of services*
	1.00		Restrictions on providing some types of internet service
	0.00	0.00	No restrictions on providing any type of internet service
0.10			*Joint venture arrangements*
	1.00		Issues no new licence and no entry is allowed through a joint venture with a domestic company
	0.50		Foreign company can enter only through a joint venture with a domestic company
	0.00	0.00	No requirement for foreign companies to enter through a joint venture with a domestic company
0.02			*Permanent movement of people*
	1.00		No entry of executives, senior managers and/or specialists
	0.80		Executives, specialists and/or senior managers can stay for up to 1 year
	0.60		Executives, specialists and/or senior managers can stay for up to 2 years

Continued on next page.

Weight	Scoring	Score	Category
	0.40		Executives, specialists and/or senior managers can stay for up to 3 years
	0.20		Executives, specialists and/or senior managers can stay for up to 4 years
	0.00	0.00	Executives, specialists and/or senior managers can stay for a period of 5 years or more
			Other restrictions
0.10			*Regulation of interconnection agreements among internet service providers*
	1.00		Interconnection is completely regulated by the authority
	0.50		Interconnection is determined by private negotiations in general, but general terms are determined by the authority
	0.00	0.00	Interconnection is completely determined by private negotiations (no regulation)
0.10			*Infrastructure*
	1.00	1.00	Providers are not allowed to either build their own network or own/lease their international data gateways
	0.50		Providers are allowed to build their own network or own/lease their international data gateways
	0.00		Providers are allowed to build their own network as well as own/lease their international data gateways
0.05			*Market structure*
	1.00		Monopoly
	0.00	0.00	Competition among plural providers
0.02			Composition of board of directors
		0.00	The score is inversely proportional to the percentage of the board that can comprise foreigners
0.01			*Temporary movement of people*
	1.00		No temporary entry of executives, senior managers and/or specialists
	0.75		Temporary entry of executives, specialists and/or senior managers for up to 30 days
	0.50		Temporary entry of executives, specialists and/or senior managers for up to 60 days
	0.25		Temporary entry of executives, specialists and/or senior managers for up to 90 days
	0.00	0.00	Temporary entry of executives, specialists and/or senior managers for over 90 days

Source: Kimura *et al.* (2003).

Table A10.4 The estimated restrictiveness indexes, 2005

Weight	Estimated score (FR index)	Category
Fixed-line		
		Restrictions on commercial presence
0.20	0.093	Licensing of fixed-line services
0.10	0.033	Form of commercial presence
0.20	0.000	Direct investment: equity participation permitted
0.10	0.000	Direct investment: restrictions on certain types of service
0.10	0.000	Joint venture arrangements
0.02	0.000	Permanent movement of people
		Other restrictions
0.10	0.000	Third-party resale of lease line
0.05	0.025	End-user tariff
0.05	0.025	Regulation of network interconnection
0.05	0.017	Market structure
0.02	0.000	Composition of board of directors
0.01	0.000	Temporary movement of people
Index value	0.193	
Mobile services		
		Restrictions on commercial presence
0.20	0.040	Licensing of mobile phone services
0.10	0.000	Form of commercial presence
0.20	0.000	Direct investment: equity participation permitted
0.10	0.000	Direct investment: restrictions on certain types of service
0.10	0.000	Joint venture arrangements
0.02	0.000	Permanent movement of people
		Other restrictions
0.05	0.025	Regulation of interconnection between fixed line and mobile or between mobiles
0.10	0.000	End-user tariff
0.05	0.000	Allocation of radio spectrum
0.05	0.000	Market structure
0.02	0.000	Composition of board of directors
0.01	0.000	Temporary movement of people
Index value	0.065	
Internet services		
		Restrictions on commercial presence
0.20	0.020	Licensing of internet services
0.10	0.000	Form of commercial presence
0.20	0.000	Direct investment: equity participation permitted

Continued on next page.

Weight	Estimated score (FR index)	Category
0.10	0.000	Direct investment: restrictions on certain types of service
0.10	0.000	Joint venture arrangements
0.02	0.000	Permanent movement of people
		Other restrictions
0.10	0.000	Regulation of interconnection agreements among internet service providers
0.10	0.100	Infrastructure
0.05	0.000	Market structure
0.02	0.000	Composition of board of directors
0.01	0.000	Temporary movement of people
Index value	0.120	

Sources: information from Tables A10.1–A10.3 and own calculations.

Table A10.5 Restrictiveness index scores for telecommunications services during 1990s

	Restrictiveness index				
	Restrictions on establishment		Restrictions on ongoing operations		
	Restrictions on direct investment in fixed and mobile network services	Restrictions on establishment total	Restrictions on cross-border trade	Restrictions on ongoing operations total	Index value
Austria	0.1333	0.1333	0.0000	0.0000	0.1333
Belgium	0.1334	0.1334	0.0667	0.0667	0.2001
Denmark	0.0333	0.0333	0.0000	0.0000	0.0333
Finland	0.0000	0.0000	0.0000	0.0000	0.0000
France	0.2100	0.2100	0.0000	0.0000	0.2100
Germany	0.0493	0.0493	0.0000	0.0000	0.0493
Greece	0.1609	0.1609	0.3000	0.3000	0.4609
Ireland	0.3533	0.3533	0.0000	0.0000	0.3533
Italy	0.1369	0.1369	0.0000	0.0000	0.1369
Luxembourg	0.1667	0.1667	0.0000	0.0000	0.1667
Netherlands	0.0300	0.0300	0.0000	0.0000	0.0300
Portugal	0.1100	0.1100	0.4000	0.4000	0.5100
Spain	0.1793	0.1793	0.2333	0.2333	0.4127
Sweden	0.1000	0.1000	0.0000	0.0000	0.1000
United Kingdom	0.0000	0.0000	0.0000	0.0000	0.0000
Turkey	0.3987	0.3987	0.4000	0.4000	0.7987

Source: Australian Productivity Commission website, http://www.pc.gov.au.

Note
The restrictiveness index scores range from 0 to 1. The higher the score, the greater are the restrictions for an economy.

Price effect (%)				
Restrictions on establishment		*Restrictions on ongoing operations*		
Restrictions on direct investment in fixed and mobile network services	*Restrictions on establishment total*	*Restrictions on cross-border trade*	*Restrictions on ongoing operations total*	*Price effect*
0.8480	0.8480	0.0000	0.0000	0.8480
0.8710	0.8710	0.4353	0.4353	1.3063
0.1985	0.1985	0.0000	0.0000	0.1985
0.0000	0.0000	0.0000	0.0000	0.0000
1.4298	1.4298	0.0000	0.0000	1.4298
0.3195	0.3195	0.0000	0.0000	0.3195
1.5778	1.5778	2.9424	2.9424	4.5202
2.6655	2.6655	0.0000	0.0000	2.6655
1.0019	1.0019	0.0000	0.0000	1.0019
1.0458	1.0458	0.0000	0.0000	1.0458
0.2025	0.2025	0.0000	0.0000	0.2025
1.3473	1.3473	4.8992	4.8992	6.2465
1.7099	1.7099	2.2247	2.2247	3.9346
0.6530	0.6530	0.0000	0.0000	0.6530
0.0000	0.0000	0.0000	0.0000	0.0000
16.7384	16.7384	16.7944	16.7944	33.5328

Table A10.6 Restrictions on banking services in Turkey, 2005

Weight	Scoring	Score	Category
			Restrictions on commercial presence
0.10			*Licensing of banks*
	1.00		Issues no new licence/no new licence is allowed
	0.75		Issues up to three new licences with only prudential requirements/licences are issued through complicated (discriminatory) and costly procedures
	0.5/0.2		Issues up to six new licences with only prudential requirements/licences are generally issued with application fee and several requirements
	0.25/0.1		Issues up to ten new licences with only prudential requirements/licences are generally issued with application fee
	0.00	0.00	Issues new licences with only prudential requirements/licences are automatically issued upon application without any cost
0.10			*Form of commercial presence*
	1.00		Measures that restrict or require a specific type of establishment
	0.00	0.00	No restriction on establishment
0.20			*Direct investment: equity participation permitted*
		0.00	The score is inversely proportional to the maximum equity participation permitted in an existing domestic bank
0.10			*Direct investment: restrictions on certain types of services*
	1.00		Restrictions on providing some types of banking services
	0.00	0.00	No restriction on providing any type of banking service
0.10			*Joint venture arrangements*
	1.00		Issues no new banking licences and no joint ventures are allowed with domestic banks
	0.50		Bank entry is only through a joint venture with a domestic bank
	0.00	0.00	No requirement for a bank to enter through a joint venture with a domestic bank
0.02			*Permanent movement of people*
	1.00		No entry of executives, senior managers and/or specialists
	0.80		Executives, specialists and/or senior managers can stay for up to 1 year
	0.60		Executives, specialists and/or senior managers can stay for up to 2 years

Weight	Scoring	Score	Category
	0.40		Executives, specialists and/or senior managers can stay for up to 3 years
	0.20		Executives, specialists and/or senior managers can stay for up to 4 years
	0.00	0.00	Executives, specialists and/or senior managers can stay for a period of 5 years or more
			Cross-border trade
0.10			*Funds raised by foreign banks*
	1.00		Banks are not permitted to raise funds in the domestic market/foreign banks are not permitted to have cross-border deposits from Turkish banks, corporations and households
	0.75		Banks are restricted from raising funds from domestic capital market/foreign banks are permitted to have cross-border deposits from only some types of Turkish resident or any type of Turkish resident with specific ceiling amount
	0.50		Banks are restricted in accepting deposits from the public/foreign banks are permitted to have cross-border deposits from Turkish banks, corporations and households with licences
	0.00	0.00	Banks can raise funds from any source with only prudential requirements/foreign banks are permitted to have cross-border deposits from any type of Turkish resident without restrictions
0.10			*Funds lent by foreign banks*
	1.00		Banks are not permitted to lend to domestic clients/foreign banks are not permitted to undertake cross-border lending to Turkish banks, corporations and households
	0.75		Banks are restricted to a specified lending size or lending to government projects/foreign banks are permitted to undertake cross-border lending to only some types of Turkish resident or any type of Turkish resident with specific ceiling amount
	0.50		Banks are restricted in providing certain services such as credit cards, leasing and consumer finance/foreign banks are permitted to undertake cross-border lending to Turkish banks, corporations and households with licences
	0.25		Banks are directed to lend to housing and small business
	0.00	0.00	Banks can lend to any source with only prudential restrictions/foreign banks are permitted to undertake cross-border lending to any type of Turkish resident without restrictions

Continued on next page.

Weight	Scoring	Score	Category
			Other restrictions
0.10			*Other business of banks – insurance and securities*
	1.00		Banks can only provide banking services
	0.50	0.50	Banks can provide banking services plus one other line of business – insurance or security services
	0.00		Banks have no restrictions on conducting other lines of business
0.05			*Expanding the number of banking outlets*
	1.00		One banking outlet with no new banking outlet permitted
	0.75		Banking outlets are limited in number and location
	0.25		Expansion of banking outlets is subject to non-prudential regulatory approval
	0.00	0.00	No restrictions on banks expanding operations
0.02			*Composition of the board of directors*
		0.00	The score is inversely proportional to the percentage of the board that can comprise foreigners
0.01			*Temporary movement of people*
	1.00		No temporary entry of executives, senior managers and/or specialists
	0.75		Temporary entry of executives, senior managers and/or specialists for up to 30 days
	0.50		Temporary entry of executives, senior managers and/or specialists for up to 60 days
	0.25		Temporary entry of executives, senior managers and/or specialists for up to 90 days
	0.00	0.00	Temporary entry of executives, senior managers and/or specialists for over 90 days

Source: McGuire and Schuele (2000).

Table A10.7 The estimated restrictiveness index for the banking services sector in Turkey, 2005

Weight in this paper	Estimated score (FR index)	Estimated score (FDR index)	Category
			Restrictions on commercial presence
0.10	0.0000	0.0000	Licensing of banks
0.10	0.0000	0.0000	Form of commercial presence
0.20	0.0000	0.0000	Direct investment: equity participation permitted
0.10	0.0000	0.0000	Direct investment: restrictions on certain types of services
0.10	0.0000	0.0000	Joint venture arrangements
0.02	0.0000	0.0000	Permanent movement of people
			Cross-border trade
0.10	0.0000	0.0000	Funds raised by foreign banks
0.10	0.0000	0.0000	Funds lent by foreign banks
			Other restrictions
0.10	0.0500	0.02500	Other business of banks - insurance and securities.
0.05	0.0000	0.00000	Expanding the number of banking outlets
0.02	0.0000	0.00000	Composition of the board of directors
0.01	0.0000	0.00000	Temporary movement of people
1.00	0.050	0.025	Total

Sources: Table A10.6 and own calculations.

Note
Estimated score is obtained by multiplying score chosen in Table A10.6 by the corresponding 'weight'.

Table A10.8 Restrictiveness index scores and price effects for banking services during 1990s

	Restrictiveness index		Price effect (%)	
	EU	*Turkey*	*EU*	*Turkey*
Licensing of banks	0.0100	0.2000	0.751510778	16.8479307
Direct investment	0.0100	0.0100	0.751510778	0.842396535
Joint venture arrangements	0.0050	0.0525	0.375755389	4.422581809
Permanent movement of people	0.0085	0.0119	0.640287183	1.002451877
Restrictions on establishment total	0.0335	0.2744	2.519064129	23.11536092
Funds raised by banks	0.0075	0.0075	0.563633084	0.631797401
Funds lent by banks	0.0075	0.0075	0.563633084	0.631797401
Other business of banks – insurance and securities services	0.0050	0.0525	0.375755389	4.422581809
Expanding the number of banking outlets	0.0025	0.0131	0.187877695	1.105645452
Composition of the board of directors	0.0119	0.0120	0.897303869	1.012560635
Temporary movement of people	0.0028	0.0074	0.213053306	0.621267445
Restrictions on ongoing operations total	0.0373	0.1000	2.801256426	8.425650143
Index value	0.0708	0.3744	5.320320555	31.54101106

Source: Australian Productivity Commission website, http://www.pc.gov.au.

Table A10.9 Restrictions on maritime services in Turkey, 2005

Weight	Scoring	Score	Category
			Restrictions on commercial presence and cross-border trade
0.15			*Conditions on the right to fly the national flag*
	0.40	0.40	Commercial presence is required in the domestic economy
	0.30	0.30	50% or more of equity participation must be domestic
	0.20	0.20	50% or more of the crew are required to be domestic
	0.10	0.10	Ships must be registered
0.10			*Form of commercial presence*
	1.00		Measures that restrict or require a specific type of legal entity or joint venture arrangement
	0.50	0.50	Shipping service suppliers must be represented by an agent
	0.00		No restriction on establishment
0.10			*Direct investment in shipping service suppliers*
		0.51	The score is inversely proportional to the maximum equity participation permitted in an existing shipping service supplier
0.10			*Direct investment in onshore maritime service suppliers*
		0.51	The score is inversely proportional to the maximum equity participation permitted in an existing onshore maritime service supplier
0.02			*Permanent movement of people*
	1.00	1.00	No entry of executives, senior managers and/or specialists
	0.80		Executives, specialists and/or senior managers can stay for a period of up to 1 year
	0.60		Executives, specialists and/or senior managers can stay for a period of up to 2 years
	0.40		Executives, specialists and/or senior managers can stay for a period of up to 3 years
	0.20		Executives, specialists and/or senior managers can stay for a period of up to 4 years
	0.00		Executives, specialists and/or senior managers can stay for a period of up to 5 years or more
0.10			*Cabotage*
	1.00	1.00	Foreigners generally cannot provide domestic maritime services
	0.75		Foreigners that fly the national flag can provide domestic maritime services
	0.50		Restrictions on type of and length of time that cargoes can be carried
	0.00		No cabotage restrictions
0.10			*Transportation of non-commercial cargoes*
	1.00		Private shipping service suppliers cannot carry non-commercial cargoes
	0.50		National flag shipping service suppliers can carry non-commercial cargoes

Continued on next page.

Weight	Scoring	Score	Category
	0.00	0.00	No restriction on access to non-commercial cargoes
			Other restrictions
0.10			*Port services*
	0.30		Some restrictions on access to ports
	0.20	0.20	Mandatory use of pilotage
	0.15	0.15	Mandatory use of towing
	0.10	0.10	Mandatory use of tug assistance
	0.05	0.05	Mandatory use of navigation aids
	0.05	0.05	Mandatory use of berthing services
	0.05	0.05	Mandatory use of waste disposal
	0.05	0.05	Mandatory use of anchorage
	0.05	0.05	Mandatory use of casting off
0.05			*Discretionary imposition of restrictions, including for retaliatory purposes*
	1.00	0.50	Governments are able to impose selective restrictions
	0.00		Governments are unable to impose selective restrictions
0.05			*United Nations Liner Code*
	1.00		Economy is party to the code and applies Article 2 of the code
	0.75		Economy is party to the code but does not apply Article 2 of the code
	0.00	0.00	Economy is not party to the code
0.05			*Government permits conference*
	1.00		Government permits the operation of conferences
	0.00	0.00	Conferences are subject to effective competition
0.05			Bilateral maritime services agreements on cargo sharing
		0.79	The score for an economy is taken from the 35×35 matrix of bilateral agreements on cargo sharing
0.02			*Composition of board of directors*
		0.51	The score is inversely proportional to the percentage of the board that can comprise foreigners
0.01			*Temporary movement of people*
	1.00		No temporary entry of executives, senior managers and/or specialists
	0.75		Temporary entry of executives, senior managers and/or specialists for up to 30 days
	0.50		Temporary entry of executives, senior managers and/or specialists for up to 60 days
	0.25		Temporary entry of executives, senior managers and/or specialists for up to 90 days
	0.00	0.00	Temporary entry of executives, senior managers and/or specialists for over 90 days

Source: Kimura *et al.* (2004).

Table A10.10 Restrictions on maritime services in Turkey, 2005

Weight	Score	Restrictiveness index	Category
			Restrictions on commercial presence and cross-border trade
0.15	*1.00*	*0.15*	*Conditions on the right to fly the national flag*
			On the national ship registry (NSR) shipping companies must be 51% owned by Turkish nationals, and masters of ships must be of Turkish nationality, while up to 30% of officers of ships engaged in international seaborne transportation excluding cabotage can be foreign nationals. Turkish International Ships Registries (TISR) are open to foreign seafarers except for cabotage. In the Turkish flagged ships registered to TISR, 30% of the crew can be employed from foreign seafarers provided that the first captain is Turkish
0.10	*0.50*	*0.05*	*Form of commercial presence*
			Those who can obtain the national flag according to NSR are either companies 51% owned by Turkish nationals, or ships must belong to legal persons set up in accordance with Turkish law, the majority of whose board of directors are of Turkish nationality. Furthermore ships that belong to trading companies, the majority of whose managerial staff and representatives are of Turkish nationality and are registered on the Turkish Trade Register, are considered as Turkish. TISR are open to foreign seafarers except for cabotage. As these considerations apply mainly to cabotage, a score of 0.5 is assigned rather than 1.00
0.10	*0.51*	*0.05*	*Direct investment in shipping service suppliers*
			To fly the national flag on NSR, 51% of equity must be owned by Turkish nationals
0.10	*0.51*	*0.05*	*Direct investment in onshore maritime service suppliers*
			According to the Ports Law No. 618, only Turkish citizens and companies that are managed and represented by Turkish citizens and for which majority voting rights are held by Turkish citizens may exercise the rights related to ports
0.02	*1.00*	*0.02*	*Permanent movement of people*
			Shipping companies on NSR must have masters of ships of Turkish nationality, while up to 70% of officers of ships engaged in international seaborne transportation must be of Turkish nationality. Shipping companies on TISR can employ up to 30% of the crew from foreign seafarers provided that the first captain is Turkish

Continued on next page.

Weight	Score	Restrictiveness index	Category
0.10	*1.00*	*0.10*	*Cabotage* Cabotage is reserved to national flag carriers
0.10	*0.00*	*0.00*	*Transportation of non-commercial cargoes* No restriction on access to non-commercial cargoes
			Other restrictions
0.10	*0.70*	*0.07*	*Port services* Mandatory use of pilotage, towing, tug assistance, navigation, berthing services, waste disposal, anchorage and casting off
0.05	*0.50*	*0.03*	*Discretionary imposition of restrictions, including for retaliatory purposes* There are various restrictions governments can impose against foreign suppliers. As such a system may result in discriminatory restrictions against foreign suppliers, but may also not, a score of 0.5 is assigned to this category instead of 1
0.05	*0.00*	*0.00*	*United Nations Liner Code* Economy is not a party to the Code
0.05	*0.00*	*0.00*	*Government permits conference* Conferences are subject to effective competition
0.05	*0.79*	*0.04*	*Bilateral maritime services agreements on cargo sharing* McGuire *et al.* (2000) considers 20 economies to obtain the score for this category: EU (15 countries), Argentina, Brazil, Canada, Chile, Colombia, Mexico, United States, Australia, Hong Kong, India, Indonesia, Japan, Korea, Malaysia, New Zealand, Philippines, Singapore, Thailand and Turkey. The procedure is as follows: each country is assigned 0 if it has a bilateral agreement with a certain country, say Argentina, and 1 otherwise. Then the sum of the score (max. 19 and min. 0) is divided by 19 (the number of the other economies) to obtain the score for Argentina. This paper basically follows the same procedure and calculates the score by adding Russia to the 20 economies. Turkey has bilateral agreements with five EU countries and two of the remaining countries. Considering the EU countries as 15 separate countries we have a total of 34 countries excluding Turkey. Hence the score is 27/34 = 0.79

Weight	Score	Restrictiveness index	Category
0.02	*0.51*	*0.01*	*Composition of board of directors*
			Those who can obtain the national flag according to NSR are either companies 51% owned by Turkish nationals, or ships must belong to legal persons set up in accordance with Turkish law, the majority of whose board of directors are of Turkish nationality
0.01	*0.00*	*0.00*	*Temporary movement of people*
			Temporary entry of executives, senior managers and/or specialists for over 90 days
Score		0.5667	

Sources: Based largely on information obtained from the Undersecretariat for Maritime Affairs and also on information contained in Kimura *et al.* (2004).

Table A10.11 Restrictiveness index scores for maritime services during 1990s

	Austria	Belgium	Denmark	Finland	France	Germany
Domestic index						
Restrictions on establishment						
Conditions on the right to fly the national flag	0.1283	0.0998	0.0143	0.0428	0.0570	0.0998
Form of commercial presence	0.0000	0.0000	0.0000	0.0000	0.0000	0.0000
Direct investment in shipping service suppliers	0.0000	0.0000	0.0000	0.0000	0.0000	0.0000
Direct investment in onshore maritime service suppliers	0.0000	0.0000	0.0000	0.0000	0.0000	0.0000
Restrictions on establishment total	0.1283	0.0998	0.0143	0.0428	0.0570	0.0998
Restrictions on ongoing operations						
Transportation of non-commercial cargoes	0.0000	0.0000	0.0000	0.0000	0.0000	0.0000
Port services	0.0000	0.0000	0.0190	0.0238	0.0238	0.0428
Government permits conferences	0.0000	0.0475	0.0475	0.0475	0.0475	0.0475
Restrictions on ongoing operations total	0.0000	0.0475	0.0665	0.0713	0.0713	0.0903
Domestic index total	0.1283	0.1473	0.0808	0.1140	0.1283	0.1900
Foreign index						
Restrictions on establishment						
Conditions on the right to fly the national flag	0.1358	0.1073	0.0218	0.0503	0.0645	0.1073
Form of commercial presence	0.0050	0.0050	0.0050	0.0050	0.0050	0.0050
Direct investment in shipping service suppliers	0.0050	0.0050	0.0050	0.0050	0.0050	0.0050
Direct investment in onshore maritime service suppliers	0.0050	0.0050	0.0050	0.0050	0.0050	0.0050
Permanent movement of people	0.0009	0.0085	0.0085	0.0085	0.0085	0.0085
Restrictions on establishment total	0.1517	0.1308	0.0453	0.0738	0.0880	0.1308
Restrictions on ongoing operations						
Cabotage	0.0050	0.0050	0.0050	0.0050	0.0050	0.0050
Transportation of non-commercial cargoes	0.0050	0.0050	0.0050	0.0050	0.0050	0.0050
Port services	0.0050	0.0050	0.0240	0.0288	0.0288	0.0478
Discretionary imposition of restrictions including for retaliatory purposes	0.0263	0.0500	0.0500	0.0500	0.0500	0.0500
United Nations Liner Code	0.0381	0.0381	0.0381	0.0381	0.0381	0.0381
Government permits conferences	0.0500	0.0500	0.0500	0.0500	0.0500	0.0500
Bilateral maritime services agreements on cargo sharing	0.0500	0.0471	0.0500	0.0500	0.0500	0.0485
Composition of the board of directors	0.0119	0.0119	0.0119	0.0119	0.0119	0.0119
Temporary movement of people	0.0028	0.0028	0.0043	0.0028	0.0028	0.0028
Restrictions on ongoing operations total	0.1942	0.2150	0.2383	0.2417	0.2417	0.2592
Foreign index total	0.3458	0.3457	0.2836	0.3154	0.3297	0.3899

Source: McGuire *et al.* (2000).

Notes
The domestic and foreign restrictiveness index scores range from 0 to 1. The higher the score, the greater are the restrictions for an economy.

Greece	Ireland	Italy	Luxembourg	Netherlands	Portugal	Spain	Sweden	UK
0.0428	0.0855	0.1283	0.0570	0.0998	0.0143	0.0713	0.0998	0.0143
0.0000	0.0000	0.0000	0.0000	0.0000	0.0000	0.0475	0.0000	0.0000
0.0000	0.0000	0.0000	0.0000	0.0000	0.0000	0.0000	0.0000	0.0000
0.0000	0.0000	0.0000	0.0000	0.0000	0.0000	0.0000	0.0000	0.0000
0.0428	0.0855	0.1283	0.0570	0.0998	0.0143	0.1188	0.0998	0.0143
0.0000	0.0000	0.0000	0.0000	0.0000	0.0000	0.0000	0.0000	0.0000
0.0428	0.0190	0.0000	0.0000	0.0000	0.0190	0.0190	0.0190	0.0000
0.0475	0.0475	0.0475	0.0475	0.0475	0.0475	0.0475	0.0475	0.0475
0.0903	0.0665	0.0475	0.0475	0.0475	0.0665	0.0665	0.0665	0.0475
0.1330	0.1520	0.1758	0.1045	0.1473	0.0808	0.1853	0.1663	0.0618
0.0503	0.1500	0.1358	0.0645	0.1073	0.0218	0.0788	0.1073	0.0218
0.0050	0.0050	0.0050	0.0050	0.0050	0.0050	0.0525	0.0050	0.0050
0.0050	0.0050	0.0050	0.0050	0.0050	0.0050	0.0050	0.0288	0.0050
0.0050	0.0050	0.0050	0.0050	0.0050	0.0050	0.0050	0.0288	0.0050
0.0085	0.0085	0.0085	0.0085	0.0085	0.0085	0.0085	0.0085	0.0085
0.0738	0.1735	0.1593	0.0880	0.1308	0.0453	0.1498	0.1783	0.0453
0.0050	0.0050	0.0050	0.0050	0.0050	0.0050	0.0050	0.0050	0.0050
0.0050	0.0050	0.0050	0.0050	0.0050	0.0050	0.0050	0.0050	0.0050
0.0478	0.0240	0.0050	0.0050	0.0050	0.0240	0.0240	0.0240	0.0050
0.0263	0.0263	0.0500	0.0263	0.0500	0.0263	0.0500	0.0500	0.0263
0.0025	0.0025	0.0381	0.0025	0.0381	0.0381	0.0381	0.0381	0.0381
0.0500	0.0500	0.0500	0.0500	0.0500	0.0500	0.0500	0.0500	0.0500
0.0500	0.0500	0.0500	0.0485	0.0500	0.0485	0.0500	0.0500	0.0500
0.0119	0.0119	0.0119	0.0119	0.0119	0.0119	0.0119	0.0119	0.0119
0.0028	0.0028	0.0028	0.0028	0.0028	0.0028	0.0028	0.0028	0.0028
0.2013	0.1775	0.2179	0.1571	0.2179	0.2117	0.2369	0.2369	0.1942
0.2750	0.3510	0.3772	0.2451	0.3487	0.2569	0.3867	0.4152	0.2394

Table A10.12 Data definitions and sources

The data used in analysis have been compiled from the following sources and transformed as described below.

X_{ij}	Exports from country i to country j, measured in million US dollars,[a] deflated by the export price index (2000 = 100).[b]
Y_i	Real GDP of country i, measured in constant 2000 US dollars.[c]
Y_i^{pc}	Real *per capita* GDP of country i, measured in constant 2000 US dollars.[c]
GD_{ij}	Geographical distance between countries i and j.[d]
$BR1_{ij}$, $BR2_{ij}$	Dummy variables to indicate whether the countries i and j are neighbours. $BR1$ takes the value of 1 if i and j are neighbours with a common land border; it is zero otherwise. $BR2$ has a broader definition and it takes the value of 1 if i and j are close to each other through sea transportation.

Sources: a, Direction of Trade Statistics (DOTS), CD-ROM, published by the IMF; b, International Financial Statistics (IFS), Online, disseminated by the IMF; c, World Development Indicators (WDI), published by the World Bank; d, Great circle distances between capitals from the website http://www.wcrl.ars.usda.gov/cec/java/lat-long.htm

Notes

1 Introduction

1 See Rodrik (2007b).
2 The Basic Agreement on Telecommunications is discussed in Chapter 4, the Energy Charter Treaty in Chapter 6 and the Basel Core Principles in Chapter 7.
3 For a discussion of the ENP see Commission of the European Communities (2003, 2004, 2006a,b) and Hoekman (2007).
4 For a discussion of these rules see Chapter 9.

2 The foreign trade regime and trade liberalization in Turkey

1 As of 2009 negotiations are in progress with the Faroe Islands, the Gulf Cooperation Council, Jordan, Lebanon and Montenegro, while exploratory talks have been held with Chile, Mexico, the Southern African Customs Union and Ukraine.
2 Because of technical difficulties and costs involved in meeting the rules of origin requirements, available evidence shows that utilization rates are often much lower than 100 per cent (Brenton and Manchin 2002).
3 The eight chapters are Chapter 1 on free movement of goods, Chapter 3 on the right of establishment and freedom to provide services, Chapter 9 on financial services, Chapter 11 on agriculture and rural development, Chapter 13 on fisheries, Chapter 14 on transport policy, Chapter 29 on customs unions and Chapter 30 on external relations.
4 Chapter 20 on enterprise and industrial policy was opened for negotiation at the end of March 2007, and two more negotiation chapters were opened thereafter, namely Chapter 18 on statistics and Chapter 32 on financial control. At the end of December 2007 Chapter 21 on trans-European networks and Chapter 28 on health and consumer protection, and during June 2008 Chapter 6 on company law and Chapter 7 on intellectual property were opened. Recently, with the opening of Chapter 4 on free movement of capital and Chapter 10 on information society and media, the number of policy chapters opened has increased to ten.
5 Articles 24.1 and 24.2 of the CUD mention the possibility of free trade in agricultural products, provided that appropriate conditions are in place, that is, Turkey fully adopts the Common Agricultural Policy (Article 25 and 27). The bottom line is that customs union arrangements apply now solely to industrial products and leave out for the time being agricultural products, although the latter may be subject to bilateral liberalization.
6 The following sections are based largely on Togan (2010).
7 We would like to thank Şinasi Demirbaş and Taşkın Barış Ergün of the Undersecretariat for Foreign Trade for explaining certain aspects of this complex tariff schedule.

8 Here it should be emphasized that, in line with the CUD, processed agricultural products imported into Turkey from the EU are subject to customs duties comprising an industrial and agricultural component. While all industrial components enjoy duty-free treatment, few agricultural components are subject to preferential treatment. MFN customs duties still apply to most agricultural components, where these components are calculated by multiplying the quantity of primary agriculture product used in processing, according to an agreed set of ratios, by the specific rate charge.

9 Note that the Mass Housing Fund levy is denominated in euros.

10 We are grateful to Rasim Kutlu of the Undersecretariat for Customs for providing the essential data required for the estimation of the ad valorem equivalent tariff rates for commodities for which the specific tariffs are stated as T1 and T2 in List III.

11 WTO definition of agriculture: HS Chapters 01–24 less fish and fishery products (HS 0301–7, 0509, 051191, 1504, 1603–5 and 230120) plus some selected products (HS 290543, 290544, 290545, 3301, 3501–5, 380910, 382311–19, 382360, 382370, 382460, 4101–3, 4301, 5001–3, 5101–3, 5201–3, 5301 and 5302). But in our calculations we use the following definition of agriculture: HS Chapters 01–24, 4101–3, 5101–3 and 5201–3.

12 Since 1996 MARA has not issued control certificates for imports from countries considered to be risks for diseases. The decision was made on sanitary grounds, and was based on the World Organization for Animal Health's risk classification for live animals (dairy and beef cattle, sheep, goats and poultry) and meat (beef, sheep, goat and poultry). As a result meat products cannot be imported from such countries.

13 Compensating products are all goods obtained from processing operations.

14 'State aid for organizing domestic fairs with international participation' provides up to 50 per cent of promotional activities, not exceeding US$25,000, 50 per cent of transportation expenses of representatives of foreign companies, not exceeding US$15,000 and 50 per cent of expenses regarding activities during the fair, not exceeding US$5,000. 'State aid for environmental protection activities' covers up to 50 per cent of the relevant certification expenses. 'State aid for research and development projects' provides a 50 per cent and up to a maximum of 60 per cent grant for R&D activities for three years. In addition, capital support is provided in the form of support for two years up to the value of US$1 million, and a soft loan up to the value of US$100,000 for one year, to be paid back in US$ with interest. 'State aid for encouraging employment in sectoral foreign trade companies' provides 75 per cent of the pre-tax salary for one manager and two members of staff with professional experience for one year. 'State aid for participation in international fairs and exhibitions' includes covering in the case of national participation 50 per cent of participation fees, not exceeding US$10,000–15,000, and 50–75 per cent of the rental cost of empty stands, not exceeding US$10,000–15,000. In addition, 75 per cent of promotional expenses will be covered, not exceeding US$80,000–120,000. 'State aid for operating stores abroad' covers 50–60 per cent of the advertising, rent, office inventory and decoration expenditures of companies operating a store abroad depending on the type of firm involved. In those cases promotional expenses up to certain limits will also be covered by the aid programme. 'State aid for promoting Turkish trademarks and improving the image of Turkish goods' provides 50 per cent of consultancy fees, rental fees, advertising, certification expenses and fees for registering of trademarks. The upper limit of support depends on the type of organization involved. 'State aid for market research projects' provides support for buying market research projects, reports and statistics, as well as financial assistance for companies participating in trade missions abroad and to become members of e-trade websites to enable them to market their products abroad. The amount of support provided depends on the type of activity. Finally, 'state aid for vocational training' covers support for improving quality, productivity, management techniques, design, international marketing and foreign trade operations. The support amounts to 90 per cent of training costs for

programmes up to six months, 75 per cent of consultancy services costs for up to one year, and one year of tuition costs for selected designers.

15 Under the prevailing regulations for operations and practices in the zones the validity period of an operating licence is for a maximum of ten years for tenant users, and 20 years for users who wish to build their own offices in the zone; if the operating licence is for production, the terms are 15 and 30 years for tenant users and investors respectively.

16 See Izmen and Yılmaz (2009).

17 As a result, on average, US$2.9 billion annually have been invested in real estate during the period 2006–8.

18 See OECD (2006).

19 See Izmen and Yılmaz (2009).

20 See Chapter 3 for a detailed analysis of technical barriers to trade.

3 Standards, conformity assessment and technical barriers to trade

1 We are grateful to Frederic Misrahi for his detailed and constructive comments on an earlier draft of the chapter.

2 The following sections are based partially on Togan (2010).

3 See National Academy of Sciences (1995), Stephenson (1997) and Maskus and Wilson (2001)

4 See Howarth and Redgrave (2003).

5 See Sykes (1995) on technical barriers to trade.

6 See Sykes (1995) and Marceau and Trachtman (2002).

7 A plurilateral agreement refers to an agreement not signed by all GATT contracting parties.

8 GATT 1947 and the Standards Code lacked an effective dispute resolution mechanism, as GATT practice before the Uruguay Round effectively required consensus before any violation of the agreement could be found. It even required consensus before a formal investigation of a complaint could be undertaken.

   For a discussion of the legal structure of the Tokyo Round Standards Code and experience under the code, see Sykes (1995).

9 Annex 1 of the TBT Agreement defines 'technical regulation' as a 'document which lays down product characteristics or their related processes and production methods, including the applicable administrative provisions, with which compliance is mandatory. It may also include or deal exclusively with terminology, symbols, packaging, marking or labelling requirements as they apply to a product, process or production method' (WTO 2002: 137). Pursuant to paragraph 2 of Annex I of the TBT Agreement a 'standard' is defined as a 'document approved by a recognized body, that provides, for common and repeated use, rules, guidelines or characteristics for products or related processes and production methods, with which compliance is not mandatory. It may also include or deal exclusively with terminology, symbols, packaging, marking or labelling requirements as they apply to a product, process or production method' (WTO 2002: 137). Although the distinction between product standards and technical regulations is useful for policy purposes, we use the term 'standards' as emphasized previously to refer to both mandatory requirements and voluntary specifications.

10 The 'conformity assessment' procedure pursuant to paragraph 3 of Annex I of the TBT Agreement is 'any procedure used, directly or indirectly, to determine that relevant requirements in technical regulations or standards are fulfiled'. Paragraph 3 further explains that conformity assessment procedures include, *inter alia*, procedures for sampling, testing and inspection; evaluation, verification and assurance of conformity; and registration, accreditation and approval as well as their combinations (WTO 2002: 138).

11 The transparency obligations include the following requirements: (1) the publication of a pre-implementation notice before the enactment of a measure that is sufficient to allow interested parties to become acquainted with a proposed measure, (2) before the enactment of a technical regulation or a conformity assessment procedure, the notification of other members through the WTO Secretariat of the products to be covered and the provision of a brief indication of the objective and rationale for the technical regulation or procedure and, for draft standards, the provision of a 60-day period for comments, (3) upon request, the provision of copies of draft technical regulations, standards and conformity assessment procedures to members, (4) before the enactment of a measure, allow members a reasonable time for written comment, and for discussions concerning proposed measures, and take these comments/discussions into consideration, (5) publish 'or otherwise make available' technical regulations, standards and conformity assessment procedures for other members and for interested parties, (6) in addition, members shall set up 'enquiry points' providing information on technical regulations. Enquiry points, which should provide information concerning a WTO member's participation in regional and international standardization and conformity assessment bodies, have the responsibility to provide certain information concerning the activities of non-governmental standardization organizations.

12 Technical barrier issues relating to agriculture were negotiated separately at the Uruguay Round of multilateral trade negotiations. The result was a separate agreement covering technical barrier issues related to agriculture, with the remaining technical barrier issues covered by the TBT Agreement. Pursuant to Annex A(1) of the SPS Agreement, an SPS measure is any measure applied: (1) to protect animal or plant life or health within the territory of the member from risks arising from the entry, establishment or spread of pests, diseases, disease-carrying organisms or disease-causing organisms, (2) to protect human or animal life or health within the territory of the member from risks arising from additives, contaminants, toxins or disease-causing organisms in foods, beverages or feedstuffs, (3) to protect human life or health within the territory of the member from risks arising from diseases carried by animals, plants or products thereof, or from the entry, establishment or spread of pests or (4) to prevent or limit other damage within the territory of the member from the entry, establishment or spread of pests.

13 See Maskus and Wilson (2001).

14 The general principle of the free movement of goods implies that products must be traded freely from one part of the EU to another. This principle is enshrined in the EC Treaty, in particular Articles 28–30, 95(4)–95(9), 296–298, as interpreted in the case law of the European Court of Justice as well as in Commission Directive 70/50/EEC and interpretative communications.

15 Technical regulations refer to 'technical specification', a specification contained in a document that lays down the characteristics required of a product such as levels of quality, performance, safety or dimensions, including the requirements applicable to the product as regards the name under which the product is sold, terminology, symbols, testing and test methods, packaging, marking or labelling and conformity assessment procedures. The term 'technical specification' also covers production methods and processes. Other requirements include a requirement, other than a technical specification, imposed on a product for the purpose of protecting, in particular, consumers or the environment, and which affects its life cycle after it has been placed on the market, such as conditions of use, recycling, reuse or disposal, when such conditions can significantly influence the composition or nature of the product or its marketing.

16 CEN (European Committee for Standardization), based in Brussels, has a membership consisting of the national standards-writing organizations of European countries and the members of the EU and EFTA. CEN develops voluntary European standards in all

product sectors excluding electrical standards, which are covered by CENELEC. The sectors are air and space, information and communications technologies, chemistry, materials, construction, measurement, consumer products, mechanical engineering, energy and utilities, nanotechnology, environment, security and defence, food, services, health and safety, transport and packaging, health care, heating, cooling and ventilation. These standards are also national standards in each of its member countries. With funding from the European Commission, CEN also writes standards to meet the 'essential requirements' for product safety mandated in EU product directives. CENELEC (European Committee for Electrotechnical Standardization), based in Brussels, has European national electrotechnical committees as members. CENELEC develops European standards for electrotechnology. CENELEC also develops standards that meet EU product directives, with funding from the European Commission. On the other hand ETSI (European Telecommunications Standards Institute) produces globally applicable standards for information and communications technologies including fixed, mobile, radio, broadcast, internet and several other areas. Currently, ETSI is recognized as an official European standards organization by the European Commission, enabling valuable access to European markets.

17 With the entry into force of the 1985 Single European Act, a qualified majority voting system was adopted in the decision-making process for internal market-related legislation. As a result, when new old approach directives or acts revising existing old approach directives are adopted, qualified majority voting is used. Furthermore, the decision-making procedure for internal market-related legislation currently is typically co-decision between the European Parliament and the Council of Ministers.

18 Notified bodies are explained in more detail in the following text.

19 Technical documentation and the EC declaration of conformity are explained in more detail in the following text.

20 Type examination is the comparison of the design specification of a product against the requirements of a standard specification, informed by physical examination of a sample and the performance of tests as may be necessary according to the particular standard.

21 The following might be required to be included in technical documentation: (1) a general description of the product, (2) overall drawing of a product, design and manufacture drawings and diagrams of components, subassemblies, control circuits, etc., together with descriptions and explanations needed to understand those drawings and diagrams, (3) risk analysis and a description of methods adopted to eliminate hazards presented by the product, (4) the essential requirements of the applicable directives, (5) a list of the standards used, in full or in part, and a description of the solutions employed to meet the essential requirements of applicable directives, (6) other technical specifications that were used, (7) results of design calculations and of checks carried out, etc., (8) test reports and/or certificates that may be available, either from the manufacturer or a third party (depending on the requirements of the directives) and (9) a copy of the instructions (for use, for maintenance, other instructions).

22 As a minimum the following information should be provided by the EC declaration of conformity: (1) the name and address of the manufacturer, (2) the identification of the product (name, type or model number, and any relevant supplementary information, such as lot, batch or serial number, sources and numbers of items), (3) all relevant provisions complied with, (4) the referenced standards or other normative documents (such as national technical standards and specifications) in a precise, complete and clearly defined way, (5) all supplementary information that may be required (for example grade, category), if applicable, (6) the date of issue of the declaration, (7) signature and title or an equivalent marking of authorized person and (8) the statement that the declaration is issued under the sole responsibility of the manufacturer and, if applicable, the authorized representative.

23　Delaney and van de Zande (2000) note that modules for active implantable medical devices could call for a type examination of the product, plus a production quality assurance system that conforms to the ISO 9002 (EN 29002) standard. Another choice for a medical device manufacturer would be a complete quality assurance programme that would conform to ISO 9001 (or EN 29001). In those cases in which the risk is high, the modules will call for the involvement of the notified body.

24　See European Commission (2000).

25　RAPEX is the EU rapid alert system for dangerous consumer products with the exception of food, pharmaceutical and medical devices, which are covered by other mechanisms. It facilitates the rapid exchange of information between member states and the Commission on measures taken to prevent or restrict the marketing or use of products posing a serious risk to the health and safety of consumers. RAPEX works as follows. When a product is found to be dangerous, the competent national authority takes appropriate action to eliminate the risk. It can withdraw the product from the market, recall it from consumers or issue warnings. The national contact point then informs the European Commission about the product, the risks it poses to consumers and the measures taken by the authority to prevent risks and accidents. The European Commission disseminates the information that it receives to the national contact points of all other EU countries. It publishes weekly overviews of dangerous products and the measures taken to eliminate the risks on the internet. The national contact points in each EU country ensure that the authorities responsible check whether the newly notified dangerous product is present on the market. If so, the authorities take measures to eliminate the risk, by requiring that the product be withdrawn from the market, by recalling it from consumers or by issuing warnings.

26　PECAs were signed between the EU and candidate states. The reason for signing these agreements was to prepare the candidate countries for full membership and to help them to prepare their test, conformity assessment and certification infrastructure and systems to match those of the EU.

27　See World Bank (2005a).

28　Within the framework of Articles 5–7 of the Association Council Decision (ACD) No. 1/95, the signatories shall eliminate not only classical trade-restricting measures such as tariffs and quotas, but also the barriers to trade arising from different regulatory practices on goods in both Turkey and the EU. On the other hand, within the framework of Articles 8–11 of the ACD No. 1/95, Turkey shall progressively adopt the relevant *acquis communautaire* on the removal of TBTs and all other related technical regulations.

29　Law No. 4703 is based on Council Directive 92/59/EEC on general product safety, Council Regulation 85/C 136/01 on the new approach to technical harmonization and standards and the Council resolution of December 1989 on the global approach to conformity assessment.

30　The legislation on market surveillance was prepared using Council Directive 92/59/EEC on general products safety, the Council resolution of December 1989 on the global approach to conformity assessment, Council Directive 88/378/EEC on the approximation of the laws of the member states on the safety of toys, and the European Commission (2000). The legislation on working principles and procedures for the conformity assessment bodies and notified bodies was prepared using the material in Chapter 6 of the European Commission (2000). The legislation on the use and affixing of the CE conformity mark is based on Council Decision 93/465/EEC on the modules for the various phases of the conformity assessment procedures and the rules for the affixing and use of the CE conformity marking. Finally, the legislation on notification procedures between Turkey and the EU for technical legislation and standards is based on Council Directive 98/34/EC, which outlines a procedure for the provision of information in the field of technical standards and regulations, and the relevant section of Decision 2/97 of the EC–Turkey Association Council.

31 The legal framework for accreditation consists of Law No. 4457 of 1999 on the establishment and tasks of the Turkish Accreditation Agency.

32 Note that, with the increase in the number of conformity assessment bodies, two associations were established: the Turkish Calibration and Experiment Laboratories Association (TUKLAB) and the Association for Conformity Assessment (UDDer). While TUKLAB aims to improve the coordination and cooperation between Turkish laboratories and provide support for its members in accreditation and certification processes, UDDer aims to serve as a platform in which the abovementioned stakeholders can effectively cooperate in tackling problems related to the conformity assessment sector.

33 The legal framework for conformity assessment in Turkey consists of general provisions covered by Articles 7, 8 and 9 of Framework Law No. 4703 relating to the preparation and implementation of technical regulations on products, published in 2001. Detailed principles can be found in the implementing Regulation on Conformity Assessment Bodies and Notified Bodies, which has been published in the *Official Gazette* on 17 January 2002, No. 24643.

34 According to the World Bank (2005a), the certification of organic nut production in Moldova for export to Germany must be renewed every six months, and each visit from an international certifying company costs US$5,000 plus US$2,000 per production test – once before processing and once after processing. This can amount to US$18,000 per year, which is a heavy burden for firms in an economy such as that in Moldova, a small economy trying to compete in international markets.

35 Istanbul Technical University does automotive testing under the authorization of the Ministry of Industry and Trade, and it performs acoustic, emissions and other tests. The Turkish Standards Institute, Tofaş-Fiat and Ford-Otosan also have engine and emissions test facilities; Seger has an audible warning devices laboratory; Tam-Test is implementing testing and certification in the case of agricultural tractors; Fren Teknik has test facilities for brakes; and Brisa has a pneumatic tyres laboratory. Turkey is implementing all relevant automotive EC directives via these facilities. We note that for automotive products, the 'e' sign verifies conformity. Crash tests, electromagnetic compatibility (EMC) and other tests on complete cars are largely conducted abroad. The National Metrology Institute was able to run the EMC tests on vehicles. It has calibration laboratories in mechanics, physics, electricity, ionizing radiation and chemicals. The laboratories under construction include EMC, acoustics and liquid flow.

36 See European Committee for Standardization (2003).

37 The Association Council Decision (ACD) No. 1/2006 was put into force on 15 May 2006 on the implementation of Article 9 of the 1/95 ACD. It regulates the rules and procedures on the allocation of identification numbers to the Turkish notified bodies.

38 The six Turkish notified bodies recognized by the EU are: (1) the Turkish Standards Institute [lifts (95/16/EC), construction products (89/106/EEC), appliances burning gaseous fuels (90/396/EEC) and pressure equipment (97/23/EC)], (2) the Turkish Cement Manufacturers Association [construction products (89/106/EEC)], (3) the Turkish Lloyd Foundation [appliances burning gaseous fuels (90/396/EEC), pressure equipment (97/23/EC) and recreational craft (94/25/EC)], (4) MEYER [appliances burning gaseous fuels (90/396/EEC) and pressure equipment (97/23/EC)], (5) the Chamber of Mechanical Engineers [lifts (95/16/EC)] and (6) the Turkish Ready Mixed Concrete Association [construction products (89/106/EEC)].

39 The report notes that, in Turkey, for a great part of product groups, there is hardly any sampling and analysis and that a large number of consumer products are not monitored at all. There is limited laboratory capacity, and this capacity is used only partially. Warnings and fines are seldom imposed, and withdrawals and recalls occur even less often. The market surveillance system is fragmented, both on a national level and even within authorities, and it is too complicated. Each authority has its own inspection body or even several bodies per type of product, and there are no obvious

transverse links between the different inspection bodies. Policy at each authority is top-down, so that management and execution are determined centrally, with weak influence from the regions. As a result, the overall coordination between the market surveillance activities is fragile. Furthermore, market surveillance is usually based on conformity and consists of checks of CE marks and documents. There are no checks on safety, and proactive risk assessment is generally lacking. Effective market surveillance requires powerful inspectors who are authorized to make quick decisions at the place of inspection according to the risk; however, inspectors are not in position to fulfil these requirements. They are reluctant to make decisions, as their legal status is not sufficiently regulated. In addition, there is no implementing authority for the non-harmonized consumer products, and market surveillance activities in the case of these products is not carried out at all. Finally, the report stresses that there are no binding or result-oriented agreements on activities such as the number of inspections to be carried out, and there is no separate budget for samples or for laboratory analysis.

40 The Decree on the Regime Regarding Technical Regulations and Standardization for Foreign Trade and its supplementary legislation were decided on 1 January 1995 by the Council of Ministers and published in the Turkish *Official Journal* on 9 March 1995

41 The Communiqué on the Imports of CE Marked Products was published in the Turkish *Official Gazette* on 14 February 2004, No. 25373. The regulation and the communiqués for 2008 were promulgated in the Turkish *Official Gazette* on 31 December 2007, No. 26743.

42 For more information on legislative alignment, see the website of the Undersecretariat for Foreign Trade, http://www.dtm.gov.tr.

43 The Turkish Standards Institute (TSE) was established in 1954 to draft standards for all kinds of products and services. The TSE is responsible for issuing and implementing technical standards. So far, it has transposed close to 90 per cent of the CEN and CENELEC standards. The TSE is a member of the ISO and IEC as well as an affiliate member of CEN and CENELEC.

44 See the *Official Gazette* of 31 December 2007, No. 26743.

45 The reasons for the non-elimination of TBTs between Turkey and the EU are various. First, the task itself is challenging. Second, the framework law and associated legislation, which is the basis for the work of harmonizing the EU's technical regulations, was put into effect only in January 2002, seven years after the formation of the customs union. Thereafter, the adaptation process accelerated for both the new and classical approach regulations, and a large number of related regulations were adopted by Turkey. At this time, however, Turkey faced another difficulty. There was no mechanism between Turkey and the EU similar to the one provided by the EFTA surveillance body, which evaluates the regulations prepared by the EFTA countries and ascertains the acceptability of these regulations by the EU. Because the EC–Turkey Association Council did not establish a similar body, the regulations prepared by Turkey were not evaluated by such a body and there was no mechanism to approve these regulations. Third, the number of personnel in the responsible ministries and governmental bodies who were fluent in English and trained in matters related to TBTs was insufficient. Finally, financial resources were limited for the harmonization of technical legislation.

46 See Undersecretariat for Foreign Trade (2008b).

4 Liberalization of telecommunications services

1 See Geradin (2006).
2 See Braga *et al.* (1999).
3 The basic telecoms service encompasses local, long distance and international services for public and non-public use.

4 The MFN principle requires that, with respect to any measure covered by GATS, each WTO member shall accord immediately and unconditionally to services and service suppliers of any other WTO member treatment no less favourable than that it accords to like services and service suppliers of any other country. On the other hand, according to the NT principle, each WTO member in the sectors inscribed in its Schedule of Specific Commitments, and subject to any conditions and qualifications set out therein, shall accord to services and service suppliers of any other WTO member, in respect of all measures affecting the supply of services, treatment no less favourable than that it accords to its own like services and service suppliers.

5 GATS, Annex on Negotiations on Basic Telecommunications (World Trade Organization 2002: 319).

6 A 'major supplier' is a supplier that has the ability to materially affect the terms of participation (having regard to price and supply) in the relevant market for basic telecommunications services as a result of (1) control over essential facilities or (2) use of its position in the market.

7 For a good discussion of the Annex of Telecommunications and the Reference Paper, see Roseman (2003).

8 Commission Directive 88/301/EEC of 16 May 1988, on competition in the markets in telecommunications terminal equipment, *Official Journal of the European Communitites*, L131/73.

9 Commission Directive 96/19/EC of 13 March 1996 amending Directive 90/388/EEC with regard to the implementation of full competition in telecommunications markets, *Official Journal of the European Communitites*, L74.

10 The undertakings are said to have significant market power (SMP) as long as the market share of the undertaking is equal to or larger than 25 per cent.

11 *Official Journal of the European Communitites* L336, 30 December 2000, p. 4.

12 Accounting separation is the weakest form of unbundling, in which a company keeps different accounts for its system and for its competitive activities and must charge competitive businesses the same fees for using the system as it charges third parties. This is intended to prevent cross-subsidies between the system and the competitive activities.

13 See European Commission (2007b).

14 The following sections draw heavily on Akdemir *et al.* (2007).

15 Between 1994 and 1998, mobile services were provided by the private companies Turkcell and Telsim under the provisions of the Revenue Sharing Contract signed individually between those undertakings and TT.

16 Law No. 4502.

17 Law No. 4673.

18 As of the end of 2008, 20 licences for satellite telecommunication services, two for satellite platform services, four for GMPCS (global mobile personal communications by satellite) mobile telephony services, 25 for data transmission services over fixed lines, 87 for internet service providers, and 32 for long-distance and international telephony services have been granted. In addition, TT was authorized under its Authorization Agreement with the Authority to supply many different services, such as a public switched telephone network (PSTN), payphones, cable television, ISDN (integrated services digital network), ADSL (asymmetric digital subscriber line), leased circuits, internet service provision, etc., and to operate the telecommunications infrastructure. On the other hand, the three GSM operators provide data services such as SMS (short message service), WAP (wireless application protocol), GPRS (general packet radio service) and MMS (multimedia messaging service) over intelligent networks, and services with added value such as geographical information, special invoicing, establishing virtual user platform, introduction of different structures for schedules of charge and options, voicemail and GSM-mail.

5 Electricity sector policy reform

1 It has been estimated in the United Kingdom that the contribution of the generation activity, including fuel costs, is around two-thirds of the overall industrial tariff: transmission activity for 10 per cent, distribution activity including the losses and unpaid consumptions for 20 per cent, and retail and wholesale activity for 5 per cent.

2 A load curve is a chart showing the amount of electricity that customers use over time. A load duration curve (LDC) is similar to a load curve but the demand data in an LDC is in descending order of magnitude, rather than chronological. The LDC curve shows the capacity utilization requirements for each increment of load. The height of each slice is a measure of required capacity, and the width of each slice is a measure of the utilization rate or capacity factor. The product of the two is a measure of electrical energy, for example in kilowatt-hours.

3 See Ramsey (1927).

4 Gate Closure refers to three-and-a-half hours before the trading period, subsequently reduced to one hour in July 2002.

5 See World Trade Organization Secretariat (2001a).

6 Directive 96/92/EC of the European Parliament and of the Council of 19 December 1996 concerning common rules for the internal market in electricity.

7 The section is based largely on Cameron (2002, 2005) and Jamasb and Pollitt (2005).

8 Guide to the Electricity Directive. Available at http://europa.eu.int/comm/energy/en/elec_single_market_market/memor.htm.

9 See Directive 2003/54/EC of the European Parliament and of the Council of 26 June 2003 concerning common rules for the internal market in electricity and repealing Directive 96/92/EC.

10 Regulation (EC) No. 1228/2003 of the European Parliament and of the Council of 26 June 2003 on conditions for access to systems for cross-border exchanges in electricity.

11 For more information on the Commission proposal, see European Commission (2007c,d).

12 Law No. 3996.

13 Law No. 4492.

14 Initially, the Authority was created under the name Electricity Market Regulatory Authority, and its jurisdiction was limited to the 'electrical' part of the Turkish energy market. However, Law No. 4628 was later amended with Law No. 4646 Natural Gas Market Law dated 2 May 2001, Law No. 5015 Petroleum Market Law dated 20 December 2003 and Law No. 5307 Liquefied Petroleum Gas (LPG) Market Law dated 13 March 2005. The jurisdiction of the Authority was greatly extended, and its current name is the Energy Market Regulatory Authority (EMRA).

15 A licence is an authorizing document that a legal entity should obtain from EMRA in order to operate in the market. Licences are required for the following market activities: generation, transmission, distribution, wholesale, retail, retail service, import and export.

16 Decision of High Planning Council No. 2004/3 dated 17 March 2004.

17 The maximum term was later reduced from 49 years to 30 years.

18 We note that Turkey is a signatory of the Athens Memoranda of 2002 and 2003 that the EC initiated to develop the regional electricity market in South-East Europe and eventually integrate it with the internal electricity market of the EU. The 2002 Athens Memorandum initiated the regional market development process commonly referred to as the Athens Process. Turkey is committed to implement the provisions of the 2003 Athens Memorandum. See Güney (2005).

19 The authors would like to thank Orhun Selçuk for helpful comments.

20 On balancing the electricity market, see Energy Market Regulatory Authority (2003).

21 Stranded costs refer to costs incurred within the previous market structure that cannot be economically recovered within a competitive market structure. They include the

high operating costs of old and inefficient generators, long-term power purchase agreements with high prices, the removal of production subsidies, and high staffing costs such as payments of redundancies resulting from the transfer of operations to the private sector, including pension liabilities for workers able to retire. Thus, stranded costs create uncertainty for new investors and risk stifling competition (Atiyas and Dutz 2005).

22 The Kayseri region is operated by a separate company in which the municipality holds the largest stake.

23 On Turkey's distribution privatization strategy, see World Bank (2007).

24 On problems encountered during the privatization of the Turkish electricity sector, see Centre for Economics and Foreign Policy Studies (EDAM 2007), Ulusoy and Oğuz (2007), Erdoğdu (2007), Bagdadioglu *et al.* (2007), Çetin and Oğuz (2007a) and the teaser prepared by Lazard for the Privatization Agency.

25 Law No. 5496 passed in 2006 allows for a uniform tariff balancing mechanism across regions with different technical loss and illicit utilization levels for the first five years of the liberalization period. Here, it should be stressed that system losses at TEDAŞ amounted to 17.8 per cent in 2005 and to 15.1 per cent in 2006. System loss levels and collection efficiency levels vary greatly between the regions. Whereas the Izmir region reported a loss level of 6.5 per cent during 2006, the Dicle and Van regions reported losses of 57.8 and 63.8 per cent respectively. This wide disparity is due to the weaker utility governance in the eastern and south-eastern regions of the country. Furthermore, arrears for the sale of electricity have been considerable, and a significant part of the arrears arises from non-payment by government agencies, particularly by municipalities for street lighting. Consequently, the implementation of regional tariffs would result in large deviations in electricity tariffs among the regions.

26 Turkey has recently enacted the Law on the Utilization of Renewable Energy Sources for the Purpose of Generating Energy (Law No. 5346). The law defines the electricity generation resources suitable for wind, solar, geothermal, biomass, biogas, wave, current and tidal energy resources together with hydraulic generation plants (either canal, runoff river type or with a reservoir area of less than 15 square kilometres) as renewable energy resources to be supported. Large hydropower plants are also considered a renewable source, but they are not included in the support mechanism defined in the law. The law provides that facilities that generate electricity from renewable energy resources will be granted a renewable energy resources certificate (the RER certificate), which will entitle such facilities to benefit from the incentives provided by the law, and that EMRA is the competent authority to grant RER certificates. The law has introduced a purchase obligation for the retail licensees in the market for renewable energy sources-based electricity generation. If renewable energy sources-certified electricity is sufficient in the market, the purchase obligation ratio should not be lower than 8 per cent of the previous year's sales. The law requires that, until the end of 2011, the price of electrical energy generated from renewable energy resources (which must be purchased pursuant to the provisions of the law) shall be the average electricity wholesale price of the previous year, as determined by EMRA; furthermore, the Council of Ministers is authorized to increase such prices by 20 per cent at the beginning of each year.

27 The initial 20 per cent limit was increased to 30 per cent with the Board Decision of 26 October 2006. If auto-producers and auto-producer groups exceed this limit, they must give up their auto-producer or auto-producer group licence and get a generator licence.

6 Policy reform in the natural gas sector

1 See Ramsey (1927).

2 See Department of Trade and Industry (2005).

3   When natural gas is cooled to a temperature of approximately –260°F (–161°C) at atmospheric pressure, it condenses to a liquid form called liquefied natural gas (LNG). One volume of LNG takes up about one-six-hundredth the volume of gaseous natural gas. LNG weighs less than one-half of water, actually about 45 per cent as much. LNG is odourless, colourless, non-corrosive and non-toxic. When vaporized it burns only in concentrations of 5–15 per cent. Neither LNG nor its vapour can explode in an unconfined environment. As natural gas takes up less volume and weight in its liquid form, it is liquefied for ease of storing and transporting.

4   This section is largely based on Musselli and Zarrilli (2005), WTO (1998a), WTO Secretariat (2001a) and Selivanova (2004).

5   MFN treatment obliges the country to accord equal conditions to all its trading partners, that is, it prohibits discrimination of trade of some members vis-à-vis other members. The national treatment obligation requires that a member accord to a product imported into its territory treatment no less favourable than that accorded to like domestic products.

6   Members of the Energy Charter Conference include Albania, Armenia, Australia, Austria, Azerbaijan, Belarus, Belgium, Bosnia and Herzegovina, Bulgaria, Croatia, Cyprus, Czech Republic, Denmark, Estonia, European Communities, Finland, France, Georgia, Germany, Greece, Hungary, Iceland, Ireland, Italy, Japan, Kazakhstan, Kyrgyzstan, Latvia, Liechtenstein, Lithuania, Luxembourg, Malta, Moldova, Mongolia, the Netherlands, Norway, Poland, Portugal, Romania, Russian Federation, Slovakia, Slovenia, Spain, Sweden, Switzerland, Tajikistan, the former Yugoslav Republic of Macedonia, Turkey, Turkmenistan, Ukraine, United Kingdom, Uzbekistan.

7   See Energy Charter Secretariat (2004).

8   The following two subsections are based largely on Cameron (2002, 2005), Albers (2005) and a background paper by Ökten (2006).

9   Gas Directive 1998, Article 3.

10   As an example of an objective tariff, a cost-of-service tariff is proposed. This tariff places all fixed costs in a capacity charge and all variable costs in a commodity charge.

11   The European Regulators Group for Electricity and Gas (ERGEG) was established by the Commission Decision of 11 November 2003 (OJ 2003 L 296/34).

12   Gas Directive 2003, Article 18.

13   The European Gas Regulatory Forum's (Madrid Forum's) participants include national regulatory authorities, member states, the European Commission, network operators, gas suppliers and traders, consumers, network users and gas exchanges.

14   EASEE-gas consists of representatives from different gas actors and provides common business practices for technical harmonization.

15   For more information on the Commission proposal, see European Commission (2007e).

16   BOTAŞ was empowered under Decree No. 397 as a monopoly on import, transmission, and sale and determination of sale prices of imported natural gas.

17   The discussion of the new law closely follows OECD and IEA (2001), OECD (2002), Mazzanti and Biancardi (2005) and Energy Charter Secretariat (2007).

18   The term 'supply security' covers several issues but suffice it to say that the EU is scared now of leaning too heavily on Russian energy sources and Russian-owned pipelines.

19   In July 2009 the European Commission adopted a new regulation to improve the security of gas supplies in the framework of the internal gas market.

20   See Pala (2006), Kılıç (2006) and Çetin and Oğuz (2007b).

21   For more information on gas storage in Turkey, see the Energy Charter Secretariat (2007).

22   See Akçollu (2006).

23 For more information on the implementation of wholesale competition by gas release, see Energy Sector Management Assistance Program (2007b).

24 For more information on initiating competitive import buying, see Energy Sector Management Assistance Program (2007b).

7 Liberalization of banking services

1 This statement, at first sight, may seem to undermine the role of the financial markets in favour of the banking system. However, it should not be forgotten that banks are indispensable institutions of the financial markets.

2 In the context of finance, adverse selection is an asymmetric information problem that occurs before the transaction because lower-quality borrowers with a higher credit risk are the ones who are most willing to take out a loan or pay the highest interest rate. Thus, the parties who are most likely to produce an undesirable outcome are most likely to be selected. Minimizing the adverse selection problem requires that lenders screen out good from bad credit risks. On the other hand moral hazard occurs after the transaction takes place because the lender is subjected to the hazard that the borrower has incentives to engage in activities that are undesirable from the lender's point of view – that is, activities that make it less likely that the loan will be paid back. The conflict of interest between the borrower and the lender stemming from moral hazard implies that many lenders will decide that they would rather not make loans, so that lending and investment will be at suboptimal levels. To minimize the moral hazard problem, lenders must impose restrictions and other contract terms on borrowers so that borrowers do not engage in behaviours that make it less likely that they can pay back the loan; thus lenders must monitor borrowers' activities and enforce the restrictive covenants if borrowers violate them.

3 Depositors, in general, are considered as uninformed public, that is, disadvantageous from the informational point of view.

4 On bank regulation, see Mishkin (2001), Dewatripont and Tirole (1999) and Barth *et al.* (2006).

5 For a recent discussion of the Basel Committee, see Claessens *et al.* (2008).

6 Capital adequacy considerations concerning financial institutions have a long history. In the United States, where the financial system was more deregulated and diversified, regulatory monitoring of capital banks goes back to the early twentieth century. Other major financially advanced countries became interested in such measures only during the late 1970s when the process of deregulation and diversification speeded up, and globalization of banking activity increased the need for coordination efforts not only in regulation but also in prudential supervision (Fratangelo 2003). The coordination work was mainly the result of two factors: (1) the risk-enhancing effect of low capital levels of internationally active banks on the stability of the global financial system and (2) the competitive inequalities created by different capital requirements of different countries.

7 See Basel Committee on Banking Supervision (1996).

8 A commodity is defined as a physical product that is or can be traded on a secondary market, for example agricultural products and minerals (including oil and precious metals).

9 VaR is a way of measuring the likelihood that a portfolio will suffer a large loss in some period of time, or the maximum amount that the portfolio owner is likely to lose with some probability, usually set at 99 per cent. It does this by looking at historical data about asset price changes and correlations, using that data to estimate the probability distributions of those asset prices and correlations and using those estimated distributions to calculate the maximum amount that will be lost 99 per cent of the time. Suppose that a portfolio owner has a portfolio consisting of equities, bonds and derivatives and that the weekly VaR is calculated as US$10 million. This

means that over the course of the next week, there is a 99 per cent chance that the portfolio owner will not lose more than US$10 million.

10 Stress testing is used to determine how much capital a particular bank will have left if the economy continues to get worse.

11 Subordinated debt is the loan or security that ranks below other loans or securities with regard to claims on assets or earnings.

12 The risk asset ratio (RAR) under the new methodology is calculated as follows: RAR=adjusted eligible capital/[banking book risk-weighted assets+trading book risk-weighted assets], where trading book risk-weighted assets are represented as 12.5×(market risk capital charge).

13 For a detailed technical discussion of internal risk rating system development under Basel II, see Özdemir and Miu (2009).

14 As was pointed out in Kashyap and Stein (2004: 18), 'in a downturn, when a bank's capital base is likely being eroded by loan losses, its existing (non-defaulted) borrowers will be downgraded by the relevant credit-risk models, forcing the bank to hold *more* capital against its current loan portfolio. To the extent that it is difficult or costly for the bank to raise fresh external capital in bad times, it will be forced to cut back on its lending activity, thereby contributing to a worsening of the initial downturn.' Banks seemed to behave in line with this explanation during the 2008 crisis, notably in the United States and in Europe. See also Brunnermeier *et al.* (2009).

15 In GATS, financial services include two broad categories of services: insurance and insurance-related services and banking and other financial services. Whereas insurance and insurance-related services cover life and non-life insurance, reinsurance, insurance intermediation such as brokerage and agency services and services auxiliary to insurance such as consultancy and actuarial services, banking services include all of the traditional services provided by banks such as acceptance of deposits, lending of all types and payment and money transmission services. Finally, other financial services include trading in foreign exchange, derivatives and all kinds of securities, securities underwriting, money broking, asset management, settlement and clearing services, provision and transfer of financial information and advisory and other auxiliary financial services.

16 MFN exemptions could have been sought with the acceptance of the GATS Agreement and, for acceding countries, at the time of the date of accession. They are contained in country-specific lists, and their duration must not exceed ten years in principle.

17 Mutual recognition allows, in principle, the maintenance of different rules in the participating countries, but the granting of market access without establishing a harmonized regulation implies that institutions from different countries will compete subject to different regulatory constraints. As these constraints will usually undermine the competitive position of banks, regulatory institutions are likely to engage in a process of competitive deregulation, attempting to ensure that the entities under their regulatory control are not handicapped relative to their competitors. Moreover, banks are likely to alter their strategies – including their location – to take advantage of a more favourable regulatory environment. It appears, therefore, that mutual recognition could foster a high degree of market integration.

18 For a discussion of the Financial Sector Action Plan, see Balling (2004).

19 To restructure the state banks, the Treasury issued government bonds to securitize the duty losses of state banks. These bonds were not marketable and were sold to the central bank. The second pillar of the restructuring strategy was the resolution of the banks taken over by the SDIF. From 1999 to 2004, the management of 21 banks was transferred to the SDIF because of their weak financial structures, which imposed serious risks on the overall economy. All liabilities of these banks were taken over by the SDIF. In addition, the banking licences of eight banks were terminated and their assets liquidated. During the same period, 11 bank mergers took place. The third pillar of the restructuring strategy was the establishment of a sound private banking sector.

Whenever necessary, the private banks' capital was strengthened through public support.

20 Article 4 of Banking Law No. 5411 specifies these permitted deposit banking activities: (1) accepting deposits, (2) granting any sort of loan, either cash or non-cash, (3) carrying out any type of payment and collection transactions, including cash and deposit payment and fund transfer transactions, correspondent bank transactions or the use of check accounts, (4) purchasing transactions of commercial bills, (5) safekeeping services, (6) issuing payment instruments such as credit cards, bank cards and traveller's cheques and executing relevant activities, (7) carrying out foreign exchange transactions, trading of money market instruments, trading of precious metals and stones and safekeeping such items, (8) trading and intermediation of forward, future and option contracts, simple or complex financial instruments involving multiple derivative instruments based on economic and financial indicators, capital market instruments, goods, precious metals and foreign exchange, (9) purchase and sale of capital market instruments and repurchasing or resale commitments, (10) intermediation for issuance or public offering of capital market instruments, (11) transactions for trading previously issued capital market instruments for intermediation purposes, (12) guarantee transactions such as undertaking guarantees and other liabilities in favour of other persons, (13) investment counselling services, (14) portfolio operation and management, (15) primary market dealing for purchase–sales transactions within the framework of liabilities assumed by contracts signed by the Treasury Undersecretariat and/or central bank and associations of institutions, (16) factoring and forfeiting transactions, (17) intermediating fund purchase–sales transactions in the inter-bank market, (18) insurance agency and individual private pension fund services and (19) other activities to be determined by the Banking Regulation and Supervision Agency.

21 In the authorities' response to the assessment, it is emphasized that BRSA is in the process of preparing regulations in line with Basel II. The risks, such as country, transfer and interest rate risk in the banking book, will be dealt with in terms of these regulations. Thus, Turkey aims to comply with BCP 11, BCP 12 and BCP 13 over time.

22 The discussion on cross-border banking as summarized by BCPs 23–24 indicates that Turkey is, in general, non-compliant with the principles.

23 For an interesting and detailed critique of the Basel II framework as a way to international harmonization of capital rules, see Tarullo (2008). Various international agencies as well as national authorities released documents to reveal their views on what should be done to prevent the reoccurrence of 2008-like crises. The following documents became available in the first half of 2009: the report of the G-20 Working Group-1 (2009), the preliminary report of the UN Commission of Experts (2009), the report of the US Treasury (2009) and the report of de Larosière *et al.* (2009) for the EU Commisison.

8 Maritime freight transport sector policy reform

1 The author is grateful to Professor Yong-Shik Lee and Professor Jai S. Mah for valuable comments. The chapter is based largely on Togan (2007).

2 Closed conference regimes mean that the right of admission and withdrawal is prescribed and that specific and varying conditions must be met. On the other hand, in open conferences, newcomers cannot be denied entry.

3 See the section on EU rules and regulations on the maritime sector for further discussion of exemptions in the EU.

4 Some bulk companies do enter into pooling arrangements whereby they share the profits and losses made by their respective fleets.

5 Although a ship owner must class a vessel to obtain insurance, and in some instances a government may require a ship to be classed, the importance of the classification certificate extends beyond insurance. It is, as stated by Stopford (1997), the industry standard for establishing that a vessel is properly constructed and in good condition.

6 The ten member societies that form the IACS are the American Bureau of Shipping (United States), Bureau Veritas (France), the China Classification Society (China), Det Norske Veritas (Norway), Germanischer Lloyd (Germany), the Korean Register of Shipping (South Korea), the Lloyd's Register (UK), Nippon Kaiji Kyokai (Japan), Registro Italiano Navale (Italy) and the Russian Maritime Register of Shipping (Russian Federation).

7 See the website of IACS, http://www.iacs.org.uk.

8 The Inter-governmental Maritime Consultative Organization (IMCO) was founded in 1958. In 1982 IMCO changed its name to IMO. As of the beginning of 2007, IMO has 167 member states.

9 Regarding maritime transport, ILO's major interest is in working conditions on ships, such as provisions for manning, hours of work, pensions, vacation, sick pay and minimum wages. Between 1923 and 2005 a total of 41 maritime labour conventions concerning seafarers and dockworkers were adopted, in addition to 33 maritime labour recommendations.

10 The Maritime Transport Committee of the OECD is the only international forum that looks at this sector from both the policy and economic perspectives. Key activities of the Committee include the development of common shipping policies and the exchange of information on shipping policy developments both within and outside the OECD, combating substandard shipping to achieve better ship safety and protecting the environment through the involvement of the entire maritime industry.

11 See OECD (2000).

12 Panamanian and Liberian registries have been among the most popular open registries since the early 1920s.

13 For an extensive discussion of maritime transport services in the WTO, see Parameswaran (2004).

14 On the Argentinean experience of privatization of ports and waterways, see Estache *et al.* (1999).

15 See Commission of the European Communities (2006d).

16 France has lodged a reservation to the OECD's Code of Liberalization of Current Invisible Operations regarding liberalization of maritime freights, including chartering, harbour expenses and disbursements for fishing vessels. Regarding the Common Shipping Principles, we note that Greece did not commit itself to accepting Principles 14 and 15 regarding auxiliary services and international multimodal transport respectively.

17 See Commission of the European Communities (2001b).

18 See Commission of the European Communities (2001c).

19 Self-handling refers to a situation in which an undertaking (a self-handler), which normally could buy port services, using its own land-based personnel (or its seafaring crew for cargo handling operations and passenger services for an authorized regular shipping service carried out in the context of short sea shipping and motorways of the seas operations) and its own equipment, provides for itself one or more categories of port services in accordance with the criteria set out in the directive. Public service requirement refers to a requirement adopted by a competent authority to secure the adequate provision of certain categories of port services.

20 Organotin compounds are chemical compounds based on tin with hydrocarbon substituents.

21 See Commission of the European Communities (2007g).

22 See Commission of the European Communities (2009b).

23 teu means twenty-foot equivalent unit.

24 See Commission of the European Communities (2006e).
25 The targeting factor is in use within the Paris MOU on Port State Control as a tool for selecting ships eligible for an inspection only. The calculation of the targeting factor is divided into two parts. While the generic factor is based on elements of the ship's profile, the history factor is based on the ship's inspection history in the Paris MOU. The generic factor is updated when the particulars of the ship change or the status of its existing flag or class changes. The history factor is updated at the end of each day.

9 Policy reform in the road freight transport sector

1 See Commission of the European Communities (2009c).
2 The signatories to UNECE agree that they will abide by all commonly agreed upon regulations. As of May 2003, UNECE had agreed to 114 regulations concerning motor vehicles and components, which fall within the following groups: (1) lights, directional signals and reflectors, (2) electrical systems, including electromagnetic compatibility, (3) noise, (4) safety protection equipment, including door latches, seat belts, seats, airbags and motorcycle helmets, (5) brakes, (6) safety glass and mirrors, (7) horns and other warning devices, (8) tyres, (9) flammability, (10) crashworthiness and general construction, including specific components such as steering columns and interiors, (11) vehicle design in terms of exterior protrusions and clearance, (12) coupling devices, for example trailer hitches, (13) emissions of pollutants, (14) measurement of fuel consumption and engine power, (15) theft protection measures and (16) instrumentation and location of controls.
3 The member countries of the ECMT are Albania, Austria, Azerbaijan, Belarus, Belgium, Bosnia-Herzegovina, Bulgaria, Croatia, the Czech Republic, Denmark, Estonia, the Federal Republic of Yugoslavia, Finland, France, FYR Macedonia, Georgia, Germany, Greece, Hungary, Iceland, Ireland, Italy, Latvia, Liechtenstein, Lithuania, Luxembourg, Moldova, the Netherlands, Norway, Poland, Portugal, Romania, the Russian Federation, the Slovak Republic, Slovenia, Spain, Sweden, Switzerland, Turkey, Ukraine and the United Kingdom. There are six associate member countries (Australia, Canada, Japan, New Zealand, Republic of Korea and the United States) and two observer countries (Armenia and Morocco).
4 The ECMT has recently been transformed into the International Transport Forum (ITF), which is an inter-governmental organization within the Organization for Economic Co-operation and Development (OECD) family. Its founding member countries include all of the OECD members, as well as many countries in Central and Eastern Europe. The aim of the ITF is to foster a deeper understanding of the essential role played by transport in the economy and society.
5 The list of individual transport operations comprises: (1) transport of vehicles that are damaged or have broken down, (2) unladen runs by a vehicle sent to replace a vehicle that has broken down and also the return run, after repair, of the vehicle that had broken down, (3) transport of goods by motor vehicle whose total permissible laden weight, including trailers, does not exceed 6 tonnes, or whose permitted payload, including that of the trailers, does not exceed 3.5 tonnes, (4) transport of supplies to meet medical and humanitarian needs, (5) transport of goods, on an occasional basis, to airports in the event of services being diverted, (6) transport of works and objects of art for fairs and exhibitions or for non-commercial purposes, (7) transport for non-commercial purposes of properties, accessories and animals to or from theatrical or circus performances, (8) transport of spare parts and provisions for ocean-going ships and for aircraft, (9) funeral transport, (10) transport of livestock in special purpose-built or permanently-converted vehicles for the transport of livestock, recognized as such by the member countries' authorities concerned, and (11) transport of goods on own account.

6 Transport for hire or reward consists of a range of transport operations, such as postal transport, transport of vehicles that are damaged or have broken down, transport of goods by vehicles whose authorized payload does not exceed 3.5 tonnes, transport of medicinal products or medical equipment and transport of emergency equipment. Transport operations for hire or reward other than those just listed require an operating certificate, namely the Community licence, which replaces bilateral licences at the EU level [Council Regulation (EEC) No. 881/92 of 26 March 1992].

7 The most important figure, as far as environmental standards are concerned, is the limit for nitrogen oxid (NOx) emissions. Note that in EURO1 standards (which correspond to the ECMT 'green' lorry), the figure for NOx emissions was 9.0 g/kWh. In EURO2 standards it was reduced to 7.0 g/kWh and in EURO3 standards it decreased to 5.0 g/kWh, which represents more or less a threefold improvement over traditional lorries at approximately 15 g/kWh. For more information on EURO vehicle classifications see footnote 21, this chapter.

8 Consider border closures between Lebanon and Israel on the one hand, and between Syria and Israel on the other, and the border closure between Morocco and Algeria.

9 The single administrative document used in the EU within the framework of trade with third countries and for the movement of non-EU goods within the EU is aimed at ensuring openness in national administrative requirements, rationalizing and reducing administrative documentation, reducing the amount of requested information and standardizing and harmonizing data.

10 While the rate of inspections at customs measured by how many inspections are undertaken among all possibilities is about 2 per cent in the EU, the rate in other countries not using the facilities is much higher.

11 United Nations Economic Commission for Europe (1956) 'Customs Convention on Containers', GENEVA: UNECE; United Nations Economic Commission for Europe (1982) 'International Convention on Harmonization of Frontier Control of Goods', GENEVA: UNECE; United Nations Economic Commission for Europe (1994) 'Convention on Customs Treatment of Pool Containers Used in International Transport', GENEVA: UNECE; United Nations Economic Commission for Europe (1957) 'European Agreement concerning the International Carriage of Dangerous Goods by Road', GENEVA: UNECE; United Nations Economic Commission for Europe (1970a) 'Agreement on the International Carriage of Perishable Foodstuffs and on the Special Equipment to be Used for Such Carriage', GENEVA: UNECE.

12 The TIR Convention has 64 contracting parties, including the European Community (EC). It covers the whole of Europe and reaches out to North Africa and the Near and Middle East. The United States and Canada are contracting parties, as well as Chile and Uruguay in South America. See United Nations Economic Commission for Europe (1959) 'Customs Convention on the International Transport of Goods under Cover of TIR Carnets', GENEVA: UNECE.

13 National treatment requires that once products have entered the market, they must be treated no less favourably than the equivalent domestically produced products.

14 According to the MFN clause, members are bound to grant to the products of others treatment no less favourable than those accorded to the products of any other country.

15 The European Conference of Ministers of Transport (1999) defines own-account transport as transport operated by the manufacturing, agriculture, trade and service industry, as an ancillary part of their business, for moving goods that relate to their main activity.

16 See Bernadet (2009).

17 There were anxieties in the sector about the possible adverse effects of running cabotage services. These focused on potentially unfair competition from lower-wage countries, which could undercut operators who have to bear greater costs in a more tightly regulated environment.

18 See Commission of the European Communities (1995).

19 See Commission of the European Communities (1998c).

20 Marginal social cost refers to the total cost to society as a whole for producing one further unit, or taking one further action, in an economy. This cost consists of two parts, namely the direct marginal costs borne by the producer and the costs to the external environment and other stakeholders.

21 EU legislation on emissions from new motor vehicles has been in force since 1970, but has only been mandatory for member states since 1993. Standards requiring the use of catalytic converters on petrol cars first came into force in 1993 with EURO1, which was replaced by EURO2 in 1997. Stricter standards have now been agreed upon, with EURO3 and EURO4 coming into force in 2001 and 2006, respectively, for passenger cars and in 2002 and 2007, respectively, for light commercial cars. Catalytic converters result in marked reductions of carbon monoxide (CO), nitrogen oxide (NOx) and hydrocarbon (HC) emissions from petrol-driven cars, and more efficient catalytic converters will ensure compliance with future, more stringent standards. For heavy-duty vehicles, standards relate to emissions of CO, HC, NOx and particulate matter (PM), and came into force in 1990 with EURO0, which was replaced by EURO1 and EURO2 in 1993 and 1996 respectively.

22 For recent developments on estimating external costs in the transport sector see CE Delft (2007).

23 The maximum daily driving period is nine hours when the driver is driving six days a week. Total driving time per week must not be more than 56 hours, and total fortnightly driving time must not be more than 90 hours. The driver must rest for at least 11 hours a day four days per week. The other three days he or she needs only to rest for nine hours. There is a stipulation for a split rest of three hours followed by a rest of nine hours (totalling 12 hours) a day. Weekly rest is 45 hours (continuous), which can be brought down to 24 hours with one 45-hour rest every two weeks. Breaks are at least 45 minutes (which can be broken into 15-and 30-minute periods) and should be taken every four-and-a-half hours.

24 A tachograph, fitted to a motor vehicle, records the vehicle's speed and whether it is moving or stationary.

25 This is supplementary to Regulation 561/2006, which outlines driving times.

26 In Directive 70/156/EEC of 6 February 1970, the categories are specified as follows:

M1: Vehicles used for the carriage of passengers and comprising no more than eight seats in addition to the driver's seat.

M2: Vehicles used for the carriage of passengers and comprising no more than eight seats in addition to the driver's seat, and having a maximum weight not exceeding 5 metric tonnes.

M3: Vehicles used for the carriage of passengers and comprising no more than eight seats in addition to the driver's seat, and having a maximum weight exceeding 5 metric tonnes.

N: Motor vehicles having at least four wheels, or having three wheels when the maximum weight exceeds 1 metric tonne, and used for the carriage of goods.

N1: Vehicles used for the carriage of goods and having a maximum weight not exceeding 3.75 metric tonnes.

N2: Vehicles used for the carriage of goods and having a maximum weight exceeding 3.75 metric tonnes but not exceeding 12 metric tonnes.

N3: Vehicles used for the carriage of goods and having a maximum weight exceeding 12 metric tonnes.

O: Trailers (including semi-trailers).

O1: Trailers with a maximum weight not exceeding 0.775 metric tonnes.

O2: Trailers with a maximum weight exceeding 0.775 metric tonnes but not exceeding 3.75 metric tonnes.

O3: Trailers with a maximum weight exceeding 3.75 metric tonnes but not exceeding 10 metric tonnes.

O4: Trailers with a maximum weight exceeding 10 metric tonnes.

27 The Directive 2002/85/EC on the installation and use of speed limitation devices on certain categories of motor vehicles requires the installation of this equipment on category N2 vehicles registered after 1 January 2005.

28 The maximum length of a motor vehicle is 12 metres, an articulated vehicle 16.5 metres and a road train 18.75 metres. The maximum width of a vehicle is 2.55 metres, while conditioned vehicles are 2.6 metres. The maximum weight is 40 tonnes for a road train or an articulated vehicle with 5–6 axles, 44 tonnes for a motor vehicle with three axles that has a semi-trailer (2–3 axles) which transports a 12.2-metrer ISO container (combined transport).

29 The roadworthiness test focuses on the breaking system; steering and steering wheel; visibility; lamps, reflectors and electrical equipment; axles, wheels, tyres and suspension; chassis and chassis attachments; nuisance, including exhaust emissions; vehicle identification; and various items of equipment.

30 European Commission News Centre. 'Stress-free motoring'. Available at http:// ec.europa.eu/research/news-centre/en/tra/01–12-tra02.html.

31 For the Law on Road Transport No. 4925, see the *Official Gazette* of 19 July 2003, No. 25173; for the By-Law on Road Transport, see the *Official Gazette* of 25 February 2004, No. 25384; for the By-Law on Training for Professional Competence in Road Transport Operations, see the *Official Gazette* of 3 September 2004, No. 25572; for Foreign Direct Investment Law No. 4875, see the *Official Gazette* of 17 June 2003, No. 25141; and for the Turkish Commercial Code No. 6762, see the *Official Gazette* of 25 July 1956, No. 9353.

32 For the Law on Road Transport No. 4925, see the *Official Gazette* of 19 July 2003, No. 25173.

33 For the Law on Establishment of General Directorate of Highways No. 5539, see the *Official Gazette* of 16 February 1950, No. 7434.

34 See the *Official Gazette* of 3 June 1977, No. 15955.

35 A vehicle is classified into one of five types based on its number of axles and the distance it is travelling. The same toll rate applies for national and foreign vehicles. Ambulances of the Ministry of Health are exempted from paying tolls following Cabinet Decree No. 2003/6254 of 23 September 2003 (*Official Gazette*, 23 October 2003, No. 25268). There are three different payment methods: manually operated tolls, contactless smart card system and non-stop electronic toll collection (ETC) system. ETC and contactless smart card subscribers receive toll discounts of 20 per cent and motorcycle drivers who are contactless smart card subscribers receive a 30 per cent discount. The dedicated short-range communications (DSRC) roadside and onboard units allow for the reading of licence plates of vehicle passing through tolls. Enforcement of this procedure is possible through cameras; violators are penalized with ten times the maximum tariff.

36 See the *Official Gazette* of 9 June 2002, No. 24810.

37 See the Law on Public Finance and Regulation of Debt Management No. 4749, published in the *Official Gazette* of 12 April 2002, No. 24721.

38 For Labour Law No. 4857, see the *Official Gazette* of 10 June 2003, No. 25134; for the By-Law on Working Time that Cannot be Divided into Weekly Working Days, see the *Official Gazette* of 6 April 2004, No. 25425; for the By-Law on Road Traffic, see the *Official Gazette* of 2 September 2004, No. 25571.

39 The by-law defines a 'reference period' as the period that is necessary to do a particular job, which can range between two and six months, as designated by the employer. The maximum weekly working time over a reference period is 45 hours. Each period of 24 hours should have at least 11 consecutive hours of rest. Alternately, 12 hours can be separated into two or three periods, but one of the periods must be at least eight consecutive hours. There can also be a reduced rest period of a minimum of nine consecutive hours, but such arrangements cannot take place more than three times a week. When there are at least two drivers for a vehicle, in a 30-hour period there must

be eight consecutive hours of rest for each driver. The weekly rest period must be at least 24 consecutive hours, which must be taken no later than at the end of six 24-hour driving periods.

40 The Labour Law stipulates that breaks be a minimum of 15 minutes for work lasting four hours or fewer, a minimum of 30 minutes for work lasting four to seven-and-a-half hours, and a minimum of one hour for work lasting longer than seven-and-a-half hours. According to the By-Law on Road Traffic, there should be a rest period of 45 minutes after four-and-a-half hours of driving, but this can be replaced by two breaks of at least 15 minutes. It further states that a driver may not carry out any other work during the break, and that breaks cannot be considered part of the daily rest period. Daily driving limits are nine hours in a 24-hour period, in which the maximum uninterrupted driving period is four-and-a-half hours. Furthermore, the by-law specifies that the weekly driving period cannot exceed 54 hours, and a fortnight's driving limit is 90 hours.

41 For the European Agreement on the Work of Crews of Vehicles Engaged in International Road Transport (UNECE 1970b), see the *Official Gazette* of 25 July 1999, No. 23766, and for the ILO Convention concerning Hours of Work and Rest Periods in Road Transport (C153) (ILO 1939), see the *Official Gazette* of 22 July 2003, No. 25176.

42 See the *Official Gazette* of 23 September 2004, No. 25592.

43 For the By-Law on Road Traffic, see the *Official Gazette* of 18 July 1997, No. 23053.

44 For the By-Law on Type Approval of Speed Limitation Devices of Motor Vehicles and Their Installation (92/24/AT), see the *Official Gazette* of 5 June 2002, No. 24776; for the Law on the Amendment of Law on Road Traffic No. 5495, see the *Official Gazette* of 10 May 2006, No. 26164; and for Fundamental Principles of International Passenger and Freight Transport by Road (Resolution of Council of Ministers) No. 8/984, see the *Official Gazette* of 29 June 1980, No. 17032.

45 For the By-Law on Amending By-Law on Road Traffic, see the *Official Gazette* of 11 April 2003, No. 25076.

46 Exemptions for speed limitation devices include motor vehicles used by the police, gendarmerie, armed forces, civil defense and fire and other emergency services; category M3 vehicles, which cannot exceed a speed of 100 km/hour, and category N3 vehicles, which cannot exceed a speed of 85 km/hour; motor vehicles used for scientific experiments and motor vehicles used only for public services in urban areas.

47 For the By-Law on Transport of Dangerous Goods by Road, see the *Official Gazette* of 22 October 1976, No. 15742; and for the By-Law on Training for Professional Competence in Road Transport Operations, see the *Official Gazette* of 3 September 2004, No. 25572.

10 Impact of economic liberalization

1 This section is based largely on Togan and Michalek (2008).

2 The number of entries varies among countries as many sectors are not included in the list of commitments of a large number of countries.

3 For a discussion of various issues related to national treatment and market access see Chapter 1.

4 The scope of GATS commitments for developed countries is usually much larger than for developing ones. In the sample analyzed by Hoekman (1995: 40) the average coverage of bound sectors/modes was 35.6 per cent for developed and 10.9 per cent for developing countries.

5 See, for example, Findlay and Warren (2000).

6 For alternative specifications of the gravity model see Francois *et al.* (2003), Park (2002) and Walsh (2006).

7 See *OECD Statistics on International Trade in Services*, Volumes I and II (OECD 2009b).

8 These data have been made available only recently.

9 The Turkish figures are based on the regulatory regime prevailing in 2005.

10 When calculating the values of q_i, and TE_i ($i=f$, m) we use the following values for the variables: $y=$US\$4210, $hd=19.2$, $wait=2.62$ per cent, $dshare=0.9$, $\eta=-1.2$ and policy variable $p=(1-FR)$. The values of the variables are obtained from the World Bank Indicators database (World Bank 2005b) and OECD (2005a). On the other hand, we get the FR value from Appendix Table 10.4, the FR value under full liberalization from Appendix Table 10.5 for the UK and Finland, and the value of the price elasticity of demand η from Albon *et al.* (1997).

11 On the calculation of tariff equivalents see Kimura *et al.* (2003a) and Dee (2003).

12 Steiner (2000) uses data for 19 OECD economies over the period 1986–96: Australia, Belgium, Canada, Denmark, Finland, France, Germany, Greece, Ireland, Italy, Japan, the Netherlands, New Zealand, Norway, Portugal, Spain, Sweden, the United Kingdom and the United States.

13 In addition to the 19 economies considered by Steiner (2000), Doove *et al.* (2001) consider 11 OECD economies: Austria, the Czech Republic, Hungary, Iceland, Korea, Luxembourg, Mexico, Poland, the Slovak Republic, Switzerland and Turkey; 12 non-OECD Asia–Pacific Economic Cooperation (APEC) members: Chile, China, Hong Kong, Indonesia, Malaysia, Peru, the Philippines, Russia, Singapore, Taiwan, Thailand and Vietnam; and eight other economies: Argentina, Bolivia, Brazil, Colombia, India, South Africa, Uruguay and Venezuela.

14 The figures are based on the regulatory regime prevailing in 2005.

15 See also Kimura *et al.* (2003b).

16 The author is grateful to Serdinç Yılmaz of the State Planning Organization and to M. Mehdi Gönülalçak and Özkan Poyraz of the Undersecretariat for Maritime Affairs for providing information on restrictions on maritime services in Turkey.

17 The sum of weights for all categories shown in column one of Appendix Table 10.9 is unity. For each restrictiveness category, a score with a range from 0 (least restrictive) to 1 (most restrictive) is assigned according to the degree of restrictiveness; the score reflects the type of restriction imposed by the economy.

18 The benefits of liberalization through harmonization of rules were studied, for example, by De Bruin *et al.* (2006) in analyzing the implications of the implementation of the Services Directive (Directive 2006/123/EC).

19 See Chapter 5 for a thorough discussion of the rules and regulations that had prevailed in Turkey before the liberalization in the electricity sector and for the rules and regulations of the EU.

20 'Consumer surplus' measures the amount that consumers gain from a purchase according to the difference between the price they actually pay and the price they would have been willing to pay.

21 Data definitions and sources are reported in Appendix Table 10.12. The end points of the estimation period, that is, 1989 and 2001, are especially important because the former marked the unification episode of the two Germanys and the latter witnessed the devastating financial crisis in the Turkish economy.

22 See Messerlin (2008) and the 'Introduction' of Hoekman and Togan (2005) for similar arguments.

References

Akarsu, M. and M. Kumar (2002) 'Turkish Container Ports: An Analysis of Problems and Potential Opportunities', unpublished paper, Maine Maritime Academy. Available at http://www.bell.mma.edu/~skumar/TurkContPorts.pdf.

Akçollu, F. Y. (2006) 'Major Challenges to the Liberalization of the Turkish Natural Gas Market', Oxford Institute for Energy Studies NG 16, Oxford.

Akdemir, E., E. Başçı and S. Togan (2007) 'Telecommunications Policy Reform in Turkey', *World Economy*, **30**, 1114–38.

Albers, M. (2005). 'The New EU Directives on Energy Liberalization from a Competition Point of View', in P. Cameron (ed.) *Legal Aspects of EU Energy Regulation: Implementing the New Directives on Electricity and Gas Across Europe,* Oxford: Oxford University Press.

Albon, R., A. Hardin and P. Dee (1997) *Telecommunications Economics and Policy Issues*, Industry Commission Staff Information Paper, Canberra: Productivity Commission, Commonwealth of Australia.

Arısan, N (1999) 'Historical Background and Evolution in Turkish–European Union Relations', unpublished manuscript, text of a lecture presented at Bilkent University, 14 April.

Atiyas, I. and M. Dutz (2005) 'Competition and Regulatory Reform in Turkey's Electricity Industry', in B. Hoekman and S. Togan (eds) *Turkey: Economic Reform and Accession to the European Union*, World Bank and Centre for Economic Policy, Washington DC: World Bank.

Bagdadioglu, N., C. W. Price and T. Weyman-Jones (2007) 'Measuring Potential Gains from Mergers among Electricity Distribution Companies in Turkey using Non-Parametric Model', *Energy Journal*, **28**, 83–110.

Baldwin, R. E. (2001) 'Regulatory Protectionism, Developing Nations and a Two-Tier World Trade System', *Brookings Trade Forum*, **3**, 237–80.

Balling, M. (2004) 'Objectives and Theoretical Foundations of European Commission's 1999 Action Plan Concerning the Framework for Financial Markets', *Journal of International Banking Regulation*, **5**, 256–86.

Banking Regulation and Supervisory Board (2005) 'Road Map for Basel II', draft document of 30 May 2005, Ankara: BRSB.

Banks Association of Turkey (2008) 'Banking Law No. 5411', published originally in *Official Gazette* No. 25983 of 1 November 2005, Istanbul: Banks Association of Turkey.

Barth, J. R., G. Caprio, Jr and R. Levine (2006) *Rethinking Bank Regulation: Till Angels Govern*, Cambridge: Cambridge University Press.

Basel Committee on Banking Supervision (1996) *Amendment to the Capital Accord to Incorporate Market Risks*, Bank for International Settlements, Basel: BIS.

—— (1997) 'Core Principles for Effective Banking Supervision', consultative paper, Basel: BIS.

—— (2006) *International Convergence of Capital Measurement and Capital Standards: A Revised Framework, Comprehensive Version*, Bank for International Settlements, Basel: BIS.

Bernadet, M. (2009) 'Report on the Construction and Operation of the Road Freight Transport Market in Europe', International Transport Forum, Transport for a Global Economy: Challenges and Opportunities in the Downturn, Leipzig, 26–29 May.

Bourguignon, R. (1990) 'The History of the Association Agreement between Turkey and the European Union', in A. Evin and G. Denton (eds) *Turkey and the European Community*, Opladen, Germany: Leske und Budrich.

Boylaud, O. (2000) 'Regulatory Reform in Road Freight and Retail Distribution', Economics Department Working Papers No. 255, Paris: OECD.

Braga, C. A. P., E. Forrester and P. A. Stern (1999) 'Developing Countries and Accounting Rate Reform:—A Technological and Regulatory El Nino?', Public Policy for the Private Sector, Note No. 173, World Bank Group, Washington DC: World Bank.

Braithwaite, J. and P. Drahos (2000) *Global Business Regulation*, Cambridge: Cambridge University Press.

Brenton, P. and M. Manchin (2002) 'Making EU Trade Agreements Work: The Role of Rules of Origin', Centre for European Policy Studies Working Paper No. 183, Brussels: CEPS.

Brown, G. and N. Sarkozy (2009) 'For Global Finance, Global Regulation', *The Wall Street Journal*, 9 December 2009.

Brunnermeier, M., A. Crockett, C. Goodhart, A. D. Persaud and H. Shin (2009) 'The Fundamental Principles of Financial Regulation', Geneva Reports on World Economy No. 11, Preliminary conference draft. Centre for Economic Policy Research, London: CEPR.

Button, K. (1990) 'Environmental Externalities and Transport Policy', *Oxford Review of Economic Policy*, **6**, 61–75.

Cameron, P. D. (2002) *Competition in Energy Markets: Law and Regulation in the European Union,* Oxford: Oxford University Press.

—— (2005) 'Completing the Internal Market in Energy: An Introduction to the New Legislation', in by P. Cameron (ed.) *Legal Aspects of EU Energy Regulation: Implementing the New Directives on Electricity and Gas Across Europe*, Oxford: Oxford University Press.

CE Delft (2007) 'Handbook on Estimation of External Cost in the Transport Sector', report produced within the study Internalization Measures and Policies for All External Cost of Transport (IMPACT), Delft, 19 December.

Centre for Economics and Foreign Policy Studies (EDAM) (2007) *Second Generation Structural Reforms: De-Regulation and Competition in Infrastructure Industries: The Evolution of the Turkish Telecommunications, Energy and Transport Sectors in Light of EU Harmonization*, Istanbul: EDAM.

Claessens, S., G. R. D. Underhill and X. Zhang (2008) 'The Political Economy of Basle II: The Costs for Poor Countries', *World Economy*, **31**, 313–44.

Clark, X., D. Dollar and A. Micco (2001) 'Maritime Transport Costs and Port Efficiency', Working Paper Series No. 2781, Washington, DC: World Bank.

Commission of the European Communities (1985) 'Completing the Internal Market: White Paper from the Commission to the European Council', COM (85) 310, Brussels: European Commission.

—— (1988) 'The Internal Energy Market', Commission Working Document COM (88) 238 final, Brussels: European Commission.

—— (1995) 'Green Paper – Towards Fair and Efficient Pricing in Transport Policy – Options for Internalizing the External Costs of Transport in the European Union', COM (95) 691 final, Brussels: European Commission.

—— (1997) 'Accreditation and the Community's Policy in the Field of Conformity Assessment', CERTIF 97/4 – EN Rev. 2, Brussels: European Commission.

—— (1998a) *Technical Barriers to Trade, Vol. 1, Subseries III, Dismantling of Barriers, The Single Market Review,* Luxembourg: Office for Official Publications of the European Communities (OOPEC).

—— (1998b) 'Financial Services: Commission proposes Framework for Action', Communication of the Commission, Brussels: European Commission.

—— (1998c) 'Fair Payment for Infrastructure Use: A Phased Approach to a Common Transport Infrastructure Charging Framework in the EU', White Paper COM (1998) 466 final, Brussels: European Commission.

—— (1999) 'Financial Services: Implementing the Framework for Financial Markets: Action Plan', Communication of the Commission, COM (1999) 232, Brussels: European Commission.

—— (2000) *Guide to the Implementation of Directives based on the New Approach and the Global Approach,* Luxembourg: Office for Official Publications of the European Communities (OOPEC).

—— (2001a) 'Completing the Internal Energy Market', Communication from the Commission to the Council and the European Parliament, proposal for a directive of the European Parliament and of the Council amending Directives 96/92/EC and 98/30/EC concerning common rules for the internal market in electricity and natural gas and proposal for a regulation of the European Parliament and of the Council on conditions for access to the network for cross-border exchanges in electricity, COM (2001) 125 final, Brussels: European Commission.

—— (2001b) 'Reinforcing Quality Service in Sea Ports: A Key for European Transport', Communication from the Commission to the European Parliament and the Council, COM/2001/0035 final, Brussels: European Commission.

—— (2001c) 'European Transport Policy for 2010: Time to Decide', White Paper COM (2001) 370, Brussels: European Commission.

—— (2003) 'Wide Europe – Neighbourhood: A New Framework for Relations with our Eastern and Southern Neighbours', Communication from the Commission to the Council and the European Parliament, COM (2003) 104 final, Brussels: European Commission.

—— (2004) 'European Neighbourhood Policy Strategy Paper', Communication from the Commission, COM (2004) 373 final, Brussels: European Commission.

—— (2006a) 'On Strengthening the European Neighbourhood Policy', Communication from the Commission to the Council and the European Parliament, COM (2006) 726 final, Brussels: European Commission.

—— (2006b) 'Expanding on the Proposals contained in the Communication to the European Parliament and the Council on "Strengthening the ENP"' Non Paper, COM (2006) 726 final, Brussels: European Commission.

—— (2006c) 'Energy Sector Inquiry, Draft Preliminary Report', Competition DG, Brussels: European Commission.

—— (2006d) 'Background Paper No. 9 on Multilateral and EC Instruments related with the Seas and the Oceans', background documents for the Green Paper 'Towards A

Future Maritime Policy for the Union: European Vision for the Oceans and Seas', SEC (2006) 689, Brussels European Commission.

—— (2006e) 'Turkey 2006 Progress Report', COM (2006) 649 final, Brussels: European Commission.

—— (2007a) 'The Internal Market for Goods: A Cornerstone of Europe's Competitiveness', Communication from the Commission to the European Parliament, the Council and the European Economic and Social Committee, COM (2007) 35 final, Brussels, European Commission.

—— (2007b) 'Electronic Communications: Common Regulatory Framework for Networks and Services, Access, Interconnection and Authorization', COD/2007/0247, Brussels, European Commission.

—— (2007c) 'Common Rules for the Internal Market in Electricity', COM (2007) 0528, Proposal for a Directive of the European Parliament and of the Council amending Directive 2003/54/EC of the European Parliament and of the Council of 26 June 2003, Brussels, European Commission.

—— (2007d) 'Cross-border Exchanges in Electricity', COM (2007) 0531, Proposal for a Regulation of the European Parliament and of the Council amending Regulation (EC) No. 1228/2003, Brussels, European Commission.

—— (2007e) 'Explanatory Memorandum of the 3rd Energy Package: Proposal for a Directive of the European Parliament and of the Council amending Directive 2003/54/EC of the European Parliament and of the Council of 26 June 2003', COM (2007) draft, Brussels, European Commission.

—— (2007f) 'Financial Services Action Plan Evaluation', Internal Market and Services DG, Financial Services Policy and Financial Markets, Brussels: European Commission.

—— (2007g) 'An Integrated Maritime Policy for the European Union', Communication from the Commission to the European Parliament, the Council, the European Economic and Social Committee and the Committee of the Regions, SEC (2007) 1278, Brussels European Commission.

—— (2007h) 'Extension of the Major Trans-European Transport Axes to the Neighbouring Countries – Guidelines for Transport in Europe and Neighbouring Countries', Communication from the Commission to the Council and European Parliament, SEC (2007) 98 and SEC (2007) 99, COM (2007) 32 final, Brussels, European Commission.

—— (2007i) 'Turkey 2007 Progress Report', SEC (2007) 1436, Brussels, European Commission.

—— (2008) 'Turkey 2008 Progress Report', accompanying the Communication from the Commission to the European Parliament and the Council 'Enlargement Strategy and Main Challenges 2008–9', COM (2008) 674, SEC (2008) 2699, Brussels, European Commission.

—— (2009a) 'Report on Progress in Creating the Internal Gas and Electricity Market: Technical Annex to the Communication from the Commission to the Council and the European Parliament', DG Tren Staff Working Paper COM (2009)115, Brussels, European Commission.

—— (2009b) 'Strategic Goals and Recommendations for the EU's Maritime Transport Policy until 2018', Communication from the Commission to the European Parliament, the Council, the European Economic and Social Committee and the Committee of the Regions, COM (2009) 8 final, Brussels, European Commission.

—— (2009c) *EU Energy and Transport Statistics in Figures Pocketbook 2009*, Directorate-General for Energy and Transport, Brussels, European Commission.

Council of the European Union (2003) 'Copenhagen European Council 12 and 13 December 2002: Presidency Conclusions', 15917/02 Polgen 84, 29 January, Brussels: Council of European Union.

Crampes, C. and J. Laffont (2001) 'Transport Pricing in the Electricity Industry', *Oxford Review of Economic Policy*, **17**, 313–28.

Cremer, H. and J. Laffont (2002) 'Competition in Gas Markets', *European Economic Review*, **46**, 928–35.

Cremer, H., F. Gasmi and J. Laffont (2003) 'Access to Pipelines in Competitive Gas Markets', *Journal of Regulatory Economics*, **24**, 5–33

Çetin, T. and F. Oğuz (2007a) 'The Politics of Regulation in the Turkish Electricity Market', *Energy Policy*, **35**, 1761–70.

—— (2007b) 'The Reform in the Turkish Natural Gas Market: A Critical Evaluation', *Energy Policy*, **35**, 3856–67.

De Bruin R., H. Kox and A. Lejour (2006) 'The Trade-Induced Effects of the Services Directive and the Country-of-Origin Principle', European Network of Economic Policy Research Institutes Working Paper No. 44, April. Brussels: European Network of Economic Policy Research Institutes.

Dee, P. (2003) 'Services Trade Liberalization in South East European Countries', paper prepared for OECD South Eastern Europe Regional Program 'Forum on Trade in Services in South Eastern Europe', Paris: OECD.

Delaney, H. and R. van de Zande (2000) 'A Guide to EU Standards and Conformity Assessment', National Institute of Standards and Technology Special Publication 951, Gaithersburg: NIST.

Department of Trade and Industry (2005) *Conditions for Truly Competitive Gas Markets in the EU*, Vols 1 and 2, London: Energy Markets Limited.

Dewatripont, M. and J. Tirole (1999) *The Prudential Regulation of Banks*, Cambridge, MA: MIT Press.

Doove, S., O. Gabbitas, D. Nguyen-Hong and J. Owen (2001) 'Price Effects of Regulation: International Air Passenger Transport, Telecommunications and Electricity Supply', Productivity Commission Staff Research Paper, Canberra: Productivity Commission.

Dutz, M., A. Hayri and P. Ibarra (2000) 'Regulatory Reform, Competition and Innovation: A Case Study of the Mexican Road Freight Industry', Policy Research Working Paper 2318, Washington DC: World Bank.

Electricity Generation Company (EÜAŞ) (2008) *Elektrik Üretim Sektör Raporu*, Ankara: EÜAŞ.

Energy Charter Secretariat (2004) *The Energy Charter Treaty and Related Documents: A Legal Framework for International Energy Cooperation*, Brussels: Energy Charter Secretariat.

—— (2007) *Turkey: Review of the Investment Climate and Market Structure in the Energy Sector*, Brussels: Energy Charter Secretariat.

Energy Market Regulatory Authority (2003) *Electricity Market Implementation Manual*, Ankara: Energy Market Regulatory Authority.

Energy Sector Management Assistance Program (2007a) 'Turkey's Experience with Greenfield Gas Distribution since 2003', Formal Report 325/07, World Bank Group, Washington DC: World Bank.

—— (2007b) 'Turkey: Gas Sector Strategy', ESMAP Technical Paper 114/07, World Bank Group, Washington DC: World Bank.

Erdoğdu, E. (2007) 'Regulatory Reform in Turkish Energy Industry: An Analysis', *Energy Policy*, **35**, 984–93.

Estache, A., J. C. Carbajo and G. de Rus (1999) 'Argentina's Transport Privatization and Re-Regulation: Ups and Downs of a Daring Decade-Long Experience', Policy Research Working Paper 2249, Washington, DC: World Bank.

EuroMed (2005) 'Towards an Integrated Euro-Mediterranean Transport System: Transport Policies and Priorities Commonly Agreed by MEDA Partners', Blue Paper, Brussels: European Union.

European Committee for Standardization (2003) *Support to the Quality Infrastructure in Turkey: Country Report 2003*, Brussels: CEN.

European Competitive Telecommunications Association (2009) *Regulatory Scoreboard 2008*, Brussels: European Competitive Telecommunications Association.

European Conference of Ministers of Transport (1999) 'Road Freight Transport for Own Account in Europe', report of the Hundred and Fifth Round Table on Transport Economics, Paris: ECMT.

—— (2001) *Regulatory Reform in Road Freight Transport*, Paris: ECMT.

European Regulators' Group for Electricity and Gas (ERGEG) (2007) 'Compliance with Electricity Regulation 1228/2003', ERGEG Monitoring Report E07-EFG-23–06, Brussels: ERGEG.

Financial Stability Board (2009) 'Improving Financial Regulation', report of the Financial Stability Board to G20 Leaders, Basel: Financial Stability Board.

Findlay, C. and T. Warren (eds) (2000) *Impediments to Trade in Services: Measurement and Policy Implications*. Sydney: Routledge.

Fink, C., A. Mattoo and H. C. Neagu (2002) 'Trade in International Maritime Services: How Much Does Policy Matter?', *World Bank Economic Review*, 16, 81–108.

Foreign Investment Advisory Service (2001a) *Turkey: A Diagnostic Study of the Foreign Direct Investment Environment*, Ankara: World Bank and the Treasury of Turkey.

—— (2001b) *Turkey: Administrative Barriers to Investment*, Ankara: World Bank and the Treasury of Turkey.

Francois, J. (1999) 'Estimates of Barriers to Trade in Services', unpublished.

Francois, J., H. van Meijl and F. van Tongeren (2003) *Economic Benefits of the Doha Round for the Netherlands*, The Hague: Agricultural Economics Institute.

Francois, J., B. Hoekman and J. Woerz (2007) 'Does Gravity Apply to Intangibles? Measuring Barriers to Trade in Services', paper presented at the CEPII-OECD Workshop 'Recent Developments in International Trade in Services', November 2007, Paris.

Frankel, J. and A. Rose (2002) 'An Estimate of the Effect of Common Currencies on Trade and Income', *Quarterly Journal of Economics*, 117, 437–66.

Fratangelo, P. (2003) 'International and European Co-operation in Prudential Supervision', *Rivista di Diritto Bancario*, December (also available as MPRA Paper No. 5539).

G-20 Working Group-1 (2009) 'Enhancing Sound Regulation and Strengthening Transparency', Final Report, 25 March. Available at http://www.g20.org/index.aspx.

Geradin, D. (2006) 'The Liberalization of Network Industries in the European Union: Where Do We Come From and Where Do We Go?', Annual Report of the European Regulation for Electricity and Gas, Helsinski: Prime Minister's Office, Economic Council of Finland.

Goodwin, P. B. (2002) 'Demographic Impacts, Social Consequences, and the Transportation Policy Debate', *Oxford Review of Economic Policy*, 6, 76–90.

Green, R. (2005) 'Electricity and Markets', *Oxford Review of Economic Policy*, 21, 67–87.

Güney, E. S. (2005) *Restructuring, Competition, and Regulation in the Turkish Electricity Industry*, Ankara: Economic Policy Research Foundation of Turkey (TEPAV).

Hoekman, B. (1995) 'Assessing the General Agreement on Trade in Services', in W. Martin and A. L. Winters (eds) *The Uruguay Round and the Developing Countries*, World Bank Discussion Paper No. 307, Washington, DC: World Bank.

—— (2007) 'Regionalism and Development: The European Neighbourhood Policy and Integration à la Carte', *Journal of International Trade and Diplomacy*, 1, 7–50.

Hoekman, B. and S. Togan (eds) (2005) *Turkey: Economic Reform and Accession to the European Union*, World Bank and Centre for Economic Policy Research (CEPR), Washington, DC: World Bank.

Howarth, P. and F. Redgrave (2003) 'Metrology – In Short', document prepared for the European Commission. Braunschweig: European Association of National Metrology Institutes.

International Labour Office (1939) 'ILO Convention (No. 153) on Hours of Work and Rest Periods (Road Transport)', Geneva: ILO.

—— (1947) 'ILO Convention No. 81 on Labor Inspection', Geneva: ILO.

—— (1976) 'ILO Convention (No. 147) concerning Minimum Standards in Merchant Ships', Geneva: ILO.

—— (1996) 'ILO Convention (No. 180) concerning Seafarers' Hours of Work and the Manning of Ships', Geneva: ILO.

—— (2006) 'Maritime Labour Convention', Geneva: ILO.

International Maritime Organization (1966) 'International Convention on Load Lines', London: IMO.

—— (1973) 'International Convention for the Prevention of Pollution from Ships (MARPOL)', London: IMO.

—— (1974) 'International Convention for the Safety of Life at Sea (SOLAS)', London: IMO.

—— (1978) 'International Convention on Standards of Training, Certification and Watchkeeping for Seafarers', London: IMO.

—— (1993a) 'The International Safety Management Code', London: IMO.

—— (1993b) 'Application of Tonnage Measurement of Seggregated Ballast Tanks in Oil Tankers', Resolution A.747(18) adopted 4 November 1993, London: IMO.

—— (2002) 'International Ship and Port Facility Security Code', London: IMO.

International Monetary Fund (2002) 'Implementation of the Basel Core Principles for Effective Banking Supervision, Experience, Influences, and Perspectives', Report prepared by the staff of the World Bank and the International Monetary Fund, Washington, DC: IMF.

—— (2007) 'Turkey: Financial System Stability Assessment', Report prepared by the Monetary and Capital Markets and European Departments, Washington, DC: IMF.

International Road Transport Union (1998) 'Final Resolution of the XXVIth Congress of the International Road Transport Union', Brussels: IRU.

International Telecommunications Union (1998) *Telecommunications Reform*, Geneva: ITU.

Izmen, Ü. and K. Yılmaz (2009) 'Turkey's Recent Trade and Foreign Direct Investment Performance', TÜSIAD-KOÇ University Economic Research Forum Working Paper 0902, Istanbul: TÜSIAD-KOÇ University Economic Research Forum.

Jamasb, T. and M. Pollitt (2005) 'Electricity Market Reform in the European Union: Review of Progress toward Liberalization and Integration', *Energy Journal*, 26, 11–41.

Kahai, S. K., P. S. Kahai and A. Leigh (2006) 'Traditional and Non-Traditional Determinants of Accounting Rates in International Telecommunications', *International Advances in Economic Research*, 12, 505–22.

Kalirajan, K., G. McGuire, D. Nguyen-Hong and M. Schuele (2000) 'The Price Impact of Restrictions on Banking Services', in C. Findlay and T. Warren (eds) *Impediments to Trade in Services: Measurement and Policy Implications*, London: Routledge.

Kaminski, B. (2005) 'Maximizing Benefits from Turkey's Integration into the EU', Background paper prepared for *Promoting Sustained Growth and Convergence with the European Union*: Turkey: Country Economic Memorandum; Poverty Reduction and Economic Management Unit, Europe and Central Asia Region, Washington, DC: World Bank.

Kaminski, B. and F. Ng (2007) 'Turkey's Evolving Trade Integration into Pan-European Markets', *Journal of International Trade and Diplomacy*, 1, 35–103.

Kang, J. (2000) 'Price Impact of Restrictions on Maritime Transport Services', in C. Findlay and T. Warren (eds) *Impediments to Trade in Services: Measurement and Policy Implications*, London: Routledge.

Kang, J. and C. Findlay (2000) 'Regulatory Reform in the Maritime Industry', in C. Findlay and T. Warren (eds) *Impediments to Trade in Services: Measurement and Policy Implications*, London: Routledge.

Kashyap, A. K. and J. C. Stein (2004) 'Cyclical Implications of Basel II Capital Standards', *Economic Perspectives*, Chicago: Federal Reserve Bank of Chicago.

Kimura, F., M. Ando and T. Fujii (2003a) 'Estimating the Ad Valorem Equivalent of Barriers to Foreign Direct Investment in the Telecommunications Services Sectors in Russia', unpublished paper, Washington, DC: World Bank.

—— (2003b) 'Estimating the Ad Valorem Equivalent of Barriers to Foreign Direct Investment in Financial Services Sectors in Russia', unpublished paper, Washington, DC: World Bank.

—— (2004) 'Estimating the Ad Valorem Equivalent of Barriers to Foreign Direct Investment in the Maritime and Air Transportation Service Sectors in Russia', unpublished paper, Washington, DC: World Bank.

Kılıç, A. M. (2006) 'Turkey's Natural Gas Necessity, Consumption and Future Perspectives', *Energy Policy*, 34, 1928–34.

Landesmann, M. and R. Stehrer (2003) 'Structural Patterns of East–West European Integration: Strong and Weak Gershenkron Effects', in *WIIW Structural Report 2003 on Central and Eastern Europe Vol. 1*, Vienna: Vienna Institute for International Economic Studies.

de Larosière J., L. Balcerowicz, O. Issing, R. Masera, C. Mc Carthy, L. Nyberg, J. Pérez and O. Ruding (2009) 'The High Level Group on Financial Supervision in the EU', Report, 25 February. Available at http://ec.europa.eu/commission_barroso/president/pdf/statement_20090225_en.pdf.

League of Nations (1923) 'Convention and Statute on the International Regime of Maritime Ports', Geneva: League of Nations.

Marceau, G. and J. P. Trachtman (2002) 'The Technical Barriers to Trade Agreement, the Sanitary and Phytosanitary Measures Agreement, and the General Agreement on Tariffs and Trade: A Map of the World Trade Organization Law of Domestic Regulation of Goods', *Journal of World Trade*, 36, 811–81.

Maskus, K. E. and J. S. Wilson (2001) 'A Review of Past Attempts and the New Policy Context', in K. E. Maskus and J. S. Wilson (eds) *Quantifying the Impact of Technical Barriers to Trade: Can it be Done?*, Ann Arbor, MI: University of Michigan Press.

Mazzanti, M. R. and A. Biancardi (2005) 'Institutional Endowment and Regulatory Reform in Turkey's Natural Gas Sector', in B. Hoekman and S. Togan (eds) *Turkey: Economic*

Reform and Accession to the European Union, World Bank and Centre for Economic Policy Research, Washington, DC: World Bank.

McGuire, G. (1998) 'Australia's Restrictions on Trade in Financial Services', Productivity Commission Staff Research Papers, Canberra: Australian Productivity Commission.

McGuire, G. and M. Schuele (2000) 'Restrictiveness of International Trade in Banking Services', in C. Findlay and T. Warren (eds) *Impediments to Trade in Services: Measurement and Policy Implications*, London: Routledge.

McGuire, G., M. Schuele and T. Smith (2000) 'Restrictiveness of International Trade in Maritime Services', in C. Findlay and T. Warren (eds) *Impediments to Trade in Services: Measurement and Policy Implications*, London: Routledge.

Messerlin, P. (2008) 'The EC Neighbourhood Policy: An Economic Review', *Journal of International Trade and Diplomacy*, **2**, 17–54.

Mishkin, F. S. (2001) 'Prudential Supervision: Why is it Important and What are the Issues?', in F. S. Mishkin (ed.) *Prudential Supervision: What Works and What doesn't*, Chicago: University of Chicago Press.

Musselli, I. and S. Zarrilli (2005) 'Oil and Gas Services: Market Liberalization and the Ongoing GATS Negotiations', *Journal of International Economic Law*, **8**, 552–81.

National Academy of Sciences (1995) *Standards, Conformity Assessment, and Trade: Into the 21st Century*, Washington, DC: National Academy Press.

Newbery, D. (2005a) 'Electricity Liberalization in Britain: The Quest for a Satisfactory Wholesale Market Design', *Energy Journal* (Special Issue on European Electricity Liberalization), **26**, 43–70

—— (2005b) 'Refining Market Design', paper presented at the conference on Implementing the Internal Market of Electricity: Proposals and Timetables, Brussels.

Official Journal of the European Communities (21 July 1998, L204) Directive 98/30/EC of the European Parliament and of the Council of June 1998 concerning common rules for the internal market in natural gas.

Organization for Economic Co-operation and Development (2000) 'Recommendations of the Council Concerning Common Principles of Shipping Policy for Member Countries', OECD document number C(2000) 124/Final, Paris: OECD.

—— (2001) *Regulatory Issues in International Maritime Transport*, Paris: OECD.

—— (2002) *Turkey: Crucial Support for Economic Recovery*, OECD Reviews of Regulatory Reform, Paris: OECD.

—— (2005a) *OECD Communications Outlook*, Paris: OECD.

—— (2005b) 'The Benefits of Liberalizing Product Markets and Reducing Barriers to International Trade and Investment in the OECD', Economics Department Working Paper No. 463, Paris: OECD.

—— (2006) 'OECD's FDI Regulatory Restrictiveness Index: Revision and Extension to More Economies', Working Paper on International Investment No. 2006/4, Paris: OECD.

—— (2009a) *Code of Liberalization of Current Invisible Operations*, Paris: OECD.

—— (2009b) *OECD Statistics on International Trade in Services*, Volumes I and II, Paris: OECD.

Organization for Economic Co-operation and Development (OECD) and International Energy Agency (IEA) (2001) *Energy Policies of IEA Countries: Turkey 2001 Review*, Paris: OECD.

—— (2005) *Energy Policies of IEA Countries: Turkey 2005 Review*, Paris: OECD.

Ökten, Ç. (2006) 'Natural Gas Sector Policy Reform in Turkey', unpublished background paper.

Özdemir, B. and P. Miu (2009) *Basel II Implementation*, New York: McGraw Hill.

Özkıvrak, O. (2005) 'Electricity Restructuring in Turkey', *Energy Policy*, **33**, 1339–50.

Özkoç, H. (2004) *The New Natural Gas Market and the Role of Regulator*, Istanbul: Energy Market Regulatory Authority of Turkey.

Pala, C. (2006) 'Turkey: Energy Bridge Between East and West', *Journal of Middle Eastern Geopolitics*, **1**, 57–60.

Parameswaran, B. (2004) *The Liberalization of Maritime Transport Services*, Berlin: Springer Verlag.

Park, S. (2002) 'Measuring Tariff Equivalents in Cross-Border Trade in Services', Korea Institute for International Economic Policy Working Paper 02–15. Seoul: Korea Institute for International Economic Policy.

Privatization Agency (n.d.) 'Privatization of Turkey's Electricity Distribution Industry', Teaser, Lazard. Available at http://www.oib.gov.tr/tedas/teaser_english.pdf.

Ramsey, F. (1927) 'A Contribution to the Theory of Taxation', *Economic Journal*, **37**, 47–61.

RAND Science and Technology (2004) 'Measuring Economic Effects of Technical Barriers to Trade on U.S. Exporters', Planning Report 04–3 prepared for National Institute of Standards and Technology, Gaithersburg: National Institute of Standards and Technology.

Rodrik, D. (2007a) 'Fifty Years of Growth (and Lack Thereof): An Interpretation', in D. Rodrik, *One Economics, Many Recipes: Globalization, Institutions and Economic Growth*, Princeton, NJ: Princeton University Press.

——— (2007b) 'Institutions for High-Quality Growth', in D. Rodrik, *One Economics, Many Recipes: Globalization, Institutions and Economic Growth*, Princeton, NJ: Princeton University Press.

Roseman, D. (2003) 'Domestic Regulation and Trade in Telecommunications Services: Experience and Prospects under the GATS', in A. Mattoo and P. Sauvé (eds) *Domestic Regulation and Service Trade Liberalization*, Washington, DC: World Bank and Oxford University Press.

Secretariat of the Paris Memorandum on Port State Control (1982) 'Paris Memorandum of Understanding on Port State Control', The Hague: Paris MOU Secretariat.

Selçuk, O. and I. E. Erten (2007) 'Analysis of Turkish Wholesale Market', unpublished paper, Ankara: Energy Market Regulatory Authority.

Selivanova, J. (2004) 'World Trade Organization Rules and Energy Pricing: Russia's Case', *Journal of World Trade*, **38**, 559–602.

Sikow-Magny, C. (2006) 'Subsidiarity and Transport Policy Co-Ordination in the European Union', in *Transport and Decentralization*, European Conference of Ministers of Transport, Paris: ECMT.

Steiner, F. (2000) 'Regulation, Industry Structure and Performance in the Electricity Supply Industry', OECD Economics Department Working Papers No. 238, Paris: OECD.

Steinherr, A., A. Tukel and M. Ucer (2004) 'The Turkish Banking Sector: Challenges and Outlook in Transition to EU Membership', Centre for European Policy Studies (CEPS) EU–Turkey Working Papers No. 4, Brussels: CEPS.

Stephenson, S. M. (1997) 'Standards and Conformity Assessment as Nontariff Barriers to Trade', Policy Research Working Paper 1826, Washington, DC: World Bank.

Stopford, M. (1997) *Maritime Economics,* 2nd edition, London: Routledge.

Sykes, A. O. (1995) *Product Standards for Internationally Integrated Goods Markets*. Washington, DC: Brookings Institution.

Tarullo, D. K. (2008) *Banking on Basel – The Future of International Regulation*, Washington, DC: Peterson Institute for International Economics.

Togan, S. (1994) *Foreign Trade Regime and Trade Liberalization in Turkey during the 1980s*, Aldershot, UK: Avebury Press.

—— (2005) 'Turkey: Trade Policy Review', *World Economy*, **28**, 1228–62.

—— (2007) 'EU Maritime Rules and Transport Sector Policy Reform in Turkey', in Yong-Shik Lee (ed.) *Economic Development Through World Trade: A Developing World Perspective*, Alphen aan den Rijn, the Netherlands: Kluwer Law International.

—— (2010) 'Turkey: Trade Policy Review, 2007', *World Economy* (forthcoming).

Togan, S. and J. Michalek (2008) 'Implications of Liberalization of Trade in Services and Network Industries', FEMISE Report on the Euro-Mediterranean Partnership, Institut de la Méditerranée. Marseilles: Institut de la Méditerranée.

Trujillo, L. and G. Nombela (1999) 'Privatization and Regulation of the Seaport Industry', Policy Research Working Paper No. 2181, Washington, DC: World Bank.

Turkish Electricity Transmission Company (TEİAŞ) (2004) 'Electricity Energy Generation Planning Study for Turkey (2005–20)', Ankara: TEİAŞ. Available at http://www.teias.gov.tr.

Ulusoy, A. and G. Oğuz (2007) 'The Privatization of Electricity Distribution in Turkey: A Legal and Economic Analysis', *Energy Policy*, **35**, 5021–34.

Undersecretariat for Foreign Trade (2008a) 'Analysis Report on Market Surveillance System in Turkey with an Emphasis on Consumer Products, "Report of the Present Situation"', Report prepared within the context of the Twinning Project funded by the European Commission on Reinforcement of Institutional Capacity for Establishing a Product Safety System in Turkey. Available at http://www.dtm.gov.tr/dtmadmin/upload/DTS/IthalatDenetimleriDb/Proje/Reports/Report_present/reportfinal.pdf.

—— (2008b) 'The Way Ahead', Report prepared within the context of the Twinning Project funded by the European Commission on Reinforcement of Institutional Capacity for Establishing a Product Safety System in Turkey. Available at http://www.dtm.gov.tr/dtmadmin/upload/DTS/IthalatDenetimleriDb/Proje/Reports/Report_Way_Ahead/ingilizcerapor.pdf.

United Nations (1974) 'Convention on a Code of Conduct for Liner Conferences', *Treaty Series*, Vol. 1334, Geneva: United Nations.

—— (1982) 'United Nations Convention on the Law of the Sea (UNCLOS)', Division of Ocean Affairs and the Law of the Sea, Office of Legal Affairs, New York: United Nations.

—— (2009) *Report of the Commission of Experts of the President of the UN General Assembly on Reforms of the International Monetary and Financial System*, New York: United Nations.

United Nations Conference on Trade and Development (2003) 'Technical Barriers to Trade', document prepared for the Course on Dispute Settlement, World Trade Organization, Geneva: UNCTAD.

—— (2006) *Review of Maritime Transport, 2006*, Geneva: UNCTAD.

United Nations Economic Commission for Europe (UNECE) (1956) 'Customs Convention on Containers', Geneva: UNECE.

—— (1957) 'European Agreement Concerning the International Carriage of Dangerous Goods by Road', Geneva: UNECE.

—— (1958) 'Agreement Concerning the Adoption of Uniform Technical Prescriptions for Wheeled Vehicles, Equipment and Parts, which can be Fitted and/or be Used on

Wheeled Vehicles and the Conditions for Reciprocal Recognition of Approvals Granted on the Basis of These Prescriptions', Geneva: UNECE.

—— (1959) 'Customs Convention on the International Transport of Goods under Cover of TIR Carnets', Geneva: UNECE.

—— (1970a) 'Agreement on the International Carriage of Perishable Foodstuffs and on the Special Equipment to be Used for Such Carriage', Geneva: UNECE.

—— (1970b) 'European Agreement Concerning the Work of Crews of Vehicles Engaged in International Road Transport', Geneva: UNECE.

—— (1982) 'International Convention on Harmonization of Frontier Control of Goods', Geneva: UNECE.

—— (1994) 'Convention on Customs Treatment of Pool Containers Used in International Transport', Geneva: UNECE.

US Treasury (2009) *Financial Regulatory Reform: A New Foundation,* Washington, DC: Department of Treasury.

Vaillancourt, F. and P. Wingender (2006) 'Decentralization, Intergovernmental Competition/ Emulation and Efficiency: Lessons from and for the Transport Sector', in *Transport and Decentralization*, European Conference of Ministers of Transport, Paris: ECMT.

Vasconcelos, J. (2004) 'Services of General Interest and Regulation in the EU Energy Market', Council of European Energy Regulators (CEER), Presentation at XVI CEEP Congress, Leipzig, 17 June.

Vickers, J. and G. Yarrow (1991) 'The British Electricity Experiment', *Economic Policy,* **6**, 188–232.

Walsh, K. (2006) 'Trade in Services: Does Gravity Hold? Gravity Model Approach to Estimating Barriers to Services Trade', unpublished paper, Department of Economics and Institute for International Integration Studies, Trinity College, Dublin.

Warren, T. (2000a) 'The Impact on Output of Impediments to Trade and Investment in Telecommunications Services', in C. Findlay and T. Warren (eds) *Impediments to Trade in Services: Measurement and Policy Implications*, London: Routledge.

—— (2000b) 'The Identification of Impediments to Trade and Investment in Telecommunications Services', in C. Findlay and T. Warren (eds) *Impediments to Trade in Services: Measurement and Policy Implications*, London: Routledge.

World Bank (2004a) 'Turkey Gas Sector Strategy Note', World Bank, Infrastructure and Energy Department, Washington, DC: World Bank.

—— (2004b) 'Transport Sector Overview'. Available at http://lnweb18.worldbank.org/ ECA/Transport.nsf/Countries/Turkey?Opendocument.

—— (2005a) *Global Economic Prospects 2005*, Washington, DC: World Bank.

—— (2005b) 'World Development Indicators Online'. Available at http://ddp-ext. worldbank.org/ext/DDPQQ/member.do?method=getMembers&userid=1&queryId=6.

—— (2007) 'Project Appraisal Document on a Proposed Loan in the Amount of Euro 205 Million to the Türkiye Elektrik Dağıtım A. Ş. (TEDAŞ) with the Guarantee of the Republic of Turkey for an Electricity Distribution Rehabilitation Project', Report No. 36341 – TR, 26 March, Washington, DC: World Bank.

World Trade Organization (1991) 'Services Sectoral Classification List', note by the Secretariat, MTN.GNS/W/120 (10 July 1991), Geneva: WTO.

—— (1998a) 'Energy Services', background note by the Secretariat', S/C/52, World Trade Organization, Council for Trade in Services, Geneva: WTO.

—— (1998b) 'Maritime Transport Services', background note by the Secretariat, S/ CSS/W/106, Geneva: WTO.

—— (2002) *The Legal Texts: The Results of the Uruguay Round of Multilateral Trade Negotiations*, Geneva: WTO.

—— (2008) *Trade Policy Review: Turkey* 2007, Geneva: WTO.

World Trade Organization Secretariat (2001a) 'Energy Services', in WTO Secretariat (ed.) *Guide to the GATS: An Overview of Issues for Further Liberalization of Trade in Services*, The Hague: Kluwer Law International.

—— (2001b) 'Maritime Transport Services', in WTO Secretariat (ed.) *Guide to the GATTS: An Overview of Issues for Further Liberalization of Trade in Services*, The Hague: Kluwer Law International.

—— (2001c) 'Road Transport Services', in WTO Secretariat (ed.) *Guide to the GATS: An Overview of Issues for Further Liberalization of Trade in Services*, The Hague: Kluwer Law International.

Index